THE
GOLDEN
DOOR

International Migration, Mexico, and The United States

Paul R. Ehrlich
Loy Bilderback
Anne H. Ehrlich

WIDEVIEW BOOKS

CONTENTS

AN UPDATE

SINCE the first appearance of *The Golden Door,* the complexity of the problems of immigration (legal and illegal) has become increasingly evident to the general public. The sudden and unexpected flow of over one hundred thousand Cubans to Florida in the summer of 1980 illustrated the lack of any coherent immigration policy or program of refugee resettlement. Otherwise, though, the new wave of Cubans is not at all typical of people entering and seeking to enter the United States. By the standards of Latin America and the Caribbean, Cuba does not have a rapidly growing population and, while life there displays the drabness, coercion, and regulation of the individual that seem to characterize Marxist countries, one does not notice the widespread hunger, unemployment, hopelessness, or political disintegration found elsewhere in the region.

The more typical pressures bringing people to the United States were seen in the story of the nine Salvadorans who died agonizing deaths while trying to enter the United States through the Arizona desert on the Fourth-of-July weekend. They were a part of a group of fifty middle-class persons who had paid $2,500 each to be brought from their Central American homes and delivered safely to Los Angeles. What went wrong in the crossing has not been established, but what propelled them from El Salvador is all too clear. El Salvador is a country that had a population of three million in 1970, has four and a half million today, and is headed for eight or nine million before the century is out. Over half that population is under eighteen years of age, and every year tens of thousands of young people come onto a job market that has no place for them. The pressure and competition for any way of earning a livelihood is intense. While the elite "Fourteen Families" which have traditionally ruled the country have recently lost control, they are still powerful enough to keep anything worthwhile from being done, assuming that anything could be done. Meanwhile, increasing numbers of youths are dropping out of society and joining guerilla and terrorist groups, usually of Marxist persuasion. Since Salvadorans have a long tradition of resolving personal and political differences by assassination, it is not surprising that the little country has achieved astounding levels of homicide. Political murders are reckoned at about thirty a week, and one never knows whether the assassins are from the right, the left, or the government. Given this situation, getting out is an attractive option for any who have the means. The United States, which, even in the doldrums of stagflation, still has a rich economy, a tradition of accepting newcomers, and a seeming lack of will and capacity to say no to anyone, is an attractive destination for those with salable skills.

Though more acute, the situation of El Salvador has much in common with that of the whole region from Mexico through Central America to Colombia and out into the Caribbean. The statistically "typical" Salvadoran going to the United States is unemployed, about thirty-one years old, and equally likely to be a man or a woman. He or she is most likely to enter the United States without inspection via southern California, will pay a *coyote*, or smuggler, $580 for assistance, and will remain some eighteen months. He or she will have $3,500 left after living expenses and paying the *coyote* out of the $7,900 earned by working 48 hours per week at $2.17 per hour. The odds are about 50/50 he or she will be apprehended and sent home by the Immigration and Naturalization Service (INS).

Countries like this—not Cuba—should be the focus of our concern. The refugee (someone who is outside his or her own country and has a justified fear of returning) has traditionally been regarded as a victim of political fortune, but now we are hearing more of the "economic refugee," who could as well be called the "demographic refugee." The idea of the "economic refugee" was popularized by those who have championed the acceptance of the illegal entrants from Haiti over the last several years. The argument runs that the inability to procure a livelihood is as destructive to the human being as political harassment and that starvation is as deadly and in many countries as certain as the firing squad. Hence, the Haitians, for example, had "a justified fear of returning" and were, therefore, refugees with a right to asylum in the United States. This line of thinking can be applied to people from a score of countries close enough to the United States for easy access.

No one seriously champions the idea that the United States should admit all these "refugees," but many such groups have some support in the United States. The black caucus in the House of Representatives champions the Haitians, the Cubans have tradition and cold-war phobias to call on, some Chicano and Mexican immigrant groups advocate a special policy toward Mexicans, the publicity given the political turmoil in Salvador has generated support for Salvadorans, and so on, and so on. Humane, responsible, enforceable immigration legislation runs the risk of being pecked to death, before it is formed, by a gaggle of geese, although no single goose wants very much.

The problem the United States faces is that its agricultural lands are no longer calling for more and more hands, and its industrial plants are no longer increasing faster than the supply of those who want work—but *still* it is admitting people at the same rate as one hundred years ago when the opportunities were here.

There have been signs of movement in the immigration field since *The Golden Door* was completed. The system of preference categories which was set up in place of the national quotas in 1965 was extended to include the Western Hemisphere (see page 88). The Refugee Act of 1980 abolished the seventh-preference category, the one under which refugees had been admitted, reduced the number of immigrants allowed under the preference system from 290,000 to 270,000, and provided for the annual admission of 50,000 political refugees. Therefore, as we enter 1981, the law provides for the lawful admission of some 320,000 immigrants annually.

In fact, all this is a sham. Exceptions built into the law and exemptions left to the President have swollen the number to over 700,000. Not all of these have been "lawfully admitted to permanent residence," but regardless of status they are here to stay.

Finally, nothing fundamental has even been proposed, much less done, to deal with the flow of illegal immigrants. The Department of Labor has stiffened its efforts to enforce employment legislation in the garment industry in the Los Angeles area and in other industries known for employing illegals, the assumption here being that such enforcement will make the employment of illegals less attractive. The fact is that employment legislation depends on voluntary compliance rather than enforcement, and the enforcement arm of the Department of Labor is not adequate to the task of a prolonged struggle to stop what is an established practice in many industries.

Otherwise, efforts to enforce our immigration laws are weaker today than previously. The INS agreed to suspend certain kinds of operations in Hispanic neighborhoods during the spring and summer of 1980 because these operations allegedly interfered with the taking of the 1980 census. It was argued that they dampened the never-very-great enthusiasm for census enumerators in those neighborhoods and thus increased the undercount typical

in poor neighborhoods, which, in turn, would affect congressional redistricting, revenue sharing, and other federal programs
based on the census. A number of court injunctions suspended
traditional enforcement tactics, particularly the practice of using
search warrants to enter places of employment to check out everyone on the premises rather than to look for specified individuals.

On the border itself the "detection and prevention of the unlawful entry of aliens into the United States," the stated mission
of the Border Patrol, has gone its usual way. The Border Patrol
has not been substantially augmented either in personnel or resources. In 1980 there were instances of the curtailment of Patrol
activities because local budgets were not increased to keep
abreast of the rising cost of gasoline. Violence and the fear of
violence have increased, particularly in the heavily traveled sections near El Paso and San Diego. The "war zone," west of
Interstate Highway 5 at San Diego (described in Chapter 7), has
continuously and increasingly been the scene of verbal abuse,
physical assault, and general harassment of Border Patrol agents.
Proven instances of brutality toward and abuse of apprehended
illegals by agents reflect this increased tenor of violence. A continued increase of violence and brutality along the United States
border with Mexico is all that can be expected in the absence of
any clarification of policy.

The general examination of immigration law and policy has
been deferred until the work of the Select Commission on Immigration and Refugees could be completed. The function of the
commission was to investigate certain aspects of the immigration
situation, listen to those who felt they had something to say on
the matter, and to write a report on what they discovered. The
commission also performed the service of keeping any significant
discussion of immigration issues out of the 1980 presidential and
congressional elections. A candidate could always say that he was
awaiting the report of the commission.

The report of the commission, expected in early 1981, will be
the point of departure for a debate on immigration policy rather
than a plan for legislative action. The elements that will be in the
report or, certainly, in the ensuing debate will present a departure—but not a radical one—from current and traditional policy.
The traditional devotion to family reunification and the proposition that the United States benefits socially and economically
from immigration will be reaffirmed. Indeed, the present six-
category preference system will probably be scrapped in favor of
two categories, one providing for each of these objectives. The

definition of the family, however, will be narrowed, perhaps to include only spouses, parents, and minor children of persons already in the United States. Refugees will continue to be treated in a category separate from other immigrants.

The most promising innovation discussed by the commissioners is the abandonment of specific annual numbers of immigrants in favor of adjustable target figures for five-year periods. It has been suggested that a commission be established which periodically, perhaps in the third year of each five-year period, would adjust levels of immigration for the fourth and fifth years in keeping with economic and demographic indicators and with consideration of the number of refugees wanting to get in. Adjustments would be made according to congressional guidelines, but without having to go back to Congress for each adjustment. While the level of admissions being discussed by the commission —two and a half to five million for each five-year period—is too high for any reasonable, long-term population policy for the United States, the general principles are sound. The adjustment of immigration levels in keeping with economic and demographic conditions, and under overall limitations, is clearly the way to go, as is the idea of addressing levels of immigration in time periods longer than a single year.

The commission will probably endorse the idea of penalizing employers who persist in employing illegal labor and will advocate the issuance of some sort of national identification card to help the employers know who is and who is not an illegal. The commission has concluded, along with everyone else who has studied the problem, that if the flow of illegals is to be controlled, the "pull" from the United States must be stopped, and that pull is the ease of employment for the illegal after he gets here. The support for "employer sanctions" and "ID cards" is growing, but so is the opposition. The United States Civil Rights Commission, after months of consideration, concluded that the danger to civil rights inherent in such a program was greater than the promise of benefits. This commission felt that a more spirited enforcement of current labor legislation, which would lessen the advantage to employers of using illegals, would produce the same benefits. Still, two of the five commissioners dissented and came out for the new approach. It seems clear that much of the debate over foreign workers in the United States will center on this issue.

Finally, the Federation for American Immigration Reform (FAIR) remains the only lobbying organization to come out of the current immigration concern, although most private groups with a traditional interest in population and labor policy are turning their attention to matters of immigration. The monthly newsletter distributed to FAIR members represents the only systematic attempt to gather the various strands of the debate and to present them to a general audience. Through the courts, FAIR focused attention on the problem of illegal aliens, the census, and congressional reapportionment. Through a letter-writing campaign it marshaled the widespread discontent with the lack of coherent policy in admitting the 1980 crop of Cuban refugees.

The 1980 elections have been interpreted as a mandate for less governmental participation in the economic and personal lives of American citizens. It remains to be seen whether this tendency will override the growing demand for some sort of coherent immigration policy that will serve the nation well in the long run. If a general retreat from government activism scotches or limits the development of such policy, it only means postponement to a time when the problems will be tougher and the remedies more painful.

Paul R. Ehrlich
Loy Bilderback
Anne H. Ehrlich
January 1981

PREFACE

Across the southern border of the United States are 67 million Mexicans. They are poor and Americans* are rich. They speak Spanish and we speak English. They are brown and we are white. They want it and we've got it: jobs, prosperity, the *Ladies' Home Journal–Playboy* life-style. As a result we are being invaded by a horde of illegal immigrants from Mexico. In the popular view, the United States is faced by a migration crisis, its economy is threatened, its way of life is on the line. Newspapers and magazines proclaim the crisis; TV does specials on it; a House Select Committee has held hearings; the President has formed a task force. The furor has attracted the attention of bigots and bureaucrats as well as concerned citizens, who ask: If we are limiting our family sizes so that our children can inherit a better nation, why should we throw open our doors to over-reproducers?

But the Mexican migration crisis, with its deep historic roots, is actually much more complex and interesting—and potentially more dangerous—than one would gather from popular accounts. It is a crisis that could erupt in ethnic strife between the dominant Anglo majority and the twelve million Hispanics inside this country and escalate into conflict and discord with foreign nations. It is also a crisis that represents, in exaggerated form, a basic problem of the global relationships between haves and have-nots. The U.S.–Mexican border is the only place in the world where a large, rich, overdeveloped nation touches a large, poor, less-developed nation. That border is nearly 2,000 miles long and only modestly patrolled. Mexico, whose population is one of the fastest growing of the major nations, entered the twentieth century with eleven or twelve million people and will have at least ten times that number when the century ends. Almost half of that increase has not yet arrived, but is due within the next twenty years. The most conservative projections indicate there will be 45 million more Mexicans in 2000 than there are today.

---

*We must apologize to those south and north of our borders who also legitimately think of themselves as "Americans" for using this word to mean "citizens of the United States." To use the latter phrase wherever needed would have substantially lengthened the book, however.

Only a little farther away are the nations of the Caribbean basin, some of which have populations that are growing at rates comparable to that of Mexico and are also contributing to the migration crisis in the United States. El Salvador, a country about the size of Massachusetts, has 4.5 million people today and may have over 9 million in 25 years. The "Soccer War" between El Salvador and neighboring Honduras in 1969 was formally (and somewhat simplistically) attributed by the Organization of American States to Salvadoran migrants being pushed into Honduras by El Salvador's skyrocketing population—the first time population pressure received official mention as a cause of war. El Salvador was the first country to establish a formal *emigration* policy designed to help its own citizens become permanently established in other countries. To assist Salvadorans in finding livelihoods elsewhere, formal agreements have been reached with Bolivia, Brazil, and Saudi Arabia. Most Salvadoran emigrants would prefer to go to the United States, however, and some of them do.

Other Latin American countries are also becoming prominent on the migration scene. Authorities in the United States have become aware of sizable Colombian and Dominican colonies in several East Coast cities, colonies quite beyond anything that could be explained by legal immigration. During the 1978 Colombian presidential elections, both major Colombian parties had campaign headquarters in New York City, and they distributed over 80,000 absentee ballots. One leader of the Dominican community in the North Bronx estimated its size at "over 100,000."

In the summer of 1978, the Bahamas suddenly expelled large numbers of Haitians who had been there for many years. Several hundred of these people took to the sea in small boats and headed for Florida, where they were promptly jailed. Many asked for political asylum on the intriguing grounds that the political regime in Haiti had created an economic situation in which it was impossible to make a living; being sent back to Haiti would have meant death by starvation. Most of the Haitians were given "parole" status, which meant they could stay freely in the country while their cases were being processed.

When we asked an Immigration and Naturalization Service (INS) official why he had arranged this, his answer was: "Hell, I'm not sending anybody back to Haiti and I'm not leaving a black man in a South Florida jail." And what was he going to do when all of Bangladesh showed up? "Look for another line of work."

Enforcement officials of the INS are now casting a wary eye outside the hemisphere, particularly at West Africa. Their intelligence sources and street experience—a lot of cabdrivers in Washington, D.C., have West African accents—indicate that a trickle is forming. It seems to run from West Africa to Canada and then, illegally, into the United States. The INS wants to keep it from becoming a torrent. In August 1978, consideration was given to the transfer of Border Patrol agents from the Mexican border to the Burlington, Vermont, sector to slow things down there.

The present crisis is not just one of numbers, but of attitudes. No one knows how many illegal immigrants there are in the U.S., but the most careful recent studies estimate there are about 4 million—less than 2 percent of the whole population. The higher numbers one sometimes sees—ranging to as much as eighteen million—were released some years ago, without foundation, in order to encourage a higher INS budget. Unfortunately, perhaps tragically, these higher numbers have sunk into the folklore along with much other misinformation about the illegal population. All responsible studies indicate that the illegals work diligently for modest wages. By and large, they do work that no one else is willing to do. Contrary to the folklore, as far as we can tell, they pay their taxes and seldom apply for or receive public assistance or services.

Nonetheless, illegal aliens do cause a variety of problems in the United States; indeed, the simple fact of their illegal presence is a problem. But there is more to it than that. The kind of life that most Americans expect puts practical limits on many things, including population size. And however desirable each individual immigrant may be, he or she increases the number of Americans. Consequently, some hard thinking has to be done about the whole picture of immigration in the United States, and the illegal immigrant is a big part of that picture.

By far the worst part of the immigration problem is that it is only beginning. Within the lifetimes of most people now living, the population of Mexico and the countries of the Caribbean will more than double. The economies of those countries, economies very largely dominated by the United States, cannot possibly accommodate those numbers. Many of the people in those countries will try to survive by migrating to a place where they have a chance to make a living, and the closest place is the United States.

Clearly, the United States is going to have to develop a new immigration policy soon. If it is to be a good policy, it must be based on an accurate assessment of the international situation and aimed at the achievement of realizable goals. However, a good policy will not come out of a discussion in which Americans tell one another that their problems stem from the presence of some ill-defined, but certainly very large legion of illegals who are taking jobs and livelihoods from American citizens and freeloading on welfare. Nor is the search for the right path likely to be advanced by promulgation of the notion that the illegal-immigrant problem can be solved simply by ousting the rascals and fortifying the borders against their return.

In this study, we focus on the Mexican immigration problem in its historical and cultural context and examine the possible consequences of various policies aimed at dealing with it. The problem is not viewed as a unique dilemma, however, but as part of a continuing pattern woven through the centuries, a pattern of mass movements as old as humanity itself. The book is thus not only about Mexico and the U.S., but about human migration in general. The first chapter presents an overview of migration in history and as a contemporary worldwide phenomenon. A great portion of the past can be interpreted in terms of people seeking greener pastures—and of the response of the already established pasture-dwellers to the seekers. The situation in which the United States finds itself today is not different in kind from dilemmas that it and other nations have faced in the past. This will become especially apparent in the second chapter, in which the focus narrows to the history of immigration to the United States.

In the next five chapters, the relationship between Mexico and the United States is examined in detail. Here again, the situation is not unique, but a dramatic example of the consequences of the increasing division of the world into rich nations and poor nations—a division with deep historical roots. Two great trends in the world today arise from this division. One is a growing tendency for people from the poor nations to seek a better life by moving temporarily or permanently to areas of greater opportunity; the other is the tendency of better-off nations alternately to encourage and attempt to stop that movement. The flow of Mexicans into the United States is one of the clearest, yet most complex and fascinating, examples of this worldwide movement. To understand that flow, one must understand its sources in the past; to view the action at the border in a contemporary "snapshot" can only lead to the wrong answers to the questions of how to deal with the illegal "problem."

In the eighth and last chapter, the subject is the future: what might happen to migration if the world turns sensibly toward a sustainable society; what might happen if it does not. The options open to both the U.S. and Mexico are described and the possible consequences of adopting them evaluated. By this point, we hope to have supplied the background necessary for an informed citizen to participate intelligently in the growing debate on immigration. It is our hope that a thorough understanding of the dilemma now facing Mexico and the U.S. will lead people to support humane policies that would benefit all the actors in the drama. Finally, we venture to suggest what sorts of policies might fit that description.

PEOPLE ON THE MOVE

Moving from one place to another—migration—seems to be almost as characteristic of *Homo sapiens* as walking erect. Hundreds of thousands of years ago, the early human form *Homo erectus* had spread from the Far East to the farthest reaches of Africa and Europe. *Homo sapiens* went even farther long before agriculture or written languages were invented. By 20,000 years ago, human beings had occupied Australia and North and South America as well as all of the Old World. Except for its own domesticated companions, the human animal became the most widely dispersed animal species on Earth. Yet the restless movement of peoples did not end with the occupation of all of Earth's land areas. It has continued to this day, and indeed in the past generation has even seemed to be accelerating.

People have moved in organized groups or as streams of individuals or families for a variety of reasons: conquest, trade, a need for more land and resources, or brighter opportunities. Some have been forced to move to escape slavery, famine, or political or religious persecution.

Each migration has unique elements based in the culture and circumstances of the migrants and of the people in the area to which they migrate. But there are also many elements in common among them. In the end, the reasons people move, voluntarily at least, boil down to the simple desire for a better life.

MIGRATIONS IN HISTORY

Of course, no record of the movements of early hunter-gatherer tribes exists, although there must have been countless occasions when a tribe had exhausted the berries and game in its territory and moved on in search of greener pastures. There is speculation that the first wave of human migrants in the New World led to the extinction, some 11,000 years ago, of mammoths, camels, giant sloths, and other groups of large mammals that had previously been prominent features of the landscape. For early agriculturalists, anthropologists have traced the dispersion of metalworking and distinctive styles of clay pots, tools, or other artifacts through time and space. How much of this dispersion was due to the actual migration of the people using the artifacts and how much to cultural diffusion—the spread of ideas from one group to another—has sometimes been a matter of debate. More often than not, the innovations seem to have been carried by the migrating people themselves, who with a superior technology could easily displace the previous residents. The agricultural revolution itself apparently spread from the Near East across Europe in this way over several thousand years. Later, the search for metal deposits and development of trade routes may have been behind the dispersal of early metalworking peoples.

Several kinds of migrations are prominent in the earliest historical records, although trade and conquest seem to have predominated as motives. The ancient world's most enterprising traders, the Phoenicians, established trading centers all around the Mediterranean basin, and the Greeks planted trading colonies in southern Italy, Sicily, southern France, Spain, Asia Minor, and almost all the way around the Black Sea. Later, under Alexander the Great, they enjoyed a brief fling with conquest. The conquests of the Roman Empire stretched from Scotland to the Sudan, from Portugal and Morocco to the Euphrates River and the Red Sea, generating mixings of peoples from all directions. Romans went to conquer and occupy the distant provinces, while great numbers of people from the hinterland came or were brought to Rome. Italians of today are largely a product of that great mixing of peoples.

Much of the migration in the ancient world was involuntary; when a territory was conquered, the conqueror customarily took slaves from the defeated population. In its heyday, between a quarter and a third of the population of Athens—the "cradle of democracy"—were slaves. A single Roman military campaign could yield as many as 50,000 slaves. Beginning in the third century B.C., the flow of slaves into Italy was so great that the economic basis of Roman society was changed, causing the failure of the Republic and the emergence of the Empire. The huge population (for its time) of Imperial Rome, perhaps a million, was built and maintained largely by immigration of people from the countryside and outlying parts of the Empire, whether they came voluntarily or not.

The Age of Conquest

Throughout the late ancient period and into the Middle Ages, Europe and Western Asia were subjected to wave after wave of "barbarian" nomadic invaders and marauders from the steppes of Central Asia. Among the invaders were Scythians, Germanic Vandals and Goths, and the Mongol Huns. Sometimes these groups merely raided the rich, established civilizations of the Mediterranean and retreated; sometimes they settled and stayed, only to be conquered in turn by the next wave of barbarians.

The various Germanic tribes moved into the western Roman Empire between the late fourth and late sixth centuries as Roman power relaxed there. The Visigoths, who entered the Roman Empire across the lower Danube in the 370s and finally settled in Spain 40 years later, could not have been very numerous since they frequently had to live off the land. The same is true of the Vandals who crossed the Rhine about 400 and finally settled in North Africa around 430. The Germans fell heir to much that was Roman, but their taste for butter and beer replaced olive oil and wine in the North. Their style of trousers for men instead of skirts came to dominate in the West, as did their political custom of hereditary kingship.

The Huns, Avars, and Magyars were all basically the same Central Asian peoples, as were the Mongols under Genghis Khan, who came later. Between the fifth and fifteenth centuries, they swept across Russia and the Carpathian Mountains to settle for a time on the Hungarian Plain along the Danube River. China, India, and the Middle East were actually conquered by the later groups. Much of Europe was terrorized by the waves of invaders, though they usually did not stay and settle.

The Huns were on the scene for only about three years, from around 449 to 452 A.D., but their raids into Northern Italy and what is now France were so savage that their name has survived the centuries. When Kaiser Wilhelm II sent the German troops off with the British, French, and Americans to kill Chinese in the suppression of the Boxer Rebellion in 1900, he exhorted them to ferocity so great they would be thought of as the Huns of old; hence the derogatory term for German soldiers during the First World War.

The Avars invaded the Hungarian Plain in the eighth century and also raided into the West, but they were much more interested in the wealth of Constantinople. Their strength was such that they managed to blackmail the Byzantines heavily, but it was Charlemagne who crushed Avar power in the late eighth century. Tales of "Avar Gold" play the same role in romantic tales of Eastern Europe as pirate treasure does in American folklore, and

now and then troves are found. Around 900, the Magyars moved
in and, after a half-century of the customary raiding, settled down
to evolve into the remarkably unfierce modern Hungarians.

In the seventh century, meanwhile, the rise of Islam in the
Arabian peninsula stimulated a new wave of invaders who within
a decade dominated Persia and the Egyptian and Syrian parts of
the Byzantine Empire. Within a century the Arabic language and
Islamic religion had been carried across North Africa and into
Spain, and Moslem conquerors occupied the Indus River valley to
the east. This was not a single migration, but a series of migrations. The Arabs, for example, were only a small part of the
Moslem army that invaded Spain in 711. This migrating army was
composed of Islamicized and Arabicized Moors. The Islamic
expansion consisted of a series of evangelical conversions, each
one serving as a base for further expansion by the newly converted.

Starting about 800 A.D., the Vikings, called Norse in Western
Europe and Varangians in Russia, launched explorations from
Scandinavia. In the next few centuries, they created a series of
political and commercial networks that, at one time or another,
reached from Kiev in Russia through Scandinavia, Iceland, and
Greenland to Newfoundland.

In the late Middle Ages, there were renewed expansions from
the Central Asian spawning ground, which were even more awesome than the earlier ones. These invaders were the Mongols,
first under Genghis Khan in the thirteenth century, and then
under Tamerlane in the last half of the fourteenth. The warriors
of Genghis Khan had crossed the Russian states, establishing
dominance over them, and besieged and bypassed the major
Polish cities. They were working their way through the Carpa-
thians on the route taken by the Huns, Avars, and Magyars when
Genghis died and the expansion stopped. The Mongols pulled
back to Russia, which they continued to dominate for more than
two centuries. It was first as chief tax collectors for the Mongols
and then as the leaders of armed resistance against them that the
grand dukes of Moscow became the leaders of the Russian states,
starting the train of historic events leading to Russian and soviet
power.

The West was always a sideshow for Genghis. His real interest
was in conquering China. It was richer, bigger, and closer. However, he was not as interested in conquering China, specifically, as
he was in expanding his Central Asian empire. Genghis was a
Mongol, and Mongols counted their wealth in horses. A very
wealthy Mongol needed a lot of pasture for his many horses.
China unfortunately was cluttered up with farms, cities, roads,

and the like. Genghis solved this problem simply by devastating the lands, killing or driving off the residents, and letting the grass take over. In his later years he allowed a subordinate to convince him that, if the people were left on the farms and in the cities, he could tax them, and with the money he could buy things almost as good as horses. Once this new idea was adopted, the Mongol conquests lost some of their qualities of awesome devastation.

There was more to the Mongol conquests under Genghis than just the desire for more grass. Genghis once said that his greatest pleasure was "to cut my enemies to pieces, drive them before me, seize their possessions, witness the tears of those dear to them, and embrace their wives and daughters." There was also a remarkable streak of puritanism in him. He railed against the Chinese, saying, "Heaven is weary of the inordinate luxury of China. I remain in the wild region of the north; I return to simplicity and seek moderation . . ." Finally, there was an element of resignation, that nothing really lasts forever and historical origins may be forgotten:

> After us, the people of our race will wear garments of gold; they will eat sweet greasy food, ride splendid coursers, and hold the loveliest of women, and they will forget that they owe these things to us . . .

Tamerlane was the last of the great Central Asian conquerors and movers of peoples. In the nineteenth century, historians tried to trace his ancestry back to Genghis or at least to some noble associate of the Khan, but in fact Tamerlane was not even a Mongol. He stemmed from one of the Turkic peoples. Nonetheless, he carried on the grand tradition of the Mongols. Between his first conquests in 1358 and his death in 1405, Tamerlane led armies from Russia to the Persian Gulf and from Greece deep into India. He was a devout Moslem and turned his capital at Samarkand into one of the architectural marvels and intellectual centers of the day. He was particularly partial to Persian poetry.

Expansion was rapid under Tamerlane because it was ruthless. In December 1378, during the siege of Delhi, he ordered the massacre of 100,000 prisoners because they had become an encumbrance. After the fall of Delhi, he granted the citizens their lives, but the conditions of the occupation were so harsh that they rose up against him. The ensuing slaughter was of such proportions that, instead of piling the skulls of the victims in a single great heap as he usually did, Tamerlane piled them in four great heaps, one at each of the corners of the city. René Grousset, the great French historian of the steppes, adds that, "So far as was possible under the circumstances, however, Tamerlane as usual spared qualified craftsmen and sent them to beautify Samarkand."

On other occasions, Tamerlane would have a low, round pit dug and then line the rim with prisoners whose hands were tied behind their backs. A rope would be run through the knots at the prisoner's wrists, looped around the neck of the next person, passed on to the third prisoner's wrists, and so on all around the circle. Now half of the prisoners had the rope around their necks, and half had the rope attached to their wrists. Then another rope would be looped around so that everyone was tied by neck and wrist to his neighbors. Then Tamerlane's soldiers would shove the prisoners into the pit. Of course, as they fell, the ropes would loosen and tighten and get snarled up, and everyone slowly strangled everyone else. Afterward, the soldiers filled in the hole so that anyone who survived the strangling would suffocate under the dirt. Tamerlane, like the Mongols before him, believed that these techniques weakened the will of his enemies so he could expand his power over people with less bloodshed.

The expansions of the Mongols and kindred Central Asian peoples came to an end at the beginning of the modern era, probably because of the development of firearms in the West and more sophisticated forms of social organization in both East and West. The strength of the surrounding societies grew to the point that they could fend off the Mongol horsemen. Even during the 1000 years that all this was going on, however, no Central Asian empire remained dominant for long.

Why these surges took place is not known. It was probably not because of periodic population explosions, as nineteenth-century historians felt. It is more likely that the appearance of men with exceptional talent for leadership and organization—Attila, Genghis, Tamerlane—coincided with some particular opportunity to conquer, setting the stage for a sudden expansion. The organizational systems of the Mongols, though, were only extensions of the personalities of their leaders, and when the leader died the empire withered.

The various movements of people just described all had conquest as their primary objective and usually did not involve transfers of very large numbers of people from one place to another. With the exception of the Germanic tribes such as the Visigoths and Vandals, who moved in to settle, most of the conquering migrants were men of the warrior class whose women and children remained behind. And even these men did not always stay and settle in the new territory. When they did, they made up a small, occupying garrison within a much larger subject population. This was true of the conquering Romans (who nevertheless did generate mass migration in the opposite direction, to Rome), the Greeks under Alexander, and the various waves of Central Asian barbarians and Mongols.

To an extent it is true also of the Arabs, who were carrying the word of Mohammed to the far corners of the world they knew. Perhaps no more than 8,000 Moslem Arabic warriors conquered Persia, for example. Later, Europe was another source of such conquest-oriented, expansionist movements, which not infrequently were motivated partly by religion. The Spanish in the New World and the British in India are two clear examples. The Crusades can also be seen in this light.

Pope Urban II preached the First Crusade at Clermont in France in 1095. He claimed that the possession by non-Christians of the holy places where Christ had walked and preached, had been born and had died, was an abomination not to be suffered. Of course, Christians had been suffering this abomination for 450 years, but suddenly it became unbearable. The response was wildly enthusiastic, and Urban found that he had to forbid certain people from going rather than continue the recruitment propaganda. Every man in Europe wanted to go forth and kill a Moslem for Christ.

By the Middle Ages, Europe had evolved one of the most curious social systems in the history of the human race. The great bulk of society—perhaps 90 percent—was locked into agricultural serfdom to support a tiny military aristocracy and a heavily bureaucratized Church. The usual description of medieval society is that it was composed of those who worked, those who fought, and those who prayed. In the eleventh century the military aristocracy—the nobility—were producing more of themselves than they had castles to fill. The growing concept of *primogeniture,* the practice of leaving the family castle and all the lands to the oldest son and allowing the younger sons to shift for themselves, was great for preserving the family estate intact and assuring that the family name would have to be reckoned with. On the other hand, it was hard on the younger sons. They were born into the warrior class and grew up with all the martial skills and manners. The classes were hermetically sealed, and no son of a warrior would think of working. One solution was the acquisition of new land somewhere. Primogeniture exerted only one of the pressures that led to the Crusades, but it did guarantee that a ready supply of experienced and otherwise unengaged killers was available for the task.

Within five years after the First Crusade was preached, Jerusalem was in the hands of the Western Christian knights, and a string of European states was set up, running from Edessa in modern Turkey almost to the Red Sea. Although Edessa, the northernmost of the Crusader states, fell almost within a generation, a Western military presence in the Near East lasted for almost two centuries, and a Western, largely Italian, commercial presence was permanently established. Chess, backgammon, and falconry were introduced into Western civilization along with a taste for decently seasoned foods. The role of spices in the history of European exploration and discovery is too well known to repeat here, but be reminded that, among other things, it led to the discovery of America. It has been argued that the crusading experience was a model for the later colonial adventures of the European nations.

Regardless of their origins, migrations for military conquest seldom lasted more than a couple of centuries at most and usually involved relatively small numbers of people, even for their times. The examples described here are by no means the only migrations known in history. They are among the best-known such episodes and most of them exerted a disproportionate and lasting influence on the culture and history of the invaded peoples. This kind of migration has persisted into the modern era, but in the last three centuries or so it has increasingly been overshadowed by other kinds of migration, particularly mass migrations. These migrations had effects that were even more profound.

MASS MIGRATION IN THE MODERN ERA

The age of European exploration beginning in the fourteenth century took men from Spain, Portugal, and England to distant parts of the globe over the next few centuries, particularly to the previously unknown, sparsely populated Americas. Yet it was more than a century after Columbus that even modest numbers of Europeans began to cross the Atlantic with the intention of establishing permanent settlements in the New World. In fact, the Spanish and Portuguese discouraged settlement, looking instead for mineral wealth (especially gold) and other resources. Eventually, however, the Europeans began exploiting the new lands to grow crops that could not be grown in Europe: sugar, cotton, tobacco, tea, and coffee, to name a few.

But the Europeans themselves were ill-suited to hard work in fields under a hot sun, and the indigenous population was small and uncooperative. So the Europeans turned to Africa to fill their labor shortage. Hence the first great wave of migration to the New World was an involuntary movement. Between 1451 and 1870 nearly ten million West Africans were captured and transported across the Atlantic. Viewers of the television mini-series *Roots* were given a glimpse of the hideous conditions under which the slaves made the long voyage—usually chained in the hold of the ship on bare-board bunks with the poorest of food and no sanitary provisions whatever. It is estimated that, overall, somewhere between 10 and 25 percent perished en route; on some trips more than half of the unwilling passengers did not survive.

Meanwhile, Europe's population had been growing steadily, and population pressures began to be felt. Before the late eighteenth century, only a few Europeans had left home to settle permanently in a new land. But after 1800, conditions for relatively large numbers of people in Europe were bad enough to encourage them to leave, while conditions of sea transport and opportunities in the New World and elsewhere had improved enough to be enticing.

After 1800, the floodgates seemed to open, and Europeans by the millions began migrating to North and South America, Australia, New Zealand, and parts of Africa to take up residence. Although it has by now slowed relatively to a trickle, and in some places (notably some African nations, in the wake of independence), even reversed itself, this great movement continues today. The United States has been by far the greatest recipient of immigrants in the world. Altogether, some 50 million people have found homes in the U.S. during its 200 years as a nation. The great majority came from Europe, but a substantial 10 million have come from other continents.

Why People Migrate

In certain respects the modern pattern of movement is a distinctly different kind of migration from the kinds that predominated in the centuries after the fall of Rome. The most important difference is that the decision to move was usually taken independently by an individual or by the head of a family for that family. Occasionally, small groups, such as the early Puritan settlers of New England, moved as a group, but they were more the exception than the rule.

This is not to say that large numbers of people from one place have not often ended up at the same destination. On the contrary, demographers have long noted the tendency of migrations to form "streams"—later migrants are more likely to follow in the footsteps of trailblazers than to go somewhere else. The first migrants find the way and by various means make it easier for others to follow. Often they even recruit their followers. Thus separate decisions made by thousands or even millions of individuals to move in the same direction produce a mass migration.

Migration is usually defined as "a permanent or semipermanent change of residence." This broad definition, of course, would include a move across the street or across a city. Our concern is with movement between nations, not with internal migration within nations, although such movements often exceed international movements in volume (especially the contemporary worldwide trend toward urbanization). Today, the motives of people who move short distances are very similar to those of international migrants.

Students of human migration speak of "push" and "pull" factors, which influence an individual's decision to move from one place to another. Push factors are associated with the place of origin. A push factor can be as simple and mild a matter as difficulty in finding a suitable job, or as traumatic as religious persecution, war, or severe famine. Obviously, refugees who leave their homes with guns pointed at their heads or with hate-filled mobs at their heels are motivated almost entirely by push factors (although pull factors do influence their choice of destination).

Pull factors are those associated with the place of destination. Most often these are economic, such as better job opportunities or the availability of good land to farm. The latter was an important factor in attracting settlers to the United States during the nineteenth century. In general, pull factors add up to an apparently better chance for a good life and material well-being than is offered by the place of origin. When there is a choice between several attractive potential destinations, the deciding factor might be a noneconomic consideration such as the presence of relatives, friends, or at least fellow countrymen already established in the new place who are willing to help the newcomer settle in. Considerations of this sort lead to the development of migratory streams.

Besides push and pull factors, there are what the sociologists call "intervening obstacles"—deterrents to migration. Even if push and/or pull factors are very strong, they still may be outweighed by intervening obstacles, such as the distance of the move, the trouble and cost of moving, the difficulty of entering the new country, and the problems likely to be encountered on arrival.

The decision to move is also influenced by "personal factors" of the prospective migrant. The same push-pull factors and obstacles operate differently on different people, sometimes because they are at different stages of their lives, or just because of their varying abilities and personalities. The prospect of pulling up

stakes and moving to a new and perhaps very strange environment may appear interesting and challenging to a young, footloose man and appallingly difficult to a slightly older man with a
wife and young children. Similarly, the need to learn a new
language and customs may intrigue one person and frighten
another.

Regardless of why people move, migration of large numbers of
people causes friction. The United States and other "receiving"
countries (the term used for countries that welcome large numbers of migrants) have experienced adjustment problems with
each new wave of immigrants. The newest arrivals are usually
given the lowest-paying jobs and are resented by natives who may
have to compete with them for those jobs. It has usually taken
several decades for each group to gain acceptance in the mainstream of society in the receiving country.

Sometimes the friction is even more serious. Virtually every
major conflict over the past two generations has contained some
element of migration at its core. Hitler justified his attack on
Czechoslovakia on the basis of protecting the Sudeten Germans
who had migrated to Bohemia centuries before. The expulsion of
Jews from Europe and their arrival in Palestine, the creation of
the State of Israel, and the expulsion of the Palestinian Arabs is a
story too familiar to need repeating here. Ultimately, some of the
Palestinians settled in Lebanon, and their concern for regaining
what to them is their Palestinian homeland rather than becoming
part of the Lebanese culture and society has turned that country,
once thought of as "the Switzerland of the Middle East," into a
bloody shambles.

The first shots of World War II in Europe were fired in the
German free city of Danzig, now the Polish city of Gdansk. Danzig
was a monument to the massive, medieval German "Push to the
East," in which the Germans slowly pushed the Slavs and others
aside to take the land for themselves. The city became Gdansk
following the ruthless expulsion of the German-speaking residents to the Soviet zone of Germany in the winter of 1945–46.
The Slavs were gaining revenge for what the Danzigers' compa-
triot Germans had done to them over the previous six years. The
bitterness of the forced emigrants from Danzig and the other,
formerly German lands of Poland remained a force in West
German affairs for twenty years, during which no German politician dared fail to express his dedication to regaining the "lost
provinces."

Along with the conflict that migration often breeds, the experiences of the migrant groups can have a disproportionate impact
on their views of themselves in later, more settled times. When

one asks the member of some group why he and his relatives are the way they are, the answer is frequently given in terms of an historical experience, real or imagined, during some earlier time of migration. Very few Americans actually have ancestors who crossed the prairie in a covered wagon, lived in a log cabin, or were involved in any of the legendary frontier experiences. But Americans are nevertheless fond of saying that their national character, with its imputed characteristics of forthrightness, honesty, self-reliance, courage, and industry, stems from their "frontier heritage."

Fantasized embroiderings on historical fact, reflecting an American self-image stemming from a migratory past, find their way into the popular culture in literature, films, and television programs. Analogous folklore can be found in every culture. An heroicized and manufactured view of history is far more important in shaping the self-image of Americans—indeed, of most people—than is the historical past as it actually was.

While many general statements can be made about migration, each migratory episode is in other respects unique. We shall now explore in some detail several migrations that have had a lasting impact on the history and cultures of the peoples concerned. The first of these really concerns an encounter between two distinct migrating peoples, each of whom were responding both to push and pull factors.

A Migratory Collision

In September 1977 newspapers revealed that the joint initiative by the Soviet Union and the United States had dissuaded the government of the Republic of South Africa from exploding a nuclear bomb. That neither of the world's super-adversaries could benefit from an augmentation of the strength of South Africa's white government underscores the anomalous nature of events unfolding there: the final sorting out of a collision between two migrant peoples.

What makes contemporary South African whites incomprehensible to almost everyone but themselves is largely explained by a sense of isolation that began more than 300 years ago and a set of practices that served them well in settling their precious *veld* during the middle decades of the last century. As one journalist has put it:

> In the nineteenth century, Boer pioneers formed their wagons into a *laager,* or circle, whenever danger threatened. Now as their

country faces increasing pressure and criticism from abroad, some conservative South African whites are repeating the old war cry, "Back to the laager."

A South African farmer is quoted:

Well, let them all come and see if they can take us. We can ride against them again. We will ride until the blood covers our stirrups.

Simple explanations of complex phenomena are hazardous, but there may be some utility in viewing contemporary South Africans as storing up inside their circle all that is needed to survive. They are already ahead of all other nations in extracting oil from coal and are still increasing this ability. With careful management, the petroleum they have stored in abandoned coal mines can last a decade. In addition to small arms and nuclear bombs, they are capable of producing the whole intermediate array of weapons, including jet fighters, armored cars, and tactical missiles. The white South African can look to his Boer heritage and see nothing novel in being alone, beleaguered, and forgotten. When it comes to promises and guarantees from great powers beyond the sea, his heritage tells him he will probably be lied to.

In the 1830s, cattle-breeding Boer trekkers moved into the lush, empty plain of the South African *veld*. Their earliest forebears had first come out from the Netherlands in 1652 as employees of the Dutch East India Company to secure a landfall and supply depot for the Company's ships en route to Dutch trading posts in Indonesia. The original party proved too small to produce enough food to feed themselves and supply the ships too. So in 1657 the Company undertook a program of land grants to immigrants who would not be its employees, but free farmers—"Boers" in Dutch—who would make their living off the land and sell the surplus to the Company ships. The plan was a booming success from the point of view of the Company. Within half a century there was a community of some 1,500 farmers producing far more than they and the Company could consume. This overproduction weakened the ties between the farmers and the Company, and the farmers started moving out from Company headquarters at Capetown.

The weakening of economic ties with the Company was accompanied by a weakening of cultural ties with the Netherlands. Their language, at the beginning the Dutch of the streets and the docks rather than the boardroom or the university, became distinctly their own as the result of normal linguistic drift and incorporation of terms and phrases from various languages of Europe,

Africa, and Southeast Asia. The Company had neither the ability nor the desire to extend political control any great distance from Capetown, so the Boers ran their own affairs. Finally, the Dutch Reformed Calvinism that the original immigrants had brought with them became distinct from that of Holland, and there emerged a fierce religion of Old Testament judgmentalism emphasizing personal rectitude and self-reliance. As the eighteenth century drew to a close, about 15,000 Boer farmers were spread over 90,000 square miles. They had come to see themselves no longer as Dutchmen but as a white African tribe and would later call themselves *Afrikaaner*.

The original indigenous peoples of the Cape of Good Hope were the *Khoikhoi* and the *San*, whom the Europeans called Hottentots and Bushmen. Their incohesive social organization and small numbers were no threat to the purposeful Boers with their firearms, who easily enslaved them as agricultural workers or simply pushed them aside. But in the late eighteenth century, two new groups intruded into the area. First the British came. After 1815 they assumed what was left of the Dutch claim and settled in to stay and govern. With British authority established on the Cape, British immigration began. Though the Boer Africans had no great trouble with the British immigrants, their attitude toward British authority was even less respectful than it had been toward the Dutch. When Britain actually tried to rule, the Boers simply packed up and headed east into the unclaimed and ungoverned *veld*. There they encountered another group of immigrants.

Unknown centuries before and 1,500 miles to the north, in the Katanga region of the Congo basin, people of the Bantu* language group began to migrate in all directions. Their knowledge of ironworking and the growing of grains gave them the base for a large population, with which they pushed aside or dominated whoever stood in their way. In the early centuries of the Christian era, another great and remarkable migration had occurred. Clear across the Indian Ocean, all the way from Indonesia, came new migrants to Madagascar and East Africa. They brought with them the foodstuffs and technology of Southeast Asia, particularly the yam, the banana, and the outrigger canoe. The enterprising

---

*"Bantu" refers only to a linguistic group and not to a tribe or ethnic group. Bantu languages are spoken by many peoples in a belt running southeast from Western Nigeria to Mozambique and South Africa. Like the Indo-European languages among which are English, Sanskrit, Persian, and Norwegian, Bantu languages can be very different and are not necessarily mutually intelligible. What is described here is only one part of the Bantu expansion, which went in all directions.

Bantu quickly adopted these innovations. The new foodstuffs increased the quantity and variety of the Bantu's food supply and set the stage for another big increase in their population. The outrigger gave this population mobility in the form of a larger, faster, and more stable vehicle to use on the extensive waterways of Central Africa.

These developments led to a new round of Bantu migration, part of which was southward through present-day Tanzania and Mozambique. In the course of all this, these rich, proud, and accomplished peoples had picked up cattle culture, not so much for the beef—blood and milk were their principal bovine foodstuffs—as for the sheer prestige of holding mighty herds. By the early nineteenth century, Bantu peoples were spread thinly over the *veld,* and more were percolating in from the east. There was a sudden surge of Bantus—the little understood "Zulu explosion"—just as the *trekboers* were pushing into the *veld* from the southwest in the 1830s. On that great, grassy plain, the proud, cattle-breeding, black Zulu met the proud, cattle-breeding, white Boer, and each wanted the grass for his own herd.

The Zulu had not been an important tribe among the Bantu nations until its chieftainship fell to a military genius named Shaka about 1810. Shaka reorganized the military structure, weaponry, and tactics of the Zulu and brought them to a position of dominance among the Bantu tribes. The Zulus increased in number because Shako offered the tribes he confronted a choice between obliteration or amalgamation. Since he was quite capable of the former, his adversaries usually chose the latter.

Shaka had only the slightest contact with the Europeans, British or Boer, and it was Dingane, Shaka's brother, murderer, and successor, who faced the *trekboers* across the *veld.* There had been conflict and skirmishes between the Boers and various Bantu groups (the most redoubtable being the Zulu) for a half-century before the Great Trek of the 1830s. But the decisive contest to determine which migration would continue was a struggle between the Zulus and the Boers (and later the British) that lasted for the next half-century. Although the conflict began with Zulu treachery—a Boer negotiating party was invited into camp by Dingane and then murdered—there was little to choose between the adversaries in terms of decency. The Boers made up for their small numbers with staying power, tight social and military organization, and firearms.

For more than a generation, the Boers and the Bantus conducted a continuous struggle. The Zulus with their superior numbers, centralized military command, and well-drilled regiments wanted fixed battles. The fewer Boers avoided this at all costs. Their military organization was typical of a people in migration. They worked in small, loosely federated, mounted and therefore mobile units, carefully picking the time and place of battle to gain the greatest return for the smallest risk. The separate units were referred to as separate commands, or *Kommandos,* and commando warfare became the marvel of turn-of-the-century military affairs when it was used against the British in the Boer War.

The British authority on the coast had three choices in dealing with the migrants on the *veld.* First, the British might ignore both Boer and Bantu, let them fight it out, and then deal with whoever was left. Or they could try to extend their authority over both and attempt to regulate affairs among them, at the risk of being drawn into the struggle. Or they could attempt to stop the flow of peoples and risk all-out war with one or both groups. In fact they vacillated among all the options in hope of finding a viable, yet economic policy.

Finally, the British felt they had to settle the matter and crushed the Zulu war machine in the Zulu War, 1879–1883. To do so, they had to commit a force of 15,000 British and African troops. The Zulus were not easily crushed. On January 22, 1879, a Zulu army of 24,000, the largest force ever fielded in black Africa, attacked a body of 950 English and 850 native troops at Isandhlwana. Only 55 of the British survived. That night the victorious Zulu impi attacked a small British detachment at Rorke's Drift. There were 4,000 Zulus against just over 100 English, but the latter held in one of the most spectacular feats of arms in military history—a story told accurately and well in Michael Caine's first starring movie, *Zulu.* On July 4, 1879, the modern arms of the British wrote "finish" to the old Zulu order at the battle of Ulundi.

After Ulundi it was all downhill for the Zulus; in 1889 the British formally annexed Zululand. A decade later the British turned to subdue the Boers, and, in three years of warfare more ruthless than anything visited on the Zulus, they managed to destroy the Boers' war-making capacity.

In 1910 the British united their colonies of Capetown and Natal with the Boer states of Transvaal and the Orange Free State to form the Union of South Africa, an independent nation under the British Crown. In 1960 the Boers led the Union out of the Commonwealth, and it became the Republic of South Africa. Today, South Africa's racist apartheid laws make it an embarrassment to most nations of the world and have marked it for extinction in the eyes of the black nations nearest it. But then, the Boers were alone 300 years ago when they went out from Capetown, and they were alone and marked for extinction when they encountered the Bantu on the *veld* in the 1830s. South Africa, even more than the United States, is a nation that has been shaped by migration, and this shaping includes a willingness to stand alone in the face of potential destruction.

A Sudden Push

The Boer and Bantu migrations were slow, evolving over centuries, with pauses and changes of direction. It is only in retrospect that one can see the pattern. In the seventeenth century, when the first Dutchmen landed on the Cape of Good Hope and the Bantu were making their way through the rivers of East Africa, neither knew that they were heading for that confrontation on the *veld* and apartheid, any more than black and white people in contemporary South Africa know where they are headed. The neat historical patterns of migration with their clear motives and directions are seen only with hindsight.

Still, some migrations are simpler than others; one of the most straightforward was the migration of the Irish to the United States. Their migration was a classic case of "push"—those people had to leave Ireland or they would have died. This event was to have a profound and lasting effect on life in both Ireland and the United States.

From 1846 to 1851, about one and a half million people died of hunger and the diseases caused by hunger in Ireland. Of the million or so who fled in that period, three-quarters came to the United States. These were followed by another three-quarters of a million between 1851 and 1855. The immediate cause of the great exodus from Ireland was the potato famine, the greatest ecological disaster since the Black Death of the fourteenth century. The fungus that caused the Irish potatoes to rot in the fields struck elsewhere too, and, though it caused great hardship wherever it struck, the hardship was not of the same proportions. Still, there was an upsurge of immigration to the United States from Germany in those same years, caused in part by the failure of the potato crop there.

The potato blight was a particularly devastating catastrophe for the Irish not simply because of the crop failure, but because their British rulers felt few qualms about Irish suffering and did very little to alleviate it. The potato-killing fungus came one day on the wind, but British heartlessness developed slowly over centuries. Which caused the migration, the fungus or the British?

Ironically, the biological part of the problem originated in the New World. The potato is a native of the cool plateaus and valleys of the Andes, where it was discovered and cultivated by pre-Incan

Indians. Fungus was also a problem for the Andean potato cul-
tivators. The Indians guarded against the problem by cultivating
several varieties in each field, even including wild varieties. More
than 400 varieties are found in the Andes even today. The Europeans borrowed the clonal cultivation, but not the diversity. As
has so often proven to be the case, disaster was entrained by
unnecessarily practicing monoculture.

How the potato reached Europe is still a mystery—its introduction is thought to have been more or less accidental, via Spanish
galleons on which dried and raw tubers were often carried as
provisions. It is not clear how potatoes managed to survive the
long hot voyage, but by the end of the sixteenth century they were
being cultivated in Spain.

At first potato cultivation spread slowly, but as the population
of Europe grew, grain crops, affected as they were by smuts and
rusts that could seriously reduce yields, could no longer be viewed
as a sufficiently dependable food source. Fortunately, a dependable source seemed at hand—the easily stored and relatively
protein-rich potato.

In one land the potato was especially welcome. That was Ireland, a land that had been troubled by foreigners ever since the
Norsemen began to invade its shores around 800 A.D. The Irish
troubles so familiar to us today began in 1155, when Pope Adrian
IV made a grant of Ireland to Henry II of England, the condition
being that Henry shape up the Irish Church and state. Toward
the end of the sixteenth century, after 400 years of trying, the
English brought the Irish firmly, if only briefly, under their yoke.
This was done by Elizabeth I, who crushed a series of rebellions,
started the systematic persecution of Catholics, and frustrated
Spanish attempts to give help and relief to the Irish. In the
process, she founded a tradition of bitterness between Protestants
and Catholics that subsequent monarchs and their prime ministers managed to build into a sturdy, even indestructible heritage
of killing, bombing, and terror that can be seen regularly today in
the streets of Belfast and throughout the northern counties.

Elizabeth's efforts were followed in the seventeenth century by
the "Plantation of Ulster"—the transplantation of Scottish and
English tenants onto land confiscated by the government in
Northern Ireland. This was intended to assure a population loyal
to the Crown and a seedbed for Protestantism, which however did
not take root in most of the country. The Irish continued to rebel.
Their uprisings were crushed by Oliver Cromwell in the middle
of the century and by William of Orange at its close. The penal
laws that followed made Catholicism illegal and denied Catholics
access to schools, professions, and public office. Progressively,

Ireland became a land of a Catholic majority ruled by a foreign nation through a Protestant minority. By the end of the eighteenth century, the Irish Catholics were typically tenant farmers or landless laborers at the mercy of an English landlord. To make things worse, most of the landlords were in England, and the property was controlled by estate agents who were even more rapacious and only rarely felt any responsibility for either the tenants or the land. Their only concept of social responsibility was to maximize immediate profits.

The French Revolution and the events that followed had dramatic consequences for Ireland. The revolutionary contagion spread from France, and in 1798 the Irish rose up again and attempted to eject the hated English conquerors. The "boys of '98" had no more success than the innumerable rebels before them. Their revolt was immortalized in the folk song, "The Rising of the Moon," but it was put down by government troops with customary savagery.

The Napoleonic wars immediately following the French Revolution had generated high food prices throughout the British Isles, which made smaller and smaller land holdings in Ireland profitable. The estate agents quickly took advantage of the situation to subdivide the estates further, thereby increasing the number of tenants paying rent.

Since potatoes could produce up to six times as much food on the same amount of ground as could grains, they were ideal for the tiny plots of the Irish peasants. The potatoes were also easy to hide from marauding British troops. The Irish became completely dependent on their potatoes, and "elegant" foods like milk and butter were reserved for rare and festive occasions.

Although civil rights had been gradually restored by the 1840s, "the government of Ireland was admittedly a military occupation, and the garrison of Ireland was larger than the garrison of India." The British had managed to reduce the Irish people to a state of abject poverty. In 1841 a census showed that nearly half the rural Irish population lived in windowless, one-room mud cabins. Furniture was a relatively rare luxury. The 9,000 people of one town in County Donegal had among them only 243 stools, 93 chairs, and 10 beds. Those who had been forced entirely off the land by the British tenancy system were in even worse shape. They usually lived in "scalps"—pits two or three feet deep covered with brush or turf.

Tragically, in the late eighteenth century, Ireland's population began a spurt of growth. Because there were no censuses, the population in 1780 can only be guessed, but the best guess is about five million. The population of Ireland had increased to just over

eight million by the time of the 1841 census. The increase is
especially impressive since it took place in the face of continuing
emigration to the New World, Australia, and Great Britain. In
1841 half a million native Irish were living in Britain. This population growth, coupled with British misrule, kept the Irish utterly
impoverished and pushed the country to the brink of famine. As
Cecil Woodham-Smith wrote in *The Great Hunger:*

> Farms had already been divided by middlemen and landlords
> but the sub-division which preceded the famine was carried out by
> the people themselves, frequently against the landlord's will. As
> the population increased and the demand for a portion of ground
> grew more and more frantic, land became like gold in Ireland.
> Parents allowed their children to occupy a portion of their holdings
> because the alternative was to turn them out to starve . . .

The children, of course, were forced to subdivide the land with
the grandchildren, and soon numerous families were living on
land that could not properly feed even one. As many as two
million Irish people did not own even a tiny plot but rented little
parcels of land communally. They were always short of food by
the late spring and early summer when the last season's harvest
was near exhaustion and the new one not yet in. The stage was set
for disaster, and it came in the form of a fungal blight that
attacked potatoes—*Phytophthora infestans*—the "terrible plant de-
stroyer." The year 1845 had a glorious spring but an unusually
cold and wet summer, a perfect season for the blight. By August
potato plants all over Europe began to sicken, and those potatoes
removed from the ground in seemingly good condition rotted
into a stinking black mess in storage. In Ireland about half the
crop was eventually lost and those Irish living in the areas worst
hit by the blight were quickly reduced to desperation. It was
obvious that something had to be done, but what to do was not at
all obvious.

In the mid-nineteenth century, the economic and social notion
of laissez-faire held sway. British politicians fervently believed
that government interference in economic affairs was virtually
immoral. They believed that the cumulative effect of the self-
interested behavior of individuals would prove best for society,
that private enterprise and private property were holy, and that
property owners had every right to exploit their property, their
tenants, or their employees as they wished. In industrializing
Britain this system had produced great prosperity for a few and
perhaps a mild improvement for the rest.

Yet the prevalence of this philosophy did not prevent Sir

Robert Peel, the British Prime Minister, from recognizing that something had to be done about Ireland. His ingenious solution was to set up a relief commission to import maize (American corn), in which there was no established trade. The government's purchase of "Peel's brimstone," as it became known, did not interfere with private enterprise. To provide the means for purchasing the maize, Irish laborers were hired on a variety of relief projects.

The plan did not work very well. The maize was hard to grind and unfamiliar to the people—but it was eaten. The relief machinery was cumbersome to set up and functioned poorly in many areas. There was more starvation than usual in early 1846, but a total disaster was avoided. On the other hand, the bitterness of the Irish increased. Poor crops meant that poor people could not pay their rents. Though some landlords forgave the rents, others were delighted to get rid of nonpaying tenants, and the pace of evictions accelerated. The tenants were not only thrown off the land but their pathetic dwellings were "tumbled"—torn down so they could not be reoccupied.

The most notorious evictions at the start of the famines were some 300 tenants of a Mrs. Gerard in a village in County Galway. The tenants were not paupers; they were quite prosperous by Irish standards. But Mrs. Gerard wanted to turn their holdings into pastureland, so they were evicted and their homes demolished with the help of police and troops. Woodham-Smith described the scene:

> . . . women running wailing with pieces of their property and clinging to door-posts from which they had to be forcibly torn; men cursing, children screaming with fright. That night the people slept in the ruins; the next day they were driven out, the foundations of the houses were torn up and razed, and no neighbor was allowed to take them in.

After such evictions, the people usually retreated to their burrow-like "scalps." But many of the landlords remorselessly winkled the evicted families out of even those.

Even more than the evictions, a second phenomenon outraged the starving Irish and further poisoned the relations between them and the English. As the grip of famine tightened, grain was still being exported from Ireland to England, and it continued to be even as the Irish died of hunger. Various excuses have been given for this by economists—just as some today try to justify the flow of protein from hungry nations to overfed ones—but the fact remains that hungry people had to sell their produce in order to pay their rents. Eviction was a death sentence. The Irish had to stand by and watch convoys of food leave their market towns for England under heavy military guard.

In the summer of 1846, the "luck of the Irish" was all bad. Due to a lack of "seed" potatoes, only about two-thirds of a normal crop was planted, and the blight returned and destroyed it all. The plants withered and blackened in a matter of hours; when potatoes were dug up, they turned into the now familiar sickening black ooze.

Only the British could save Ireland now, but Sir Robert Peel's Tory government had been replaced by the Whigs under Lord John Russell, who was even more infatuated with the doctrine of laissez faire than Peel had been. The relief of the Irish was, in essence, to be left to private charity; hence there was essentially no relief. The financial resources of the Irish landlords were not up to the task, even if the landlords had been willing to expend them. The government was forced to continue expanding programs of public works in order to provide income to the destitute so they could buy food. But it was too little and, for many, too late. A great many of the hungry could not find work, and those who did were often not paid. For example, one Denis McKennedy of County Cork died by the side of the road when he was owed two weeks' wages. A jury determined that he "died of starvation due to the gross negligence of the board of works." By late 1846 death by starvation was common. A visitor to the country wrote to the *Illustrated London News:*

> At a poor nailor's cabin; his wife some time dead; two children on a miserable bed, some scanty covering thrown over them, but destitute of clothes; one of them so weak from want of food, as to raise himself with difficulty for the purpose of shewing his emaciated limbs. A labourer, with his wife and two children, sitting round a bit of fire; a younger child lying dead in its cradle, much emaciated from the insufficiency, as it was supposed, of maternal nourishment, the poor woman herself suffering from want; and the family unable to provide a coffin for the deceased. At Aghadown the police informed us that the night before, while on patrol, they were attracted to a cottage by an unsteady light; on proceeding to ascertain the cause, they found a father and son were lying dead whilst the survivors, being unable to purchase even a candle, were endeavouring to keep up a light with straw pulled from the thatch.

At Clare Abbey in December, Captain Wynne, the Board of Works inspecting officer, described a scattered crowd of women and children foraging over turnip fields "like a flock of famished crows, devouring the raw turnips, mothers half naked, shivering in the snow and sleet, uttering exclamations of despair while their children were screaming with hunger."

Things were especially bad around Skibbereen in Cork, where starvation had been reported in September. In mid-December, a magistrate, Nicholas Cummins, visited the Skibbereen district and graphically reported the horrors he saw: in one hovel he saw "six famished and ghastly skeletons, to all appearances dead . . . huddled in a corner on some filthy straw . . . they were alive—they were in fever, four children, a woman and what had once been a man." In a short time, because he had brought some bread, he was "surrounded by at least 200 such phantoms, such frightful spectres as no words can describe . . . their demonic yells are still ringing in my ears, and their horrible images are fixed upon my brain."

Hundreds of people died of starvation in Skibbereen in November and December of 1846, even though a well-stocked market was there. People starved, as happens in so many places today, not for lack of food but for lack of money to purchase it. In this case they were at least partially victims of the laissez-faire philosophy of the British government, the official view that "the famine in Ireland offered traders an opportunity to make profits of which it would be unjust to deprive them."

In early 1847 horrors piled on horrors. Soup kitchens were established, but they often dispensed faintly flavored water. Individual reports give only a hint of the suffering. For instance in County Cork, "a woman and her two children were found dead and half-eaten by dogs; in a neighbouring cottage five more corpses, which had been dead several days, were lying." A priest discovered one dying man surrounded by his dead wife, two dead children, and a dead infant being devoured by a starving cat. Masses of bodies were buried without coffins in shallow graves.

Starvation was accompanied in that awful year by typhus (known as "black fever" by the Irish), relapsing fever, scurvy, and dysentery, which ravaged the starving population. Even a good crop year was to bring no relief. Because of the shortage of seed potatoes, only 10 to 20 percent of the usual acreage could be planted, and the famine continued against a background of declining British and world interest. Then as now, drawn-out suffering ceases to be news, especially when, as for the British of that era, it is the suffering of a despised enemy.

In 1848 there was a complete crop failure again, and the suffering was reported as worse than in 1846–47. There were more failures in the years ahead, including a disastrous one in 1879, and starvation long remained a part of Irish life. But it was the events of 1845–48 that are conventionally called the Irish Potato

Famine, and the events of those years again confirmed the Irish as mortal enemies of the British.

Some have claimed that the British purposely tried to exterminate the Irish, that their behavior was fundamentally genocidal. A more reasonable judgment and the one accepted by most serious scholars today, including those from Ireland, is that the major elements were incompetence, callousness, and devotion to laissez-faire. The treatment of the Irish was not different in kind from that often meted out to poor and powerless Englishmen.

Whatever the motivations of those in power, it is clear that conditions for most of the people in Ireland became unbearable in 1846. It is hardly surprising then that many of the Irish attempted to flee their native land. Of course, there had been a steady flow of Irish overseas for years. From 1841 through 1845, an average of about 50,000 people left annually for the United States, Canada, and Australia, with two-thirds going to the United States. Almost all of these emigrants sailed in the spring and early summer when conditions for the crossing were best. The dramatic effect of the 1846 blight was evidenced by the unique autumn exodus that year—a sudden change from planned emigration of a few to a large-scale flight of refugees.

The need to "get out" was widely and quickly recognized in Ireland. In December 1846 the Marquis of Clanricarde wrote to Lord Russell:

> Nothing can effectually and immediately save the country without an extensive emigration. And I have not met in town, or in country, a reflecting man who does not entertain more or less the same opinion.

Between 1846 and 1850, almost 200,000 people emigrated annually to distant lands, and in 1851 over 260,000 left. Altogether, well over a million departed. In those same years, somewhere around one and a half million people died in Ireland of starvation and disease. A population that should have grown to more than nine million in 1851 was abruptly reduced to about six and a half million. Ireland's population continued to decline, largely because of continued emigration, for over a century. At present, there are only slightly over three million people in the country—about the number there were 200 years ago.

Hundreds of thousands of Irish also fled to not-so-distant lands, primarily to England, some to stay, some to sail on. In the first part of 1847, 300,000 hungry Irish descended on Liverpool, more than the city's native population. They traveled in utter misery—one witness before a government committee said that "the pigs are looked after because they have some value but not the migrants." They found squalor in Liverpool and brought fever with them.

Descriptions of conditions on long voyages to other continents make it seem that fleeing was little safer than staying. Ships were unsafe, overcrowded, and underprovisioned—"coffin ships" they were called. Passage was cheap, but the risks were great. At least ten percent mortality was not uncommon on trips that stretched to as long as two months. The most hideous conditions were found on ships financed by landlords trying to rid themselves of "a dead weight of paupers." When one ship, the *Lord Ashburton,* arrived in Quebec at the end of October 1847 carrying, among others, Lord Palmerston's tenants, conditions aboard were especially deplorable—"a disgrace to the home authorities," the *Quebec Gazette* said. Of 584 emigrants who boarded her, 107 died of disease on the *Lord Ashburton* and 60 were ill on arrival. Lord Palmerston's 174 tenants were virtually naked, and half of them had to receive clothes from charities before they could leave the ship without offending the public decency.

The reception the migrants received in North America was hardly warm—in part because they brought typhus with them. Ships were backed up for miles at the Canadian quarantine station at Grosse Isle in the St. Lawrence, near Quebec City, and hundreds died on the waiting vessels. More than 5,000 died at the makeshift hospital on Grosse Isle, taking many doctors along with them as the typhus spread. An avalanche of sick, dying, and penniless people descended from Grosse Isle on Quebec and Montreal, where many perished on the wharves and in makeshift sheds. Of some 100,000 people who left Ireland for Canada in 1847, an estimated 20,000 died.

No such horrors overtook emigrants headed for the United States. This was ensured to a great extent by the "Passenger Acts" passed by Congress in early 1847, which made passage to this country relatively expensive. Rigorous enforcement of the prohibition against landing the sick or destitute except under heavy bond saw to the rest. Groups desperate enough to storm ashore were forced back on board. The well-known inscription on the base of the Statue of Liberty says, in part:

> Give me your tired, your poor
> Your huddled masses . . .
> The wretched refuse of your teeming shore.
> Send these, the homeless, tempest-tost to me,
> I lift my lamp beside the golden door.

By and large those words have held meaning in American history, but in the years of the Irish Potato Famine, the very tired and the very poor, the very huddled and the very wretched were sent on to Canada.

Despite the obstacles, a great many of the Irish did reach the United States, a million and a half in the decade after the first blight and nearly five million altogether. Those who made it, like other immigrant groups before and after them, had to weather decades of rejection and scorn. Even the willingness of the Irish to do hard work was turned against them. The dumb "Mick" and the Irish washerwoman were standard items of ridicule on the stage well into this century. One joke ran that the wheelbarrow was invented to teach a Mick how to walk on his hind feet.

The Irish nevertheless worked hard to become assimilated. In times of war they fought and died for the United States. During the Civil War, entire units of the Union Army were composed of Irishmen. The great Irish actor, Victor McLaglen, very nearly made a career from the role of the Irish sergeant-major in almost every cavalry regiment John Wayne ever commanded. On the plains of Ellis County, Kansas, are six graves still carefully maintained by the Central Pacific Railroad, each containing the body of an Irish section hand. They had been killed by Indians who just did not see subtle distinctions among whites. What a long way to travel just to be killed by Indians.

The Irish settled mainly in the Eastern cities, where they quickly learned the power of the vote and of voting in a bloc. By the end of the Civil War, they were a force to be heeded. A generation later they dominated many local political scenes and were slowly moving up to state and national politics. Similarly, they came to dominate the police forces of the Eastern cities. The police science program at Fordham, New York City's largest Catholic university, became in effect the command and general staff school of the New York Police Department.

Finally, 115 years after the first potato blight, an Irish-American Catholic became President of the United States. They had made it.

The story of the struggle of the Irish to be accepted and assimilated into the mainstream of political and social life can be repeated for every immigrant group to enter the United States. Each wave of foreigners—the Germans, Scandinavians, Poles, Russians, Italians, Chinese, and Japanese—has met resentment and discrimination. In this generation, the Mexicans and Caribbean peoples are encountering the same difficulties. This problem is by no means limited to the United States; similar reactions have been seen in virtually every country that has admitted large numbers of immigrants with a different language and cultural background. By and large, the more "different" from natives the newcomers seem in terms of appearance, language, customs, and religion, the stronger the reaction is likely to be.

The Greatest Migration

The most spectacular sudden movement of human beings in great numbers was not an event of the distant past. No crusade, no advance of Mongol hordes, no press of barbarians toward Rome came close to matching in scale and rapidity the migrations in the fall and winter of 1947–48 on the Indian subcontinent, involving more than 12 million people.

At midnight, August 14, 1947, Great Britain's dominion over that subcontinent was voluntarily ended. In the wake of the British Raj, the colony of India was partitioned into India, a country ruled and dominated by Hindus, and Pakistan, a country ruled and dominated by Moslems. Partition came as a result of a long tradition of conflict and mistrust between Moslem and non-Moslem (principally Hindu and Sikh) communities. Its immediate cause was the insistence by the Islamic political organization—the Moslem League—that Moslems be given a separate nation of their own.

Led by the dour Mohammed Ali Jinnah, politically active Moslems feared for the fate of their people in a united India governed by the Congress Party of Jawaharlal Nehru, representing the Hindu majority. The majority of Indian villagers of both faiths would quite possibly have been willing to live together in peace if left alone. Unfortunately, however, various fanatic groups periodically stirred passions. This led to a communal bitterness that, in the end, even the saintly Mahatma Gandhi could not keep from erupting into the bloodiest rioting the world has ever seen.

On several occasions, both before and after partition, Gandhi managed to end Hindu-Moslem strife by his presence and example. A typical Gandhian tactic was for that frail old man to threaten a fast to the death if violence did not end. Another was to go and live among villagers where massacres were threatened and preach his gospel of nonviolence to both Hindus and Moslems. Sometimes Gandhi's tactics succeeded.

Hindu-Moslem riots starting in Calcutta on the Moslem League's Direct Action Day (August 16, 1946) resulted in the loss of some 6,000 lives in that city alone. During the winter of 1946–47, Gandhi went to live in the Noakhali district of East Bengal, where stories of Moslem suffering in the Calcutta riots had turned the Moslem majority against the Hindu minority. As

Larry Collins and Dominique Lapierre described it in their fascinating book, *Freedom at Midnight:*

> They had slaughtered, raped, pillaged and burned, forcing many of their neighbors to eat the flesh of their sacred cows, sending others fleeing for safety across the rice paddies.

Gandhi walked barefoot through the villages of Noakhali, which were dotted with burned huts. He lectured the people, held interfaith prayer meetings, brought Moslem and Hindu leaders together as guarantors of peace, and restored the area to relative tranquility. But despite such successes, in the end he lived to see his dream of a peaceful, united India shattered in a horrifying bloodbath. Geography and ancient religious hatreds were against him.

The British, led by Viscount Louis Mountbatten, undertook the task of fractionating the old India because even Jinnah, head of the Muslim League, and Nehru realized that the Moslems and Hindus could not agree on the new boundaries. Mountbatten, great-grandson of Queen Victoria, Empress of India, was appointed Viceroy of India in early 1947. He was given extraordinary powers to end the British colonial presence. They were needed. Even Mountbatten's tribulations during World War II as organizer and leader of the commandos and, later, Supreme Allied Commander in Southeast Asia seemed rather minor in comparison to what faced him as Viceroy.

His basic problem was that the antipathetic Moslems and Hindus were not geographically segregated on the subcontinent. Therefore, any plan of partition would inevitably leave millions of Moslems in Hindu-dominated India and millions of Hindus in Moslem-dominated Pakistan. The job of determining the new border was given to a distinguished British barrister, Sir Cyril Radcliffe. He had to complete this daunting task almost singlehandedly within a few months. Radcliffe was chosen specifically because he was ignorant of India—a condition thought necessary to avoid accusations of favoritism. But even if he had known India well and had been given years, Radcliffe could not have done it right. To do it right was impossible.

The rich, irrigated, agricultural plains of the Punjab in Northwestern India, Bengal, and the region of the Ganges Delta in the Northeast were the principal natural regions that had to be divided. Imagine the problems that would be presented by trying to divide the United States into Catholic and Protestant countries along a line running roughly between New York and San Francisco. Imagine also that it had to be done in two months, maximizing the number of Catholics north of the line and Protestants to the south. Finally, assume that many thousands of Americans had recently been killed in Catholic-Protestant rioting. That will provide some feel for the task confronting Radcliffe.

Inevitably, after partition, some farmers would find their fields in one country and their homes in another. One nation would contain the main components of irrigation systems designed to water crops growing in an area now in the other nation. There would be factories in India designed to process raw materials produced in Pakistan. Jute was, and still is, the main export crop of Bengal. But the mills that processed Bengali jute were in Calcutta, where there was a predominantly Hindu population. The Moslems expected Calcutta to become part of Pakistan, and the Hindus assumed that the great city of Lahore in the Punjab would remain in India. Both groups were to have their hopes dashed. From the start Radcliffe decided that Calcutta would remain in West Bengal (India), and he gave Lahore to Pakistan because "they had to have a big city in West Punjab." So Radcliffe left the great industrial center of Bengal in India and left the jute growers of East Pakistan (now Bangladesh) without the mills to handle their crops. In short, partition automatically led to myriad personal and regional economic dislocations that in turn would contribute to a great human tragedy.

In the years prior to partition, the Indian subcontinent had been no stranger to tragedy. Failure of the rice crop in the winter of 1942 led to the Bengal famine of 1943–44, in which over one and a half million people died. Almost 100,000 Indians were killed or wounded in World War II. Moreover, premature death from malnutrition and disease had been the lot of millions of Indians annually for as long as anyone could remember.

But for unmitigated horror, few, if any, periods of human history can match the events of late August and September 1947. Accurate records do not exist, but all sources estimate that between 200,000 and 500,000 human beings were slaughtered in a few months following partition. More than twelve million people were uprooted from their homes and forced to migrate between Independence Day and March 1948—some 6.5 million Moslems from India to Pakistan and six million Hindus and Sikhs from Pakistan to India. Later, problems in Bengal led to the migration, by 1950, of about four million more Hindus to India from East Pakistan, while roughly a million Moslems moved in the opposite direction.

There is no way to allocate blame for the brutal events that swept the subcontinent in the fall of 1947. Moslems in the Punjab, misled by the propaganda of the Moslem League, assumed that, after Pakistan was established, the hated Hindus and Sikhs would disappear, leaving their property behind. When they did not disappear, Moslem mobs set out to make them disappear.

On the other side of the line that Radcliffe had sliced through the Punjab, the Sikhs prepared to expel their Moslem neighbors. They wanted to make room for their coreligionists who were expected to flood in from the Moslem part of the Punjab, now in Pakistan. Sikh and Hindu refugees did start arriving, carrying with them lurid tales of slaughter, rape, and forced conversion to Islam. These stories added fuel to the flames of religious strife already burning brightly in the Indian portion of the Punjab. Collins and Lapierre wrote: "The people of the Punjab set out to destroy themselves with bamboo staves, field hockey sticks, ice picks, knives, clubs, swords, hammers, bricks and clawing fingers."

An eyewitness described events in the city of Ramgarh in the Pakistani section of the Punjab:

> Here we saw the most ghastly sights and the most organized butchering of Hindus and Sikhs. The technique was as follows. First the Baluch soldiers and police came and shot at everybody on the road or in the houses. Following there were persons carrying tins of kerosene oil, etc. These people soaked rags in petrol or kerosene oil and set fire to the houses. When the houses were ablaze the inmates either came out on the road, where the military got them, or they crossed over to the adjacent houses and thus caused congestion in particular localities. This especially occurred in the Government quarters of the Clerical Establishment. The stabbers were then let loose on these houses. These fiends broke open the doors with axes and hammers and butchered the inmates, men and women, and abducted the girls within their sight. Whosoever tried to run away fell a victim to the shots of the Baluchis and the policemen. . . . We heard woeful cries of Hindu and Sikh children as they were done to death by the Muslim mob. The cry of one child was particularly heartrending. At about 2 P.M. we heard the cry, "Do not cut my throat. Do not cut my throat. You have already killed my parents. Take me with you." He was killed in the hospital verandah about twenty paces from us.

Such scenes were repeated thousands of times throughout the Punjab and to a lesser extent in other parts of India. People were shot, stabbed, and beaten to death singly or in groups. Many were cremated alive in homes, temples, and other buildings. Mutilation was commonplace—in one hospital the dominant types of wounds treated were:

(1) amputation of limbs, hands, and forearms, (2) skull and temple injuries, (3) stab wounds penetrating the abdomen and chest, (4) bullet and gunshot wounds, (5) amputation of breasts of women (six such cases of chopped off breasts were brought to the refugee camp and all of them proved fatal), (6) circumcision wounds performed on the male organs of many young men and old men, (7) cut throat cases and (8) burns. . . .

Refugees fleeing the bloodbath were preyed upon on the road. Stragglers were picked off; entire groups were massacred. Trains arrived in stations awash with blood, the passengers slaughtered. Between September 20 and 23 alone, some 2,700 Moslems and 500 non-Moslems lost their lives or were wounded on trains in the Punjab.

The creation of two nations on the Indian subcontinent and the subsequent massive exchanges of population did not bring an end to ethnic strife. Partition was immediately followed by conflict over Kashmir, and fighting between the two nations continued in 1948. The UN intervened to obtain a cease-fire, but Kashmir remains to this day a bone of contention between the two nations. So did India's possession of the headwaters of the two great rivers essential to the lives of both countries, the Ganges and the Indus. In August 1965 the tensions led to an open war which reached a stalemate in September, after which a UN-sponsored cease-fire was negotiated.

Meanwhile all was not well within Pakistan. Although the people of two parts of the country were bound together by the common faith of Islam, they were separated by 1,000 miles of Indian territory and by a cultural gap that was even more difficult to bridge. As Collins and Lapierre put it, "Punjabis and Bengalis . . . were as different as Finns and Greeks. . . . Neither history, nor language, nor culture offered a bridge by which these two peoples might communicate."

East Pakistanis chafed under the political domination of the West, until in early 1971 the Bengalis of the East revolted and declared themselves independent. The Pakistani military regime of General Yahya Khan attempted to suppress the revolt in another ghastly bloodbath. It is estimated that as many as one million Bengalis were killed in battle or murdered after the fighting ended. Some ten million refugees fled across the border into India, causing severe economic problems for that already overburdened nation.

At the end of 1971 India intervened militarily, invaded East Pakistan, and defeated Yahya Khan's army of West Pakistanis. East Pakistan then became a third independent nation on the subcontinent, the poorest of all, Bangladesh. Once again millions of refugees were on the move; this time Bengalis were returning to their homes in Bangladesh. Several years later another migration was arranged; Biharis, a minority group in Bangladesh, emigrated to Pakistan.

With all the bloodshed that accompanied partition and continued in the subsequent decades, the suffering caused by these migrations has tended to be overlooked. To put it in perspective, an American might consider what it would be like for all the people in California, Washington, and Oregon to be forced to leave their homes, taking only what they could carry, and walk scores, or even hundreds of miles to settle in a foreign land among total strangers.

The refugee migrants, as so often happens, were the victims of political troublemakers such as Jinnah. It will never be known whether the migrations will prove to be a benefit in the long run. Certainly they were a hardship in the short run. But might the bloodbath have continued and even intensified if the people had remained where they were? Or might Gandhi's ideas eventually have prevailed and brought peace to the subcontinent? No one can say.

The Soccer War

A more recent migration was considerably smaller in scale and effect than either the Irish emigration or the consequences of India's partitioning. The migrants in this case were responding to both push and pull factors, unlike the Irish and the people of South Asia, who were clearly pushed out of their homes. Like the Indian partition, however, this migration led to a war, if only a brief one. Since the incident that touched off the powder keg was a soccer game, the conflict has come to be known as the "Soccer War."

The regional semi-finals of the World Cup soccer competition were played in San Salvador on June 15, 1969, between the national teams of El Salvador and Honduras. El Salvador won. There is nothing in American sport comparable to World Cup soccer competition for Latin Americans. On Sunday, throughout Latin America, almost everyone is either playing soccer or watching it. The only bullring in Mexico City seats 55,000 people, but the two principal soccer stadiums together hold over 200,000. The popularity of the game and the portion of the population involved in it is even greater in the small, impoverished Central American republics.

It has the great advantage of being a cheap game to play. To be sure, Americans, who are just learning the game, can make it expensive with special shin guards, knee socks, and prescribed dress; but on the municipal playing fields and in the town squares of Honduran and Salvadoran towns and cities, only the ball is needed. Goalposts can be improvised. We have seen poor children in Tegucigalpa, the capital of Honduras, playing without even a ball. They used a bundle of tightly knotted rags.

Soccer, or *fútbol*, is a fast-moving, low-scoring game that builds up tension in spectators as steadily as it wears down the players. It is a game where great skill, an extra ounce of endurance, or a lucky break can turn defeat into victory and where even the very best fail regularly. The World Cup competition has a drama and builds tensions all its own. That the teams represent their countries is very important, particularly in small, poor countries that never get much positive recognition otherwise. In these countries, winning a silver medal in any event at the Olympics guarantees that the bearer will be a celebrity for life. In the heart of every Salvadoran and Honduran—indeed, in the hearts of the citizens of almost every small country in the world—is the fantasy that their national team will ultimately win the World Cup and for a brief moment they will shine with reflected glory. So a lot more than soccer is involved in the World Cup competition.

In 1969, the match between Honduras and El Salvador had even more behind it than the usual supercharged atmosphere of the sporting event itself. In previous years, over 300,000 Salvadorans—almost 10 percent of the Salvadoran population—had moved into Honduras in search of land for subsistence farming, and the Hondurans wanted them out. The only place for them to go was back to El Salvador which, with well over 400 people per square mile, simply could not accept them. Such crowding and poverty had been basic factors in the migrations in the first place.

As an indication of the level of poverty in El Salvador, the Institute of Nutrition of Central America and Panama estimated that in 1969 as many as *80 percent* of Salvadoran children showed signs of malnutrition, and that half of these were more than 25 percent under normal weight for their ages. The great majority of Salvadorans thus are so poor that they cannot provide their children with even a minimally adequate diet. This poverty is not only a consequence of a simple population/resource squeeze, however; it is exacerbated and perpetuated by a social and political system of remarkable venality and insensitivity.

El Salvador is governed by a military committee (*junta*), which first represents the interests of the army and secondarily serves the interests of a small industrial, commercial, and agricultural elite. One compassionate member of the Salvadoran oligarchy told us in 1976 of his efforts to get something done in El Salvador about the malnutrition among children:

> They just don't realize how important a little piece of meat or an egg once a week is to the children. They are colonels, and when you talk to them about nutrition they think only of rice and beans. They don't know about brain development and IQ development and how nutrition fits into that.
>
> I wouldn't care if the population of El Salvador were nine million or 90 million so long as they were intelligent human beings, but the way we are going, by the end of the century we are going to have nine million apes, nine million monkeys, and it could all be prevented.

The political climate in El Salvador in 1979 is not encouraging. The political system appears to be breaking down under charges of electoral fraud, social inequity, and schism between Church and state. The Inter-American Human Rights Commission has completed an on-site inspection of conditions in El Salvador; and *New York Times* and *Washington Post* accounts of the report indicated that the human rights situation in El Salvador might be worse than that in Nicaragua. Senior officials in the State Department have expressed concern about the Salvadoran situation, and one told us that he perceived a frightening pattern in the scores of political murders there. It seemed to him that a systematic effort was underway to kill, isolate, or incapacitate those progressive members of the "fourteen families" and the small middle class who might provide leadership for positive, beneficial change in the sociopolitical system. It is unclear whether the killings are by paramilitary groups like *"Orden"* and the "White Warriors Union," alleged to draw support from the military and the far right, in order to forestall change, or from one of three or four revolutionary groups on the *izquierda,* the left, aimed at setting the stage for violent revolution.

El Salvador is also characterized by its extreme disparity of income between rich and poor. Wealth is heavily concentrated in the hands of the oligarchy. This applies as well to land in rural areas, where in the past large landowners have expanded at the expense of small subsistence farmers. The most productive land in valleys is owned by the rich; the poor are mostly crowded onto tiny plots on the hillsides. In addition, there has been expansion in planting of export crops, which are mainly grown by large landholders, at the expense of food crops for local consumption, grown mainly by small farmers. There is little opportunity for the landless poor to rent land or to support themselves by working for large landowners.

The situation in Honduras is somewhat better. It, too, is run by a military committee that represents the army first and then the status quo, but the system is not as repressive, and the condition of the people is marginally better. As in El Salvador, 40 percent of the children are estimated to be at least 25 percent underweight, but another 40 percent do not show evident signs of malnutrition, as compared with less than 20 percent in El Salvador. In the 1960s there was land still available for peasants to rent, and jobs could be found on large plantations. If 10 percent of the population of El Salvador slipped illegally into Honduras to find a better life in the 1950s and 1960s, their condition in El Salvador must have been comparatively hopeless.

The situation in two villages, Tenancingo, a donor village in El Salvador, and Langue, a recipient village in Honduras, have been studied in detail by William Durham of the Department of Anthropology at Stanford University. He discovered that Tenancingo had long ago exceeded its carrying capacity for milpa (slash and burn) agriculture (indeed, a mid-nineteenth-century census observed that the village had exhausted its supply of firewood). He found that people had been leaving it throughout the twentieth century and that the rate of emigration had increased in recent years. Moreover, about a quarter of the young people from moderately well-off families (those with two to ten acres of land) were leaving the village. But, surprisingly, the children of very poor families (those with less than two acres) and the very well-off families (more than ten acres) were both leaving in far greater numbers; about half the children of these families were leaving.

In other words, the greatest emigration was among those so poor they could not stay and those who were well enough off to afford to go. The rich migrants, relatively speaking, were trying to break into the middle class in San Salvador, the capital city, while the poor ones went off looking for work in other rural areas or for land to farm. Some decades earlier, these young people might well have crossed the border into Honduras to find temporary work on banana plantations. Indeed, some were still going to work on cotton plantations in southern Honduras. But many of the young migrants to Honduras rented plots of municipal or privately owned land; some simply settled on apparently unoccupied land as squatters.

Certain principles of Hispanic property rights are very different from the corresponding principles of the Anglo-Saxon tradition. One difference is that, while the ownership of land is inviolable in our tradition, Hispanic law holds that the owner can lose his land if he does not "use" it. Land that is not being used for anything reverts to the nation and can be claimed by someone who will use it. Obviously, many arguments can arise from what "use" means, and they do. This principle means that "squatter's rights" are very real in Latin America. A deep understanding of the Latin American squatter can be gained from reading the delightful *Shepherds of the Night* by the great Brazilian author, Jorge Amado.

The attitude of many large landholders is indicated by the term used for the squatters in Costa Rica, *parasitos* (parasites). Parasites they may be to some, but they are still a force to be reckoned with. Often the easiest way to deal with squatters is to buy the land once from whoever has the title recorded in the national capital and then buy it again from the squatter. Another technique is for the large landholder to use his political influence to get the police and the army to oust the squatters.

In the 1960s the Honduran population grew very rapidly, and the Salvadoran illegals kept coming. At this same time there was a boom in the Honduran cattle industry, largely caused by an increase in beef consumption in the United States and other industrial countries, and a boom in cotton caused by rising market prices. Hence Honduran cattlemen and cotton planters, like planters in El Salvador earlier, were expanding at the expense of the small subsistence farmers—many of them squatters—and accelerating the land squeeze for those farmers. In the decade of the 1960s there were almost a hundred violent clashes between big landowners and peasant groups, and there were many hundreds of lawsuits.

There was no animosity, nor even any very deep sense of being different, between the Honduran and Salvadoran peasants. They felt they were all in the same boat and that their enemy was the large landholder. By and large, they were at least holding their own until the *Federacion Nacional de Agriculturas y Ganaderos de Honduras* (FENAGH), the national federation of big farmers and ranchers, hit on a new tactic—blaming the Salvadorans.

A Honduran law against the foreign ownership of land had been successfully ignored up to that time by United Brands and other U.S. fruit companies who had gigantic holdings in the north-coast tropical banana country. Now, though, FENAGH decided it could be used against the Salvadoran squatters. On November 24, 1967, FENAGH petitioned the President of Honduras to help them and stated in part:

> This problem of land invasions and future land grants obliges the Federation to denounce before the President of the Republic that, in considerable number, it is the foreigners who are usurping rural properties, especially foreigners of Salvadoran nationality.

FENAGH kept pounding on this theme. In another petition, presented less than three weeks before the World Cup semi-finals, it escalated the blame of the Salvadorans, saying, "a majority of the land invasions have been made by foreigners." "Foreigner" had become another word for Salvadoran.

The technique worked. In May 1969, the Salvadoran tenants on property that had been set aside for use in government land-reform projects were given 30 days to vacate their land. El Salvador broke diplomatic relations with Honduras as soon as the expulsion started, after closing the border to Salvadorans attempting to return. El Salvador then filed a petition with the Inter-American Commission on Human Rights, claiming that numerous rights violations had been committed by Honduran security forces against more than 500 Salvadoran families.

The defeat of the Honduran *fútbolistas* on June 15 in San Salvador was followed by scuffles and widespread abuse of Honduran spectators. Honduras reacted by increasing the rate of Salvadoran land evictions and went on to order the Salvadorans out of the country. El Salvador did not want to take in another 300,000 peasants of any nationality, so the army was dispatched to the border to block the entry of the returning Salvadorans, in the hope of forcing the Hondurans to keep them. When the Hondurans continued to return the Salvadorans to their native land, the Salvadoran government decided to attack and on July 14, 1969, invaded Honduras, "to defend the human rights of our countrymen." These were the same countrymen they had been prepared to keep out of the country by force a week earlier. Perhaps 2,000 people were killed in the skirmishes that followed.

The real purpose of the invasion may have been to induce intervention by the United States. If so, it worked. Operating through the Organization of American States, the United States arranged a cease-fire and a withdrawal of Salvadoran troops within three days after the invasion. Now, ten years later, the two countries still have no diplomatic relations and are still in a "state of war," with very little exchange of any kind. Unfortunately, these are neighboring countries in a region where all countries need to work closely and harmoniously with one another if they are going to survive.

Even more unfortunately, however, the fundamental causes of the migration and of the Honduran expulsion of Salvadoran peasants are still in force. The population in El Salvador continues to grow rapidly—currently, it is increasing by about 3.5 percent per year, which would double it in only 20 years. The pressure on the land, especially the fraction of land available to the poor, increases accordingly. Feeble attempts at land reform have been severely quashed. The social system is as inequitable and as repressive as ever, offering little hope that conditions for the poor majority will soon improve. In Honduras, the outlook is only slightly better. Wealthy landowners are no more tolerant of squatters and peasant tenant farmers than they were ten years ago, but there has been some movement toward land reform favoring small farmers. Whether this movement will be suppressed by wealthy interests or will gain momentum is still in doubt.

THE RISE OF THE MIGRANT WORKER

With the exception of the Boers and Bantu, the series of migrations just described have been motivated primarily by push factors. The Irish were pushed by famine, the Moslems, Sikhs, and Hindi of India and Pakistan by religious intolerance, and the Salvadorans by scarcity of land. But, within the past generation, expansion of industrialization in rich countries and the widening income gap between rich and poor countries have given new impetus to another kind of migration, in which the migrants are responding largely to pull factors. This newly prominent form of migration has increasingly come to replace the earlier ones. Conquering warriors have essentially faded from the scene, except perhaps in some tropical regions such as the Amazon Basin and Central Africa where remote tribes still survive and are free to conquer one another. Before 1940 (apart from political refugees, another large category of migrant that unfortunately shows no sign of becoming extinct), most migration consisted of individuals and families moving permanently from the populous Old World to the sparsely populated New World, Australia, or New Zealand. But since World War II, and especially since the mid-1950s, apart from refugees, the likeliest migrant has been a young man in his twenties who moves to a relatively more developed area or country to get a better job or better pay. Our discussion will center on those who move to another country.

Most migrant workers plan to stay in their destinations for a few months or a few years at most. Of course, some of them end up as permanent residents if the host country allows it, bringing their families to join them or marrying local people. The majority, however, see the stay as temporary, send some part of their earnings home to wives or parents left behind, and make little effort to become assimilated in their new surroundings. Those who do not speak the host country's language may learn only enough to do their jobs and survive.

Migrant workers are not a new phenomenon; they have existed

in parts of Latin America and Africa for perhaps a century or more, though not in as large numbers as today. Migrant workers can be found today in virtually all industrialized countries and in many of the more advanced less-developed countries (LDCs). For instance, workers migrate from Bolivia, Chile, Paraguay, and Uruguay to relatively industrial Argentina; from Colombia to oil-producing Venezuela; from Mexico and the Caribbean to the United States. They go from Lesotho, Malawi, Mozambique, and other black southern African countries to work in the mines and factories of South Africa. They move from Upper Volta to Ghana and the Ivory Coast to work on plantations or in mines. But, apart from the stream of Mexicans into the United States, perhaps the best-known examples are the roughly twelve million "guest workers" (including their families) in Northwestern Europe who have moved there mainly from Southern Europe, Turkey, and North Africa.

The rural populations of most less-developed countries and many of the less advanced of the developed countries in Southern Europe are growing rapidly or have been growing rapidly until quite recently. The result is that there are many more young people looking for land or for farming jobs than there are places for them. Rural unemployment rates are very high. The circumstances are similar to those that led to the migration of Salvadorans to Honduras—although usually not so extreme. The result is that, in nearly every country in the world that is not already fully urbanized, people in very large numbers are flocking to cities, seeking jobs. The only major exceptions to this are the People's Republic of China and the Communist regimes of Indochina where there are specific government policies and programs aimed at increasing rural employment and keeping their young people down on the farm.

Many cities in LDCs are consequently being all but overwhelmed by the influx of migrants from the countryside. But their fledgling industries are generally incapable of providing employment to so many job-seekers.

In overdeveloped countries the situation is different. Their populations have had relatively low birthrates for many decades, and therefore the numbers of young people entering the job market each year are relatively small and are significantly compensated by the older people who retire. Rapid post–World War II economic expansion in Northern Europe produced a serious labor shortage there. Even in overdeveloped countries like the United States, where there has been no absolute labor shortage (thanks to the postwar baby boom of the 1940s and 1950s), there has been a shortage of people willing to do hard, unpleasant, low-paying work. Thus unemployed workers in developing countries have been attracted to developed countries where jobs are available, apparently solving some serious problems for both sending and receiving countries.

Europe's Guest Workers

From the late 1950s until the recession of 1974, the flow of migrant workers into Northern Europe increased rather steadily year by year. In 1975 the number of guest workers (not including families) was over 6 million (down from a peak of 7.5 million in 1973). The principal host countries were West Germany (with over 2 million guest workers in 1975), France (1.9 million), the United Kingdom (three-quarters of a million) and Switzerland (a half-million). The guest workers made up over 8 percent of the 1975 work force in both West Germany and France, and an impressive 17 percent in Switzerland. In Luxembourg the number was deceptively small (only 47,000), but migrant workers accounted for a conspicuous 31 percent of the labor force. In England, though the number was large, only 3 percent of the labor force was made up of foreign workers in 1975. Moreover, nearly two-thirds of them came from Ireland. Other countries with significant numbers of guest workers are Austria, Belgium, the Netherlands, and Sweden, with work-force percentages ranging from 4.2 to 6.9.

By far the most generous donor country is Italy, which in 1975 had exported nearly a million workers to Northern Europe. The second is Turkey, with about 700,000, followed by Yugoslavia with slightly fewer, then Spain and Portugal (a half-million each), Algeria, Morocco, and Greece (over 200,000 each). Smaller numbers have come from other parts of Africa, Asia, and Latin America, mainly to France, England, and the Netherlands.

The first migrant workers came predominantly from Italy's impoverished south. Italy is a member of the Common Market, a factor that simplified the recruitment and immigration processes. Spain, Portugal, and Greece soon followed in sending forth their excess workers. These countries, like Southern Italy, were still relatively undeveloped in the 1950s and 1960s and had more rapidly growing populations than did their northern neighbors. More recently, these Southern European countries have been catching up as industrial nations while their birthrates have declined considerably, with the result that their surplus labor pools have shrunk. So countries that are further behind on the development/growth-rate continuum—Yugoslavia, Turkey, Morocco—have increasingly been filling the Northern European labor gap in the 1970s.

In many cases, workers have been actively recruited from their home countries by industries and governments of host countries. They are mainly hired for low-paying, low-skilled jobs as construction workers, factory workers, farm hands, waiters, dishwashers, and janitors, etc. Usually, a prospective migrant worker must pass a physical examination and then is given a work permit for a specific job with the company that hired him or her. (Although the majority are men, many women also migrate. They, too, generally are young and unmarried, and they commonly take jobs as factory workers, waitresses, hotel maids, or domestic workers.) The work permits are required for entry into the host country and are time-limited, though often renewable. This procedure has been followed by West Germany and Switzerland.

Alternatively, the workers may be citizens of former colonies who are attracted to the brighter opportunities in the former colonial powers—Algerians who go to France, for instance, or West Indians and Pakistanis who go to England. As a rule, entry into the host country is relatively easy for former colonials.

A migrant worker's lot is not an easy one. To begin with, beyond assuring the prospective migrant's health and that he or she has a job, most host countries until recently have done very little to help the migrant get settled and adjust to a foreign country. Most new arrivals have been faced with finding housing and learning the rules and customs of a strange society on their own. Usually they do not even speak the language when they arrive. Some countries have assigned housing projects (mostly of deplorable quality) for migrant workers, which in effect are ghettos. Elsewhere, migrant workers must fend for themselves in the housing market, though they often are helped by previous immigrants from their home countries, who settle newcomers in their own neighborhoods. Because of this tendency for migrants from a given country to cluster together, maintaining their own language and ethnic identity, and helping each other when problems arise, they form their own ghettos.

The people attracted to industrialized countries often are among the brightest and most enterprising in their home societies, but, as immigrants in a "more advanced" country, they are at a severe disadvantage from the start. The majority of migrant workers are semi-skilled or unskilled and often illiterate, and they are hired for the least prestigious jobs. Yet, though these jobs pay poorly and usually have long hours and unpleasant working conditions, they are better than what may have been available in the home country.

Because they are foreign and therefore have different habits and customs, speak the local language poorly or not at all, and compete with natives for jobs (or so it is believed), migrant workers are apt to be received by the native population with suspicion and prejudice. As workers have come from more distant lands outside Europe, with more distinctly different cultures, the prejudice has grown stronger. Resentment against migrant workers, naturally enough, is strongest among lower-class, poorly educated natives who are most likely to be competing for the same sorts of jobs. This hostility has sometimes led to outbreaks of violence. In Rotterdam in 1972 some Dutchmen attacked and beat up a group of Turkish workers. In 1973 in Marseilles a group of Algerians was so savagely beaten that four of them were killed.

The British journal *The New Internationalist* has published some case studies of migrant workers in Europe. One, featured in 1976, was a 28-year-old Algerian named Mohammed, who was working as an electrician in a Paris factory. He had learned his trade in France during an earlier work tour. Because Algeria is a former French colony, Algerians can migrate easily, even without guaranteed jobs. But since the 1974–75 recession, finding work, even the most unpalatable jobs, has been difficult; some of Mohammed's friends had spent up to six months job-hunting.

Mohammed was living in a "foyer," a rather spartan, badly built hotel that the French government provides for migrant workers, most of whom are men living alone. Several men were sharing a bathroom, kitchen, and a "day room" in Mohammed's foyer, though each had his own tiny bedroom. The foyer housed about 200 men, 30 percent of them Algerian. The remainder came from Southern Europe and the Middle East. The foyers are partly subsidized by the government, but the migrants are also charged some rent plus utilities.

Mohammed was working a ten-hour day, seven days a week, earning about 320 dollars a month. At least a third of his income was needed for his living expenses. At the time of the interview, Mohammed was still getting settled and had not yet sent money home to the wife he had married after his first three-month work tour in France. Bringing his family to France would have cost him more than he could afford. Mohammed's comments on the hardships of such family separation are worth considering:

> It's difficult being alone here. If someone's sick, who makes the food? Who will give us something to drink? It's very difficult for older people to be separated. There are many marriages which break up. The French could not live like we do, and leave their wives far away.

As might be expected, most of Mohammed's friends were from his home country. When asked about the French, he said:

It's difficult to make French friends if you are an immigrant worker. People have very little respect for us. It always depends on the people. Some of them don't mind foreigners, but they are now saying that they don't need us here.

It should be added, of course, that these young men have little opportunity to make French friends or otherwise become integrated into the local society, living as they do in segregated housing projects, working very long, often irregular hours, and many of them having to commute additional hours to their jobs daily.

Mohammed's experiences and feelings seem to be fairly typical of the guest-worker situation in most European countries. Some host countries, notably Sweden and the Netherlands, have made greater efforts to help guest workers become oriented and gain access to job benefits and social services than Mohammed found in France. Other countries have done even less in the past. As the trend toward making guest workers permanent residents unfolds, more countries are likely to provide such services and try to integrate the newcomers into the larger society. This will make life for immigrants much easier, particularly if their families join them, but it may create new problems for the host societies.

England: A Special Case

England's migration situation is somewhat different from that of continental Europe, and there are several interesting aspects to it. Since World War II, England has been both a significant exporter and an importer of people. English natives are still emigrating in fairly large numbers to Australia, New Zealand, Canada, the United States, and until recently South Africa. During the same period, large numbers of people from elsewhere have entered the United Kingdom, most of them to stay. There was a time in the 1950s when Britain imported migrant workers from Southern Europe, as France and Germany have continued to do. But, beginning in the 1950s, there has been a flood of immigrants from former colonies—India, Pakistan, Bangladesh, East and West Africa, and the Caribbean—as the colonies achieved independence. These immigrants soon exceeded the number of Southern European immigrants.

For much of the three-decade period, immigration exceeded emigration for Britain, contributing significantly to its population growth rate. Unfortunately, the British keep notoriously poor migration statistics, so numbers are hard to come by, but since the early 1970s emigration has at least equaled immigration, and in 1977 Britain lost some 17,000 through net emigration. In combination with low fertility rates, this reversal of migration rates has brought England to zero population growth.

The principal difference in England's case is that most of the immigrants from less-developed countries have brought their families and intend to stay permanently. Many of them were essentially refugees with no place else to go. The reaction against them by the English seems generally to have been more intense than that of natives of other host countries. Much of the resentment is undoubtedly racist in character (complaints about the half-million Irish are seldom heard). The immigrants to England, many of whom are conspicuously dark-skinned, are more noticeably "different" from natives than would be Southern Europeans, Turks, or North Africans.

There are three other probable reasons for the intense reaction. First, Britain's economy during the 1970s has been considerably less robust than those of many continental countries, especially Germany and Switzerland, and the need for foreign workers to make up a labor shortage has been less obvious. Second, the presence of wives and children, who require schools, health care, and other social services, is probably a source of resentment. Third, the new arrivals from the colonies have tended to congregate in Britain's larger cities and most often take jobs in service industries (as waiters, taxi and bus drivers, bellhops, etc.) where they are highly visible to the public. As English intolerance of the growing presence of non-European aliens has risen, there have been several outbreaks of violence and a good deal of nastiness shown toward immigrants. Yet the non-European aliens in England in 1978 numbered only 1.8 million—less than four percent of the total population.

Discriminatory behavior has not been limited to the public; officialdom has also participated. In early 1979, the British government admitted, with some embarrassment, that immigration officials had been until then carrying on the Victorian practice of performing virginity tests on young women from India, Pakistan, and Bangladesh, who were entering as fiancées of British citizens and legal residents. The tests were discontinued after newspapers published an interview with an Indian schoolteacher who had undergone the test.

In response to the growing public intolerance of immigrants over the past two decades, the government of the United Kingdom has progressively tightened restrictions on immigration. In January 1978, Conservative Party leader Margaret Thatcher stated on television that many people in England were afraid of "being swamped by people of a different culture" and called for policies leading to "an end to immigration." A public poll taken in

Britain that month reported that 86 percent of the people felt that there were already too many immigrants in the country. The British government is now considering adoption of even more stringent limits and restrictions on immigrants and a crackdown on the small number of illegal immigrants, of whom less than a thousand were apprehended in 1977. A deadline may be set for entry of the thousands of Asians who hold British passports, were expelled from Kenya and Uganda a few years ago, and want to go to England. Margaret Thatcher became Prime Minister in May 1979, which may accelerate the trend in England toward slamming the door.

In many ways, the situation in England can be seen as a bellwether for other overdeveloped countries with substantial subpopulations of foreigners. Immigrants from clearly different cultures almost always generate some friction. When times are good and foreign workers fill a genuine economic need, they may be tolerated fairly well; but when the economy turns sour, trouble is likely to follow. And immigrants have traditionally served as convenient scapegoats for everyone's problems.

Advantages to Host Countries

There are a good meny advantages to the host countries in the guest-worker system. First and foremost, guest workers are filling a genuine labor shortage and gladly take low-paying, low-status jobs that natives will not accept—or at least not enough of them will. Relatively little in the way of costly fringe benefits— unemployment, health, or accident insurance, pensions, etc.— are provided. Many social services available to citizens have not been provided to guest workers, let alone special services to help them adapt to the new environment. Finally, in hard times when unemployment rises, host countries can "export" excess labor by declining to renew work permits and by reducing or shutting down recruitment activities in sending countries.

In 1974, in response to the oil-crisis recession, virtually all Northern European countries clamped strong restrictions on foreign labor recruitment, with a view to holding the post-recession guest-worker population constant while their economies recovered. The influx of migrant workers in 1975 was about one-fifth what it was before the recession, and a large portion of these were Italians, who as Common Market members can move relatively freely to other Common Market countries.

Today, West Germany is maintaining its ban on recruitment, allowing only a trickle of new workers each year. Switzerland's efforts to restrict the foreign worker population has persuaded some multinational companies not to locate there. France has taken a slightly more liberal view but is exercising control over both imports of workers and "involuntary returns." In general, throughout Europe, recruitment is being allowed at a rate that will just replace or very slightly exceed the number of people who have returned to their birthplaces.

The host nations' economic troubles were thus eased, but in the donor countries unemployment jumped and other dislocations occurred as thousands of emigrants returned. Curiously enough, although over a million workers left industrial Europe between 1973 and 1975, those who remained had lower rates of unemployment than did natives. It appears that the foreign element of the work force really is essential to the economies of the host countries.

Those guest workers already in residence in Northern Europe are being encouraged to stay permanently and to bring their families to join them. The host countries have realized that the resident foreign-worker populations, which have higher birthrates than the native populations, can further augment labor supply through spouses and offspring. In France, for example, some 50,000 wives and children of migrant workers enter the labor force each year. Consequently, to encourage workers to stay, fringe benefits are being extended, and orientation services to help workers and their families become assimilated are being increasingly offered in some countries.

The only catch is that the children of foreign workers, who have grown up and been educated in the host countries, may then be no more willing to take low-paying, low-status jobs than the natives are.

The Donor Countries

While migrant workers are responding primarily to pull factors—namely job opportunities in developed countries that far outclass what is open to them at home—there are push factors operating as well, principally the lack of good jobs. Most migrant workers are from rural areas with rapidly growing populations. Since not all can inherit the family farm, many are being squeezed off the land. The migrant-worker movement thus can be seen as an extension of the worldwide trend of rural-to-urban migration. Ordinarily, the migrants would move only as far as the nearest large city. But in these countries, the growth of the labor pool has been much greater than growth in the number of jobs. Thus, exporting surplus workers to an overdeveloped country with a labor shortage is often seen as a benefit to both countries.

Of course, things are never that simple. Some of the problems that can develop in host countries have been described; donor countries also suffer disadvantages as well as advantages. The most obvious disadvantage is the loss—even temporarily—of some of the nation's brightest, healthiest, and often better-educated young citizens, whose efforts might be more usefully employed at home than doing menial jobs in an overdeveloped country. The difficulty is finding a way to employ those talents when there is an abundance of young people needing work. Exporting excess labor thus may seem to work very well for a less-developed donor country—until the host country has a recession and sends its guest workers home, as happened in 1974 in Europe. Since recessions often hit poor countries with weaker economies even harder than rich ones anyway, a sudden flood of returning emigrants into the job market at such a time is no help at all.

It is usually assumed by donor-country governments that exporting migrant workers is a way of giving them free vocational training. Supposedly, the returning migrant has learned a useful skill or two and something about the mysterious ways of industrialism. But it often turns out that the new skill is not appropriate to conditions in the home country. And what the migrant may have learned about life in the host country only makes him (or her) discontent when he returns. His attitudes and values have inevitably been influenced by his tour abroad, and his native land may now seem backward and overburdened with tradition. In turn, he may seem very sophisticated and foreign to his friends who stayed home. Returning women often have even more acute problems of readjustment. After being abroad on their own for some time, picking up strange ideas about freedom and equality between the sexes, young women find it difficult to return and fit into the traditional dependent female role.

The money sent home by migrant workers is often rightly considered an advantage to the donor country—a partly hidden subsidy paid by rich countries to poor ones. The amounts in total can be substantial and contribute significantly to the donor countries' balance of payments. In 1974, some $7 billion were transferred from industrial Europe to migrant-worker donor countries. But when migrants are suddenly returned to their home countries, as they were from Northern Europe in 1974–75, the flow of funds is also reduced, just when it may be badly needed.

Some economists have expressed concern about the effect on the balance of payments of the host countries that this uncontrolled outflow of cash represents, arguing that it would be better to export jobs by corporate investment in the poor countries than to import workers. This, of course, would avoid the problems—and abuses—of the migrant-worker system, but other resulting economic dislocations might be just as bad for both investing and recipient countries. Such overseas investment is now taking place on a grand scale, and its benefits to the poor countries are often questionable, since both the goods produced and the profits usually go back to the rich investing country. Nor does such investment seem to have had much effect in stemming the flow of migrant workers.

The greatest disadvantages of the migrant-worker system obviously fall on the migrant's family, particularly if the migrant is a married man, even though the family benefits from the extra money sent home. Apart from the hardship of long separation—several months, perhaps even a year or more—the wife must care for the children and home unaided. If, as is often the case, the absent worker is a farmer, she and the children must keep the farm going. Or she may have to work to support herself and her children if the money sent back is undependable or inadequate for support.

Sometimes this burden is spread through a larger community when all or most of the young men in a village or rural area go elsewhere for temporary work and the farming and other work is left to the women, children, and old people. This has been a problem for many donor countries at various times. It is now a serious problem for some of the black nations in Southern Africa that send workers to South African mines and factories. In response, some donor countries have imposed restrictions on the numbers of men who can be recruited from a single village, on the time they can be away, and how often they can go.

The argument has been raised that emigration from less-developed nations functions as a sort of demographic safety valve, allowing those countries to postpone reducing their birthrates. Many demographers believe that this happened in Europe in the nineteenth century. They have pointed out that England, Scandinavia, and Germany all exported large numbers of emigrants—mostly young unmarried adults and young couples—to the New World. Birthrates in those countries declined considerably later and more slowly than did that of France, which did not have a high rate of emigration.

There is little evidence, however, that this is happening in less-developed countries today. To be really effective in relieving population pressures, far larger numbers of people would have to leave most LDCs than are leaving today. For migrant workers, one can even make the opposite argument, namely that long absences of young married men and of both unmarried men and women (who obviously have postponed their marriages) operate directly to reduce the birthrate in the home country.

Whether or not the movement of young workers from poor to rich countries significantly relieves population pressures in the former (and adds significantly to it in the latter), it is a worldwide movement of considerable consequence. Such migrations can be found on every continent, even when the difference between levels of development between sending and receiving countries do not seem very great: Ivory Coast to Ghana, for instance, Guatemala to Mexico, Colombia to Venezuela, or Italy to Switzerland. Wherever they occur, though they ease some economic problems—especially employment problems—they create a host of others, economic as well as social. And it is becoming clear that, like the closely related trend of urbanization in LDCs, the migrant-worker movement is increasing. As long as there are large differences between countries in income, opportunity, and population growth rates, migrant workers can be expected to result, and the consequent problems will continue to plague both donor and host societies.

One poor-to-rich migration that has created some of the thorniest problems for Americans is the movement of Mexicans and Caribbean peoples into the United States, a large portion of it clandestine and illegal. But understanding the ramifications of this issue, particularly the Mexican migration, requires illumination of its place in the worldwide scheme of things and also some perspective on the history of the United States as a traditional immigrant-receiving nation and the historical relationship between the United States and Mexico.

[2]

NOT QUITE A NATION OF IMMIGRANTS

THE United States frequently styles itself as a nation of immigrants. In fact it is not now and never has been. At no time in the history of the United States was more than one out of six residents of the nation foreign-born, and never has the number of foreign-born and their offspring amounted to more than one out of three. Historical demographers calculate that only about one-half of Americans are descendants of post-1789 immigrants; that is, if there had been no immigration since George Washington was inaugurated as president, the population of the United States would be about half of what it is today.

On the other hand, almost 50 million individuals have immigrated to the United States since 1789. No nation has ever accepted so many foreigners, and even today none accepts as many as the U.S. does. But the total volume of immigration is just too large to picture easily. It becomes even more incomprehensible with the realization that typically each individual in the total made his or her decision alone or as part of some very small group.

The decision to cut oneself off from the familiar and the dear and to risk all in a new land was sometimes made in hope, sometimes in fear, sometimes in desperation. In his first *Essay on Population,* written in 1798, Thomas Robert Malthus considered the possibility of people migrating to new lands as a means of escape from the crowding and wretchedness of a Britain starting to undergo industrialization and concluded:

We well know from repeated experience how much misery and hardship men will undergo in their own country before they can

50

determine to desert it, and how often the most tempting proposals of embarking for new settlements have been rejected by people who appeared to be almost starving.

Perhaps the hardships and misery worsened in Britain, or the temptations of the New World increased after Malthus expressed that opinion. Certainly ocean crossings became easier and safer with the development of steamships after about 1820. Whatever the reasons, in the century after Malthus about two and three-quarters million people deserted England and Scotland and crossed the sea to America.

Any study of immigration must rely on official records, and these unfortunately list only "political" nationality, not the more useful "ethnic" nationality. For example, the official record tells us that well over three million "Russians" came to the United States, but this number includes a score of readily identifiable and distinct nationalities and ethnic groups such as Poles, Baltic peoples, Finns, Germans, Jews, Ukrainians, and others, who never for a moment considered themselves Russians but who were ruled, at one time or another, from St. Petersburg or Moscow. The same record tells us that over four million immigrants to the U.S. entered from Canada, but most of these in fact were from other lands and had simply paused in Canada on their way to the United States.

Even though Americans like to think of the U.S. as a nation of immigrants, a good deal of time and effort has been expended, especially in this century, in trying to stop immigration or at least reduce the flow. Attempts at restriction have usually focused on certain groups who at various times were perceived as threatening: the Irish, Chinese, Japanese, Southern and Eastern Europeans, etc. Today Mexicans are the object of this kind of attention. To understand what is happening today, it is instructive to examine the history of the United States as an "immigrant nation."

During most of America's history, concern about immigration has largely been directed toward the flow of immigrants from Europe and Canada, which has accounted for over 85 percent of immigration since 1789. In the nineteenth century there was also a significant influx from Asia, which aroused considerable opposition, much of it racist in character. Racism against blacks in the United States has been a centuries-old problem, but it has not played a part in immigration policy. The ancestors of most black Americans were already in the United States by the earliest years of the republic (legal importation of slaves was forbidden after

1808), and thereafter blacks were a minuscule part of the U.S. immigration picture until the last decade or so.

THE WHITE FLOOD

Official records of immigration to the United States begin in 1820. Starting that year, the master of any vessel arriving from abroad was required by law to make a list of all passengers taken on board during the voyage and turn it over to the local customs officer. This list was to designate the age, sex, and occupation of each passenger, "the country to which they severally belonged," and the number who had died during the voyage. These lists were sent to the Secretary of State, who reported the information periodically to Congress. In 1820 very few immigrants came overland, so this system worked pretty well.

The problem remains, however, of estimating the migration component of population growth of the United States for the first three decades after independence. It is customary to estimate immigration in that period at 8,000 or 9,000 per year, or a quarter million for those 30 years. This number is consistent both with the known numbers of immigrants entering in the early years of the 1820s and with the degree of population growth from census to census, 1790 to 1820. The flow of immigrants accelerated rapidly in the early nineteenth century. It is assumed that about 80,000 arrived in each decade from 1790 to 1820. Then in the 1820s about 140,000 immigrants entered the United States, and almost 600,000 came in the 1830s. But the real immigration began in the 1840s, as the rate of inflow nearly doubled again.

The Old Immigration

Between 1840 and 1881, well over 9 million people came to the United States from other nations. The task of absorbing some quarter of a million additional foreigners every year for 40 years should not be shrugged off lightly. The total number of newcomers during this period equaled roughly 30 percent of the U.S. population at the midpoint in 1860. But there were factors that mitigated the impact of all these strangers. Ninety percent of them came from Canada, Britain, Ireland, or Germany, and their ways and origins were familiar to Americans. Moreover, the United States contained expanses of potential farmland that could not soon be brought under the plow by the native-born population alone; nor could that population hope, without augmentation, to realize the mystical "manifest destiny"—the rapid settlement of the continent from sea to sea.

Still the welcome mat had some rough spots. There was resentment against the Irish for their Catholicism and because they depressed wages in the Eastern cities. There was anger against the Germans and Scandinavians for not speaking English. Immigrants in general were not immediately accepted by natives and usually were given the least attractive jobs.

In the early 1840s, even before the great influx of the Irish who fled the potato famine, a distinctive form of American xenophobia known as "nativism" appeared. It first took the form of the "Order of the Star-Spangled Banner" (the OSSB), which evolved into the American Party (commonly called the "Know-Nothings"). This small group had little public support, however. Their candidate, former President Millard Fillmore, ran a poor third in the 1856 presidential election. Outside of the OSSB, there was no serious talk of limiting the number or kind of immigrants.

Out of the Old Immigration developed an idea, never enacted in law nor even clearly articulated, that America needed the world, that America could absorb the world, and, perhaps most important of all, that the world needed America. In 1630 John Winthrop, aboard the *Arabella* in mid-Atlantic, had penned the sentiment that he and his fellow Puritans were going forth into the new land "to build a city on a hill, a beacon to the world." This early Puritan attitude explains much of American behavior, past and present, from its self-righteousness in foreign affairs, which ally and adversary alike find mind-boggling, to its seemingly contradictory attitudes toward immigrants.

A naturalization ceremony in a federal court has a dignity in keeping with the tone of a judicial process, but it is not simply the sober, stately atmosphere of the courtroom. The proceedings have the air of a religious ceremony, giving witness to the transfiguration of men and women into the Community of the Elect, the Congregation of True Believers. Since God's capacity to accept is infinite, so, too, should be the capacity of the land of his blessing. Acceptance of all who came to America was virtually a theological necessity. And it was as reasonable in the mid-nineteenth century to think that the vast reservoir of resources possessed by the middle third of the North American continent was inexhaustible as it is foolish to think so today. No one then knew the limits to the resources nor the numbers of people who would come.

The New Immigration

The differences between the New Immigration and the Old are

few in number but profound in character. The most important distinction is the sheer magnitude of the immigration. The Old Immigration had averaged a quarter million per year, but between 1881 and 1920 more than 23 million people entered the United States, or almost 600,000 per year. It is a common misconception that immigration from Northwestern Europe and Canada diminished in this period. In fact, over 10 million persons came from these lands in the New Immigration as compared with less than 9 million during the Old. Only Germany and Ireland sent fewer than before, while the other countries, particularly Scandinavia and Canada, more than made up the difference. Most of the staggering increase, though, was made up of inhabitants of Mediterranean lands and Slavic peoples from Eastern Europe. The Old Immigration had included relatively small numbers from Italy, the Austro-Hungarian Empire, and Russia; the New Immigration included well over three million from each of these.

By one measure, the New Immigration was not larger than the Old; immigrants represented about 30 percent of the population of the United States in both 1860 and 1900, the midpoints of the two eras. The proportion of newcomers to natives, though, is not the only factor that determines the reception of immigrants. The strangeness of so many who came in the New Immigration, their exotic languages, religious observances, dress, food, and customs stirred fear in the native breast. Scorned by the bulk of society, the New Immigrants clustered together in urban ghettos where maintaining the old ways made life less strange and the problems of coping less menacing. Mario Puzo's *The Fortunate Pilgrim* presents the struggle of the New Immigrant very well and certainly better than his more popular *Godfather*.

The America that received the New Immigrant was also different from the America that had taken in the Old. The 1890 Census remarked that the open public lands—that is, the frontier—were about gone. Three years later, at the Chicago World's Fair celebrating the four hundredth anniversary of Columbus's accomplishment, historian Frederick Jackson Turner read his essay, "The Significance of the frontier in American History," and thus not only signed the frontier's death certificate but began an autopsy that continues to this day. In Europe the word "frontier" had always signified an end, a closing, a place to stop. In America it had meant a place to begin. Now that beginning place had disappeared, but a new technology had replaced the old. While the cheap land "of such extraordinary fertility that a very slight amount of toil expended on it affords returns that might have satisfied even the dreams of Spanish avarice . . ." had ceased to be, the intensification of resource exploitation known as industralization was in full swing, and America's capacity to accommodate the newcomer was still largely intact. But now the immigrant's livelihood would come more commonly from mine and mill than from tilling the soil.

THE YELLOW PERIL

The story of immigration from Asia is significant both because it resulted in the first serious attempts to exclude people and because of some fascinating parallels with the current Mexican "problem." The two principal Oriental groups to come to the United States were, of course, the Japanese and the Chinese. The official records report that about half a million persons entered from each of these countries. Two-thirds of the Chinese came between 1850 and 1890. The Japanese came a bit later, mainly between 1880 and 1920, with the heaviest inflow occurring in the 1890s. The subcontinent of India has never contributed great numbers of immigrants to the United States. In all, fewer than 100,000 persons have come from this region, and the vast majority of them have come since 1965.

The cultural richness that the Japanese and Chinese have brought to America (and the wealth they have created), particularly in the Western states, is far out of proportion to their numbers. Their industry, their rectitude, and the integrity of their families have been exemplary. Today it is very hard to understand the causes or the intensity of the hatred and hysteria that the greater society directed against these few people. At the turn of this century, the words "peril," "horde," and "scourge" were commonly used to describe them. Some of this opposition grew from racial and religious bigotry on the one hand and fear of cultural extinction at the hands of the "Heathen Chinee" on the other. Because China's population was so large, the white people of the United States were intensely fearful they would be "swamped." In fact this fear had no rational basis, for relatively small numbers of Chinese came to the United States even in the days when work was plentiful and Asian immigration was unlimited.

But bigotry needs no rational basis. As the authors of the *Annals of San Francisco* wrote in 1854, "It was admitted on all sides, that the Chinese were naturally an inferior race, both mentally and corporeally, while their personal habits and manner of living were peculiarly repulsive to Americans." In the last half of the nineteenth century, Californians acted as if the Chinese were subhuman:

John Chinaman was buffeted from pillar to post. He was everywhere discriminated against; he was robbed, beaten, and frequently murdered, and no punishment was meted out to his assailant; he was brutally and unceremoniously ejected from whatever mining or agricultural property he managed to acquire; in the courts he was classed lower than the Negro or the Indian; and scores of laws were enacted for the sole purpose of hampering him in his efforts to earn an honest living.

Official reaction in California to the Chinese began early. Governor Begler urged legislation to restrict or completely block Chinese immigration in 1852. The great robber baron Leland Stanford, who was governor a decade later, followed Begler's lead. In 1862 he sent a message to the California legislature urging that the flow of Chinese be staunched by every legal means since "the presence of numbers of that degraded and distinct people would exercise a deleterious effect upon the superior race." Stanford, never one to permit his principles to interfere with his business operations, was at the time employing a sizable number of those "degraded and distinct people" to build his Central Pacific Railroad—and a quarter of a century later was still using Chinese labor to run his estate in Tehama County.

The California State Constitution, which was ratified in 1874, was openly anti-Chinese. It did not give the Chinese the vote, would not allow corporations to employ them, and severely restricted the conditions under which they could reside in the state. Meanwhile, the city of San Francisco passed a series of ordinances in the 1870s designed to make the lives of the Chinese miserable. One of them forbade the carrying of baskets suspended from poles across the shoulders—the way dirty clothes were transported by Chinese laundrymen. Disinterment of bodies was forbidden to prevent the Chinese from following their ancient custom of shipping bodies home for permanent interment. Another law placed a 50-dollar fine on anyone sleeping in a room with less than 500 cubic feet of space per person—which led Herbert Asbury, historian of the Barbary Coast, to comment that the law "made the slumbers of practically every Chinaman in San Francisco illegal." But the ultimate indignity was a law that made pigtails on men illegal. This one was challenged in court by a Chinese who had had his queue cut off in jail, and the ordinance was declared invalid. Even so, that such laws could even be proposed indicates the xenophobia that has characterized the "nation of immigrants" for so much of its history and that so easily can become virulent.

On March 2, 1875, the Supreme Court of the United States decided that the interstate-commerce clause of the Constitution brought immigration under the jurisdiction of the federal government. The next day Congress passed a law forbidding the immigration of "obnoxious" Orientals. This class included prostitutes and Chinese contract labor (which was really a form of slavery). The furor over Asian immigration escalated to hysteria over the next few years. In 1876 both the Republicans and the Democrats included anti-Chinese planks in their platforms, and a Committee of Congress reported from California that the Western United States had to be saved from the Chinese "scourge."

An obstacle to curbing immigration from China was the Burlingame Treaty of 1868, which provided for the free migration and transfer of political allegiance between the two countries. The Constitution provides that a treaty with a foreign nation properly concluded and ratified is above acts of Congress and on a par with the Constitution itself. This forced President Rutherford Hayes to veto a Chinese exclusion act in 1879, but the President, sensitive to the mood of the country and staring into another election year, hastened to renegotiate the treaty to accommodate Congress. In that same year California voted over 150,000 to 800 to exclude all immigration from China.

By 1881 the treaty had been renegotiated so that the United States could "limit, suspend, and regulate" the immigration of Chinese laborers. Chinese people other than laborers were untouched by the new treaty. This is not what the American people wanted, but the Chinese government could not be talked into allowing the United States to exclude all Chinese. China had to be heeded in this matter because a lot of Americans were getting rich out of the China trade, and, if the United States completely excluded the Chinese, China might respond in kind and the profits would stop. Armed with the new treaty, Congress promptly passed an act "suspending" all Chinese immigration for 20 years. The new President, Chester A. Arthur, wearily vetoed the act on the common-sense grounds that a categorical, twenty-year suspension was in fact a prohibition and violated the treaty just ratified by the Senate. Congress then went back to work and in 1882 came up with a bill that would suspend the immigration of Chinese contract labor for ten years. President Arthur saw this act as being within the limits of the treaty and signed it into law. The Chinese did not retaliate.

Marion T. Bennett, who has written the most thorough account of American immigration policy, characterized the 1882 act as "an embarrassing negation of the treaty with China." Thus was established the principle of exclusion by race which would remain a shameful part of U.S. immigration policy for 70 years until removed by the Immigration and Nationality Act of 1952.

One sees in the politics of Chinese exclusion a century ago the same faulty thinking and the same predictable sequence of events that have cropped up in U.S. immigration debates ever since. Congress and the people seem incapable of realizing that immigration is a part of foreign relations as well as being a domestic matter. If the United States discriminates against peoples of selected countries by restricting immigration and status of residence, it cannot reasonably expect U.S. citizens to be welcomed in those same countries to do business and make profits. Furthermore, the pattern of events is dangerous within the United States. Some group is declared a "scourge" by someone or other; the press becomes aroused and proceeds to exaggerate the problem; jurists and learned authorities from the universities hasten to affirm that the republic is in danger; and Congress rushes into action. In the 1870s it was the Chinese, in the 1920s it was the Slavs and the Italians, in the 1950s it was some ill-defined, undifferentiated "them," and today it is the Mexicans. A few years after the hysteria has run its course, no one can remember what the scare was all about and the country is left an unworkable immigration policy.

The situation with regard to the Japanese was somewhat different from that of the Chinese. Xenophobia seems the only explanation for American fear of the Japanese. Unlike China, Japan was not a populous nation—nor was its population growing rapidly. As with the Chinese, free immigration had not caused any threatening crowds descending on American shores. Indeed, unlike the Chinese who had a long history of emigration, Japan had deliberately shut herself off from the world until the United States had threatened her with war if she did not enter into intercourse in the community of nations. Even after Admiral Perry and the Meiji Restoration had started Japan on the road to world prominence, the Japanese government discouraged emigration. Nonetheless, the government and people of the United States perceived a threat, and people and their governments respond not to what is but what is perceived to be.

This xenophobia was further complicated by elements of Japanese culture that were generally misunderstood by white America. In the first place, the priorities of personal responsibility in the Code of Bushido and the Shinto religion were emperor first, family second, and self last. The figure of the emperor was understood primarily as the bonding force of the culture rather than as a political leader, but this led to the assumption that Japanese political loyalty to the United States was suspect. While cultural integrity and political loyalty were separate and differentiated in modern Western civilization, they were regarded as

the same in Japan. That nation refused to recognize the transfer
of political allegiance inherent in the American tradition of immigration. The Japanese government insisted at the very least
that overseas Japanese return to Japan for compulsory military
service. Rather than humiliate relatives in Japan, many young
Japanese did return for this reason and then went back to the
United States. It was a demonstration of respect for the family
and their culture more than it was a political act, but it could be
reasonably misunderstood since in Western nations military service is the ultimate test of political loyalty.

In order to avoid the humiliation of having their nationals
barred from entry to the United States, the Japanese government
in 1907 entered into what was known as the "Gentlemen's
Agreement" with the United States to restrict the flow of Japanese
by limiting the number of exit permits issued to those wishing to
come to the United States. The Gentlemen's Agreement was in
fact an informal arrangement worked out in semisecret between
the Empire of Japan and the executive branch of the United
States Government. The Senate of the United States saw the
Gentlemen's Agreement as an abridgement of their power and a
violation of the Constitution, which provides that treaties with
foreign nations can be concluded only with the "advice and con-
sent" of the Senate. In addition to seeing the Agreement as an
improperly arranged treaty, the Senate, along with the House of
Representatives, considered immigration policy a domestic, legislative matter and not a matter of foreign policy to be negotiated by
the president with foreign governments. For these reasons Congress excluded further Japanese immigrants in the National
Origins Act of 1924. President Coolidge signed it, but with an
expressed reservation about the annulment of the Gentlemen's
Agreement. The Japanese government and people were outraged because they felt the integrity of their government and the
value of their culture had been impugned.

Throughout this period the principal foreign-policy objective
of the United States and other Western nations in the Far East was
the "opening up" of Japan and China. The story of Admiral Perry
and the Black Ships threatening to bombard Japanese cities if
they did not trade with the U.S. is too well known to warrant
recounting, and the coolness with which the first American con-
sul, Townsend Harris, was received in that country was the subject of a 1958 motion picture, *The Barbarian and the Geisha*, starring
no less an item of Americana than John Wayne.

By the turn of the century, the "opening up" policy led to
creation of an international garrison, including United States
troops, in Peking. The attempt of the Chinese to dislodge it was

the subject of another motion picture, *Fifty-five Days at Peking*. This one was released in 1963 and cast Charlton Heston as the prototypical heroic American and David Niven as the prototypical understated Englishman. At the moment of the deliberations leading to the National Origins Act of 1924, in which the terms "yellow peril" and "Asiatic hordes" were commonly used (and much concern was expressed about the dangers of letting Orientals into the United States), there were 4,000 American Protestant missionary stations in China, each one flying the United States flag and every American in them enjoying immunity from Chinese law. At the same time, the United States, along with Japan, France, and Great Britain, maintained the Yangtze River Patrol to make certain that American and other foreign missionaries and businessmen would remain unfettered by Chinese authority. While American missionaries were trying to subvert their culture, while American businessmen were trying to exploit their economy, while American gunboats imposed the law of the United States in their land, the press, the government, and the people of the United States were worrying about the threat posed by the Chinese!

Against this background it is extremely difficult to sustain the argument that immigration is an issue for consideration only by the recipient country. In the cases of both China and Japan, the United States Government had deeply involved itself in their internal affairs. The immigration of Asians into this country was part and parcel of that involvement. The United States Government had allowed its nationals to recruit labor in China without restriction for the exploitation of mineral deposits and the building of railroads in the United States. Considerable economic and social dislocation had taken place in China and Japan as a result of aggressive, even bellicose American policies directed at them. The notion, then, that the consequences of this meddling were the business of the United States alone was ridiculous. Here again, the Asiatic immigration situation of 50 to 100 years ago parallels the Mexican immigration "crisis" of today in that many Americans fail to recognize the role played in the creation of the crisis by American meddling in Mexico.

In all, fewer than one million Asians came to the United States, but they caused a furor far out of proportion to their numbers. And this furor derived not from anything they did or anything they were, but arose exclusively from the imaginary fears of white Americans. Imaginary fears are a very poor basis for policymaking, but policy was made anyway.

No discussion of Asian immigration would be complete without mention of the relocation and internment of the Japanese in

1942. In that year the old yellow-peril hysteria re-emerged with a vengeance. To be sure, as Franklin Roosevelt said, the United States of America had been suddenly and deliberately attacked by the naval and air forces of the Empire of Japan. There had been severe damage to American naval and military forces, and over 2,000 American lives had been lost. This is not the place to discuss the threat to their national existence that the Japanese perceived. The point to be made here is that three-quarters of a century of irrational hate-mongering in the United States prompted the government to adopt, and conditioned the people to accept, an entirely inappropriate, inhumane, and unnecessary policy.

All residents of the states of Washington, Oregon, and California who were of Japanese ancestry were relocated outside those states whether they were United States citizens or not. The euphemism for a United States citizen was "non-alien."

Relocation—being sent to camps outside the three Western states—was the lot of all residents of Japanese descent, but those who fell under any sort of suspicion were subjected to the stricter confinement of internment. One case was that of the family of Izumi Taniguchi of Stockton, California. The elder Taniguchi had been born in Japan and therefore was not eligible for United States citizenship. As mentioned before, the Japanese government required all overseas Japanese to meet their military obligation. Since Taniguchi could not gain U.S. citizenship, he had to dispatch the obligation to the Japanese government in order to keep his Japanese citizenship. Like thousands of others, he had long before effectively transferred his political loyalty to the United States, but there was no persuading the government to accept it. The Japanese government did allow its citizens abroad to meet their military obligation through nonmilitary service programs, which did not require the person to return to Japan, take a military-service oath, or to bear arms. Taniguchi chose this option and was asked to raise money for morale programs and prepare packages of small personal comforts for Japanese troops during the Sino-Japanese War. These activities were completely within the laws of the United States and did not represent any sort of political compromise. By 1942, however, this was enough to result in his internment. The families of internees were given the choice of accepting relocation for themselves or accepting internment in order to remain with the suspect family member. It is a tribute to the integrity of the Japanese family that most accepted internment rather than suffer separation.

Although some honest Americans may have been motivated by considerations of military security, war hysteria was simply used as a smoke screen for a policy of economic confiscation. Residents of Japanese ancestry in Hawaii or Alaska, whether alien or citizen, were not relocated; nor was Canada so harsh with the Japanese in British Columbia. Moreover, Americans of German and Italian ancestry were not restricted or persecuted.

Probably the most ironic element of this national disgrace was the feverish attempt to recruit young Japanese-Americans out of the relocation camps and internment centers for service in the United States Army. The government, faced with a major Pacific war, discovered to its dismay that the only sizable source of Japanese/English bilinguals in the nation was behind barbed wire. Incredibly, the Japanese-Americans responded to the pleas of those who had persecuted them and enlisted. The 442nd Regimental Combat Team, composed primarily of Americans of Japanese ancestry from Hawaii, sustained a 300-percent casualty rate in Italy and France and emerged as the most decorated unit for its size in the United States Army. In 1947, a white barber refused to give Daniel Inouye, now a United States senator, a haircut. Inouye had recently returned from the European theater of operations, having lost his right arm, and having been nominated for a Congressional Medal of Honor. When the haircut was refused, he was in uniform and wearing ribbons indicating he had been given the Distinguished Service Cross, the Bronze Star, the Purple Heart with cluster, five battle stars, and four unit citations.

Not a single incident of treason or disloyalty to the United States on the part of a resident of Japanese ancestry, alien or citizen, was ever brought to court. Unfortunately, when the constitutionality of the internment was brought into question, the courts saw fit to sustain the government's action in a time of national emergency. In short, the legacy of yellow-peril immigration hysteria is alive and well in the law of the republic. It should not be a matter of concern only to people with an Asian heritage that the government can arrest and imprison an American of Japanese ancestry without evidence or trial. It could do the same to a WASP citizen. If the government can do this to one group of Americans, it could do it to any group.

RESTRICTION AND LIMITATION

There is an important distinction between the restriction of immigration and its limitation. *Restriction* is the barring of certain categories of people from entering the United States; the object is to ensure that only the "right kinds" of people are admitted. *Limitation* is a matter of brute numbers. The attempt to restrict immigration began in the earliest years of European settlement;

the attempt to set an absolute numerical limit did not begin until 1965.

In 1639, a scant nine years after Winthrop alighted from the *Arabella,* Massachusetts restricted immigration with legislation aimed at excluding or controlling paupers, criminals, and the diseased. Those who today are concerned about law and order on the one hand and the increasing welfare burden on the other are upholding a long tradition. In the next century no less an eminence than Benjamin Franklin would say of the Germans, 60,000 of whom had moved into Pennsylvania by the time of the Revolution, that

> Those who come hither are generally the most stupid of their own nation, and as ignorance is often attended with credulity when knavery would mislead it, and with suspicion when honesty would set it right, . . . it is almost impossible to remove any prejudices which they may entertain.

In the same passage, Franklin expressed his fear that the ignorant greenhorn was dominating the local elections. Elsewhere Franklin asked,

> Why should the Palatine* boors be suffered to swarm into our settlements and, by herding together, establish their language and manners to the exclusion of ours?

Here the fears of political dominance and cultural extinction at the hand of foreigners appear in addition to the earlier concerns over the character, economic status, and health of the immigrant. These five worries, plus religious and ethnic bigotry, have been the primary wellsprings of restriction throughout American history, and they still are.

The Constitution of the United States exhibits only a limited trust of foreigners. Of course, none but the native-born may aspire to the presidency (Art. II), and a foreign-born citizen must experience seven years of citizenship before he or she can find a place in the House of Representatives (Art. I, Sec. 2) and nine for the Senate (Art. II, Sec. 3). The only direct reference to immigration in the Constitution is confounded with the prohibition of the slave trade and seems to make the regulation of immigration a matter for the states:

---

*Germans from the Rheinland-Pfalz. In fairness to Dr. Franklin, he also said, "Their industry and frugality are exemplary. They are excellent husbandmen and contribute greatly to the improvement of a country."

The migration or importation of such persons as any of the States
now existing shall think proper to admit shall not be prohibited by
the Congress prior to the year one thousand eight hundred and
eight. (Art. I, Sec. 9)

While the federal government remained inactive in the field of
immigration, it did, in 1798, assume the right to deport aliens. In
that year, fear of the ideas of the French Revolution led to the
Alien and Sedition Acts, which, among other things, allowed the
president to deport aliens suspected of wrongheaded politics.
Although this law was allowed to lapse, the principle of federal
jurisdiction in matters of deportation was established. The federal government assumed the regulation of immigration on
March 2, 1875, when the Supreme Court extended the always-
useful Interstate Commerce Clause of the Constitution to this
field.

The first efforts of the federal government in the field of
immigration were the prohibition against importing Chinese contract labor in 1875 and the Chinese Exclusion Act of 1882. The
first general immigration legislation, also passed by Congress in
1882, simply codified the old Puritan worries of 1639 by forbidding the entry of convicts, lunatics, idiots, and those likely to
become public charges.

Immigration policy was one of the principal political issues of
the late nineteenth and early twentieth centuries. Everyone
seemed to have some category of people they wanted restricted or
prohibited from entering the country. As so often happens in
national debates, the legislative product became increasingly
complex while the legal effect bordered on the insignificant. In
the first decade of this century, when nearly 9 million immigrants
arrived in the U.S., only about one and one-quarter percent were
turned away. Of over 13 million foreign-born in the country in
1910, fewer than 3,000 were deported.

One of the most hotly debated means of restriction was a
literacy test. This requirement was vetoed by Presidents Cleveland and Taft and twice vetoed by Woodrow Wilson. When it was
finally passed over Wilson's second veto in the Immigration Act of
1917, the test was limited to the ability to read a simple forty-word
passage in any language, and even then it did not apply to children under 16 years of age or to most close relatives of legal U.S.
residents over the age of 55. Indeed, the Immigration Act of 1917
is a monument to the American lawmakers' capacity to confound
the simplest of issues. It contained 33 categories of persons who
were not to be admitted—including anarchists and
polygamists—and then turned around and listed 10 categories of

exceptions. The act was so complex that despite the intentions of those who agitated for its passage, it did more to guarantee the right of immigration than to restrict it. For example, in its eagerness not to limit the cultural life of the republic, Congress included a provision for the free immigration of artists, including singers. While the act barred the entrance of an indigent, anarchistic polygamist with a criminal record, it allowed his admission if he could sing grand opera. This led enterprising Italians to form large "opera companies" which had a strange way of dissolving soon after they cleared immigration. Congress did not get around to plugging this loophole until 1934, allowing it and other sievelike qualities of the 1917 Act to persist through the 1920s.

The most important detail of the 1917 Act was the creation of the "Asiatic Barred Zone." This zone, defined by lines of latitude and longitude, included virtually all of the Asian continent and beyond, from Arabia through the Polynesian islands. Along with the Chinese exclusion acts and the Gentlemen's Agreement with Japan, the creation of the Asiatic Barred Zone all but closed the door to all Asians and it remained closed for a generation.

THE QUOTAS DEBATE

The Immigration Act of 1917 had no discernible effect on the volume of immigration. In 1920, the first year of free travel after World War I, 800,000 persons entered the United States as immigrants. That year, as immigration again approached prewar levels, concern over its volume became a significant issue along with its character. Although Congress was still more than 40 years from setting an absolute numerical limit on legal immigration, the Emergency Immigration Act of 1921 did place an annual limit of 350,000 persons from Europe with the plain intention of limiting the total number of immigrants.

In addition to limiting the number of all Europeans (immigration from most of the Western Hemisphere was unlimited and would so remain until 1968), this law set limits for each of the various nations of Europe. The system for these national quotas was very simple. Each year, the number of immigrants from a given country could not exceed three percent of the number of persons resident in the United States in 1910 who had been born in that country. As its name implies, the Emergency Immigration Act of 1921 was never intended to be permanent, but it began a generation and a half of fiddling with quotas, tightening here, loosening there, plugging one loophole, and carving out another. In order to get a place within the quota, of course, the prospective immigrant had to meet all the criteria contained in the 1917 Immigration Act.

The cornerstone legislation of the quota system was the National Origins Act of 1924. A more curious piece of legislation has seldom issued from the halls of Congress. It had as its two aims the severe limitation of total immigration on the one hand and the preservation of the distinctive American character on the other. It achieved the first of these by dropping the total annual number of European immigrants to be admitted ultimately to 150,000. The quota was fixed in a two-step system because, although a majority of the Congress agreed that immigration should be sharply curtailed, no one could agree on how this was to be done.

For the interim quotas, the system used in the Act of 1921 was finally adopted, except that the number of immigrants was to be two percent of the various nationalities resident in the United States instead of three percent, and the base census was to be that of 1890 instead of 1910. This revision ignored post-1890 immigration and loaded the figures against Southern and Eastern Europeans. Had the interim quotas simply scaled down the quotas of 1921, about 55 percent of the immigrants admitted would have been from Northwestern Europe and 45 percent from Central, Southern, and Eastern Europe. With the 1890 Census used as a base, however, 87 percent of the immigrants were allotted to Northwestern Europe and a pathetic 13 percent to the rest. Clearly, the second aim of the act, the preservation of the distinct American character, was to be served by restricting to the point of extinction the flow of Mediterranean and Slavic peoples with their strange religions and languages.

With the second, "permanent" quotas, which were not established until 1929, the alloy created in the American melting pot was to be forever stabilized. The European nationalities would be admitted in numbers that would preserve the ethnic mix existing in 1920. The flow of immigrants would not be stopped, but it would be reduced and regulated so that British, Italian, German, Irish, and Polish "blood" would forever be mixed in the American mainstream in the "correct" proportions.

The dynamics of the great immigration debate of 1923–24 cut across the usual ideological lines of "liberal" and "conservative." Both sides publicly proclaimed the loftiest of ideals while whispering their baser motives into the ears of congressmen. Samuel Gompers, himself an immigrant, led the American Federation of Labor into the restrictionist ranks along with the nativist standard-bearers of the American Legion and the Ku Klux Klan. On the other side stood the immigrant groups, from the Sons of Italy to the Sons of Norway, making common cause with the

National Association of Manufacturers, the American Mining Congress, the Associated General Contractors, and the National Industrial Conference Board. The business groups cited the inscription at the base of the Statue of Liberty and defended the need for the continued availability of labor at "satisfactory" wage rates. The nativists, who wanted to keep America pure, and the trade unionists, who did not want to compete for wages with any more foreign-born workers, were thus allied against the immigrant groups, who wanted to bring their relatives in, and the employers, who wanted to keep wages down.

Surely the most reprehensible contribution to the debate, however, came from the scientific community. Some members of that community were quite happy to produce "scientific" evidence that non-WASP immigrants were inferior—to formalize the kind of nonsense Senator Stanford had spouted about the Chinese a half-century before. Paramount among these scientists was psychologist Henry Goddard, who in 1912 "went to Ellis Island to see if the methods used in keeping out defectives could be improved." Although he spent quite a bit of time trying to determine whether he and others could tell "defectives" simply by looking at them (very often, it seems, he was able to do so), he eventually had some tests administered to immigrants through translators.

The results, reported in 1917, were astonishing. Goddard found that 87 percent of the Russians, 83 percent of the Jews, 80 percent of the Hungarians, and 79 percent of the Italians were "feeble-minded." Goddard's findings became a prime weapon of the nativists in their fight to restrict the numbers and kinds of immigrants admitted. Interestingly enough, while Goddard could not see that his test results were preposterous, he tended to assume that this epidemic of feeble-mindedness among immigrants was not hereditary but a "defect due to deprivation." He personally was not necessarily in favor of their exclusion, citing the need in society to do an "immense amount of drudging . . . for which we do not wish to pay enough to secure more intelligent workers." He asked, "May it be that possibly, the moron has his place?"

In spite of Goddard's touching concern for the "place" of morons, in 1917 he was able to report that:

> . . . beginning at about the time of our experiment, the numbers of aliens deported because of feeble-mindedness (not insane or epileptic) increased approximately 350 percent in 1913 and 570 percent in 1914 over what it had been in each of the five preceding years.

He further noted:

This was due to the efforts of the physicians who were inspired
by the belief that mental tests could be used for the detection of
feeble-minded aliens and in spite of very inadequate facilities in the
way of room, interpreters and a sufficient force of medical officers
to do the work. All of this means that if the American public wishes
feeble-minded aliens excluded it must demand that Congress provide the necessary facilities at the ports of entry.

Considering the level at which the debate was conducted, it
should not be amazing that the resultant legislation was both very
complex and, in the event, not very useful. Once some agreement
was reached, the National Origins Act of 1924 was passed overwhelmingly by both houses of Congress. What opposition there
was came from congressmen whose constituencies were heavily
immigrant. Almost half of the nays were by congressmen from
New York, Chicago, Boston, Cleveland, and Detroit, where the
foreign-born had heavy clout. Nearly two-thirds of the votes cast
against the act in the House were from the four states of New
York, Massachusetts, Connecticut, and New Jersey, where the
1920 Census had shown that two-thirds of the population were
immigrants or first-generation citizens.

Many who voted for the act did so only because they were trying
to avoid something even more restrictive. The worst aspect of
restriction—the separation of families—was avoided by the creation of the non-quota category, which waived restrictions for
spouses and minor children of immigrants and citizens. The
non-quota immigrant category was particularly valuable to
Southern and Eastern Europeans, and through it poured hundreds of thousands of Mediterranean and Slavic peoples who
otherwise would never have been admitted. In the most restrictive years of the interim quotas, 1925 through 1929, only 12
percent of those admitted under the quotas were Southern and
Eastern Europeans. But non-quota admissions increased their
numbers to over 22 percent of the immigration from Europe.

The whole business of quota and non-quota immigrants, preferences within quotas, and so on was very complex and led to
some remarkable wording, such as:

> . . . the term 'quota immigrant' means any immigrant who is not a
> non-quota immigrant. An alien who is not particularly specified in
> the Act as a non-quota immigrant or a non-immigrant shall not be
> admitted as a non-quota immigrant or a non-immigrant by reason
> of relationship to any individual who is so specified . . .

The so-called permanent quotas were not specified in the National Origins Act, nor was the method for determining them.

The problem of figuring out how much and what kinds of "blood" ought to be admitted was left to a committee composed of the Secretaries of State, Commerce, and Labor. These busy men had something better to do with their time than to pursue this particular Congressional fool's errand, and, although the "permanent" quotas were to have been established by 1927, the committee did not get the job done until 1929. These National Origins Quotas redressed the unfavorable balance against Southern and Eastern Europe a bit. While the total number of Europeans to be admitted dropped by 11,000, the portion allotted to Northwestern Europe fell even more, while that allotted to Southern and Eastern Europe actually rose by 3,000. These quotas endured, more or less, until 1965.

A curious aspect of the quotas debate was that it focused completely on direct immigration of Europeans from Europe. Immigration from the Western Hemisphere was left without numeric limitation, and if a European wanted to come to the United States badly enough to reside for a time in Canada or a Latin American country (by the end of the 1930s it took five years), he or she could enter with no attention at all paid to native origin. Immigration from Latin American countries before then had been trivial, and American involvement in the internal affairs of many of them was so profound that it was easier for everyone if the United States simply ignored the comings and goings from this half of the globe. The desire for cheap Mexican labor in the Southwest, particularly in South Texas, was another incentive to ignore the flow of people in that quarter.

There are a good many parallels to be found between the immigration debate of the 1920s and the one in progress today over limiting the inflow of Mexicans. Now, as before, labor unions are in the forefront of the groups who are urging stricter measures against illegal immigrants from Mexico. And, as before, among their allies are the Ku Klux Klan. On the other side, predictably, can be found businessmen's groups, who are anxious to have their supply of Mexican labor remain available.

Chicano groups, like the earlier ethnic associations, also tend to favor an open-door policy. But such groups have traditionally played a somewhat ambivalent role. There has always been a tendency for immigrant groups to want friends and relatives to be able to enter easily, but also to want to slam the door in the face of others. Some of this ambivalence is doubtless rooted in fear of economic competition from the newcomers. In the case of Chicanos some comes from fear of harassment by the INS in search of illegals. In part, restrictionist tendencies in ethnic groups may also be traced to a desire to appear "more American than thou." In spite of the ambivalence, though, their general stance is usually anti-restrictionist.

Fortunately, some of the less attractive aspects of the earlier debate have not, so far at least, been prominent in the current discussion. This is partly because foolish notions about "national character" and the genetic transmission of national characteristics are neither as strongly nor as universally held today as they were 50 years ago, although some of this kind of thinking is still found. It is difficult to imagine that a great national debate could take place now in which the genetic inferiority of this or that national group was generally assumed and the idea went unchallenged. This is not to say that essentially racist arguments to exclude Mexicans and other immigrants have not been raised. They have and no doubt will continue to be, unfortunately.

The ultimate irony of the National Origins idea was that no sooner was it in operation than a quarter-century of economic depression, world war, and cold-war politics rendered it inappropriate. Within a year of the establishment of the permanent quotas, the Great Depression began, and within two years not a single European country was filling its quota. During the 1930s Italy and Germany were the only major European countries to feel any real restriction from the quotas, and Germans felt the pressure only in 1938 and 1939 as religious and political persecution in their homeland became intolerable. Immigration from Poland fell below the quota from 1931 through 1963. As a whole, European immigration in the 1930s was about a third of a million, although the quotas would have accommodated more than a million and a half. Indeed, more foreign-born left the United States during that decade than arrived.

The quotas were by no means the only impediment to immigration. The jungle of restrictions and exceptions contained in the 1917 Act was still in force, by and large, and the bureaucratic regulations for administering the laws were restrictive in themselves. For example, an immigrant visa had to be procured in the applicant's home country; that is, a German could not get an immigrant visa in Norway. This made it very difficult for refugees from Hitlerian or Stalinist persecution to make their way to the United States.

World War II, of course, brought an almost complete halt to European immigration. During the years of full-scale hostilities, 1940–45, fewer than 100,000 Europeans came to the United States, and most of these came from Western Hemisphere countries where they had been living.

THE REFUGEE ERA

An entirely new set of forces came into play on United States immigration policy with the close of World War II—which to date represents the ultimate "push" factor in migration to the United States. Tens of millions of people in Europe were without homes, employment, or any way to care for themselves. Over seven million of these were designated as "Displaced Persons" (DPs), people who had been uprooted by the war and were outside their native lands. One million of them were living in the crudest conditions in DP camps. The Soviet presence in Eastern Europe made it impossible for many of these people to go home, yet they could not be accommodated where they were. Soviet ascendancy in the East was seen more and more as a threat to Western Europe and therefore to the United States. The establishment of stability, order, and prosperity in Western Europe replaced the prosecution of the war as the principal foreign-policy objective of the United States. Some kind of long-term accommodation of the DPs was essential to the achievement of this objective.

The United States involvement in the reconstruction of Europe sprang from many sources and was propelled by many motives. This involvement was not without altruism and it was not without self-service. Sometimes altruism and self-service conflicted with one another in the same program or effort, but often they did not. The only important point here is that since the close of World War II, refugees, their creation and their disposition, have been intertwined with American foreign-policy efforts, and their accommodation has been a nagging problem in the development of U.S. immigration policy.

As the magnitude of the DP problem became evident in 1945 and 1946, President Harry Truman issued a Presidential directive giving precedence to these people within the existing quota system. This was all he could do under the existing law, and Congress did not change the law until 1948. Under the Displaced Persons Act of that year, Congress authorized 202,000 immigration visas for the refugees over the next two years. These were visas in addition to those that would have been issued under the quotas, but they were to be counted against future quotas. Consequently, quotas for some of the smaller Eastern and Southern European countries were simply "mortgaged" out of existence. President Truman signed the act but sent a message to Congress expressing his "very great reluctance" and stating that he felt that the refugees should have been admitted as non-quota immigrants. In 1957 the Congress came around to Mr. Truman's way of thinking and canceled the mortgages against the quotas.

The problem of large-scale refugee immigration was a new one for the United States and other nations. Though the world has been confronted with the problem repeatedly since 1945, no one has learned how to deal with it. The United States and other nations want a controlled flow of immigrants, if any at all; yet the political upheavals of our time can create within a few months pools of hundreds of thousands of persons with no place to go. In an age of mass murder, refusal to accept these people or a decision to "send them back where they came from" is simply a death sentence. Indeed, it was a death sentence for hundreds of thousands of Russian citizens forcibly repatriated after World War II.

The DP problem of the late 1940s was created by World War II, but its resolution took so long (there were still 400,000 persons in the DP camps in 1949) because of the reorganization of Eastern Europe under Soviet hegemony. More DPs ended up in the camps fleeing from the Soviets than from the Nazis. In the view of Americans, these people stopped being victims of "Nazi barbarism" and became victims of "Communist aggression." The Orwellian swiftness with which the Russians replaced the Germans as adversaries in the American mind in those years is nowhere seen more clearly than in perceptions of refugees. In 1945 and 1946 a DP typically was perceived to be a Pole or Ukrainian whose family had been murdered by the Nazis and who himself had been taken away, starved, beaten, and worked nearly to death in some Ruhr factory. Many such cases were real. By 1948, however, the refugee was seen as a Pole or a German from the eastern provinces whose sister had been raped by Russian soldiers and whose political past or social position had marked him for consignment to a work camp in Siberia where he would be starved, beaten, and worked to death. Many such cases were also real.

To Americans these two sources of refugees blended into a single force—totalitarian aggression—and the United States was pushed and pulled by various, sometimes contradictory, attitudes. On the one hand, U.S. immigration policies were underlain by the restrictionist attitudes of the 1920s and 1930s. But, following the war, humanitarian considerations, strengthened by guilt over the failure of the U.S. to offer help to refugees in the 1930s, strongly affected American attitudes and led to recognition of a need for new policies.

The Immigration and Nationality Act of 1952

In the early 1950s, against the background of the Korean conflict when the cold war was at its worst, Congress undertook its first, full-length consideration of immigration policy since the 1920s. The product of this concern was the Immigration and Nationality Act of 1952, called the McCarran-Walter Act after its two principal sponsors. For the first time in history, the laws concerning how many and what kinds of people would be allowed to enter and live in the United States were codified in a single law. Up to this time Congress had enacted over 200 pieces of legislation on the subject with very little consideration in any one of them for any of the others. Immigration was governed primarily by the Immigration Act of 1917 and the National Origins Act of 1924 and its amendments. The 1952 Act went far toward sweeping all of the previous legislation away in the narrow legal sense, but in fact, although the law was changed, the principles remained the same.

The battle in Congress was less rambunctious than the earlier one, but the lines drawn were very nearly the same. On one side were those who wanted to abandon the National Origins idea and increase the numbers admitted. On the other side were those who still held to the old ideas of maintaining the American character and wanted things to stay as they were. The latter group eventually carried the day. The principal characters who shaped the act were Senator Patrick McCarran of Nevada, Representative Francis E. Walter of Pennsylvania, and Richard Arens, Staff Director of the Senate Sub-committee to Investigate Immigration and Naturalization.

Senator McCarran was at that time chairman of the Senate Judiciary Committee and of its subcommittee on Immigration and Naturalization as well as the one on Internal Security. Representative Walter was the ranking Democrat, after the chairman, of the House Judiciary Committee and chairman of its Immigration and Naturalization subcommittee. He was also the chairman of the House Committee on Un-American Activities, and the author of the Internal Security Act of 1950, which bears his name and is the chief instrument for the prosecution of subversives whenever any appear. Arens had been a member of the staff of the Judiciary Committee of the Senate and subsequently became staff director of the House Committee on Un-American Activities. In these posts he directed staff work on the Internal Security Act of 1950 and the Communist Control Act of 1954 as well as the Immigration and Naturalization Act of 1952.

These three Middle Americans were staunch defenders of

what they saw as basic American values against what they perceived as enemies, foreign and domestic. All three of them considered their work on immigration and naturalization as an extension of their work on "internal security." They felt it was their duty to keep out all those people who would sap the vital juices of Americans and make them easy prey for foreign ideology.

Senator McCarran said it best when he stated in defense of the Act:

> The cold, hard truth . . . is that today, as never before, untold millions are storming our gates for admission. Those gates are cracking under the strain. The cold, hard fact is, too . . . that this nation is the last hope of Western civilization, and if this oasis of the world shall be overrun, perverted, contaminated, or destroyed, then the last flickering light of humanity will be extinguished.

One wonders if Senator McCarran, in the dark of night and the peace of solitude, ever reflected that a scant generation before his birth those very sentiments had been used to justify the harassment and persecution of Irish-Catholic immigrants like his parents! Be that as it may, these sentiments in 1952 were shared by the overwhelming bulk of the United States Congress and the public. Arens characterized critics of the act as members of "four principal groups":

[1.] out-and-out Communists . . .
[2.] the pinks and sincere but misguided and uninformed liberals who are captivated by the emotional Communist slogans . . .
[3.] the professional immigration promoters [who] pressure for more public funds to bring over more immigrants of the various types they are particularly interested in . . .
[4.] professional vote solicitors who fawn on nationality groups, appealing to them not as Americans but as hyphenated Americans . . .

Among those who criticized the Act, and thus were characterized as Communists, dupes, wastrels of the public treasure, or dividers of the republic, were Herbert Lehman, Senator from New York; Hubert Horatio Humphrey, Senator from Minnesota; and Harry S. Truman, President of the United States.

The bill passed the House resoundingly, and support in the Senate was so strong that its opponents complained that there was no one in the Senate Chamber to hear their arguments or to answer their questions. Of the nine members of the Senate Judiciary Committee which had unanimously endorsed it, none bothered to speak for it on the floor save the chairman, Senator McCarran. President Truman vetoed the bill, but it became law when Congress overrode the veto.

What is truly remarkable about this debate is that passage of the Act changed matters so very little. Very few persons were turned away, expelled, or had their naturalization revoked because of the far-reaching powers given by it to the Attorney General. Immigration from the independent nations of this hemisphere was left without numerical restriction, and the quotas for European nations were virtually unchanged. One change the Act did bring, and one generally applauded, was the abandonment of racial discrimination in the areas of immigration and naturalization. The Asiatic Barred Zone, established in the 1917 Act and subsequently called the Asia-Pacific Triangle, was forgotten, and the independent nations of this area were given quotas. To be sure, the quotas were small—less than 2,300 for all the peoples from Arabia to Malaya, China, Japan, and on through the Pacific Islands—but the principle was important.

Of far greater immediate consequence was the simple provision that the "right of a person to become a naturalized citizen of the United States shall not be denied or abridged because of race or sex." When Congress passed the first naturalization act in 1790, this right was offered only to "any alien being a free white person." Then in 1870 the right to naturalization was extended to "aliens of African nativity and to persons of African descent." In 1940 American Indians, Eskimos, and members of other groups inhabiting North America before the coming of Europeans were made eligible; then in 1943 a wartime gesture of goodwill opened citizenship to the Chinese. Filipinos and the peoples of the Indian subcontinent were given their chance in 1946. Only in 1952 was race finally eliminated as a criterion for citizenship eligibility.

Sexist restrictions on naturalization were more complex and applied primarily to women who were native-born United States citizens but had lost their citizenship by marrying men of certain categories. Never did men lose their citizenship by marrying women of those categories. The removal of the sex bar on naturalization by the McCarran Act applied primarily to women who had thus lost their citizenship, opening the way for them to regain it through the naturalization process.

The McCarran Act was not otherwise a forward-looking piece of legislation. It provided solutions of the past for the problems of the past. It attempted to enshrine the National Origins principle even while acknowledging that the principle had never worked. It established an elaborate and humiliating procedure for immigration in order to protect the United States from those who would contaminate and pervert, without stating the nature of the contamination or of the perversion. Finally, it failed to work into the fabric of our immigration policy any general, systematic treat-

ment of the refugee problem. The Act did, however, recognize
that, now and then, there might be a person or group of persons
who needed admission to this country on short notice and in
situations wherein this admission would be in the interest of the
United States. Therefore the Act provided for the Attorney General, with congressional overview, to "parole" persons into the
United States. The status of the parolee was not made clear, but
he was certainly not an immigrant. It was a special legal status in
which to place someone while deciding what to do with him.

When the McCarran-Walter Act was written, it was generally
assumed that refugees were a temporary phenomenon caused by
World War II and the reorganization of Eastern Europe. The
failure of the 1952 Act to recognize refugees as a major and
continuing source of immigrants led to a perversion of the Attorney General's parole power. Originally intended for occasional
use in individual cases, it soon became the principal avenue for
entry into the United States for hundreds of thousands of people.
Once they were admitted, ways could be found for them to
remain.

Refugees of the Cold War Era

An essential distinction between the DPs of the years immediately after World War II in Europe and the later refugees of
the eras of decolonization and the cold war is that the DPs' plight
was part of a worldwide upheaval, the causes of which were so
complex and the responsibility so diffused that there was no one
particular source of the disaster. The United States absorbed
several hundred thousand DPs, but millions of them remained in
Europe. The Germanies, East and West, did a splendid job of
absorbing the German-speaking peoples who fled westward in
1945–46, and West Germany has tried to indemnify others whose
lives were uprooted by Nazi barbarism.

Once the DPs were accommodated, however, the world, not
surprisingly, has looked increasingly to the countries that have
been traditional recipients—the United States, Canada, Australia, and some of the Latin American republics—to do the right
and humane thing for refugees. Meanwhile the countries that
have long been traditional migrant donors have looked the other
way. There are exceptions of course. France accepted hundreds
of thousands of Algerians when Algeria won its independence—
but those "Algerians" were French citizens. Britain has absorbed
thousands of refugees from former colonies, but in recent years
has been increasingly reluctant to take any more. For a complex
of reasons, Arab countries have been unwilling to accommodate

the Palestinians whose cause they claim to champion. Consequently, the Palestinians have remained homeless refugees in "temporary" camps for over three decades, and their plight continues to be a major obstacle to peace in the Middle East.

It is not entirely unreasonable for countries to be reluctant to admit refugees, even when those countries had a hand in generating the problem in the first place. Refugees, particularly those whose movement has resulted from decolonization or revolution, frequently make poor immigrants. They tend to view themselves as persons only temporarily displaced from their true homes, not as permanent settlers in a new land. Many such refugees also harbor a sense of having been betrayed, a feeling that may or may not be justified.

The most sensational contemporary example of the mischief these attitudes can cause is that of the South Moluccans in the Netherlands. The South Moluccans remained loyal to the Dutch colonial authority during the Indonesian war of independence, now over for some 30 years, on the promise of their own independence when the Dutch successfully won the war. But the Dutch lost the war. Were the South Moluccans betrayed?

The South Moluccans living in the Netherlands have simply failed to realize that, regardless of any promises, real or imagined, made years ago, the Netherlands can do nothing for them now except to take them into the mainstream of Dutch society. But many of the Moluccans do not want to be assimilated. Certainly, assimilation does not come easily to short Asians in a land of tall Dutchmen, nor is it easy for them to see their native heritage—language, religion, diet, and family patterns—die out among their own children. In order to ensure that their traditions would not be lost to their children, our Pilgrim forefathers rejected comfortable asylum in Holland in favor of the wild New England coast. Unfortunately for the Moluccans and scores of other refugee groups spread over the world today, there are no more wild New England coasts for them to populate, and most of them can never go home.

The South Moluccans are by no means the only refugee group that has felt betrayed. In the late 1950s, when East African nations were throwing out the British, the large population of South Asians who had been brought in by the British at the beginning of this century were a stumbling block to the British withdrawal. They opposed it, expressing concern over their future under black African rule. In order to eliminate this opposition, the British issued passports to any who wanted them and assured the takers that they could move to Britain when things got rough. A decade or so later, when things got rough in East Africa, the British became increasingly reluctant to let them in. Now the government is considering setting a deadline after which the passports will not be honored. This pretty clearly would be betrayal.

These characteristics of refugees in general have also at times been a problem for the United States, which since 1952 has been a destination of refugees from a variety of homelands. The U.S. was not a colonial power taking in people who were unwelcome under newly independent regimes, but it nevertheless played a role in generating the exodus of refugees in several cases. United States immigration policies continued to reflect the conflict between restrictionism and humanitarianism, but they also have increasingly included a measure of political self-interest. Many of the refugee movements generated since passage of the McCarran-Walter Act were outgrowths, one way or another, of cold-war politics. And, in the view of many observers, the United States had some obligation toward those refugees.

Hungarians. The first acute refugee crisis of the cold war began in the streets of Budapest on October 23, 1956, when demonstrations and rock-throwing sparked a general, nationwide uprising of the Hungarian people against the Soviet-installed, Stalinist government of Mátyás Rákosi, which had ruled since 1946. This uprising gave the world the term Freedom Fighter. For the next three weeks the world watched a grand performance of the sort of political theater that is now commonplace. The United States hesitated while the Soviet Union tried to patch things up. After three weeks of indecision by everyone except the Hungarians, the Soviets dispatched their tanks into Budapest, arrested the members of the provisional government, took them to Russia, and ultimately shot most of them. Still, for three weeks the Freedom Fighters controlled Hungary and its western border with Austria, and in this time tens of thousands of Hungarians fled to the West. The first, ironically, were Hungarian Communists fleeing the Freedom Fighters; then came the pragmatic types who knew that the whole thing was not going to work and simply wanted out; and at the end, as the Soviet tanks rolled west to seal the border once more, came those who had resisted. The poignancy, tragedy, and heroism of those few days is well captured in James Michener's *The Bridge At Andau.*

The Hungarian uprising of 1956 was a turning point in the cold war. Since 1948 the United States had been posturing as the intrepid foe of "Communist tyranny." CIA front groups had mounted radio barrages to iron-curtain countries through Radio Free Europe and Radio Liberty, which had spewed the strident cold-war rhetoric throughout Eastern Europe. The talk had been particularly tough in the summer of 1956 because Dwight Eisenhower wanted a second term as president of the United States. When the people of Hungary took the talk seriously, President Eisenhower and his Secretary of State, John Foster Dulles, sat on their hands. The Hungarian disaster could not have been better timed if it had been planned by the Republican National Committee. The uprising took place before the election, the Freedom Fighters were in full control on election day, and the Eisenhower-Dulles betrayal took place after the election. Probably the United States should not have assisted the Hungarians. Certainly it should not have encouraged them.

The Eisenhower administration had to do something to save face. It had just granted *de facto* recognition to Soviet dominance of Eastern Europe and communicated to the more perceptive members of the American public that cold-war rhetoric was for internal consumption only (the less perceptive continue to believe in it to this very day). There was still the matter of 100,000 or so displaced Hungarians, mostly in Austria, who had to go somewhere, and back to Hungary was not the place. On November 8, 1956, President Eisenhower authorized the admission to the United States of the first few thousand Hungarians under the Refugee Relief Act of 1953. Later he authorized the admission of additional tens of thousands, mostly as parolees under the 1952 act. By June 30, 1957, nearly 34,000 Hungarians had been admitted to the United States.

The suddenness with which this pool of potential immigrants came into existence and the speed with which they were admitted to the United States created some short-run problems, but by and large the Hungarians made splendid immigrants. They brought skills, they dispersed themselves widely over the United States, learned English, and were thankful. (It is very important to Americans to be thanked.) Furthermore, the Hungarian refugees had had quite enough of politics, and they did not sit around plotting their return.

Cubans. The second bout of the United States with cold-war refugees began about two years after the Hungarian influx. In January 1959, Fulgencio Batista, who had ruled Cuba on and off for a quarter-century, announced that he was capitulating to a vast array of forces opposing him and would leave the country. The most conspicuous element in the opposition was the Twenty-sixth of July Movement, M-26 (or M-26-7) for short, headed by Fidel Castro. At first Castro appeared to be a standard Latin American reformist politician. He was the son of a prosperous landholder from the farthest reaches of the island, a university graduate and lawyer who was entitled to style himself "doctor."

He programmed his opposition to Batista largely as a political and military operation but partly as a media event as well. He conducted small-scale military operations in the area where he had grown up, the mountains of Oriente Province, 600 miles from where the action was in Havana. But it was his skill at public relations that made him an international figure and recognized as the leader of the anti-Batista faction. In February 1957, he managed to smuggle Herbert Matthews of the *New York Times* into the Sierra Maestra so he could be interviewed, and the following April he managed to get two CBS newsmen in for a television interview. The latter interview was particularly significant because Batista had announced some weeks earlier that Castro had fled the country. It was embarrassing in Havana. Fidel's public relations efforts were not restricted to a North American audience. By far the most important piece of equipment he had was a radio transmitter powerful enough to cover the island, and his *Radio Rebelde* broadcast continuously, describing the real and imagined defeats he had inflicted on the Batista forces.

In fact, Batista's capacity to resist was profoundly limited. In the last months it was necessary to send someone politically reliable up with each military pilot for fear that he would otherwise fly off to Miami with his airplane. In September 1957, Batista was even forced to bomb the Cienfuegos Naval Base in order to put down an antigovernment mutiny.

Throughout the late months of 1958, Batista's position deteriorated very rapidly. The United States suspended arms shipments to the Cuban government on March 13, 1958. Batista was under great pressure from forces in Cuba that formerly had supported him to hold elections and to absent himself from them. Castro and others in armed opposition to Batista were flourishing. Arms and men to fight Batista came into Cuba from many sources, the arms mostly from the United States. In an unparalleled act, the Venezuelan government made a gift of $50,000 to M-26 and allowed the organization to set up radio-telephone service between Caracas and the Sierra Maestra where Castro was. At the beginning of 1958, Fidel Castro commanded no more than 300 armed men, but by the middle of the year he could launch attacks at will in the mountains and could send columns out of the mountains onto the plains. Batista had no support outside Cuba, and his support within Cuba was eroding daily, so he simply threw in the towel on New Year's Day 1959 and left the country. Castro was clearly the best-known figure in the fight against Batista and probably the most able. In any event, it was to him that the Cuban people turned, and, after a slow triumphal march across the island, he set about to build a new Cuba.

In the early months of 1959, Fidel Castro enjoyed a greater popularity in the United States than any foreigner since Winston Churchill in the early days of World War II. He visited the United States smoking a big cigar and wearing his combat fatigues, and his flamboyance only added to his popularity. Rough times were ahead, however, and as 1959 unfolded, Castro ceased being a comic or romantic figure and emerged as a real force that had to be contended with. He announced an indefinite postponement of elections, began the systematic purging of the government of alleged Batista followers, executed many of Batista's police and some military personnel, and undertook the confiscation of certain foreign-owned, particularly American, properties. It became evident that Castro was not just another Latin American politician, but was determined to rebuild Cuban society; if this threatened the interests, economic or political, of foreigners, so be it.

The exodus of Cubans to Miami was composed of all sorts of people with all sorts of motives. Only a few fled because their past made their future in Cuba downright dangerous. Many were former Castro sympathizers—including his sister—who had worked hard for the downfall of Batista but now felt left out or betrayed. Most were people who simply wanted out of Cuba to escape the dislocation and inconvenience of the revolutionary changes taking place there. They were middle-class sorts with skills and education and saw no reason to put up with the problems of the new Cuba when they did not have to. After all, Cuba was not being reorganized for their benefit. Regardless of the reasons, they came to the U.S. in very large numbers throughout 1960—about 1,600 per week. The number of Cuban refugees quickly made the numbers of Hungarians seem inconsequential.

Almost all of the Cubans were staying in Miami, however. This concentration resulted in part from the basic refugee attitude of the Cubans—that they would soon go home when affairs in Cuba went back to normal. The United States Government was not altogether pleased when large numbers of Cubans began streaming into Florida. But, as American attitudes toward Castro hardened, it became increasingly difficult to turn the Cubans away. Seeing that the Cubans might instead be useful, the government encouraged them to believe that they would soon go home and thus reinforced their tendency to stay in the Miami area.

On January 3, 1961, in the very last weeks of the Eisenhower Administration, but with the full knowledge and approval of the

incoming Kennedy Administration, the United States broke off
diplomatic relations with Cuba. Well before this, however, the
United States Government had decided to bring down the Castro
government by force, intrigue, and subversion. For almost a year,
elements of the 2506 Assault Brigade had been training in the
jungles of Guatemala for their landing at the Bay of Pigs on the
morning of April 16, 1961. These men then fought for three days
on the beaches without the air support they had been promised
and without even being resupplied. When they ran out of ammunition, they put down their arms and became prisoners.

Ultimately, the CIA spent $45 million on this disaster with no
formal consultation with Congress, with no special appropriation
of funds, and with no accounting for the money when it was all
over. A year and a half later, another $62 million from ostensibly
private but only vaguely specified sources was spent to ransom the
captives from Cuban jails.

The Cuban refugee community in Miami was absolutely essential to this operation and continued to be to all such operations so
long as it was the policy of the United States Government to
subvert the government of Cuba. The men who fought and died
and were captured at the Bay of Pigs came from this community.
After open invasion failed, the CIA shifted its efforts to internal
subversion and annoying but largely inconsequential
commando-style raids. Again, the personnel came from the
Miami Cubans.

In order to keep these people in a situation where they would
be useful to its secret and violent policy, the United States Government violated the basic, historic, first principle of immigration. This principle is, very simply, that it is the primary objective
of the United States Government to facilitate the assimilation into
American society of those who come permanently into the country. In the case of the Cubans, however, the United States Government resolved to follow paths calculated to impede assimilation. It might be argued that the government did not then regard
the Cubans as permanent residents. But then, in this instance,
who or what was "the United States Government"? It was certainly not the Immigration and Naturalization Service, nor the
Congress, nor anything else that saw the light of day. It was a
small, inbred group of men with too much money, too little
supervision, and a complete lack of the essential humility it takes
to ask oneself, "What if I am wrong?"

Three basic techniques were used to keep the Cuban refugee
community intact and amenable to directions from Washington.
First, the hundreds of thousands of Cubans were kept uncertain
about their exact legal status in this country. Many who came

legally entered only on visitor's visas and were not technically entitled to hold employment. After the U.S. broke diplomatic relations with Cuba in January 1961, no more visas of any kind could be issued. But "visa waivers" were given to those who made their way here anyhow, and those who entered via the airlift were paroled. None of these people had any right to seek employment, but since they had to survive they were not only allowed to work but actually assisted in finding employment. Of course, at any moment this courtesy could have been withdrawn.

The second way the Cuban community was kept together was by officially and unofficially encouraging the Cubans to believe that, somehow, the United States would get them back to their island. President Kennedy went to Miami personally to welcome the returning prisoners from the Bay of Pigs. There he returned the flag of the Assault Brigade, which had somehow made its way to Washington, and promised that he would again meet these men, but in Havana. Unofficially, the CIA remained active in the community, using it to recruit raiders and generally encouraging the Cubans to believe that their return was just around the corner.

Finally, the United States Government made public assistance available to the Cuban refugees on a lavish scale, but available only in Miami. These programs were run with federal money but administered by Florida or Dade County. This effort was so successful that as late as 1976 almost half of all Cuban aliens reporting their residence were still in Florida.

The impact and magnitude of this contrived immigration is something that is seldom discussed. All told, the number of Cubans who came to the United States as refugees exceeded 600,000 persons, or about eight percent of the Cuban population at the time Castro took power. Almost two-thirds of this number arrived in this country via the airlift from Cuba, which was paid for by the United States Government. Census results show an increase in the number of Cuban-born residents in the United States from 80,000 to 440,000 between 1960 and 1970.

The exodus from Cuba is frequently cited as an indication of the failure of the Cuban Revolution or rejection of it by a large part of the Cuban people. Castro's answer to this is that if the United States prepared the same welcome for the citizens of any other Latin American or Caribbean country, the exodus would be even larger. He is probably right.

The consequences for the United States of the Cuban immigration and of the calculated campaign to keep the refugees confined to the Miami area have been several. First of all, with over 200,000 persons who consider themselves primarily Cuban, Miami, or at least large parts of it, has become an Hispanic Caribbean city, and not one of the more picturesque. There are simply too many Cubans clustered in South Florida to achieve anything like the degree of assimilation that has been achieved by the Hungarians. Furthermore, the efforts of the United States to encourage the refugees to think of themselves as Cubans who are only temporarily in this country has made the problem even worse. U.S. policy created in the Cuban community a political underworld inside this country for the purpose of overthrowing the Castro regime and sanctioned the Cubans to break U.S. laws and commit acts of war outside the country.

It is therefore not surprising that, when the United States Government finally saw the folly of all this and withdrew its support, many of the Cubans went right ahead with their political outlawry both here and abroad. When Richard Nixon's White House burglars needed additional personnel for their mischief in the Democratic National Headquarters in the Watergate apartment and office complex in June 1972, they turned to the Cuban refugee community in Miami. No one knows to this day what the burglars wanted in there, but the leaders—themselves veterans of the good old days down in the Florida Keys—sold the line to the Cubans that they were somehow fighting Fidel Castro by bugging Larry O'Brien's office. That grown men could believe this is but a measure of the unreality that has been fostered in the Cuban community in Miami.

As time passed and reality became more and more intrusive both in the United States Government and in the Cuban refugee community, the Cubans finally began to become assimilated. In November 1966, Congress extended to the Cuban refugees who had entered the country without immigration visas—and this was virtually all of them—the right to seek "adjustment of status." This meant that they could become immigrants and ultimately seek naturalization. In 1976 almost 8 percent of all "immigrants" were in fact Cubans who had achieved adjustment of status but had been in the United States for many years. Since it usually takes five years for an immigrant to qualify for citizenship, the impact of the Congressional action of 1966 was not felt until the early 1970s. Every year from 1971 through 1976, Cubans were the largest national group receiving naturalization. Their numbers in those years totaled over 125,000, representing one-sixth of all naturalizations. After a very long time the Cuban refugees are making their way into American life.

Vietnamese. "In late March and early April 1975, prospects of a political settlement to the conflict in South Viet Nam had begun to fade." With this monument of understatement, the 1975 *Annual Report* of the Immigration and Naturalization Service began its account of the Indo-Chinese Refugee Program. The United States had been fighting the war there for twenty years, one way or another, to one degree or another, and now was defeated. During those twenty years, tens of thousands of Vietnamese had compromised themselves totally with the now victorious North Vietnamese Army and the Viet Cong by serving the interests of United States policy. To remain behind seemed to mean execution at worst or an uncertain and probably unpleasant future at best. These people had to be brought out and resettled somewhere, and most of the nations of the world were not willing to take them.

In addition to the number the United States had to accommodate in order to do the right thing by those who had served its interests, another sizable number of refugees was generated by continued ranting of traditional cold-war rhetoric. Instead of pursuing a course that would help the Vietnamese to accept the fate that Americans had sealed for them, the United States Government followed actions that only heightened their understandable concern. In the first weeks of April 1975, the U.S. Government undertook the evacuation of over 2,000 small children to the United States. Allegedly, these were children without families in Vietnam scheduled for adoption into American families. In fact, the operation was carried out in such disorder that it may never be known who many of those children were. Still, it allowed President Gerald Ford and his Secretary of State, Henry Kissinger, to save face. A few days later the American public was treated to the sight of the last United States ambassador to Vietnam alighting from a helicopter onto the deck of an aircraft carrier with the American flag in a plastic pouch under his arm. Ford used the Vietnamese children and the other Vietnamese refugees just as Eisenhower had used the Hungarians and Kennedy had used the Cubans—to put something of a decent face on the ugly consequences of a vacillating and deceitful foreign policy.

Apparently there were no contingency plans for the orderly evacuation of those South Vietnamese to whom protection was owed. There was just a mad rush. On April 18, 1975, President Ford asked 12 federal agencies to "coordinate . . . all U.S. Government activities concerning evacuation of U.S. citizens, Vietnamese citizens, and third country nationals from Vietnam and refugee and resettlement problems relating to the Vietnam conflict." On April 25 the advance party sent out to Guam, where the civil and military authorities had been instructed to prepare accommodations for 50,000 persons for 90 days, arrived there to begin their preparations. They discovered that the evacuation had started two days earlier and that over 10,000 Vietnamese refugees were already there. Instead of 90 days, the processing on Guam and at an overflow facility on Wake Island took six months; and instead of 50,000 persons, the number eventually exceeded three times that number.

The reception these people met in the United States was mixed, perhaps partly reflecting American ambivalence toward the Vietnam War itself. Since a fair number of the refugees were former police and other government officials in Vietnam, they were often looked upon with suspicion or outright hostility, particularly by Americans who had actively opposed the war. A number of volunteer organizations sprang up to help the new arrivals find homes and employment. Like the Hungarians before them, the Vietnamese have dispersed themselves throughout the country, harbored no notions about going home, and have made every effort to become assimilated. And they have succeeded to a remarkable degree. Most of the original hostility has faded as the Vietnamese have established themselves in the public view as industrious, productive members of their new society. Gail Kelly has chronicled their rapid assimilation in her book, *From Viet Nam to America*. The story she tells is well worth reading.

Yet the story of the Indochinese exodus is not yet over. Political upheavals in Cambodia, Laos, and Vietnam have continued to generate a stream of migrants who have attempted to find refuge in other Asian countries. The hostility they have encountered makes what the first refugees found in the United States seem trifling. In July 1977, a group of 47 Vietnamese, including 20 children, were forced to sail 2,500 miles in a fishing boat to Australia in order to find a place that would accept them. On their way, they had been turned away from Thailand, Singapore, and Indonesia. In late 1977, over 100,000 Indochinese refugees were stranded in various places throughout Southeast Asia, and others were fleeing at the rate of 2,000 per month.

In 1977, two years after the processing centers on Guam and Wake Island had been closed down, the United States agreed to admit another 15,000 Indochinese refugees through the parole power of the Attorney General. About half of these have been "boat people," who were stranded on the high seas because no one would let them in, and the other half were persons with "dangerously close prior connections with the U.S." Congressional reaction was not enthusiastic, and Representative Joshua Eilberg, chairman of the House Judiciary Committee's subcommittee on immigration sought to restrict the Attorney General's parole power by requiring him to consult with Congress before admitting any more refugees. But nothing seems to have come from this attempt so far.

Meanwhile the boat people are still streaming out of Indochina. Between 1965 and early 1979 some 800,000 people left Indochina altogether. Some 20,000 boat people had been admitted to the United States by early 1979 and hundreds more were arriving on the West Coast each week. The pressure to let in more of the boat people continues, as does pressure to keep them out. In no other recent case has the union of foreign policy and immigration policy been more evident.

Since the close of the Second World War, over one million individuals have been officially admitted to the United States as refugees. About three-fourths of these were Europeans whose lives were uprooted by Nazi and Soviet imperialism. To this number should be added about 600,000 Cubans, who arrived here as refugees-in-fact if not refugees-in-law, and perhaps a quarter-million Indochinese.

Over a dozen different pieces of major legislation or presidential directives have touched on the problem of the refugees. One of the more curious was the Azores and Netherlands Relief Act of 1958, which provided for special admission as immigrants certain persons who were displaced from their homes by volcanic eruptions and earthquakes in the Azores Islands and certain persons uprooted by political changes in Indonesia. In all, over 20,000 people were admitted under this piece of legislation.

Legislation always lags behind social need, and certainly the problem of the refugee-immigrant is no exception. The United States ignored the refugees of the 1930s, and for 20 years following World War II the prevailing attitude was that each upheaval was unique and had to be dealt with on its own terms. President Eisenhower's use in 1956 of the parole authority granted by Congress to the Attorney General to admit Hungarian refugees wholesale set an important precedent. The authority was intended for sparing use in individual cases, but it was the only option available to Eisenhower for dealing with the refugee problem. It was subsequently used by every succeeding administration for the Cubans, Indochinese, and other refugees.

In no other single detail has the inadequacy and unreality of U.S. immigration policy been more obvious than in the failure of Congress to provide for refugees in the 1952 law. This failure forced every president subsequent to Truman to bend the law to carry out his mandated responsibility for conducting the nation's foreign policy and to meet the demands of simple humanity. Until recently, no outcry was heard from Congress or the public, indicating that admission of the refugees was not considered outrageous. But one might well ask why Congress has been so slow to enact legislation that would bring the law into congruence with practice as it emerged. Evidently, Americans simply could not admit that world politics and the consequences of their own foreign policy could so repeatedly force them to breach their own principles of immigration.

In 1965 Congress finally enacted legislation that abandoned the idea of preserving ethnic purity through the national-origins principle. This law also belatedly extended to political refugees a fixed claim to immigration to the United States, with an annual allotment of 17,400, and specified that they must be refugees from communism or from "the general area of the Middle East." In February 1979, the Carter Administration was preparing a legislation proposal that would rationalize and liberalize policies toward admission of refugees. The proposed bill would raise the limit to 50,000 per year, giving priority to those toward whom the U.S. might feel special responsibility, such as the Vietnamese. It would also broaden the eligibility of refugees to conform with the United Nations' definition of a refugee: "anyone outside his or her own country with a justified fear of returning, or someone uprooted by military operations, civil disturbances or natural calamity."

LEGAL IMMIGRATION SINCE 1965

Today, the immigration policy of the United States is embodied primarily in Public Law 89–236, which was passed by Congress on October 3, 1965. Technically an amendment to the Immigration and Nationality Act of 1952, the law in fact completely changed the basis on which immigrants were admitted to the United States. The new law abolished the system of national quotas that had governed immigration for 40 years, abandoned the national origins idea as the basis for immigration, and for the first time in U.S. history placed a numerical limit on the number of immigrants that could come from Western Hemisphere countries. Immigration from the Western Hemisphere is limited to 120,000 persons annually on a first-come, first-served basis, but with no more than 20,000 from a single country.

Effective December 1, 1965, immigration from the Eastern Hemisphere has been restricted to 170,000 per year without reference to any particular nation, but with the provision that no more than 20,000 immigrants could come from any one country in any one year. A prospective immigrant from the Old World could apply for an immigration visa in any one of seven categories. Four preferential categories were created for relatives of United States citizens, and these were allotted first claim on 74 percent of the total visa numbers available. Two categories of occupational preference were allotted 20 percent of the visa numbers, and the seventh "non-preference" and refugee category was given the remaining 6 percent plus any unused numbers left over from the other categories. Within all categories, qualified applicants are assigned numbers on a first-come, first-served basis. There has long been agitation to remove the distinction between the hemispheres and place the world under a single 290,000-person limit using these categories.

In practice, the proportions of people admitted in each of the preference categories have been quite different from the assigned percentages. In 1976, for example, 60 percent of the immigrants admitted from the Eastern Hemisphere were in the close-relative categories, 18 percent were admitted under the occupational preferences, and 22 percent were non-preference immigrants and refugees. In addition to the maximum of 290,000 immigrants who enter the United States in the various numerically limited categories, the spouses, parents, and minor children of United States citizens as well as certain others are admitted without reference to the limitations. In 1976 these people represented almost one-third of all immigrants, or 113,000 persons.

Since the implementation of Public Law 89–236, the level of immigration has increased. During the period 1961–65, the last five years of the old system, immigration averaged about 290,000 persons per year; but in the period 1972–76, the most recent five-year period for which figures are available, the number averaged about 390,000 per year. These represent *gross* immigration figures—the total number of legal immigrants admitted. No one knows what the *net* immigration might be—that is, the number who actually end up spending their lives here—because no one knows how many of the immigrants decide to go back home or on to some other country. The number is certainly considerable, perhaps a third of the gross immigration.

There are more qualified applicants for immigration visas in many of the preference categories than can be accommodated under the law, and for people with approved applications this has resulted in the phenomenon of "waiting for your date." This means waiting for the date on which a visa application was approved to come up on the list of oversubscribed categories in the monthly *Visa Bulletin* of the Immigration and Naturalization Service. The date of September 15, 1968, came up for Filipinos approved under preference category number five—brothers and sisters of United States citizens—only in July 1978. Because of changing patterns of demand and vagaries of the law, it is impossible to know when one's date might come up. A United States District Court decision ordered the INS to make generally available to non-preference applicants from the Western Hemisphere with a "date" prior to July 1, 1975, nearly 145,000 visa numbers that had been reserved for Cubans. Hence, the date for many Western Hemisphere immigrants will be coming up sooner than anyone expected. In July 1978, the date for non-preference applicants from the small British Caribbean dependency of St. Christopher-Nevis—the birthplace of Alexander Hamilton—was December 8, 1961. Seventeen years is a long time to wait for a chance to go to the promised land.

Public Law 89-236 has had a profound impact on the balance between European and Asian immigrants to the United States. During the period 1961–65, total immigration from Europe averaged about five times as high as that from Asia. In the period 1972–76, there were 62 percent more Asians than Europeans.

The new immigration rules were praised in the mid-1960s because they abandoned the national-origins idea with its racist implications and based eligibility for immigration largely on preserving the integrity of the family and on the capacity of the immigrant to contribute to American life. On the other hand, the law was condemned out of fear that the occupational-preference categories would draw professional people and skilled workers out of the Third World where they were desperately needed. There is some reason for concern here, but only 34,000 of the visa numbers allotted to the Eastern Hemisphere are for occupationally preferred immigrants, and these have to serve not only the qualified individuals themselves but also all their immediate families. In 1976, for example, about 27,000 persons were admitted under the occupational-preference categories. But only about half of them were the applicants themselves and half were their relatives.

It is absolutely scandalous that the United States of America, the richest and most powerful nation on Earth, should import so many of its skilled workers from some of the poorest parts of the world. But the occupational-preference categories do not seem to be the major villain. In 1976, of the over 12,000 physicians and registered nurses admitted to the United States as immigrants, only 30 percent of the doctors and 40 percent of the nurses came in as "beneficiaries of occupational preference." The rest came in from the Western Hemisphere as relatives of U.S. citizens, as refugees, or as non-preference immigrants.

Undoubtedly the immigration policy of the United States will continue trying to straddle the inherent contradictions that have always beset it. On the one hand, motives of humanitarianism, self-interest, and tradition will tend to push the door more widely open, while other aspects of self-interest, nativism, and bigotry will tend to shove it shut.

Two elements in the current debate on immigration policy are new. For the first time in United States history, overpopulation is a concern. In the late 1940s, President Truman argued for the admission of displaced persons to alleviate overpopulation in Europe, but no one even brought up the problem of overpopulation in the U.S. Cheap foreign labor causing unemployment among native Americans who refuse to work for the modest wages acceptable to the foreigner is an old refrain, but today it is the illegal immigrant who is the focus of debate. Whether there are really more illegal immigrants in the country today than there have been before is an open question. Indeed, how many there really are is not known. Overpopulation and the illegal immigrant are both new elements in the old debate about immigrants, and both are going to be increasingly important in coming years. Powerful, perhaps preponderant, forces in Congress will argue that United States immigration policy is a purely domestic issue and must be decided on the basis of domestic concerns, not on the need to live together peacefully with others in the family of nations. Others will take the opposite, broader view.

The developing migration debate, however, has already focused on the topic of illegal immigrants, and that focus can be expected to become increasingly sharp as the debate proceeds. To most Americans, "illegal immigrant" means "wetback Mexican." Illegal immigrants are viewed by many uninformed people as a substantial threat to the character and economy of the United States. In order to understand fully how this perceived threat arose, it is necessary to have a grasp of the history of the Mexican nation and of the border that separates it from the United States.

[3]

TWIXT STRENGTH AND WEAKNESS, THE DESERT;* THE DEVELOPMENT OF MEXICO AND THE U.S.–MEXICAN BORDER

International borders vary tremendously in their character and meaning. Some are distinct and undeniable, marked by a river or the crest of some mountain range. Others are totally indistinguishable, being nothing more than a surveyor's line on a map. Crossing some, like the United States–Canadian border or most of those between Western European nations, is little more trouble than crossing a state line in the U.S. Others are nearly impenetrable barriers. Sometimes borders divide peoples of markedly different languages, cultures, and heritage. The tightest border in the world, that between East and West Germany, divides peoples of identical language and culture. Most borders are intended to keep people out; that one, with its watchtowers, searchlights, minefields, and multiple fences, is intended to keep people in.

The United States–Mexican border today extends a bit less than 2,000 miles, from the mouth of the Rio Grande to the Pacific Ocean. For about 1,250 of these miles, the border is the Rio Grande. The rest is a totally artificial surveyor's line running through trackless desert, splitting an occasional border settlement. It contains only three metropolitan areas that would have any substantial existence were they not on the border—

---

*A quotation attributed to Sebastian Lerdo de Tejado, who became president of Mexico in 1872.

Brownsville, Texas/Matamoros, Tamaulipas near the mouth of the Rio Grande; El Paso, Texas/Juárez, Chihuahua, 750 miles northwest; and San Diego, California/Tijuana, Baja California. The rest of the 25 or so border towns make an industry out of being on the border.

The U.S.–Mexican border, like all others, has no intrinsic existence. It was established piecemeal as the result of warfare, compromise, exigency, and, occasionally, common sense. What that border divides is two distinct New World cultures. A century before the English settled that wild New England shore and tidewater Virginia, the Spanish were already spreading out from their base in the Central Valley of Mexico. It is impossible to pinpoint a specific moment when the English stopped being English and the Spanish stopped being Spanish, but the process of becoming "Americans" and "Mexicans" began on the first day of arrival when the men and women of both groups started dealing with problems and exploiting opportunities that were not to be found in England or Spain.

The Spanish in Mexico spread out north and south, linking up with a similar expansion from the other Spanish base in Peru. Eventually, they created an empire that stretched from Tierra del Fuego in southernmost Chile to the Columbia River. The English did not do much in their first couple of centuries in the New World except grow tobacco and build Protestant churches, confining their activities mainly to the Eastern Seaboard until the Revolution. But once the westward movement began, it was pursued with an enthusiasm and a purposefulness that overreached itself into ruthlessness more than once.

In the process of each of these expansions, the Mexican and American national characters were formed, first by the new experiences and then by absorbing the views and ways of new peoples. The Spanish and the Indian cultures interbred and intermingled (with a sprinkling of blacks brought in to work mines on the northern frontier) to form the distinctive *mestizo*, or mixed, Spanish-speaking nationality. The English killed or pushed aside the Indians, absorbing little of their wisdom except some agricultural ways, but the mammoth, nineteenth-century immigration of European peoples created an equally mixed English-speaking nationality. Yet, until the 1820s, there was almost no contact between the two peoples and therefore no border separating them.

In 1848 the Treaty of Guadalupe Hidalgo, which ended the Mexican War—or the American Intervention as it is called in Mexico—and the Gadsden Purchase in 1853 of the Mesilla Valley and other lands in the far northwest of Mexico established the present U.S.–Mexican border. Yet it remained a phantom until population growth, economic development, national jealousy, and political turmoil made it into something of consequence. And even today that border is the most disregarded and the most violated of any marking the boundaries of major nations.

Despite the flow of people across the border, not much information about Mexico seems to reach the United States. To most Americans, Mexico is an undifferentiated area south of the border—a land of "Frito banditos," mariachi music, tropical resorts, corruption, siestas, spicy food, marijuana, and poverty. It also seems a land without a history, for the average American is unaware of the epic, four-hundred-year struggle of the Mexican peoples to form a nation and free themselves from foreign domination. How many Americans concerned about illegal Mexican immigration and the Chicano minority realize that it is the Anglos who are the more recent immigrants to the Southwest, occupying by right of conquest nearly half the territory once recognized as Mexico? Ignorance, prejudice, and romanticism blend to form a view of Mexico, Mexicans, and Mexican history that has little to do with reality, but goes a long way to explain why many Americans are fooled by jingoistic presentations of the Mexican "problem."

Since Mexico today is the chief donor of immigrants, legal and illegal, to the United States, it is important that Americans understand how the present situation developed.

The political history of Mexico is violent. In the National Historical Museum in Chapultepec Palace, the work of the great Mexican muralist José Clemente Orozco interprets the course of the Mexican Revolution of 1910. At one end of the mural—it covers several walls and can only be viewed in parts—is a large detail of dead bodies laid out neatly, side by side, in a row that seems to stretch to infinity. It looks like a road, and in fact Orozco has thus explained his message: those who died on all sides in the Revolution paved with their bodies the avenue that would carry Mexico forward. This violence does not stem from anything inherent or innate in the Mexican psyche; a person is safer on the street in any Mexican city than in any comparable city in the United States. The average level of interpersonal violence— people assaulting, stabbing, and shooting each other—is much lower in Mexico than it is in the United States. The political violence stems from deeply rooted social and economic problems of such awesome magnitude and complexity that their solutions have bred equally awesome and complex conflict.

A NATION WHOSE HEROES WERE SHOT

The story of the U.S.–Mexican borderlands really began over

450 years ago. In 1519 Hernán Cortés and a band of a few hundred adventurers landed at the present-day site of Veracruz and began the conquest of Mexico. The *conquistadores* were superb horsemen. Grandly mounted and equipped with the latest armor and weapons—swords, lances, knives and arrowheads made from steel, and firearms—the Spaniards outclassed their horseless, steel-less Indian opponents as completely as the German panzers and Luftwaffe outclassed the Polish cavalry in 1939. The Indians were terrified by the explosions of gunpowder and at first thought the mounted *conquistadores* and their horses were single, unnatural creatures. The Spaniards were also imaginative campaigners. They took advantage of various weaknesses in Indian culture and society, recruited Indian allies, and put them to good use.

The technological superiority of the Spanish was based primarily on their horses, which allowed armored men to move long distances rapidly. Just as important as this technology was the political situation they found in central Mexico. The dominant Aztec culture, so admirable in many respects, ruthlessly dominated other peoples in an exploitative and oppressive manner. Many of these other Mexican peoples saw the *conquistadores* as the tool that would rid them of their oppressors. Pressing their advantages, the Spaniards soon established themselves as the successors to the Aztecs.

The greatest ally of the Spanish, however, had nothing to do with their political acumen. That ally was disease—in particular smallpox and measles—which came with the Spanish and ravaged the Aztecs. From slightly over 25 million in 1518, the population of central Mexico dropped to a little over 6 million in only 30 years. By 1605 it was estimated to be just over one million. The decline was a "demographic holocaust" virtually without precedent. It took the population of Mexico more than four centuries to return to the pre-Conquest level, which may go a long way toward explaining the persistent strong emphasis on large families in Mexican culture.

From their base in Mexico City, the *conquistadores* reached out north and south. A single man, Francisco Vásquez de Coronado led conquerors and explorers on expeditions ranging over 4,000 miles of North and Central America, from Kansas to Costa Rica. In 1542, the year Coronado was in Kansas, Juan Rodríguez Cabrillo traveled by sea to the future sites of San Diego and Los Angeles. By 1700 New Mexico had been successfully colonized. By the earliest years of the nineteenth century a string of 21 missions had been established along the California coast, the garrison towns of San Diego, Santa Barbara, Monterey, and San

Francisco had been founded, and pueblos established at San Jose and Los Angeles.

Additional colonies were started in Arizona and Texas, but colonization of *el Septentrión*, the north, never went well. The greatest Spanish success in the north was the domination of the Pueblo Indians of the upper Rio Grande in New Mexico in the early seventeenth century. But even there they were thrown out for over a decade by an Indian uprising in 1680, which wiped out all the settlements and killed some 400 Spaniards. As the Spanish moved north in these years, the Navajo were moving south, and this collision made settlement of Arizona difficult. The Navajo and the Apache, as well as the Comanche farther east on the plains of Texas, were nomadic. Unlike the peoples of Mexico and New Mexico, these groups did not live in towns that could be surrounded and conquered. Despite their best efforts, the Spanish could not retain their monopoly on horses and firearms. Once the nomadic Indians were mounted and armed, they could force the Spaniards to hole up in fortified towns just as they had forced the Pueblo Indians to do before the coming of the Spanish. As Carey McWilliams has written:

> Spanish colonization in the Southwest proceeded, from the out-set, under the cloud of Apache terror. The fifth-century Europeans felt no greater fear of the Huns of Attila than the fear which the Apaches inspired in the Spaniards and the Pueblo Indians.

The failure of the Spanish against the Indians was rooted in the system the *conquistadores* brought with them from Spain. Like the Anglos who moved into the area a century or two later, the Spaniards were true frontiersmen, with traditions based on the 800-year struggle to retake the Iberian Peninsula from the Moslems. That struggle, known as the *Reconquista*, was a political and military exercise, but it was also a phenomenon of an advancing frontier, a colonization of a hostile area, not unlike the frontier movement in the United States. But the system the Spanish frontiersmen brought to the Western Hemisphere was based, as McWilliams put it, "on the presidio, the mission and the hacienda—the conquistadores to conquer; the priests to convert; and the encomenderos to exploit." The *encomenderos* were privileged Spaniards to whom Indian groups were "entrusted"—and all too often were simply treated as a source of forced labor.

The system worked like a charm with the sedentary Indians of the Mexican plateau and to a degree with the Pueblo Indians of New Mexico. But it was a disastrous flop at dealing with the warlike nomadic tribes of the Southwest or the elusive Seminole and Cherokee in the Southeast. It is a historic irony that Native Americans helped to contain the Spanish advance into what is now the United States. They so ill fitted the Spanish design that the borderlands were still virtually empty nearly 300 years after Coronado.

Still, wild Indians do not explain all of the Spanish failure to settle the north, for their attempts to move into Florida and Georgia from Cuba and up the California coast from Mexico were never really successful either. Another explanation may simply be that the population base was not large enough to support a really effective expansion and full occupation of the territory. Following the population decimation caused by the Spanish conquest, recovery was very slow. As late as 1800, the population of what is now Mexico was still less than six million.

The inability of the Spanish during the colonial period to become firmly established in the north was a recurring concern of the Council of the Indies, which sat in the Spanish port city of Cádiz and ruled all of the Spanish New World. One waggish historian with a broad perspective has suggested that what the United States is experiencing today is only the ultimate success of a Spanish colonial policy that failed in the sixteenth and seventeenth centuries. The Cubans have taken over Miami and the Mexicans are finally moving into the north, just as the Council of the Indies planned.

The determined but impotent push to the north created a Spanish (later Mexican) presence in what today is United States territory, a presence that was strong enough to hang on only so long as it was not seriously challenged by someone else who wanted the territory. In the early nineteenth century, Americans, egged on by the notion of Manifest Destiny and a desire to annex territory, and later by the discovery of gold in California, began to expand into the area. The population of the young United States in 1820 was nearly ten million and, unlike the Spanish, growing very rapidly. This rapid growth no doubt gave impetus to the push westward. (In turn, of course, high rates of immigration and high birthrates both were encouraged and approved because of the perceived need to populate the continent.)

The discovery of gold in California came too late for the Spanish. Prior to that discovery, there had been little incentive for the Spanish to increase their efforts in what was basically a peripheral, poor, and dangerous area—the "tail" of the Spanish dog in the New World. Had there been no Apaches or Comanches, if the Spanish expansion had been from a larger population base, or if gold had been discovered earlier, the flag of Mexico might well be flying today over San Antonio, Albuquerque, Tucson, Los Angeles, and San Francisco.

The Spanish conquest not only began 400 years of foreign domination over Mexico, it also began the racial stratification of that nation. At the top were the Spanish overlords—the *gachupines*—who represented the power of Imperial Spain on the other side of the Atlantic. Below them were the creoles (*criollos*), people born in Mexico of Spanish parents. At the bottom of the heap were the pitiful remnants of the original Indian tribes that had occupied Mexico when Cortés destroyed the Tenochca (Aztec) Indian civilization.

Cortés's victory gave Mexico its first national hero, the last Tenochca ruler, Cuauhtémoc. Cuauhtémoc is revered today in Mexico for his valiant last-ditch battle against Cortés, while Cortés is reviled as the plundering foreign invader. That Cortés himself married an Indian princess, Malinche, "who played mother to Cortés's father in founding the Mexican nation" has not softened the modern Mexican view of him. Indeed, today a pejorative term for a Mexican who sells out to foreigners is a *malinchista*.

It was of course inevitable that there would be intermarriage between the Spanish, who had left most of their women at home, and the Indians. The offspring of these marriages were the start of another racial class in Mexico—the *mestizos* ("mixed"), lying between creoles and Indians in the social hierarchy. At the risk of oversimplification, the struggle for independence and nationhood in Mexico could be cast in terms of a series of class and racial conflicts. First, the creoles fought the *gachupines* for political power. Then the *mestizos* (with help from a few thoroughly Hispanicized Indians like Benito Juárez, who was a full-blooded Indian) wrested power from the creoles. Today Mexico is a *mestizo* nation; the question remains whether the Indians' time will ever come.

The Coming of Mexican Independence

At 7 A.M. on the sunny morning of July 30, 1811, a middle-aged creole faced a firing party of Spanish soldiers in the small town of Chihuahua. Because he was a priest, the man was allowed a private execution and the right to face his killers rather than be shot in the back. He uttered a few sentences forgiving those about to kill him, passed out candy to them, and waited while the Spanish officer gave the fatal commands. Afterward, the man's head was severed from his corpse and was taken to Guanajuato, hundreds of miles to the south, along with the heads of three comrades. At Guanajuato the heads were put into iron cages, and one was hung on each of the four corners of the *Alhóndiga de Granaditas,* the municipal granary, in the middle of town. The heads would rot there for a decade. This priest, Miguel Hidalgo y Costilla, who fifteen months earlier had become the father of Mexican independence, had now paid for it with his life—as had his lieutenants, Ignacio José Allende, Juan de Aldama, and Mariano Jiménez. The roar of musketry, rifles, and automatic weapons would echo and re-echo through the next twelve decades of Mexico's history and do much to influence her political development. During that time, most of Mexico's heroes would die by the bullet: Morelos, Iturbide, Guerrero, Ocampo, Madero, Zapata, Carranza, Villa, and Obregón, to name just the outstanding ones. It was as if not only Lincoln, Garfield, McKinley, and Kennedy, but also Washington, Jefferson, John Adams, Ben Franklin, Andrew Johnson, Teddy Roosevelt, and Woodrow Wilson had all been shot to death.

Ironically, this first movement toward Mexican independence had its roots in Europe. The outbreak of war between Spain and Great Britain on December 12, 1804, had profound consequences for the viceroyalty of New Spain, as Mexico was then called. The financial squeeze caused by the war pushed Spain to extract all the money she could from her colony—and she decreed a sort of forced loan that led to the ruin of many creoles and destroyed the sources of income of poorer parish priests and many friars. Landowners *(hacendados),* merchants, and others found common cause with the lower clergy. In 1808, Ferdinand VII was forced to abdicate by Napoleon, who attempted to establish his brother, Joseph Bonaparte, on the Spanish throne. Spain lapsed into a civil war, and the creoles in New Spain started to call for self-government, while proclaiming loyalty to Ferdinand.

Events in Mexico then moved rapidly toward violent revolution. The leader of the revolt was the creole priest, Miguel Hidalgo. His hand forced by increasing pressure by the *gachupin* government on potential insurgents, Hidalgo declared the revolution to his parishioners in the village of Dolores, near Guanajuato, on September 16, 1810. His actual words cannot be known with assurance, but one reconstructed version goes like this:

> My children, this day comes to us as a new dispensation. Are you ready to receive it? Will you be free? Will you make the effort to recover from the hated Spaniards the lands stolen from our forefathers three centuries ago? Today we must act! The Spaniards are bad enough themselves, but now they have sold our country to the French. Will you become Napoleon's slaves? Or will you, as patriots, defend your religion and your homes?

He finished with a cry that probably included all or some of the following phrases: "Long live Ferdinand VII! Long Live America! Long Live Religion! Death to bad government!" That cry, usually summarized as "death to the *gachupines*," would go down in Mexican history as the *Grito de Dolores*—the cry of Dolores.

The same day, in the nearby village of Atotonilco, the independence movement acquired a crucial symbol to go with its battle cry—a picture of the Virgin of Guadalupe, the dark-complexioned patron saint of the *mestizos* and Indians. The banner of the Virgin of Guadalupe rallied the masses to what originally was basically a creole cause, uniting them against the *gachupines* who venerated the light-skinned Virgin of Los Remedios.

Hidalgo's revolt spread like wildfire, with Indians and *mestizos* flocking in large numbers to his banner. The Spanish garrison at Guanajuato, holed up in the *Alhóndiga,* refused to surrender. The granary was stormed by an insurgent mob, and some 300 *gachupin* defenders (almost the entire garrison) were slaughtered. The rebels lost about 2,000 men, but not their momentum. Hidalgo's peasant armies sacked Guanajuato and then quickly occupied most of the fertile valley known as the Bajío, northwest of Mexico City.

With the Bajío under his control, Hidalgo turned toward the capital itself. On November 2, he defeated a much smaller, but highly skilled and determined government army of about 2,500 men at Monte de las Cruces, almost at the gates of Mexico City. Then, after moving onto the heights above the city, he turned back. He did so against the recommendation of his one experienced general, José Allende, for reasons that are still disputed. A strong case can be made that the revolt was already starting to fall apart. It lacked creole support after the sacking of Guanajuato—many upper-class creoles felt more threatened by the peasant revolt than oppressed by the Spaniards. Furthermore, Hidalgo's army was weakened by massive desertions after Monte de las Cruces, as peasants fled, appalled by the slaughter inflicted upon them by the disciplined royalist troops.

A few days later Hidalgo's army was split by troops under the *gachupin* general Félix Calleja and forced to retreat westward toward Guadalajara. Calleja waged a ferocious campaign of reoccupation in the Bajío, and at Calderón Bridge near Guadalajara, he ended the insurrection on January 17, 1811, by crushing the huge but ill-trained and undisciplined rebel army. Hidalgo and the other leaders escaped and fled northward, only to be betrayed and captured two months later at a place ironically called Our

Lady of Guadalupe of Baján. They were tried in Chihuahua, far from centers of rebellion on the central plateau. The Virgin of Guadalupe could not protect Hidalgo and his associates from *gachupin* vengeance or from the display of their heads at the place of their first victory—the *Alhóndiga* in Guanajuato.

Hidalgo bungled his revolt, and there is evidence that in the end he felt that the suffering and bloodshed it caused had been in vain (his capture had been accompanied by widespread rejoicing). But Hidalgo had planted the seeds of Mexican independence. After his death, the mantle of leadership in the struggle for an independent Mexico was transferred to another priest, a *mestizo* who had been one of his lieutenants in the south.

José María Morelos proved to be a much more effective leader than his former chief. Morelos continued the battle, aided by skilled fighters such as Vicente Guerrero and Nicolás Bravo, and soon was in control of substantial portions of the south and west. In September 1813, Morelos convened a constitutional convention at Chilpancingo, a town on the road from Mexico City to Acapulco. The Congress of Chilpancingo produced the Mexican equivalent of the United States' Declaration of Independence— supporting the first recommendation of Morelos's program, "that under the present circumstances in Europe, . . . the dependence on the Spanish throne should be dissolved."

This declaration of independence had no effect on General Calleja, who kept his troops in the field against the insurgents. The harassed rebels reconvened the Congress in Apatzingán in October 1814 and ratified Mexico's first formal constitution. But Calleja soon triumphed. Morelos was captured on November 5, 1815, and forced to watch as 27 of his colleagues were executed. He was then defrocked by the Inquisition and tried by the state. On December 22, 1815, at San Cristobal Ecatépec just north of Mexico City, bound, blindfolded, and on his knees, Morelos was shot by a four-man firing squad. Still a devout Catholic, his last words were "Lord thou knowest if I have done well; if ill, I implore thy infinite mercy."

The rebellion did not die with Morelos, although by 1820 a new viceroy, replacing Calleja, seemed to have the situation well in hand. Only in the South Center did Guerrero (foreshadowing the behavior of another from that area, Emiliano Zapata, almost a century later) carry on the armed revolt.

In that fateful year, Spain herself was gripped by a liberal revolution, accompanied by a series of anticlerical measures. This dramatically changed the alignment of forces in New Spain. The Church, feeling its privileged position threatened by the liberal revolution, now saw in independence a chance to maintain its position. So did rich *gachupines* who wanted nothing to do with a liberal Spain.

Suddenly, the creole liberals, who wished to build an independent nation similar to the United States, and the conservative *gachupines* and clerics all wanted independence. What was needed was a military leader, and he appeared in the form of the royalist colonel Agustín Iturbide. Iturbide has been described as the first *caudillo,* or "man on horseback." The *caudillo*

> was to dominate the Mexican scene, with rare exceptions, for more than a century, despoil the country for his own glory and aggrandizement, and leave it disorganized and weak, thereby delaying immeasurably the growth and maturity of Mexico.

Iturbide was a creole, a descendant of a noble family from Navarre, who had fought on the *gachupin* side against Hidalgo and Morelos. Like Morelos, he was born in Valladolid, and his forces had inflicted an especially punishing defeat on Morelos near Valladolid just after the first congress had declared the independence of Mexico from Spain. In the engagement Morelos had narrowly escaped capture. In one of those ironies in which Mexican history abounds, it was Iturbide's victory that started Morelos on the road to the firing squad, and it was Iturbide who eventually made possible the fulfillment of Morelos's dream.

Iturbide and Santa Anna: the Troubled Years

The man immediately responsible for Mexico's independence was thus a creole who had fought against the creole-inspired independence movement and was chosen by the Spanish viceroy to command the royalist army operation against the southern guerrilla forces under Guerrero. Iturbide, however, immediately began to seek a reconciliation with Guerrero and Bravo (who was then in a royalist prison). He moved south and, rather than attack Guerrero, turned on his Spanish masters. He announced on February 24, 1821, the famous *Plan of Iguala,* proclaiming Mexican independence and calling for racial equality and defense of the Catholic Church.

The Plan of Iguala struck the right chord. It united such disparate elements as Guerrero's hard-bitten guerrillas, rich landowners, clergy, liberal creoles, and royalist officers. Although the viceroy sent troops against Iturbide, it was in vain. Spanish power disintegrated, a treaty was signed with Spain, and Mexico became independent. Iturbide, Mexico's liberator, became its *de facto* ruler. It is a further irony that Iturbide, who achieved Mexican independence in a nearly bloodless revolution, is not commemorated in Mexico today. His birthplace, Valladolid, was renamed Morelia after its other native son, and although states are named after Hidalgo, Morelos, and Guerrero, there are no monuments to Iturbide, and no city or state is named after him.

Iturbide's vision of an independent Mexico ruled by a local monarch came to pass on May 18, 1822, a little more than a year after the declaration of independence, when he engineered a coup that installed him as emperor. His "empire," however, was largely in ruins after a dozen years of internecine wars, and the dominant political forces were republican—the spiritual descendants of Hidalgo and Morelos.

An ambitious military commander at Veracruz soon went into revolt and declared a republic. Guerrero and Bravo supported him, taking up arms against Iturbide in the south, and an era of instability—revolts, wars, and political turmoil—that historian Jan Bazant christened the "troubled years" (1821–1855) began. Iturbide was deposed, shipped off to exile, and declared a traitor and subject to execution if he should return. Unaware that he was condemned in advance, Iturbide returned with hopes of restoring his empire, landing on July 17, 1824. He was immediately captured and two days later faced a firing squad. He died bravely, declaring that he was not a traitor and, in the tradition of Hidalgo, forgiving those who killed him.

The ambitious young officer from Veracruz who first revolted against Iturbide was Antonio López de Santa Anna, destined to become the paramount *caudillo* of Mexico—a man so involved in the events of the next 30 years that that period of Mexican history is sometimes called the "age of Santa Anna."

During this period in Mexico there was a continual political struggle. On one side were the more conservative Centralists (such as Santa Anna eventually became), who with the support of the army and the Church attempted to establish a strong central government in Mexico City. In opposition were the Federalists, a more liberal group hoping to reduce the influence of the army and Mexico City and form a republic modeled after the United States, with countervailing power resting in state governments and militias.

Economic turmoil added to the political as Mexico constantly struggled to repay its foreign debts, all too often contracted by generals in power attempting to enrich themselves. The Spanish made an attempt at reconquest in 1828 and were defeated near Tampico by yellow fever and Santa Anna. The latter became a national hero. There were revolts and counterrevolts. For the fourth time, Guerrero took up arms against the central government and was defeated by Bravo, his old ally from the days of the battle for independence. Like so many other Mexican heroes, he was promptly shot.

In 1833 Santa Anna was elected president by Congress, but he retired to Veracruz, leaving his liberal vice-president Valentín Gómez Farías in Mexico City pushing anticlerical policies. The army and the Church pressured Santa Anna to return, and in the late spring of 1834 the army revolted. When the dust had settled, Santa Anna had double-crossed the liberals and had become dictator of Mexico. Those who had looked to the United States as a model had lost, just as relations with their increasingly powerful northern neighbor moved to center stage in the Mexican drama.

By then, Texas, the most northeastern portion of Mexico, was directly in the path of an expansionist United States. Americans at that time were obsessed with the notion of Manifest Destiny—that it was their destiny to occupy the continent from coast to coast. Thus it was inevitable that the U.S. should try to absorb much of the Mexican possessions in the South and West.

THE BEGINNING OF THE BORDER

There had been almost no contact between the Mexicans and Americans before the 1820s and therefore no border between them. But soon after 1800, the mountain men from the Rockies occasionally visited Taos and Santa Fe to buy supplies or just look around. Before long, however, the Americans established the Santa Fe Trail from Independence, Missouri, and did a brisk business carrying goods in both directions.

An important way station on the Trail was Bent's Fort in southeastern Colorado. The Bent family typified the ease of the time and the casual nature of the borderland area. Some members of the family settled in Santa Fe and married Mexican women, had Mexican families, and dabbled in Mexican politics. One became the first U.S. governor of New Mexico after it was taken by the Americans; he was murdered in an Indian uprising aimed at throwing them out. Others stayed in Colorado and did business out of the fort. Yet another member of the family rejected both cultures and went off to live with the Comanche, joining in their depredations against both groups of settlers. In the 1820s Americans started moving into Texas, too, and the same casualness characterized the scene there that marked it in New Mexico.

The Mexicans themselves were in large part responsible for the flow of migrants from the U.S. into their territory. Many Mexicans believed that populating the borderlands would discourage their annexation by the United States, and the Mexican government accordingly encouraged settlers. Stephen Austin's father, Moses Austin, had a concession from the Mexican government to found a colony of Roman Catholic Anglo-Americans in Texas. When Moses died before the colony could be established, Stephen carried on with the explicit approval of Iturbide. Under an agreement reached between them on April 14, 1823, and later ratified by the Mexican Congress, Austin was to supervise the colonization of Texas by Americans, luring them with large land grants and seven years' exemption from taxes.

In 1825, under Austin's urging, the first immigrants from the U.S. were entering Texas—to Austin's great gain since, in addition to a land grant, the Mexican government paid him a bounty for each colonist. But the influx of immigrants soon made the Mexican government nervous, and attempts were made to restrict the flow. By 1834, Anglo-Americans outnumbered Mexicans in Texas 30,000 to 5,000.

From the outset the two groups kept apart; the Anglos lived largely on ranches, the Mexicans largely in towns. There was a great deal of friction between them. The Mexicans were wary of the Anglos' power, and the Anglos typically were unwilling to accept the Mexican culture, which they viewed with a contempt similar to that they had for Indian cultures. Santa Anna's dictatorial policies did not improve the situation.

One of the issues that drove a wedge between the Anglos in Texas and the government in Mexico City was slavery. Texas and Coahuila were fused into a single state, and the new state constitution, over the objections of the Texans, contained a strong anti-slavery article. The Texans petitioned for separate statehood and for a series of reform measures, but were turned down by the Mexican Congress. More maneuvering and demands followed, but Santa Anna, in the process of setting himself up as dictator of Mexico, rejected the most important of them and attempted to bring the Texans under control by sending General Martín Perfecto Cos north with a small army.

The Texans, partly in reaction to this military threat, partly to demand the restoration of the Federalist Constitution of 1824, and partly because of ethnic prejudice, declared themselves an independent nation. Cos arrived with less than a thousand men, divided his forces, and in December 1835 was defeated by the Texans in five days of street fighting in San Antonio—then known as Béjar. Santa Anna then marched northward at the head of an army of 3,000, determined to make the Texans pay for their victory at Béjar. His state of mind before leaving Mexico City can be inferred from his statement to the British and French ambassadors that, if the U.S. were aiding the rebels, "he would continue to march his army to Washington and place upon its Capitol the Mexican flag." Some claim that experiences as a young officer fighting in the borderlands had given Santa Anna a contempt for Texans and the notion that they were best handled by terror. If so, these attitudes did not serve him well when he moved to put down the rebellious Texans.

Santa Anna never made it to Washington, but on March 6, 1836, he won a permanent place in American history and legend by launching his army of perhaps 5,000 men against the 183 defenders of the Alamo in Béjar. The Texans and Mexicans fighting under the Mexican flag of 1824 were, as every schoolchild knows, killed to the last man. Santa Anna lost some 300 to 400 troops. Two weeks later, one of Santa Anna's generals, José Urrea, overwhelmed another Texan force of more than 300 men at Goliad and forced their surrender. To the great consternation of Urrea and his men (who knew the Texans thought the conditions of their surrender were that their lives would be spared), Santa Anna ordered them all executed. The result was a slaughter much like that of U.S. troops at Malmedy during the "Battle of the Bulge" which was to enrage Americans more than a century later.

Santa Anna, contemptuous as ever, became careless in victory, and on April 21, 1836, his army was taken by surprise at San Jacinto by the attack of some 800 Texans under Sam Houston. Caught asleep, Santa Anna fled ignominiously. His second-in-command was forced to surrender the Mexican army, which suffered several hundred killed and wounded. The Texans lost six men. Santa Anna was soon captured, but astonishingly, after several close calls, he was able to sweet-talk his way out from in front of the firing squad most Texans dearly wanted him to face. Thus avoiding the usual fate of Mexican heroes (and rightly so, for he was not much of a hero), Santa Anna was forced to recognize formally the independence of Texas before he and the remains of his army were allowed to return south across the Rio Grande.

Most historians seem to agree that the eventual transfer of Texas from Mexico to the United States was inevitable. The cultural ties of the majority of the population were clearly with the U.S., as were the geographic ties. Mexico City is 700 miles from San Antonio, with much inhospitable desert and mountain terrain intervening; New Orleans is 500 miles from San Antonio, with no such barriers interposed. But Santa Anna's heavy-handed tactics were to cost Mexico more than Texas, for they led directly to the war with the United States. They also helped to poison relations between Mexicans and Anglos in the borderlands. To this day the Alamo remains a symbol in the American mind of the Mexican as a cruel barbarian and part of the excuse for a much more enduring barbarism toward Mexicans on the part of the Anglos.

The Mexican War

In the decade that Texas existed as an independent republic, chaos continued to reign in Mexico. Santa Anna, in what was to become another *caudillo* tradition, "retired to his hacienda." This maneuver permitted a real strongman to retain his influence while dodging responsibility for events in the capital. A succession of generals "ruled," and for awhile it appeared that Santa Anna would actually remain without influence.

Then the insane—which was the norm for this period of Mexican history—happened in 1838. A French pastry chef demanded compensation from the Mexican government for the looting of his store in Mexico City by soldiers. The government refused to pay, and the French used this as an excuse to invade Mexico! Santa Anna dashed back from his hacienda to lead the Mexican forces in the "Pastry War." He skirmished with the French at Veracruz, losing a leg in the process, and sent outrageous reports of his "victories" to the Minister of War. From this launching pad, he managed, in a complex series of intrigues, to make himself dictator again, only to be exiled "for life" after another coup in 1844. One of his accomplishments during this brief reign was to have his amputated leg buried with appropriate ceremony.

With things so chaotic in Mexico City, it should be no surprise that Mexico could not deal effectively with events along its northern border. Armed conflict with the Texans continued sporadically, reinforcing hatred on both sides. The aggressively expanding United States first recognized Texas in 1837 and annexed it in 1845. Everyone on both sides of the border realized that annexation very likely would lead to war. A series of issues, many of them related to Mexico's inability to meet its financial obligations, had darkened relations between the two nations since the Mexicans had won independence from Spain. But the big issue was Texas, and now its annexation gave the U.S. and Mexico a common, if undefined border.

The stage was set for a direct conflict between the United States and Mexico, one that would establish the Rio Grande as the eastern part of the border between the two nations. During Texas's brief independence, the Mexicans had been suspicious that its annexation was part of a planned expansion of the U.S. and had continually threatened to retake the lost territory. The

U.S. Government at first would not guarantee protection to Texas, because northerners were opposed to the entry of another slave state into the Union. The worried Texans went to Great Britain and France for aid. The prospect of strong European influence in Texas changed the minds of enough Northerners that the U.S. Congress agreed to annex Texas in early 1845.

The Mexicans had repeatedly stated that if the U.S. annexed Texas it would mean war, but it seems clear that, if the Americans had been conciliatory, Mexico's pride could have been soothed and the conflict averted. But the new U.S. president, James K. Polk, "a strong-willed and unimaginative small-town lawyer," was not the man to smooth ruffled feathers south of the Rio Grande. Polk wanted to trade U.S. financial claims for an agreed boundary on the Rio Grande, and also to purchase California. Polk bungled his attempt at negotiations and, as tensions increased, prepared to establish the border where he wanted it as a *fait accompli*.

At that time, the Rio Grande did not divide anything. The Mexican state of Tamaulipas extended north to the Nueces River, which reaches the Gulf of Mexico at Corpus Christi, about 120 miles north of the Rio Grande at Brownsville, and west to the 100th meridian. The Texas Declaration of Independence mentioned the Rio Grande as its southern border, but in its ten years of national existence, the Republic of Texas made no attempt to extend its jurisdiction south of the Nueces, and what government there was came from Mexico. So few people lived there—the Census of 1850 showed fewer than 10,000 people in its 20,000 square miles—that it was pointless to talk about who ruled it.

The Rio Grande became a border in fact during the early months of 1846 when President Polk sent General Zachary Taylor south to occupy the north bank of the river. Taylor had served in the military continuously since 1808, seeing action against the Indians, especially in the Seminole War which started in 1835. The general, known as "Old Rough and Ready," was ordered to cross the Nueces River and occupy what is now the southern part of Texas. The plains between the Nueces and the Rio Grande thus became part of the United States by a military occupation.

The Mexicans naturally considered the southward movement of U.S. troops an act of war, one they were determined to resist. In late March and early April, Taylor blockaded the city of Matamoros and drew up his artillery in preparation for its bombardment. Later in April a unit of Mexican cavalry crossed the Rio Grande and engaged some United States dragoons, killing some and capturing the rest. On May 11, Polk sent a war message to Congress, saying that Mexico had "shed American blood upon the American soil." Congress gave Mr. Polk his war. He did not care about the uninhabited strip of semidesert between two far-away rivers, but he did care about California, and the war would supply an excuse for its annexation.

Many voices were raised against the war and against expansion. Among these were spokesmen of such varied interests and regions as John C. Calhoun, Henry Clay, and Martin Van Buren. But public enthusiasm was too high and the leaders could only follow. One of the most ringing indictments of the war and its pretext was from a one-term congressman from Illinois named Abraham Lincoln. He was a "lame duck" at the time, and his stand on Mexico did not increase his popularity. He returned to Springfield, certain his political career was ended.

The Americans, using their artillery to great effect, soon captured Matamoros on the south side of the Rio Grande on May 18. The U.S. Navy blockaded Mexico's Gulf ports. Then after a two-month delay, Taylor moved south. Santa Anna was brought back from his "exile for life." He conned Polk into letting him through the American blockade by promising to agree to a peace favorable to the United States. He raised an army and in February 1847 fought Taylor to a bloody draw at Buena Vista, west of Monterrey. Raw Mexican recruits, exhausted from a long march north, fought with great courage. Santa Anna, with perhaps 1,800 killed or wounded and unwilling to risk his tired army in another day's battle, withdrew under cover of darkness, claiming a great victory. Taylor, who had been hard pressed the day before when he had lost some 700 troops and was planning to retreat himself, was astonished and delighted to find his enemy gone. He reported a great victory to Washington.

The Mexican nation, meanwhile, was in disarray—primarily over how the war was to be financed. The government was determined to get the funds from the Church, leading some clerics to hope for an American victory. Santa Anna, as usual, was heavily involved in the Church-state political maneuvering. Soon, however, he had to rush toward the Gulf port of Veracruz where General Winfield Scott had landed an army. Scott was sent by Polk, it is said, to offset the growing popularity of Taylor. (Taylor was a Whig, and Polk was a Democrat; Polk's fears later turned out to be well-founded when Taylor was elected President in 1848.)

Scott defeated Santa Anna and marched on to Mexico City while the numerous political factions in Mexico struggled with each other. But when Scott reached the Valley of Mexico, the Mexicans at last united behind Santa Anna and put on a valiant last-ditch defense at the Churubusco River. Best remembered are the 13-to-15-year-old military cadets *("Los niños heroes")* who, under the command of Bravo, the old hero of Independence, died at their posts defending the fortress of Chapultepec. It was to no avail—a month later, on September 14, 1847, the city was taken and the Mexicans were forced to sue for peace.

The Treaty of Guadalupe Hidalgo recognized in law what Zachary Taylor's artillery had established in fact, namely that the Rio Grande would form part of the border with Mexico. In addition, the United States gained territory encompassing the present states of California (invaded in July 1846 by John Charles Fremont), Arizona, New Mexico, Nevada, Utah, and part of Colorado. Amazingly, Polk did not listen to the Manifest Destiny extremists and take *all* of Mexico—he just settled for somewhat more than half. He did generously "compensate" Mexico by a payment of $15 million and the assumption of all debts owed by Mexico to American citizens!

Several factors added to the legacy of bitterness left by the Mexican-American War. The discovery of gold in California immediately after the signing of the treaty sharpened the sense of loss of what otherwise might then have been viewed as a vast but relatively worthless territory in the far Northwest. And the behavior of the American troops in Mexico was execrable, even in the context of those rough-and-ready times. General Scott himself admitted that the volunteers who made up the majority of the army had:

> committed atrocities to make Heaven weep and every American of Christian morals blush for his country. Murder, robbery and rape of mothers and daughters in the presence of tied-up males of the families have been common all along the Rio Grande.

George C. Meade, then a young lieutenant and later commander of the Army of the Potomac, referred to his own men as "Goths and Vandals."

Anti-Catholic prejudice was at a high point in the U.S. during the war, and there was much desecration of Mexican holy places by American troops. Some 250 American soldiers, many of them Irish Catholics, went over to the Mexican side, forming the San Patricio (Saint Patrick's) battalion. Eighty-five of these deserters were captured at Churubusco when they tried to block Taylor's advance on Mexico City. Fifty of them were hanged in a manner that made them martyrs to the Mexicans. Thirty were forced to stand on the scaffold for hours watching Taylor's assault on Chapultepec Castle. When the Stars and Stripes were raised, the American officer in charge ordered the traps sprung.

Even with an army of occupation in Mexico City, the United States could not dictate a border that would satisfy the Americans, and in 1853 it was necessary to dispatch James Gadsden to Mexico City to bargain for another chunk of Mexico. The era of railroad building had begun, and its usefulness in binding together a nation expanding so rapidly was evident. The plan was to build a railroad westward from New Orleans through Texas and the Southwest to California, but the negotiators at Guadalupe Hidalgo had left the only route, one that ran through the Mesilla Valley of southern Arizona, in Mexican hands. Mr. Gadsden was supposed to do something about this and he did. Since Mexico had just lost a war with the United States and was heavily involved in subduing the Indians in Yucatán, the readjustment was not that difficult to arrange. A price of $10 million was agreed upon, and the territory was transferred to the United States. The boundary established by the Mexican War and the Gadsden Purchase became a legal reality, and with minor adjustments, most recently in 1965, it has endured.

During the nineteenth century and the very earliest years of the twentieth, the essential fact about this border was that so few people lived along it that it did not really divide much. The 1880 United States Census records that the whole area between the Nueces River and the Rio Grande, the territory that the U.S. Army had invaded 35 years before and that Mexican revolutionaries would invade 35 years later, contained just over 50,000 human beings. The next settlement of any size along the border to the west was El Paso, where the whole county numbered fewer than 4,000 persons. Beyond El Paso there was only San Diego, California, with fewer than 3,000 in the city and just 8,000 persons in the county. The largest city anywhere near the border was Tucson, the metropolis of Arizona Territory and the whole Southwest, with its 7,000 souls.

ROCKY ROAD TO REVOLUTION

Meanwhile in Mexico, Santa Anna managed to hold on to power until 1855, when a number of events, the most important being his willingness to go along with the Gadsden Purchase, brought him down. One of Guerrero's old lieutenants, Juan Álvarez, started a successful revolt in the south. Exiled again, Santa Anna made two unsuccessful attempts to regain power. As a man of 78, he was allowed to return to Mexico City in 1872, where he died four years later, ignored and impoverished. Shortly before his death the Mexican government held ceremonies commemorating the thirtieth anniversary of the Battle of

Churubusco where the Mexican forces, under their commander-in-chief, Antonio López de Santa Anna, had fought the Americans. The old man was not even invited to attend. These words of Mexican historian Rafael Muñoz are inscribed over the exhibit on the "Age of Santa Anna" in the National Historical Museum in Chapultepec Castle:

> Eighty-two years of age
> Eleven times President of the Republic
> Exiled by all America
> Millionaire and Pauper
> Venomous and Persecuted
> Tyrant and Captive
> Patriot and Traitor
> Hero and Villain!

La Reforma, Juárez, and Maximilian

Following Santa Anna's exile, Álvarez, the last surviving leader of the revolt against Spain, took over the presidency. Soon, however, a youthful group began to move Mexico toward modernity. The outstanding men in this group were a Zapotec Indian lawyer from Oaxaca, Benito Juárez, considered by many the greatest of all Mexican leaders, and a well-off *hacendado*, Melchor Ocampo. The liberals fought to free the country from the unbalanced power of the Church and the army. The Church was the biggest landowner in the nation, and parish priests (who had a monopoly on rites of passage) charged exorbitant fees for baptisms, marriages, and funerals—so high that in fact many peons could not afford them and "lived in sin." Both the Church and the army had ancient rights, or *fueros,* which exempted them from trial in civil courts.

The liberals moved against these bastions of privilege, starting a period (1856–1867) called "the Reform." It was a time of violent transition away from a basically feudal system toward a constitutional system. The start of the Reform came when Juárez, Minister of Justice under Álvarez, promulgated a law, the famous "Ley Juárez," which ended the *fueros.* This act immediately induced the clergy and conservatives to start yet another civil war. Álvarez resigned, and the liberals, under a new president, Álvarez's old comrade-in-arms General Ignacio Comonfort, beat the reactionaries.

The liberals then moved against Church property with a complex plan known as "disentailment," the Ley Lerdo. Separation of Church and state were proclaimed, the wealth owned and administered by the Church was confiscated, activities of the clergy were severely curtailed, and parish fees were abolished. The need for agrarian reform was recognized, but, apart from redistributing the Church's property, no mechanism for instituting it was established. The liberals needed the help of *hacendados* against their principal enemy—the Church. Many *hacendados* therefore were allowed to take advantage of the sudden availability of Church land without much opposition from the liberals.

Both the Ley Juárez and the Ley Lerdo were included in the new liberal constitution of 1857—a document that survived for 60 years and established most of the legal basis of modern Mexico. Taken together, these acts are *la Reforma,* the Reform, from which the main street of Mexico City today takes its name. But it was not established peacefully.

The new constitution led, through another complex series of events, to a new civil war between the reactionaries and the proponents of the Reform. Liberal elements, led by Juárez and Ocampo at Guanajuato, were strong in the outlying states; the conservatives were strong at the center—Mexico City, Puebla, Queretaro. After almost two years of war, Juárez's troops occupied the capital on Christmas Day 1860, and the liberals had won. But conservative guerrillas kept up the battle in some areas, and in March 1861 Ocampo was captured by one band and shot.

Juárez was elected president of the war-weary nation and was immediately faced with overwhelming financial problems. He was soon forced to suspend all foreign debt payments. As a result, France, Spain, and England intervened militarily, invading Mexico just one year after the end of the bloody civil war. It soon became clear that France wanted more than payment of debts, and Spain and England withdrew. A French army advanced on Puebla, where, on May 5, 1862, its incompetent general launched it needlessly against the relatively amateur, but strongly entrenched, Mexican forces. The general thereby succeeded in adding a new national holiday, *Cinco de Mayo,* to the Mexican calendar. The French suffered a catastrophic defeat, losing more than 1,000 men and being forced to retreat all the way to the coast. Mexico once more became a nation united against a foreign invader—this time under Juárez. In spite of the early reversal at Puebla, however, the reorganized French soon captured Mexico City, and Juárez and his government were forced ever farther northward toward the borderlands.

Napoleon III, the French Monarch, anxious to stabilize his hold on Mexico, did not restore the privileges of the Church as the conservatives expected. Further, to provide a façade of respectability for his conquest, he held a phony plebiscite and in

1864 installed Archduke Maximilian of Austria as Emperor of Mexico. In yet another ironic twist, Maximilian turned out to be astonishingly liberal, and surrounded himself with liberal ministers (Maximilian was also naive enough to believe that the Mexican people had actually voted him in). It looked like the end of Mexico's brief independence. French troops had forced Juárez to the border; only the indomitable Álvarez remained in the field with liberal troops in the hard-to-conquer "south," the Pacific slope that had given the nation heroes like Morelos and Guerrero and would later give it Zapata.

But the spirit of independence still burned bright among the Mexicans in general and in Juárez in particular. While the French brutally attempted to root out Juárez's supporters in the field, Maximilian alienated powerful conservative groups with liberal laws and a generally bungled administration. The event that was to spell Maximilian's doom, however, took place on April 9, 1865, some 1,900 miles northeast of Mexico City at the Appomattox Courthouse in Virginia. The United States until then had been too busy with its own civil war to exercise the Monroe Doctrine; Lincoln had been supportive of Juárez, but was unable to help him. Now the Johnson Administration told the French to get out of Mexico, and began to provide modern arms to Juárez, whose tenacious battle against the French had won great admiration for Mexico in the United States. Juárez's military pressure on the French increased, and they soon pulled back and then left Mexico.

In June 1867, Maximilian and his conservative army made a last stand at Querétaro and were defeated. In the tradition of no-quarter battling that characterized Mexican civil wars, Maximilian and his two conservative generals were promptly shot. The death of Maximilian marked the end of an era by making clear the existence of a true Mexican nation, free from the interference of European nations and free from the medieval domination of the Church.

The Reform was now complete. Juárez embarked on the task of rebuilding the exhausted economy of the nation, but he died in bed (contrary to the tradition of Mexican heroes) in 1872. His passing, shortly after being re-elected President, paved the way for Porfirio Díaz, who ousted Juárez's successor in 1876. From then until 1910, Díaz dominated Mexico, converting the presidency into a dictatorship. During the 34-year Age of Díaz, United States military and political involvement in Mexico largely gave way to commercial involvement.

Rising Tensions Along the Border

Throughout this period there were intermittent outbreaks of violence and tension on the U.S.–Mexican border. Ever since the Rio Grande had become the border, adventurers on both sides had raided across it. In 1853, for example, one William Walker led a filibustering expedition into Baja California, and in 1857 Henry Alexander Crabb invaded Sonora. Walker actually set himself up briefly as the president of a short-lived "Republic of Lower California."

"Filibustering" (private invasions of foreign territory) was not restricted to Americans invading Mexico. A series of incidents in the 1850s had produced great tension between the Mexican and Anglo communities in south Texas. Slaveholding Texans resented the opposition of Mexico to slavery, and suspected, probably correctly, that escaping slaves were being helped across the border by Mexicans. This was in part a two-way problem, since debt-ridden peons were simultaneously fleeing into Texas. In the quarter-century following the Treaty of Guadalupe Hidalgo, the Mexican government estimated the loss in unpaid debts represented almost a half million dollars, no small sum in those days.

A planned slave revolt was exposed in Colorado County (which lies between Houston and San Antonio) in 1856. The slaves plotted to kill their owners and, with the help of local Mexicans, flee south across the border. Anti-Mexican sentiment flared, and Mexicans were expelled from Colorado County and Matagorda County to the south of it. At Goliad, site of the massacre of Texans by Mexicans greater even than that at the Alamo, a resolution was passed, stating that "the continuance of the greaser or peon Mexicans as citizens among us is an intolerable nuisance and a grievance which calls loudly for redress."

Tensions generated by the abortive slave-revolt incident were kept high by the so-called Cart War which began in 1857. Anglos, jealous of the thriving business of Mexican ox-cart operators moving freight between San Antonio and points on the Gulf Coast and in Chihuahua, attempted to drive out the Mexicans. The freight trains were attacked by predatory bands of Anglos, the drivers often were killed, goods plundered, carts burned, oxen driven off, and business generally disrupted. The assaults were cheered on by public opinion, and Texas lawmen "made no efforts whatever either to suppress the crimes or to bring the criminals to justice." Only after the local Anglo citizens began to suffer from the violence did the local authorities restore order.

Against this background, the first Mexican filibusterer to achieve fame burst on the scene in Brownsville on September 28, 1859. Late in the day, the citizens of the sleepy Texas border town were startled by cries of "Viva Cortina! Kill the gringos!" Juan Nepomuceno Cortina had returned with an armed force to resolve a two-month-old dispute with Texas lawmen. Cortina's men killed five Anglos, released some Mexicans from the local jail, and indulged in some looting of shops. It was the start of the "Cortina War."

Cortina, a reddish-blond-haired man, became known as either the "Robin Hood" or the "Red Robber" of the Rio Grande. He proclaimed his objective to be:

> to chastise the villainy of our enemies, which heretofore has gone unpunished. These have connived . . . to persecute and rob us, without any cause, and for no other crime on our part than that of being of Mexican origin . . .

Cortina successfully fought both Mexican troops and American troops on several occasions, while raiding throughout the borderland from Rio Grande City to the Gulf for fifteen years.

The French adventure in Mexico and the U.S. Civil War generated more chaos along the border, as did various and sundry Indian tribes, who of course did not recognize any border. Much of the area was extremely wild and inhospitable—an ideal refuge for nomadic peoples being pressed by two alien cultures. The Kickapoos, Lipons, Seminoles, Mescalero Apaches, and remnants of other tribes raided back and forth across the border. This led to American troops penetrating Mexican territory and vice versa, causing international incidents.

Right after the Civil War, the Kickapoos caused the most trouble. They were originally a tribe of the Kansas plains, but they had moved to Tamaulipas during the war. In 1873 they made an especially destructive raid into Texas and were pursued back across the border by Colonel R.S. Mackenzie and four companies of the Fourth U.S. Cavalry. Mackenzie and his troopers followed the Kickapoos through the night and launched a surprise dawn attack on their village. Some 20 Indians lost their lives, more were captured, and the cavalry retreated across the Rio Grande before Mexican militia could organize and oppose them.

The raid caused a storm of protest in Mexico, and the tension heightened in succeeding years as U.S. troops continued to cross the border without Mexican permission and Mexican troops occasionally made unapproved northward raids into American territory.

At the start of the Díaz regime in late 1876, relations between the two nations were sorely strained. The U.S. was not inclined to recognize another revolutionary government in Mexico after the constitutional stability under Juárez and his successor Lerdo de Tejada (who had gone into exile after Díaz's military victory). The U.S. State Department had been pressing for an agreement allowing reciprocal crossings by troops along the whole border, but the Mexicans interpreted this as an aggressive move. As historian Robert S. Gregg wrote:

> Immediately, flames of resentment leaped high in the Mexican press against the hated gringo. These were fanned into a blaze when the American Border Commission Report of 1876 was made known with a proposal for unilateral action by the United States in case Mexico refused a reciprocal agreement.

The congressional resolution permitting such action did not pass, fortunately; for if it had it might have meant war.

Thus Díaz inherited from Lerdo a difficult and dangerous situation on his northern frontier and a public in a higher than usual state of animosity toward the nation on the other side of that frontier. As he consolidated his power in 1877, however, the U.S. ambassador to Mexico, John M. Foster, became convinced that Díaz should be recognized. Foster saw that the delay of recognition after it had been granted by other major powers was embittering the Mexican government. But Rutherford B. Hayes replaced U.S. Grant as American president in 1877, and various factions in the U.S. wanted to use the presence of new administrators on both sides of the border to get new written agreements on the border problems as a precondition of recognition.

A combination of these forces—Texans, who wanted more U.S. forces on the border, plus American business and military interests—led to the notorious "Order of June 1." The order from Secretary of War George W. McCrary to Civil War hero General William Tecumseh Sherman, then commanding general of the army, first noted a report on recent raids into Texas and then stated:

> The President desires that the utmost vigilance on the part of the military forces in Texas be exercised for the suppression of these raids. It is very desirable that efforts to this end in so far at least as they necessarily involve operations on both sides of the border, be made with the cooperation of the Mexican authorities; and you will instruct General Ord, commanding in Texas, to invite such cooperation on the part of the local Mexican authorities, and to inform

them that while the President is anxious to avoid giving offense to
Mexico, he is nevertheless convinced that the invasion of our
territory by armed and organized bodies of thieves and robbers to
prey upon our citizens should no longer be endured.

General Ord will at once notify the Mexican authorities along the
Texas border of the great desire of the President to unite with
them in efforts to suppress this long continued lawlessness. At the
same time he will inform those authorities that if the Government
of Mexico shall continue to neglect the duty of suppressing these
outrages, that duty will devolve upon this government, and will be
performed, even if its performance should render necessary the
occasional crossing of the border by our troops. You will, therefore, direct General Ord that in case the lawless incursions continue he will be at liberty, in the use of his own discretion, when in
pursuit of a band of marauders and when his troops are either in
sight of them or upon a fresh trail, to follow them across the Rio
Grande, and to overtake and punish them, as well as retake stolen
property taken from our citizens and found in their hands on the
Mexican side of the line.

Prior to the Order of June 1, incursions of U.S. troops into
Mexico had been by order of local commanders and tacitly approved by the War Department. Now crossings were officially
sanctioned by Washington, a change in policy that caused another
outburst of rage in Mexico. *La Epoca,* a newspaper supporting
Díaz, declared that "neither reason nor right" was on the side of
the United States. A paper supporting the exiled Lerdo thought
the order "a serious offense to the national dignity, and to the
sovereignty and Independence of Mexico." A Spanish journal in
Mexico City, *El Colonia Española,* saw the issue as a clash between
two races. The papers wrote of resisting by putting millions of
men in the field or opting for guerrilla warfare against the powerful enemy in the north.

Foster soon realized that the U.S. had committed a gross diplomatic blunder in issuing the order, an opinion based on official
Mexican reaction which included orders to General Jerónimo
Treviño, commanding the Mexican Army in the north, to repel
any unauthorized incursions by force. Fortunately, however, the
commanders in the field were less warlike than the folks back
home. Both Ord and Treviño avoided confrontations and con-
ferred with each other to maintain order along the border
cooperatively. Their cool-headed behavior carried the day. In the
two years the order was in force, there was only one incident (out
of a dozen or so U.S. penetrations of Mexican territory) that
nearly led to a battle between American and Mexican troops.

Ironically, then, the order that so inflamed public opinion in Mexico led not so much to conflict as to cooperation along the border. It aroused Mexican pride, focused attention on the border, and speeded its inevitable pacification. On April 9, 1878, less than a year after the order and following complex negotiations by Ambassador Foster, the United States extended diplomatic recognition to the Díaz regime.

In 1882 Mexico and the United States reached an informal agreement allowing troops of either country to cross the border in hot pursuit of Apache raiders. The agreement was a result of the great difficulties both nations were having in suppressing the Apaches. The Apache leader Victorio (who succeeded the great Cochise) had fled U.S. Government harassment and operated mostly well south of the border. Hundreds of people were killed by his raiders, and at one time he was pursued by as many as 2,000 cavalrymen. In late 1880 his band of 100 braves and 400 women and children had been surrounded by Mexican forces and decimated, with Victorio himself being killed. His successor, Nana, rallied the remnants, gathered reinforcements from reservations in the U.S., and continued raiding there until forced back across the border by the U.S. Cavalry. By April 1882 the hostiles in Mexico had been joined by Geronimo and his Chiricahua Apache followers. By the end of July, the two nations had agreed that "regular federal troops . . . may reciprocally cross the boundary line . . . when they are in close pursuit of a band of savage Indians."

The last great spurt of hostilities with the Apaches (and with any native Americans) occurred between May 1885 and September 1886, when nearly half the Chiricahua Apaches left the reservation and joined Gerónimo in a bloody series of raids in Arizona, New Mexico, and Old Mexico. More than 70 Americans and 24 Mexicans were killed, as well as a large number of "friendly" Apaches. Brigadier General Nelson Miles pursued Geronimo relentlessly for over 1,300 miles, finally forcing him to surrender and ending Indian raids as a major factor in U.S.–Mexican relations. It is noteworthy, however, that not all the Indians were pacified. There continued to be sporadic incidents through the 1890s. In 1900 Apaches attacked a Mormon settlement in Chihuahua, and rumor had it that one Apache leader, El Chico, was still alive and untamed in the inaccessible Sierra Madre in the 1920s.

The last decade of the *Porfiriato*—as the 34-year reign of Porfirio Díaz was known—was one of relative stability along the border. The populations on both sides grew rapidly with the introduction of railroads and the great water projects of the early decades of this century. As the populations grew, the two societies changed. Before then there had been very little distinction between the peoples on either side; now they began to be differentiated. What had been a rather casual border honored primarily in the breach evolved into a barrier that admitted goods and people selectively. The selection was determined primarily by the economic needs of the United States and the development plans of the Díaz government.

The relative stability of the border during the end of the *Porfiriato* was short-lived, as events related to the Mexican Revolution and World War I were soon to demonstrate.

Díaz and Madero

Díaz believed profoundly in improving the social and economic situation of Mexico through industrialization and technology imported from and financed by foreign interests. Accordingly, he and his planners, called *científicos,* set about creating conditions favorable to foreign investment, which ultimately led to the grossest forms of economic exploitation serving only the foreign investors and a technical/managerial elite of Mexicans.

The overthrow of the Díaz regime was engineered by a most unlikely revolutionary, Francisco I. Madero. He was a wealthy, idealistic advocate of evolutionary change who never could have succeeded except for an incredible mistake made by Díaz himself. In 1908, Díaz gave an interview to a highly recommended American reporter, James Creelman, for *Pearson's Magazine.* Creelman was extraordinarily lavish in his praise of Díaz, whom he described as "the master and hero of modern Mexico," who had a "slender, erect form . . . strong soldierly head and commanding but sensitive countenance." The reporter stated that, although the dictator could stay in office as long as he wanted, Díaz had told him that he would retire at the end of his term (in 1910):

> I have waited patiently for the day when the people of the Mexican Republic would be prepared to choose and change their government at every election without danger of armed revolutions and without injury to the national credit or interference with national progress. I believe that day has come.

Why Díaz made these statements when he clearly had no intention of stepping down is open to debate. But when the interview was reprinted in *El Imparcial* and other Mexican papers, the result was to destabilize the Mexican political situation. The political opposition took heart, believing (or pretending to believe) that

Díaz was serious about retirement. Soon discussions of issues such as unlimited re-election (of which Díaz repeatedly availed himself) and the need for political parties (which Díaz had suppressed) began to appear in print. And not long after the Creelman interview was published, Madero himself began to write a book called *The Presidential Succession in 1910*, which was published in January 1909. Madero praised Díaz personally but criticized many of his policies. His prescription for Mexico was that the re-election of Díaz should be accepted, but that a new party of independents be organized to select a vice-president democratically.

It was a peculiarly noninflammatory and mediocre book to be, as historian Charles Cumberland described it, "one of the major contributing causes of the growth of the tidal wave which engulfed the Díaz administration and swept it from power." But *The Presidential Succession in 1910* was an immediate success and quickly made Madero the darling of those opposed to Díaz. Eventually an Anti-Reelectionist Party was founded, and Madero, emboldened by his popular success and ignoring his own prescription, became its presidential candidate. Díaz badly misjudged Madero and what he symbolized. He announced his own candidacy for re-election and again selected Ramón Corral, an ally of the *científicos*, as his vice-presidential candidate. Corral, the tough former governor of Sonora, had become vice-president in 1904 and was one of the most hated men in the administration.

As the election neared, however, Díaz became nervous. There was no way he could lose the count; "even the concept was foreign to the Mexican mentality." The government fully controlled the counting process. But Díaz did not like the enthusiasm Madero's candidacy engendered and had his opponent arrested on a pretext in the midst of a campaign trip and imprisoned in San Luis Potosí. While Madero was in prison, Díaz "won" the election on July 8 as expected. Madero was released on bail in late July, but was required to remain in San Luis Potosí. On October 6, Madero jumped bail and slipped out of the city. Disguised as a railroad mechanic, he was smuggled onto a train to the border. He entered the U.S. at Laredo the next day and went on to San Antonio. There he spent part of his time organizing a revolution and the rest of his time denying that he was organizing a revolution.

Madero was not the only prominent opponent of the Díaz regime to base himself in the U.S. portion of the borderlands. Ricardo Flores Magon and his younger brothers Enrique and Jesús were sparking a Liberal-Anarchist attack on Díaz from Los Angeles. The Liberals, with a much broader view of revolution than Madero's, hoped to establish a socialist state. They inevitably split from the Maderistas, but their movement met with some success, especially in Baja California. Nonetheless, it was the wealthy evolutionist, not the struggling revolutionists, who eventually toppled the aging tyrant.

As soon as Madero reached Texas, he proclaimed the "Plan of San Luis Potosí," declaring the re-electionist victory null and void and announcing that he was becoming provisional president. He set November 20 as the date for the start of an armed uprising against Díaz and his government. The start of the revolution was a fiasco. There were widespread disturbances on the announced date, but everywhere the revolutionaries were defeated or repulsed. Madero, who had recrossed the border, was forced to retreat hastily to Texas.

All was not lost, however. The state of Chihuahua in the north had suffered grievously under Díaz. Abraham Gonzales, the anti-reelectionist leader in the state, found plenty of tough and talented guerrilla chieftains among the bandits and cowboys of the state. Gonzales's second-in-command was an ex-mule skinner, Pascual Orozco, who began to wage a widespread guerrilla campaign against the Díaz forces. With Orozco rode a former bandit named Doroteo Arango. Arango would become a hero to the downtrodden of Chihuahua for his daring and success at stealing cattle from the huge ranches of the Terrazas family. He was known to the peons and would become known to the world under his assumed name, Francisco (Pancho) Villa.

THE MEXICAN REVOLUTION, 1910–1920

On November 27, 1910, after Madero's ignominious retreat to Texas, Orozco and Villa won an important victory over Díaz's troops at Pedernales in Chihuahua. Madero re-entered Mexico in February 1911 and in May was with Orozco and Villa as they shot their way into the important border city of Ciudad Juárez. Madero, typically preferring to avoid violence, was negotiating with Juan Navarro, the commander of the federal garrison, when a minor accident triggered the rebel attack. Madero barely managed to save Navarro from execution and had a face-off with Orozco and Villa in which he prevailed through a display of personal courage.

After the loss of the port of entry at Ciudad Juárez, Díaz's situation deteriorated rapidly. On May 12, 1911, Emiliano Zapata, legendary fighter for agrarian reform, led his Indian army into the city of Cuautla in the state of Morelos. By late May, cities seized by revolutionary leaders or mobs included Cuernavaca in Morelos; Nogales, Agua Prieta, Hermosillo and

Guaymas in Sonora; Acapulco and Chilpancingo in Guerrero; Pachuca in Hidalgo; Torreon and Saltillo in Coahuila; and Colima in Colima. From a purely military point of view, it was clear that Díaz was doomed; and after long and complex negotiations with Madero, an official treaty ended the rebellion on May 21.

The document was signed outside of Ciudad Juárez on a table illuminated by automobile headlights. It provided for the resignation of Díaz, Corral, and José Limontour, minister of finance and best known of the *científicos*. A provisional president was named under the assumption that Madero would be elected to succeed him.

News of the treaty reached Mexico City on May 23, and the next day mobs roamed the streets shouting for Díaz to resign. Díaz (in agony with an abscessed tooth) still refused, and, in a final tragedy of his regime, his troops fired on the crowd before the National Palace and killed 200 people. The next day Díaz resigned and on the 26th left for exile in Europe.

Madero made a triumphant entry into Mexico City on June 11, but almost immediately began to make serious mistakes. He did not consolidate his power, but left much of the machinery of the old Díaz regime grinding on while he awaited official election in October. Francisco de la Barra, the conservative provisional president, used the still-intact federal armies to suppress revolutionary forces. De la Barra sent General Victoriano Huerta to Morelos to put down the Indian peasants who had followed Zapata in the hope of regaining their lands, and Madero himself met with Zapata to persuade him to lay down his arms and trust Madero to institute reforms after his election.

Madero was duly elected in October, but it soon became clear that his notion of the pace and scale of needed reform was a long way from that of Zapata and other revolutionaries. Madero was not a man of the people, but rather a wealthy proponent of gradual reform who had revolted against a dictator. He clearly never understood the motives of men like Zapata and Villa, and this was to cost him his life. By the end of the year, Zapata rebelled again, demanding in his *Plan de Ayala* the immediate restoration of lands stolen from the villages during the Díaz regime and confiscation of one-third of the lands from the *haciendas*. Madero's moves toward land reform were much too small and slow for Zapata. As uncompromising a revolutionary as the world has ever seen, Zapata resisted both the assaults and the blandishments of General Huerta, who again went to Morelos, this time under the nominal control of Madero, to subdue the Zapatistas.

Perhaps, though, Madero should not be condemned for not understanding Zapata's motives. The traditional view of Zapata fostered by John Steinbeck, brought to the silver screen in the form of Marlon Brando, and most recently celebrated in the biography by John Womack, is being quietly undone by French historian Jean Meyer. Examining the period of intense Church-state conflict and civil war in the 1920s, known as the Cristero Movement, Meyer found genuine land reform in Zapata's Morelos to have occurred only then. In the 1910s Zapata installed his "Indians" on *hacienda* land only by expelling other "Indians" who did not adhere to his banner. Meyer suggests that rewarding one's followers with the spoils of victory at the expense of others equally downtrodden is somewhat less than revolutionary.

Soon Madero was faced with further revolts. He had failed to give a satisfactory post to the most popular hero of the early Revolution, the man most people believe toppled Díaz by his brilliant capture of Ciudad Juárez in 1911, Pascual Orozco. Orozco revolted in early 1912, supplied with cash by northern cattle barons who were as infuriated by Madero's attempts at land reform as had been Zapata. For those like the Terrazas family who held nation-sized ranches, Madero's small and slow reforms were too big and too fast. Eventually, Madero dealt with Orozco by sending General Huerta against him. Huerta suppressed the rebels with ferocious efficiency and pushed Orozco into exile in Arizona. When Huerta returned, he would not account for a million pesos of government money he was responsible for, and Madero had him put on the retired list.

One problem followed another for Madero. In October, Félix Díaz, nephew of the deposed dictator, rebelled in Veracruz but was quickly captured. Instead of following the tradition and having him promptly shot, the gentle Madero had him imprisoned, as he had done with Bernardo Reyes who had attempted an earlier rebellion. Díaz and Reyes formed the focus of forces uniting against Madero, forces that were being prodded by Henry Lane Wilson, U.S. Ambassador to Mexico. Wilson was associated with the Guggenheims, who along with the Rockefellers competed with the wealthy Maderos over guayule rubber and copper interests. Wilson represented a common attitude in American officialdom—a longing for the return of the stability of the *Porforiato*. Later, that attitude was turned into action that greatly weakened Madero's position.

Throughout January 1913, extremist elements in the Mexican Army plotted to free Reyes and Félix Díaz, overthrow Madero, and make Reyes president. The plot was almost common knowledge, and Madero's relatively hard-headed brother Gustavo tried to warn him and assumed the task of organizing mass support for him. Finally, Sunday morning, February 9, 1913, the rebel plan was put into effect, but the insurgents met unexpected resistance from loyal troops, and Reyes was cut down by machine-gun fire. Madero then made a final, fatal mistake: he turned to General Huerta to command the loyalist troops. Huerta was an admirer of Reyes and secretly negotiated with Díaz and Henry Lane Wilson while fighting a prolonged artillery duel with Díaz's troops. For the "tragic ten days" of February 9–18, 1913, the two forces pounded the main business district of Mexico City to rubble in an attempt to make the citizens of the city accept peace at any price.

Huerta went as far as deliberately sending regiments loyal to Madero on suicidal attacks. On February 18 he made his move, luring Gustavo Madero away from his brother for a luncheon engagement and then having Madero and his vice-president, José Pino Suárez, arrested. During the luncheon with Gustavo, Huerta excused himself for a moment, and his men then entered and arrested the President's brother.

Gustavo was delivered to the followers of Félix Díaz as a sign of Huerta's good faith. That night he was thrown to the mob, blinded with a sword or bayonet, beaten, and shot to pieces. Madero and Pino Suárez were then persuaded by Huerta to resign their offices—a mistake Madero characteristically made to avoid further bloodshed. When the Congress was informed of the resignations, it accepted Huerta as the legitimate successor. Then on February 22, Madero and Pino Suárez were awakened shortly after retiring and told they were to be transferred to the penitentiary. Outside the brightly lighted walls of the penitentiary, they were removed from their cars and shot by the officers guarding them. The cars were then riddled with bullets to provide evidence of an attack, but no one was fooled. Although it was never proven that Huerta gave the orders, the blame for the assassinations was clearly fixed on his administration.

Huerta did not last long—his reign was characterized by his constant drunkenness (which apparently did not interfere with his ability to govern) and the murder of those of his enemies he could get his hands on. But in the north there were enemies he could not get his hands on. In Coahuila Venustiano Carranza rose against him, claiming he wanted to avenge Madero. (Others said he would have rebelled against Madero if Huerta had not beaten him to it!) In Sonora, revolutionary forces coalesced under the able military leadership of Alvaro Obregón. In Chihuahua, Villa abandoned the legitimate butcher's business he had established after Madero's election and returned to the field determined to conquer Mexico. Villa in particular hated Huerta, under whom he had served in the campaign against Orozco. Huerta had tried to have Villa executed for disobeying orders, and only a last-minute reprieve engineered by Madero's brother Raúl had saved him. And, of course, the indomitable Zapata was soon back in the field in the south. Thus by 1914 the diverse forces were in motion that would tear Mexico apart, induce thousands to flee to the United States, and involve the U.S. in further border troubles.

It would be hard to find a period in the history of the United States to equal the complexity and brutality of the events of the next few years in Mexico. Partly as a result of an American invasion of Veracruz (about which more later), Huerta was forced to flee the country in July 1914. Armies of both Villa and Obregón were converging on the capital, and the war was turned into a race to determine whether the *Villistas* or the *Carranzistas* (under Obregón) would occupy Mexico City. The *Carranzistas* won because Carranza controlled the coal necessary to run Villa's trains, and he cut off the supply. As a result of this bit of treachery, Villa promptly declared war on Carranza.

In October 1914 the military chiefs, Obregón, Zapata, and Villa, met at Aguascalientes in an attempt to make a peaceful settlement. Villa's big contribution to the prolonged sessions was the suggestion that much could be accomplished if he and Carranza both committed suicide! The congress failed. In the end Villa was declared commander-in-chief and Carranza was found in rebellion. Mexico went up in flames. Plot and counterplot, maneuver and countermaneuver were the order of the day, while anarchy spread throughout the nation, and bands of "revolutionaries" (mostly bandits) looted, raped, and murdered.

On December 6, 1914, Villa and Zapata jointly occupied Mexico City. The *Zapatistas,* long painted as ogres in the propaganda of those controlling the capital, turned out not to be cruel bandits but well-behaved, humble peasants. They politely begged for food at the homes of the rich. The *Villistas,* in contrast, were an amalgam of bandits, cowboys, and drifters from the north, and, according to some reports, they did their share of killing and plundering.

The struggle between Villa and Carranza now escalated. Operating out of Veracruz, Carranza tried to rally peasant support by calling for return of the lands stolen from the Indians. In response to this swing to the left by Carranza, himself a *hacendado,* conservative elements shifted their support toward the former cattle thief Villa. American business interests concluded that Villa, with his vague revolutionary aspirations, would be the easiest of the leaders to control.

Obregón then denounced Villa, proclaimed the wealthy Carranza the only true revolutionary leader, and moved against Villa's forces. Obregón prevailed at Puebla and reoccupied the capital. Villa meantime had returned to Aguascalientes and Zapata to Morelos. Early in April 1915, Villa moved south toward the capital and Obregón north from it. They met at Celaya in the bloodiest battle in Mexican history.

Obregón had his men dig in and string barbed wire. Villa chose to use his previously invincible cavalry in frontal assaults. The *Villistas* were slaughtered by Obregón's machine guns. Some 40,000 men were engaged, 25,000 under Villa and 15,000 under Obregón, and many thousands died. Even approximate casualty figures are not known, but Obregón claimed 4,000 *Villistas* killed and 6,000 taken prisoner. Outside of the American Civil War, it was the bloodiest battle ever fought in North America. It finished the "Centaur of the North," as Villa was known, as a major force in Mexico. Obregón drove him steadily northward along the route Villa had so recently traveled triumphantly in the opposite direction. Repeated defeats pushed Villa back into Chihuahua, where on his own "turf" he could resist indefinitely. From Chihuahua he could take his revenge on the United States, for he blamed Woodrow Wilson, who had recognized Carranza as head of the *de facto* government in October 1915, for his defeat.

It is against this tumultuous background that the final series of border incidents began. The first event concerns an obscure gentleman named Aniceto Pizaña and an equally obscure scheme known as "the Plan of San Diego."

The Plan of San Diego

Aniceto Pizaña found exactly what the last few years along the border had conditioned him to expect when he and his heavily armed Mexican raiders captured the construction crew working on the Fresnos Pump Canal. It was September 2, 1915, and the place was in the countryside outside Harlingen, Texas. The foreman, technicians, and supervisors—the ones who wore the clean clothes, got the good pay, and gave the orders—were Anglos, and the ones who moved the dirt and lifted the loads were Mexicans. It had not always been this way, but ever since the St. Louis, Brownsville, and Mexico Railroad had pushed down from San Antonio and the spurs had been built, one going east to the Gulf at Port Isabel and another westward up the Rio Grande Valley, things had changed. The southern part of the Lower Rio Grande had been "opened up," which meant that the agricultural potential of the region would be realized and its harvests of fruits and vegetables would increase and be sent north to the large and prosperous markets of the Eastern and Midwestern United States. The soil was fertile and American, and it could be watered out of the river without interference from the Mexicans who were absorbed in their four-year-old civil war.

By the summer of 1915, the situation along the border was tense. The *Carranzistas* more or less controlled Tamaulipas, Nuevo León, and southern Coahuila up to Villa Acuña, across from Del Rio, Texas. The *Villistas* held the rest of Coahuila, Chihuahua, and Sonora, although there were *Carranzista* garrisons in most of the towns. North of the border a very nervous General Frederick Funston commanded the Southern District of the United States Army. He held command of 20,000 men and responsibility for over 1,700 miles of border—everything from the Gulf of Mexico to the California state line.

After Pizaña and his raiders had set fire to a storehouse and an automobile and wrecked some machinery, they started toward the border, eight miles to the south. Along the way Pizaña ordered the Anglo captives to be shot. One of Pizaña's men had worked for the foreman, S.S. Dodds, knew him to be a good and honest man, and interceded for him. Pizaña excused Dodds from the group, asked the rest if any of them were German, and when they said they were not, had them murdered. A few hours later the raiders met a mixed group of civilians and U.S. Army troops. Dodds escaped, and Pizaña and his men fled across the river.

Pizaña's puzzling last question, "Are any of you German?" indicates that something from outside the hemisphere was intruding into the politic of the Mexican–American border. A dreadful war was being fought in Europe, and the Germans felt that they could win if the United States just stayed out. Even though there were over two million persons of German birth in the United States, Imperial Germany concluded that if the United States came in, they would come in on the side of England and France. While thumping for neutrality on the official level, the Germans had a slender, secondary hope of involving the United States in the Mexican chaos. This could be done only if the United States were strongly provoked, so German interests set about arranging the provocation. Through incredibly good luck or even more incredible skill, the Germans had a loyal agent on the staff of Pancho Villa. The agent, Dr. Lyman B. Rauschbaum, functioned as Villa's physician and incidentally was one of the few men in the entourage who could read and write. Rauschbaum would prove useful later, but in the summer of 1915 Villa had no reason to attack anything in the United States.

Aniceto Pizaña had been a small farmer near Los Tulitos, Texas, but the previous June he had been recruited as Chief of Staff of the Army of Races and Peoples, subject to the Provisional Directorate of the Plan of San Diego. San Diego was a small town

near Corpus Christi, Texas, and its only connection with the
bizarre Pizaña affair seems to have been that one of the early
supporters of the Plan had taught school there once. The Plan
was hatched by a small group of Huerta supporters while they
were in jail in Monterrey, Mexico, but it was necessary to make it
look as if it were inspired by ethnic dissatisfaction north of the Rio
Grande. The Plan was signed in the jail on January 6, 1915, and
called for an interracial uprising of blacks, Orientals, Indians, and
Latins against the United States. This uprising would commence
on the following February 20, and every Anglo male over the age
of 16 in much of the southern and southwestern United States
was to be murdered. Upon completion of the racial purge, the
territories lost in the Texan and Mexican Wars of the 1830s and
1840s—Texas, New Mexico, Colorado, Arizona, and
California—would be returned to Mexico. Between the reconsti-
tuted Mexico and the remnant United States, a buffer state would
be created, controlled by blacks, Latins, and Orientals. The Indians would have their lands restored.

When February 20 came without the scheduled uprising, the
plotters in Monterrey did what most revolutionaries do in such
circumstances—they rewrote the Plan. But in the month between
the first and second Plans, the cabal had fallen completely into the
hands of German mischief-makers.

With German guidance and financial support, the Plan slowly
moved toward action. On the propaganda front, Heinrich Albert,
commercial attaché of the German Embassy in Washington,
started a systematic collection of accounts of lynchings and racial
violence against blacks and forwarded it to Mexico. From Mexico
a black American physician named Mosley was sent into the
southern United States to recruit for the Plan. On the border
itself, Dr. Alberto Krumm-Heller made a lecture tour with en-
gagements on both sides. Though he was ostensibly a propagan-
dist for Venustiano Carranza, his lectures were anti-gringo
diatribes. In Monterrey he told a receptive audience that they had
nothing to fear from U.S. troops because they were of German
descent and would never fire on their Latin friends.

Although the Plan was known to United States officials, no one
took it seriously. The repeated protestations of innocence by the
German consuls in Matamoros and Monterrey were apparently
believed, and no one was prepared for the military phase of the
Plan, which began, symbolically, on July 4, 1915.

For almost a year—until June 16, 1916–the followers of the
Plan attempted to incite race warfare. They launched at least 27
separate military actions, of which Pizaña's was just one. Thirty-
three Americans and 31 raiders were killed, 24 Americans and

eleven raiders were wounded, and 22 raiders were captured. The damage to property was considerable, particularly that of the railroads, and the economic activity of the four southernmost Texas counties was totally disrupted.

But the real cost of the Plan of San Diego went far beyond this military balance sheet. The United States Army was hopelessly insufficient in numbers to deal with the problem. The initiative always lay with the raiders, and the army could only respond. The State of Texas had no force capable of helping, and something had to be done. The men and women of the region undertook to defend themselves, but against whom? Who were these raiders and why were they so hurtful? Since they only killed Anglos, any Latino was suspect. Texas quickly—indeed haphazardly—recruited provisional Rangers from whomever was available. Drifters and toughs, kids looking for a last-frontier hurrah, and an occasional sadist hoping to kill some Mexicans rode into south Texas in the name of law and order. While the body count from the raids stood around 65, the casual shootings among the resident Latino population probably exceeded 200—despite repeated protestations by the Latino community deploring the raids and the total lack of any evidence that anyone living north of the Rio Grande was involved in any of this. Fear of the raiders among the Anglos and fear of the Anglos among the Latinos compounded animosity that had already developed over the rights to Rio Grande water and the social and economic changes that had come with the railroads and the canals. In the short year of the Plan of San Diego, the ethnic antipathy that had been developing in Texas for decades became set. It endures to influence attitudes toward immigration today.

Villa at Columbus

In 1916 Carranza decided to do what he could to stop the raiders. His choice up to this time had been to remain neutral—which is to say allow the raids to go on under his protection—or see the followers of the Plan turn their guns on him. Furthermore, the raids performed a limited service to him. They reminded people in the United States that chaos in Mexico was a problem and that establishment of law and order south of the border would be of benefit to them. Carranza's change of policy came about suddenly and unequivocally because on March 9, 1916, the *Villistas* under the personal command of their general attacked the town of Columbus, New Mexico, with a force of 485 men.

Villa's presence near the border had already added to the

apprehensive atmosphere on the American side of the border. On January 10, 17 American miners were returning to reopen a mine in Chihuahua under the "guaranteed" protection of Carranza's government. Near the cattle station of Santa Ysabel, they were taken from the train by a gang of *Villistas*. Colonel Pablo López, the commander, told the Mexicans on the train, "If you want to see some fun, watch us kill these gringos." The Americans were then slaughtered, some shot trying to run away, others point-blank by soldiers who fought for the privilege.

Villa's degree of responsibility for the Santa Ysabel massacre has never been established, but it is suspected by some that his policy was to kill any Americans in the area Carranza claimed to control. Others think he did not order the massacre, but that his hatred of Americans was inflamed by the reaction against him. Whatever the motivation, Americans within Villa's reach promptly fled Mexico. There was outrage in the United States, but it soon faded as public attention focused on the European war. Still, Santa Ysabel marked the end of any friendly feelings toward Villa in the United States.

In the winter of 1915–1916, Villa's fortunes were at a low ebb. In mid-December, he told some newspapermen that he was retiring from politics, and this was duly reported in the American press. In fact, Villa was already well into the planning of the Columbus raid. In a letter dated January 8, 1916, before the Santa Ysabel massacre, he invited Emiliano Zapata to bring his force north to support him in the incursion. Why did Villa want to attack the United States? Even if that question were answered, why did he pick Columbus, New Mexico?

The testimony of Major José Orozco, who had been a member of Villa's bodyguard during the Columbus raid, given over 50 years after the event, sheds some light on the reasons. According to Major Orozco, the general had at least two matters outstanding in the town of Columbus. One of the reasons Villa was in trouble was that $2,500 worth of supplies bought and paid for through the hardware store of the Ravel Brothers, Sam and Luis, had not been delivered, and ammunition delivered to him by the Ravels contained sawdust instead of gunpowder. There was also the matter of some $10,000 on deposit to the credit of General Villa in the Columbus State Bank. When he asked to withdraw the money, the bank said the account was without funds. Major Orozco found the attitude of the bank beyond understanding. After all, the money had come from the sale of cattle, and the cattle had not been stolen in the United States.

The general's view of his dealings with the business element of Columbus was refracted through the teutonic prism of Dr.

Rauschbaum, physician to the general and his staff, corresponding secretary, and keeper of account books. If his name and
position were not enough to suggest that the good doctor was
serving the Kaiser at least as well as he served the goals of the
Mexican Revolution, there is the matter of his connection with
Felix Sommerfeld. Herr Sommerfeld was a reserve officer in the
Imperial German Army and something of an adventurer who
had made his living as best he could in Mexico for several years.
One of his vocations was that of journalist, and in the employ of
the Associated Press he met and became close to Francisco Madero, who appointed him as his purchasing agent for munitions
in the United States and chief of his secret service. Sommerfeld
dispatched these duties from El Paso, where he was affiliated with
the Constitutionalist Junta, a pro-Madero propaganda group, a
prominent member of which was none other than Dr. Lyman B.
Rauschbaum.

With the murder of Madero, Sommerfeld transferred his services to General Villa, who rewarded him with the dynamite
concession for the State of Chihuahua. Dynamite was a very
valuable commodity at that time and in that place. Between April
5 and December 1, 1915, Sommerfeld paid over $380,000 to the
Western Cartridge Company of Alton, Illinois. The funds were
paid from an account in the Mississippi Valley Trust Company of
St. Louis, Missouri, and the goods were shipped to Hipolito Villa,
a younger brother of the general, at El Paso, Texas. Agents of the
U.S. Department of Justice subsequently concluded that the
source of these funds was the Imperial German Embassy in Washington.

Finally, there is the curious appearance in Columbus of one
George Seese on March 6, 1916, three days before the raid. Mr.
Seese was a news reporter assigned to the Los Angeles office of
the Associated Press. Sommerfeld had worked for the AP, and his
superior seems to have been George Seese. This might or might
not have been a remarkable coincidence. It seems likely, though,
that Sommerfeld arranged the press coverage while Rauschbaum
arranged the raid.

Villa's force entered the United States in the early morning
hours of March 9, 1916 and by 3 A.M. were in position near the
town. At 4 A.M. the attack was launched, with one column going
into town and another moving to contain the garrison. The men
of the Thirteenth Cavalry, though caught completely by surprise,
reacted quickly and effectively. They repulsed the column intended to check them and moved immediately to the relief of the
town.

In town, Villa himself and a small band went to the bank to

withdraw his funds. Villa did not rob any other bank in town, and though the amount he took from the Columbus State Bank is unknown, it seems that he did not clean it out. Another group under Pablo López went to the Commercial Hotel seeking its owner, Sam Ravel, whom López had been ordered to take, dead or alive. Unable to find Ravel, López robbed and murdered some, but not all, of the guests and then burned the structure. By 7:30 A.M., Villa recrossed the Mexican border with elements of the Thirteenth Cavalry in hot pursuit.

The raiders had killed nine United States soldiers and eight civilians, wounding five soldiers and three civilians. Villa lost 90 dead and seven captured, six of whom were subsequently hanged. There is no official account of any booty taken, but contemporary reports said a large number of horses and mules were taken—around 100—and one account speaks of 300 Mauser rifles. One wonders how the remaining force of less than 400 men could carry an extra 300 rifles while riding hell-for-leather across the Sonoran desert pursued by the United States Cavalry.

There were no reports of rapes or mutilations of bodies. Had Villa wanted simply to raise hell, he would have killed more than seventeen people. He released at least two prisoners in the course of the raid.

On March 10, 1916, General John J. Pershing was ordered to prepare a military column to enter Mexico to pursue and disperse the *Villistas*. He succeeded in this but failed to capture Villa. Under the same order, General Funston's men along the Rio Grande were ordered to pursue the raiders of the Plan of San Diego into Mexico. In one such operation, Major George Langhorne led elements of the Eighth and Fourteenth Cavalry Regiments in hot pursuit for 135 miles into Mexico. The last Plan of San Diego raid into the United States occurred on June 16, 1916. On June 11, Carranza had started arresting those associated with the Plan of San Diego, thus ending that episode.

Pershing's and Funston's punitive expeditions into Mexico ended the era of bloodshed and terror along the border but not the bad feelings between the two countries. In January 1917, German Foreign Minister Alfred Zimmermann sent a telegram to President Carranza of Mexico proposing an alliance between their nations. Germany would guarantee the return of the land previously lost to the United States in exchange for another Mexican-American War. The telegram was intercepted by the British, who passed it on to the United States Government. The Zimmermann telegram became a *cause célèbre* on its release to the public in March 1917 and was certainly an important factor in the decision of the United States to enter World War I in April.

There is a curious affinity between the Zimmermann telegram and the Plan of San Diego. The resentment in Mexico over the loss of its former territory had roots extending over three generations back. From the uprising of Juan Nepomuceno Cortina a decade after the Treaty of Guadalupe Hidalgo to the political formulations of the *Partito Liberal* and its founders, the Flores Magon brothers, after 1906, agitation for redress of the Mexican loss had been a constant in border and national Mexican life. Indeed there are some militants today who view recent Mexican migration to the U.S. Southwest as, in effect, a reclamation of land wrongfully seized.

The Zimmermann proposal, having been exposed, of course came to nothing. With the end of fighting and terrorism along the border, the turbulence elsewhere in Mexico abated and the government began trying to set its house in order. In the fall of 1916, a national congress was assembled to draw up a new constitution for Mexico. The new Constitution of 1917 was based in large measure on the one of 1857, but with some important differences.

The groundwork for a significant land and agrarian reform was laid in Article 27. The aim was to restrict large landholders and encourage small and medium-sized farms. Land was to be restored to villages, some of which had been lost in the disentailment under the *Ley Lerdo*. Only Mexican citizens or companies were permitted to own land. Unfortunately, the changes hoped for by the liberal authors of Article 27 have not been fully realized, even though the legal basis for them still exists. Other important parts of the Constitution vested all mineral rights in the government, gave some protection to workers, further restricted the Church, and reorganized and stabilized the chaotic monetary and financial system of the country.

Carranza accepted the new Constitution and continued to rule as president with declining support until 1920. In that year Obregón challenged him for the presidency, but Carranza was determined to install his own puppet. Obregón's supporters found an excuse to revolt, and in May Carranza was forced to flee the capital. On the way to Tampico, Carranza was murdered in his sleep in an Indian hut.

Carranza's death effectively brought an end to the Revolution in Mexico. After a few more incidents, Obregón was elected president in November 1920, introducing a period of peace. The great revolutionary figures were all but gone. Zapata was betrayed and murdered by an agent of Carranza in 1919. He was tricked by a colonel who captured and executed a detachment of his own army in order to convince Zapata he was sincere. Villa outlived both Carranza and Zapata, returning to his *hacienda*. But on June 21, 1923, he was killed by a burst of machine-gun fire as the open car in which he was riding slowed at an intersection. The assassins were never officially identified, but it is known that in 1923 only the government in Mexico City had machine guns. Obregón lasted until 1928 when he was assassinated less than three weeks after being reelected president. His death ended the era of political assassination in Mexico.

The ten years of revolutionary turmoil were a disaster for the Mexican people. Untold thousands were killed in the fighting or simply as innocent bystanders. Toward the end of the decade, the worldwide influenza epidemic of 1918–1919 took its toll. Many thousands of additional Mexicans fled across the border to the United States, and many of them stayed there permanently. Although demographic records are far from complete, it appears that altogether Mexico's population (in 1910 about 15 million) declined by a million during the decade.

With the end of the revolutionary era, the U.S.–Mexican border took on essentially its modern character, that of a peaceful dividing line between strength and weakness. But there remains consideration of one crucial topic to complete the background of today's illegal-immigration situation—how the strong have meddled in the affairs of the weak, and what things are like on "the other side."

[4]

EL OTRO LADO

G IVEN the historical background of Mexico and the borderlands just presented, it should be apparent that the flood of immigrants from Mexico is not a flow from some exotic less-developed country that just happens to be on the other side of the southern border of the United States. First and foremost, the movement is across a boundary created by force and conquest in the middle of an area claimed by Spain and Mexico for centuries before the Americans arrived. Moreover, it is a two-way movement created by a complex array of pushes and pulls. Beyond the crude facts of the U.S. Acquisition in 1848 of more than half the territory claimed by Mexico and the subsequent development of the dual-culture "borderlands," there is another reason that the "problem" of Mexican immigration is unique: the special role that the United States has played in Mexican internal affairs virtually since Independence. President Adolfo López Mateos (1958–1964) hit the nail on the head when he said that the United States was Mexico's "biggest problem."

UNITED STATES INVOLVEMENT IN MEXICO: THE BEGINNING

Direct American meddling in Mexican internal affairs began with the arrival of Joel R. Poinsett in 1822 as a special envoy of President Monroe. Poinsett was an unabashed fan of republican government with no sympathy for Iturbide's imperial regime, and he quickly made his feelings known in words, gestures, and reports. His attempts at helping the republican forces that wanted to model Mexico's political structure on that of the United States had the eventual effect of making him thoroughly disliked by

136

Mexicans of all political persuasions and heightening Mexican nationalism and apprehension about the intentions of the United States. His instructions to negotiate treaties both to recover Texas (the U.S. had given up its clouded claim on Texas to Spain in 1819 as part of the deal for the acquisition of Florida) and to provide for the return of runaway slaves tended to produce in Mexican minds an association between slavery and American expansionist ambitions. And those ambitions seemed all the more ominous after Monroe promulgated his famous Doctrine in late 1823. In the era of Manifest Destiny, it is hardly surprising that Monroe's warning to European powers to keep their hands off the Western Hemisphere was interpreted (in no small part correctly) to mean that the U.S. was intending to build its own empire there. Poinsett's part in creating the frictions that eventually led to the Mexican-American War is memorialized today by the ornamental Mexican plant with blood-red bracts that bears his name— *Poinsettia.*

Until the era of Díaz, the expansionist activities of the United States were the major bone of contention in U.S.–Mexican affairs. Even after the Mexican-American War and the Gadsden Purchase, the threat of the U.S. engulfing ever more Mexican territory remained. Indeed, in 1859 a desperate Juárez agreed, virtually under threat of invasion, to the McLane–Ocampo Treaty. The treaty gave Baja California to the United States, gave the United States rights-of-way from a point on the Rio Grande to Mazatlán and from El Paso to Guaymas, and gave Americans the perpetual right to free travel across the Isthmus of Tehuantepec. Furthermore, the document in essence gave the United States permission to intervene in Mexican affairs whenever it wished (on the excuse of protecting Americans in Mexico). Justo Sierra, the first Mexican historian to sympathize with the Mexican masses and one of Díaz's *"científicos"* who was serving as Secretary of Public Instruction, wrote of the treaty:

> That such a pact should have appeared feasible to men of such patriotic mettle as Juárez and Ocampo is shocking, and but for the attenuating circumstances, the delirium caused by political fever in crisis, no one would boggle at calling it a political crime.

The U.S. Senate refused to ratify the treaty because Northerners felt it would strengthen the South, then on the verge of secession. It was also rejected by the Mexican Congress.

Foreigners during the Porfiriato

The Age of Díaz, known as the *Porfiriato,* brought a new level of foreign intervention in Mexico. Porfirio Díaz set out to rebuild the Mexican economy, and in many respects he succeeded. Like an early Mussolini, he not only made the trains run on time, he also built the railroads. During his reign from 1876 to 1910, Díaz expanded the Mexican railroad system from almost nothing to some 15,000 miles of track. He also expanded many of Mexico's industries. For instance, the smelting of precious and semiprecious metals was icreased fourfold, petroleum and textiles industries were developed, and exports and imports were multiplied tenfold. Díaz greatly reduced the national debt and generally put the country on a sound financial footing. For the most part, Mexico was peaceful and prosperous during the Age of Díaz. The Mexican population doubled during those 34 years, after centuries of very slow growth.

The price of this peace and prosperity, in addition to a repressive dictatorship, was the granting of outrageous concessions to foreigners, accompanied by a demeaning of everything Mexican, and "the near adulation of everything foreign" by the elite who were running the country. The price also included some serious economic problems, the alienation of most Mexicans from their own government, and ultimately an extremely bloody revolution.

From the beginning of the Age of Díaz, French, British, and United States interests were given various kinds of land, mineral, railroad, and banking concessions. For instance, the railroads of the north of Mexico were financed by American capital, those of the south by European capital. The terms had to be very favorable to the foreigners, since recent Mexican history had not made that nation appear to be an especially advantageous place for long-term investment.

Díaz also intervened in the age-old Mexican conflict between the communal landholding villages (ejidos) and the semifeudal haciendas, siding with the latter and thus reversing the efforts of mid-nineteenth century liberal reformers. The científicos enforced the liberals' earlier land laws, which, although well-intentioned, had worked against the Indians and their ejidos. Communal lands were divided, and most found their way into the possession of large landholders. These, and an 1883 law governing the surveying of "unoccupied" national lands, provided a new means for unscrupulous landgrabbers to enrich themselves at the expense of the peasantry. As a result, by the end of the Porfiriato, no more than three percent of the rural population owned land: "there were eight hundred and thirty-four hacendados and perhaps nine million landless peasants living in miserable peonage." Much of the land, of course, passed into the hands of American and other foreign investors. Much of the land expropriated from the Church under the Ley Lerdo was sold, not to landless peasants, but to *hacendados* and foreign investors. And much that by tradition belonged communally to villages was also taken and sold to *hacendados*. The Marxian North American Congress on Latin America (NACLA) described the *científicos'* agrarian policy as one "to eradicate Indian land tenure and replace it with capitalist agriculture."

For instance, shortly after the turn of the century in the state of Jalisco, over 96 percent of the farm families were landless, while the largest *hacienda* covered almost 100,000 hectares (385 square miles). In Veracruz 98.9 percent of the people owned no land. In the state of Mexico, less than one percent of farm families owned 99.8 percent of the land. The mind-boggling scale of the holdings of some *hacendados*—owners of the *haciendas*—is exemplified by the lands owned by the Terrazas family in northern Mexico. Their "Encinillas" *hacienda* covered almost 2,000 square miles; a second smaller *hacienda* was only a little more than 1,300 square miles.

Most of Mexico's *peones* (farm workers) lived in near serfdom on the gigantic *haciendas*. The *hacendados* controlled the lives not only of the *peones* on their *haciendas* but of small local landholders as well. One Mexican analyst wrote in 1895 that *hacendados*

refused absolutely to rent pasture land to their weak neighbors, who have seen their cattle die of hunger in the years of prolonged drought, while before their eyes lay vast stretches of grassland hardly trod by the light foot of the deer.

Since they controlled the irrigated land, *hacendados* were less affected by drought than were the poor farmers, and this, combined with the food-storage capacity of the *hacienda*, allowed them to manipulate the market and maximize their profits.

Life for the *peones* in the *haciendas* ranged from moderately bad to hideous. Keeping the *peones* in continuous debt to the *hacendado*, often by crooked bookkeeping practices, was standard operating procedure, at least in Yucatán. On the worst *haciendas*, brutal treatment of the *peones* was routine. As one observer summed it up:

Many overseers regarded the peon as an animal and often treated him worse. He was beaten and tortured. And if the majordomo beat an incorrigibly lazy peon to death, the local authorities understood the difficulties perfectly. The peon's daughters, if comely, were the victims, willy-nilly, of the overseer's lust.

Disastrous as it may have been for the peasants, the policy of the

Díaz Administration was quite successful from the standpoint of American investors. By 1890 some 27 million hectares of Mexican land were in the hands of foreign companies largely based in the United States. These "colonizing companies" (to use NACLA's term) controlled between one-fifth and one-seventh of Mexico's farmland. In the Northwest, for example, the New York–based Alameda Sugar Refining Company purchased some 13,000 hectares of land for sugarcane at under two pesos per hectare, and the Sinaloa Land Company and United Sugar Company also established large holdings. No heed was taken, naturally, of the Indians who thought they owned the land.

The local Indians, Yaquis and Mayo, met the land push with a series of uprisings just as the land companies were advertising their wares in U.S. newspapers at $25 per acre, as having the "richest and deepest soil in the world," "lovely climate," and "early ripening of all produce at high prices." Since newspaper stories of farmers slaughtered in Indian raids might tend to dampen the land boom, Díaz and the U.S. Government moved to put down the Indian rebellion. In spite of the enslavement of large numbers of Yaquis and their sale to plantation owners in Yucatán, the rebels organized under an 18-year old Yaqui-Mayo woman, who became known as "La Santa de Cabora," and resisted for five years until they were finally defeated by Mexican and American troops at Nogales in 1896.

It is popular, especially for Marxian analysts, to picture Díaz and the *científicos* retrospectively as monsters, men utterly without redeeming social value. They were only men of their times—sometimes greedy, sometimes cruel—faced with an appalling task, that of reconstructing and modernizing Mexico's economy after a half-century of chaos. But the contempt in which they held the native agriculturalists was hardly unique to their time or place. It persists today nearly worldwide, as it has for a century and not only in capitalist countries. The twentieth-century destruction of the small-plot agricultural systems in Russia, China, and Cambodia employed far more draconian methods than were ever dreamed of by Díaz and his colleagues. In Russia, the result has been a concentration of wealth and power not unlike that in Mexico. The end result in China and Cambodia remains to be seen.

In order to guarantee the safety of foreigners and their investments, part of Díaz's effort toward "national development" was the extension of central authority into the countryside, much of which was in reality ruled by local strongmen not responsive to Mexico City or by outright bandits. The local strongmen were recognized by Don Porfirio and allowed to keep their power so long as they more or less recognized him. The instrument used against the bandits was the *rurales,* a mounted, rural police force who would fight the bandits if the bandits chose to fight, or let the bandits join them if they chose to do that. Often the establishment of the *rurales* in an area amounted to little more than enlisting the local bandit chieftain with his followers and giving them uniforms. After that the bandits were the *rurales,* and things went on pretty much as before. This process of nationalizing banditry probably decreased the level of violence in remote corners of Mexico; it certainly extended the authority of Mexico City. Díaz did not create repression in the countryside, he simply organized what he could not eradicate.

The *rurales* generally shot first and asked questions later. So many suspects were "shot attempting to escape" that Mexicans cynically called the system under which the *rurales* operated the *Ley Fuga* ("the law of flight"). Historian Stanley Ross observed that, with the establishment of the *rurales,* "legally sanctioned oppression supplanted irregular brigandage."

The U.S. and the Mexican Revolution

The resentment of the mass of Mexicans, especially the younger technical and middle-class types, toward these developments can well be imagined. (Suppose, for example, that an American president had encouraged foreign investment in and exploitation of the United States and then created a special uniformed branch of the FBI recruited from the Mafia to shoot any Americans who raised a fuss about it.) In contrast, of course, the foreigners, including the Americans, loved it. They made a mint of money in the new, stable Mexico. Keeping Mexico a safe place for American investment was a guiding principle of U.S. foreign policy around the turn of the century, and it still is today.

It is particularly tragic that the instrument of American policy at the end of the Díaz era was Henry Lane Wilson. President Taft wished to remain strictly neutral in the Díaz-Madero conflict, but Ambassador Wilson was strictly on the side of the Díaz regime and the American robber barons intent on exploiting Mexico. He loathed Madero and urged United States intervention "to protect foreign elements against possible outbreak of criminal classes here," the "criminal classes" being Madero's revolutionaries.

After failing in his efforts to keep Díaz in power, Wilson proceeded to plot the overthrow of the legally elected Madero, bombarding the U.S. State Department with anti-Madero propaganda and pleas for intervention, promoting the arming of the American colony, and berating the Mexican government with claims of the maltreatment of American citizens and corporations. In a final ignominious act, he plotted successfully with Huerta and Félix Díaz to overthrow Madero. Then he either assented to the murders of Madero and Pino Suárez or at least did not go out of his way to prevent them.

Henry Lane Wilson and his friends had good reason to be concerned about the disappearance of Díaz and the ascendancy of revolutionaries like Madero, Zapata, and Villa. When Díaz was forced to flee, the Mexican economy was dominated from north of the border. American investments in Mexico then amounted to more than $1 billion (at a time when the average American earned about $300 annually). United States corporations owned by, among others, the Rockefellers, Guggenheims, and Hearsts controlled more than 75 percent of Mexico's minerals. More than 50 percent of Mexican oil was in American hands, thanks largely to the pioneering of Edward Doheny, who was quickly followed by John D. Rockefeller in the ruthless exploitation of Mexican land and labor with the blessing of the Díaz regime. In addition to huge parcels of land held by the oil companies, other American interests owned many millions of hectares of prime cattle ranches and sugar, coffee, and cotton plantations. As much as one-fifth of the land surface of Mexico was under foreign, mainly American control. The holdings of William Randolph Hearst in Chihuahua alone amounted to some three million hectares.

Huerta turned out to be a bush-league Díaz, who was unable to suppress the revolutionary movements of Zapata in the south or of Carranza and Villa in the north. In spite of Henry Lane Wilson's determined efforts to gain recognition for Huerta by picturing him as the savior of Mexico from the devil Madero, the U.S. State Department, to its credit, refused to go along. Finally, as the battle between Carranza and Huerta escalated, Wilson was forced to resign. In the early 1950s Daniel James wrote that, during Wilson's term as ambassador:

> Wilson probably did more than any single American of the time to create in the Mexican mind an image of the American as arrogant, patronizing, exploitative, and imperialistic. If Mexican leaders today still fear the gringo, and still do not quite trust him, much of that fear and mistrust can be attributed to the incredibly destructive role of Henry Lane Wilson in Mexico.

Ironically, however, the badly motivated meddling of Henry Lane Wilson in Mexican affairs produced less anti-American feeling than the well-motivated meddling of President Woodrow Wilson. In 1913 Wilson began to put pressure on the Mexicans to end their civil war with an armistice and to hold free elections. He also embargoed the shipment of arms to Mexico, which helped Carranza because he controlled the border and could smuggle arms into Mexico, while Huerta was dependent on legal shipments that could be cut off. President Wilson enraged both sides by his attempts to meddle in the internal affairs of Mexico, and Huerta bluntly told him to mind his own business. Wilson reacted by demanding Huerta's resignation and, in early 1914, he lifted the arms embargo, apparently thinking it would help Carranza and Villa. His attempts to help the revolutionaries soon backfired, however.

Huerta was using money raised by foreign loans to import weapons through the port of Veracruz. Wilson wanted to cut that lifeline. He used as a pretext a minor incident at Tampico involving nine American sailors. The sailors had come ashore in a whaleboat from a gunboat, the *U.S.S. Dolphin,* flagship of the squadron lying off the port to protect American citizens there in case the *Carranzistas* attacked the Federal troops guarding the port. The sailors had been arrested by mistake and released with a verbal apology by the *Huertista* general, Morelos Zaragoza, commanding the Tampico garrison. The American commander, Rear Admiral Henry T. Mayo, was incensed that American sailors had been removed at gunpoint from their ship (the whaleboat). He demanded a formal apology, a raising of the American flag in Tampico, and its salute with 21 guns. The State Department pushed Huerta to accede to this, perhaps suspecting that no Mexican leader could knuckle under to such a demand and survive in office. When Huerta refused, Wilson ordered marines and sailors to invade Mexico at Veracruz, which they did on April 21.

Contrary to American expectations, the landing was greeted by effective, though unorganized opposition from civilians as well as from *Huertista* soldiers. The Americans were at first slowed down, but the marines, backed by a heavy naval bombardment, finally carried the day. The U.S. "victory" cost 19 American lives and wounded 47, while at least 200 Mexicans gave their lives defending Veracruz from Wilson's democratizing force. Huerta immediately struck a pose as the great defender of Mexican nationalism, and Carranza (whom Wilson presumably had wanted to help) condemned the occupation as a violation of national sovereignty.

Wilson's full motivation in invading Veracruz may never be known. Some have pointed out, for example, that Veracruz is near the Mexican oil fields at Tampico, and Wilson's move may have been an attempt to establish some sort of permanent U.S. presence there. Others think it was a combination of personal stubbornness and ineptitude and that even the interception of arms shipments was a pretext—that Wilson thought U.S. national "honor" was at stake. Whatever his motives, Wilson did not agree to evacuate until mid-September, and the troops remained through November, even though Huerta, the invasion's putative target, had resigned and fled the country in July.

The overall result of Wilson's intervention was to rekindle Mexican hatred of the U.S., which, ever since the events of 1846–48, was still smoldering. The public response was vehement: newspapers called for vengeance against Yankee pigs; there were numerous violent attacks on Americans and American property; and schoolchildren marched through the streets of Mexico City shouting, "Death to the gringos!" Wilson apparently learned nothing from this experience. He continued his meddling, and, while refusing to recognize anyone, "generously" offered to negotiate between Carranza, Zapata, and Villa. He finally recognized Carranza over a year after American troops left Veracruz.

There followed, of course, the border disturbances discussed in the last chapter, climaxed by Pershing's expedition into Mexico in 1916. However, the increasing involvement of the United States in World War I soon ended Carranza's worries about another invasion from the north. The turmoil of the years of revolution had made Mexico a much less attractive place for either foreign intervention or investment. Yet confrontation with the United States was far from over. In late 1916, with his control assured, Carranza convened a constitutional convention in Querétaro. The new Constitution, under which Carranza was elected first president in March 1917, contained the seeds of further U.S.–Mexican disagreement.

ARTICLE 27 AND THE FOREIGN OIL COMPANIES

The crucial portion of the new Constitution of 1917 was Article 27, which stated that, "In the Nation is vested direct ownership of all minerals . . . [including] petroleum and all hydrocarbons—solid, liquid or gaseous." It also gave the Mexican nation:

> the right to impose on private property such limitations as the public interest may demand as well as the right to regulate the development of natural resources, which are susceptible to appropriation, in order to conserve them and equitably to distribute the public wealth.

Article 27 provided the legal basis both for agrarian reform and for the expropriation by the Mexican government of mineral rights held by foreigners—thus permitting the heritage of the Díaz era to be swept away. Only "Mexicans by birth or naturalization and Mexican companies" could now own Mexican land or exploit Mexico's mineral wealth, although the government could cede that right to foreigners *if* they gave up the right of protection by their own government and placed themselves under Mexican law with regard to their rights of ownership. Article 27 was not altogether the result of revolutionary enthusiasm and anti-Americanism. In many respects it was only a return to old Spanish legal principles which held that subsurface rights were always retained by the crown for the national good. The enthusiasm for foreign investment and development of natural resources by Don Porfirio and the *científicos* had led them to disregard these principles during the *Porfiriato*.

The situation in the oil fields in the years just after the promulgation of the new Constitution seemed especially disadvantageous to the Mexicans. Oil wells had been allowed to flow very rapidly, producing a yield of 40 million barrels annually. By 1921 annual production reached 200 million barrels. This made Mexico the world's largest petroleum producer after the United States, whose production had reached 40 million barrels only in 1910, and was still below 1,000 million barrels in 1921. The rapid flow rates, which generated huge profits for the oil companies, had been catastrophic for the Mexican oil fields. Letting the oil flow too fast often permitted salt water to invade the field or left in the ground vast pockets of oil that could no longer be exploited with the technology of the day. To add insult to injury, the oil companies sold their oil for higher prices within Mexico than they did abroad.

The Mexican government also had to deal with the complaints of many Mexicans who claimed that the oil companies were cheating or abusing them—invading their land, terrorizing them, and refusing to pay royalties. Similar complaints came from small independent producers, Mexican and foreign. The giant companies were accused of stealing oil by offset drilling (drilling at a slant so as to extract oil from under a neighbor's land), hiring "bandits" to harass their competitors' workers and sabotage their fields, and generally trying to push the small firms into bankruptcy so they could be engulfed.

If only a small portion of the accusations were true, the major foreign producers were hardly "good neighbors" to those who lived or operated in their vicinity. They were hardly good citizens either—scoffing at or evading reasonable attempts at regulation and regularly trying (often with great success) to bribe Mexican officials. Their entire demeanor, both in dealing with the gov-

ernment and Mexican citizens and in their treatment of Mexican
workers in the fields (Mexicans were paid less than Americans
doing the same job), was tinged with a racism completely inappropriate to revolutionary Mexico.

Then in 1918 Carranza first applied Article 27 to the oil companies, setting a tax and proposing to convert their titles to concessions. This caused an enormous furor in the United States.
U.S. Senator Albert B. Fall, always a servant of the oil interests
(and who later went to prison in the Teapot Dome scandal),
actually proposed to the Senate that the United States invade and
occupy Mexico. The intransigent attitude of the American leadership horrified the Mexicans, but a *Gotterdämmerüng* was avoided
when the Mexican Supreme Court ruled that Article 27 could not
be applied retroactively. The first victory thus went to the
foreigners in what was to be a 20-year battle over who owned and
controlled Mexico's oil.

After Carranza's overthrow and murder in May 1920 and a
brief interim presidency, Alvaro Obregón took office as duly
elected president. Obregón wanted both to restore the economy
of a nation devastated by a bloody civil war and to honor his
commitments to social reform. Since the oil industry was still
functioning, Obregón tried to pacify the oil companies—but it
proved a difficult task. The United States refused to recognize
Obregón's "bolshevist" government, and the oil companies and
other Americans with interests in Mexico orchestrated a press
campaign against him.

In order to obtain recognition, Obregón was forced to make a
variety of concessions, after listening to a humiliating series of
demands presented by Secretary of State Charles Evans Hughes.
The most difficult group to satisfy were the oil companies, which,
while complaining loudly of maltreatment on the part of the
Mexican government, were actually making enormous fortunes
in their Mexican operations. Finally, in a series of meetings
known as the "Bucareli Conferences" (held at No. 85 Avenida
Bucareli, in Mexico City), Obregón made the key concession,
unofficially ceding to oil companies the subsoil rights they sought.
He then got the official recognition *he* needed.

Obregón had pulled off a considerable coup, to which this brief
discussion cannot do justice. He managed to prevent an invasion
of Mexico and win recognition for his government while giving
the appearance of not allowing the United States to dictate the
terms. Obregón also beat off an attempted coup by Adolfo de la
Huerta and in 1924 arranged the legal election of Plutarco Elías
Calles, his own choice as successor. The 1917 Constitution forbade a president to succeed himself. The Mexican nation was
intact and the Revolution could continue.

The issue of the oil companies remained, however, as did persistent American attempts at intervention. The bones of contention were laws intended to implement Article 27 and in particular U.S. attempts to dictate the form of that legislation before it passed the Mexican Congress. The tension built to a high level as the Hearst newspapers, ever a bastion of recklessness, jingoism, and greed, screamed for military intervention. A quote from the Hearst New York *American* of the 1920s gives one the flavor of William Randolph Hearst's sentiments:

> There will never be a stable government in Mexico until the United States imposes one and sustains it with . . . American bayonets. . . .
>
> Custom and tradition in international relations . . . justify intervention by a country for the purpose of putting an end to prevalent disorders in a neighboring country.
>
> There is no human power anywhere that can re-establish order in that unhappy country except the power of the United States of America. Early or later, our government must do what the Hearst newspapers for three years have suggested it do: Intervene in Mexico energetically, dignifiedly, and in sufficient force, not in order to suppress the Mexican people but to save them . . .

The kind of "order" that Hearst longed for was the kind found during the *Porfiriato,* when foreigners had been encouraged to rape Mexican resources for fun and profit. One can imagine the reaction in Revolutionary Mexico when President Calvin Coolidge, missing the point of the Revolution, ruminated nostalgically about the good old days when Don Porfirio ran a tight ship south of the border:

> During the more than thirty years of President Díaz we were especially encouraged to make investments. . . . After he was driven from office by revolution, much disorder existed, with presidents following one another in rapid succession.

The oil companies, with this sort of encouragement from America's jingoistic press and under the "protection" of a friendly State Department, simply rebelled against the Mexican government and refused to obey Mexican laws. Under one order the government prohibited them from drilling without a permit. The oil producers continued to drill without permits. Then the government locked the wells. The companies broke the locks and continued drilling. Then the government sent troops to surround the wells and stop the drilling. It amounted to a gigantic face-off between the government of Mexico on one side and the foreign oil companies and an interventionist U.S. State Department on the other.

General Lázaro Cárdenas was placed in charge of the Mexican military force around Veracruz. His orders from President Calles were that, in case of invasion, he was first to burn the oil fields and then to fight the United States troops.

It turned out that after the Teapot Dome scandal, the worst scandal in U.S. history between Grant's whiskey ring and Nixon's Watergate, public support in the United States for big oil companies evaporated. The presidents of two of the five oil companies that were behaving atrociously in Mexico were principals in Teapot Dome—an affair in which the Secretary of the Interior took bribes to give oil companies leases on government oil reserves without competitive bidding. With no support from home, the oil companies finally backed down, assuming, among other things, that the loss of revenue would soon force the Mexican government to give in to them.

Then the State Department replaced its old-style ambassador with Dwight W. Morrow, a Wall Street lawyer, a partner in the J.P. Morgan Co., and a most unlikely candidate to do what he did— establish the first period of friendly relations between the U.S. and Mexico by initiating what Franklin Roosevelt later christened the "Good Neighbor Policy." Still, the tensions eased too late for foreign oil companies, for what Lázaro Cárdenas saw during his tour of duty in the Veracruz area (including, reportedly, an unsuccessful attempt to bribe him) was to seal their doom a decade later.

Calles and Morrow reached a compromise on the oil question, with Calles agreeing to modify the Petroleum Law so that oil lands purchased prior to 1917 would not be affected by Article 27. With this the threat of American intervention receded even further. Calles, who has been called the last of the *caudillos*, continued to control Mexican politics through three subsequent presidencies until Cárdenas, by then Minister of War, was nominated by the official party and elected to a six-year term in 1934.

The Expropriation of Oil

As president, Cárdenas revitalized the Mexican Revolution. He did not use Chapultepec Castle as his official residence, thus breaking away from a tradition started by Díaz. Although he had been elected because of Calles' support, he would not let Calles run things; and when Calles turned against him, a struggle for power ensued. In a series of maneuvers, Cárdenas smashed Calles' political machine and in early 1936 expelled him from the country. Things were settling down in Mexico; the last *caudillo* was removed without violence.

Cárdenas's first big moves in what was to become known as "The Second Revolution" were in the direction of land reform. In November 1936 the Expropriation Law was passed by Congress and put into effect, empowering the government under Article 27 of the Constitution to expropriate any property that had "public utility." It seems clear that Cárdenas originally had no intention of using the law to expropriate the foreign oil holdings, but events were to change his mind.

Mexican oil workers, living and working under the most miserable of conditions, had belonged to 21 small unions. In 1935, at Cárdenas's instigation, they were joined together into the National Petroleum Workers Syndicate. In 1936 they became part of the Mexican Worker's Confederation (CTM), a government-sanctioned, almost paramilitary organization of 200,000 workers. The syndicate threatened to strike in November 1936, but Cárdenas intervened and persuaded the union to put off their strike for a six-month "cooling-off" period until May 1937. In a long series of meetings, the companies claimed they could not afford to meet the worker's demands, even though their rate of profit in Mexico was almost three times that in the United States and the real wages of the Mexican oil workers had fallen while those of American oil workers had risen.

The oil companies were unyielding, even when confronted with these statistics, and in late May 1937 the oil workers struck. The Petroleum Workers Syndicate then petitioned the government to declare that the strike was not a strike but an "economic conflict"—a situation defined in Mexican law as one where the balance of power is so uneven that a normal strike would be ineffectual. It was so declared by the Federal Board of Conciliation and Arbitration. The government, operating under something resembling Taft-Hartley legislation, suspended the strike and appointed a fact-finding commission under leftist economist Jesús Silva Herzog. The Herzog Commission's findings were not only favorable to the strikers, but the commission also censured the foreign oil companies for operating against the national interests of Mexico.

The oil companies immediately protested to Cárdenas, threatened to shut down their operations, and attempted to get their governments to intervene. They started pushing their governments even before the board had handed down its decision, to the great disgust of the nationalistic Mexicans. Experience apparently had taught the oil companies nothing about the sensitivity of the Mexicans to outside pressure.

The final decision of the board, supporting the Herzog Commission recommendations, was handed down in December 1937, and the following January the board ordered the foreign oil companies to comply. On March 1, the Mexican Supreme Court, considering an oil-company appeal but under enormous popular pressure not to rule for the foreigners, ruled in favor of the Board of Conciliation and Arbitration. The oil companies defied the government and refused to comply with the orders of the board and the Supreme Court. They also rejected a final compromise offered by Cárdenas and managed to insult him by refusing to accept his word. This was the straw that broke the camel's back. On March 18, Cárdenas nationalized the foreign oil companies, most of which were American. They were to be taken over immediately. The companies were told they would be indemnified within ten years as required by the Expropriation Law.

Expropriating the oil companies was the most popular single move ever made by a Mexican president. Cárdenas was not merely supported by all segments of the Mexican public, he was lionized. Mexican women of all classes offered their jewelry to the state to help ease the financial burden of indemnifying the oil companies. The Catholic Church, including the Archbishop of Mexico, gave the government its support, even though the lengthy Church-state confrontation in Mexico had only recently ended with the state triumphant. A magnificent fountain and monument commemorate the event on Mexico City's El Paseo de la Reforma, and public schools have been named after *la expropriación*. March 18, 1938, has become one of the most important dates in Mexican history—vying with September 16, 1810, the day of the "Grito de Dolores;" with May 5, 1863, when the French were defeated at Puebla; and with November 20, 1910, the date designated in the Plan of San Luis Potosí as the start of the Mexican Revolution.

The oil expropriation was viewed somewhat differently in the United States. Largely oblivious of the nationalistic past and present of their own nation, the oil companies and their friends in the United States viewed Mexico's behavior as a colossal act of *chutzpah*. How dare a banana republic expropriate property belonging to some of the richest American thieves? The yellow press raged about the Bolshevik threat south of the border, and the oil companies, squealing like the stuck pigs they truly were, struck back with economic warfare (boycotts, slapping liens on Mexican oil cargoes and claiming they were "stolen goods," blacklists, and other pressures).

The companies launched a propaganda campaign demanding that the U.S. Government take action. But the U.S. Government's options were limited. Franklin Roosevelt, in a tradition that went all the way back to Thomas Jefferson and in the spirit of Dwight

Morrow's ambassadorship, had formally announced the Good Neighbor Policy in his first inaugural speech. He had explicitly pledged that armed intervention by the U.S. in the affairs of Latin American nations was a thing of the past. (Would that it had been.) Furthermore, Roosevelt's eyes were on the gathering storm in Europe—he wanted a secure southern flank, not trouble with Mexico.

Roosevelt's response to the problem of the oil expropriation was very different from what the oil companies demanded in their massive public relations campaign. The Roosevelt Administration openly allied itself with the goals of the Mexican Revolution and only expressed concern that the companies be properly compensated. The Mexican position was that, although just compensation was due under international law, expropriation could not wait until Mexico was in a position to pay. The Mexican Secretary of Foreign Relations, Eduardo Hay, told Secretary of State Cordell Hull in a note that social justice in Mexico had priority over the oil barons' right to more quick bucks.

A lengthy debate ensued between Hay and Hull, mostly couched in general terms about rights of expropriation and proper compensation. Even today the exchange throws considerable light on fundamental differences in point of view between poor and rich nations. On one side was the urgent need of a poor nation for social reform, on the other were the legal property rights of a corporation and individuals who were attempting to thwart that reform. The issue is likely to arise ever more frequently in the future, especially as the impact in less-developed countries of the operations of gigantic multinational corporations becomes better understood.

The Mexican position was not appreciated by most Americans, especially since most of the American newspapers presented the expropriation as the act of a communist dictator and claimed that the Mexicans would be unable to operate the oil fields. This claim proved about as accurate as the claim by the British almost two decades later that the Egyptians would be unable to run the Suez Canal, and, we daresay, as accurate as claims by the American press four decades later that the Panamanians will not be able to run the Panama Canal.

In spite of all the fuss and furor, no international confrontation took place. After complex negotiations, the major differences between Mexico and the United States were settled shortly before Pearl Harbor, and the basis of an agreement was reached for compensating the oil companies. In April 1942, the amounts of compensation were settled and schedules of payment set up. Mexico fulfilled her obligations on time. Although for more than a decade after expropriation the oil industry in Mexico was plagued by problems, the situation was turned around, and, under the direction of an autonomous national corporation, *Petroleos Mexicanos* (PEMEX), the oil industry 20 years after nationalization had expanded far beyond the pre-expropriation scale. It has continued to expand since then.

The settlement over oil in 1941 brought to an end the open interference of the United States in the political affairs of its southern neighbor. During the Second World War, Mexico gave the United States the secure southern flank that Roosevelt desired and supplied it with farm labor. Since the war, American financial involvement in Mexico has continually increased. The Mexican Revolution has become institutionalized, and the government once again has provided the kind of "stability" that attracts foreign investors. Most of those attracted quite naturally have been from Mexico's powerful northern neighbor.

THE AGRICULTURAL SECTOR

A major cause of the Mexican Revolution was the overwhelming need for agrarian reform and improvement of the conditions of life for the peasants who made up the majority of the population. But the struggles of the Mexican *peones* to free themselves from the bondage that had been promoted in the last part of the nineteenth century by the dictator Porfirio Díaz still had not been successful by 1920. The leaders of the Revolution were mostly dead by then. Reaction against the Revolution grew in the countryside, and many *peones,* fed up with conditions on the *haciendas,* or driven off newly redistributed lands, or, above all, sick of the violence and terror, began looking north for refuge and employment. This was the beginning of Mexican migration to the United States.

Pablo Mares, a miner from Jalisco, went north "because it was impossible to live down there with so many revolutions." Drunken soldiers almost killed him in one incident, and he was then pressed into Pancho Villa's revolutionary army. In 1915 he ran away to El Paso.

Luis Murillo from Monterrey began running errands for federal troops when he was thirteen years old and was quickly conscripted by the government forces of the dictator Huerta. After Huerta's defeat he was demobilized, but in the economic chaos of revolutionary Mexico, there was no work.

> With the farms burned there weren't even any tortillas to eat, nothing but maguey leaves and there wasn't anything else to do

when Carranza [leading revolutionary troops] drew near, but once again join the army.

Murillo served through the confusion of revolutionary action in northern Mexico, first under Venustiano Carranza, then under Pancho Villa, then under Carranza again. He began to grow disenchanted with the Revolution while in Villa's army, and then after a second tour with Carranza's forces, he returned home. "But I kept my taste for adventure from being a soldier so much and on the 2nd of August 1920 I crossed the bridge [to Texas]."

Mares fled Mexico hungry and in terror, and Murillo went north because he had become footloose and restless in military service. They are only two, but their stories dramatize some of the "push" factors that launched Mexican emigration to the United States. During the seven years of Mexican revolutionary struggle, 1911 through 1917, 120,000 Mexicans went north, and in the next seven years the number rose to over 300,000.

President Cárdenas became a Mexican hero for nationalizing the oil fields in 1938, but his activities in agrarian reform may have had an even more profound and lasting effect on Mexican life. During his administration (1934–1940), the land-reform program mandated by the 1917 Constitution, but until Cárdenas only halfheartedly implemented because of lack of funds and personnel, was greatly accelerated. Parcels of land were taken from the *hacendados* and redistributed to small farmers. The redistributed parcels could not be sold or mortgaged, and in many cases they were to be cultivated communally (a sort of return to the *ejido* system). The new *ejidatarios* (land-reform farmers) were given preference for irrigation water, sources of credit, and technical assistance. Sizable tracts of land, including some foreign-owned properties in the irrigated districts of the northwest, were expropriated and distributed. The lands of the United Sugar Company were among the giant holdings that were dismembered.

In addition, the *ejidatarios* received other services, such as education, health care, and communications. Some agricultural research, conducted locally, was improving indigenous strains of corn and wheat, and developing better farming methods for local conditions. By 1940 the beneficiaries of land reform in Mexico had produced measurable increases in food production; on 47 percent of the farmland they accounted for 52 percent of the value of Mexico's agricultural production.

Unhappily for Mexico, this trend toward supporting agriculture and benefiting the rural poor proved to be short-lived. Cárdenas's policies had enemies in several camps: Mexico's large landowners, whose land was taken over; the urban rich, who wanted the government to invest in services for them; and American investors in industry, who wanted similar services and plenty of cheap, docile, urban labor. At the same time, food production relative to population growth was faltering. Unrest in rural areas, attendant to land reform, hindered production. Large landowners, expecting their land to be confiscated, were reluctant to invest in land improvement and modern agricultural techniques. In the early 1940s crop failures, followed by scarcity and high food prices, led to riots in Mexican cities and towns.

Cárdenas's presidential successors largely catered to the interests of the rich and the foreign investors at the expense of agricultural development, particularly the small farmer. Credit and other rural services remained available mostly to large landholders, who used their advantage to buy out smaller private holders and co-opt *ejidos* by renting the land.

Government funds were spent for the electric power, highways, airports, communications, and other amenities desired by the rich. Investment of domestic and foreign (mainly U.S.) interests in industry was encouraged by government policies. An important element of this was a deliberate policy of maintaining food supplies in cities at low prices to keep urban workers satisfied and their wages low. Because of rapid population growth and urbanization, the labor pool has constantly expanded, which also helped to keep wages down. But this policy also kept farmers, other than large producers of commodities for export, in poverty. Forty percent of the Mexican people still live on farms, but only 10 percent of the gross domestic product is accounted for by agriculture today.

The redistribution of land did not come to an end after Cárdenas, although it was substantially slowed, especially in the 1940s and 1950s. Relatively little land remains available for expropriation today. There are several serious problems with the system as it has evolved both in terms of equity and of agricultural efficiency. In 1960, *ejidatarios* slightly outnumbered private landowners, but the private owners held nearly three-quarters of the land and the majority of cultivated and irrigated acreage. The overwhelming majority of both *ejidatarios* and owners (roughly 85 percent) have less than 10 hectares of cultivable land, and many have far less. Many of these parcels of land are too small to be economically productive even with simple methods, let alone to provide a financial base for modernization. In addition, the majority of *ejidatarios* do not have clear title to their lands, which makes them ineligible for credit and other extension services.

Since the Revolution, some three million peasants have acquired land, either as owners or *ejidatarios*. But the rural population, despite heavy migration to Mexico's cities, has nonetheless grown faster, and today there are well over four million landless peasants, who constitute more than half of the rural work force.

Mexico is a splendid example of a two-tiered society—one in which the upper fraction of the population has grown rapidly richer, while the poorest fraction has gained very little. While Mexico's gross national product grew in the neighborhood of 7 percent per year between 1958 and 1973 (about twice as fast as the population), the incomes of the poorest 20 percent of families increased by just over one percent per year, and the richest 20 percent gained over four percent per year. From 1950 to 1969, the income gap between the richest and poorest fifths of the population widened, with the poorest group receiving a 2 percent smaller share of national income than before.

This widening of the income gap has been especially pronounced for people living in the countryside. During the 1950s, while the average per-capita annual income of Mexicans rose from $308 to $405, the average yearly income of landless farm workers fell from $68 to $56. As the rural population expanded, workers were being replaced by machines, and days worked per year by landless farm workers fell from an average of 194 in 1950 to 100 in 1960 and to 75 in 1970.

There are other indications that there has been no significant improvement in living conditions for the poor in Mexico; between 1965 and 1975, mortality among infants and small children due to malnutrition *rose* by 10 percent. Malnutrition in general is not as severe in Mexico as it is in some other less-developed countries. Extreme malnutrition has been found in less than five percent of the people even in the poorest areas in the country. Yet a substantial portion—perhaps half or more of the population—is inadequately nourished to some degree, and the government has only lately felt some concern about it. Between 1965 and 1975, in the face of a population growth rate close to 3.5 percent per year, acreage planted in staple food crops (corn, beans, rice) was reduced by 25 percent. By the mid-1970s from 15 to 45 percent of these staples had to be imported. At the same time Mexico was providing the United States market with half or more of its supply of many fresh vegetables and fruits in winter and spring.

Once again, the United States has played a role in shaping Mexico's development policies. First, as investors primarily in industry, Americans encouraged the Mexican government's neglect of the agricultural segment of the economy in favor of urban development. Secondarily, Americans have been involved in what agricultural development there has been since 1940, starting with the Green Revolution.

The Green Revolution and U.S. Investment in Agriculture

One of the ironies of U.S.–Mexican affairs is that American involvement in Mexican agriculture has had a considerable impact on the flow of Mexicans across the U.S. border. Landless peasants have been squeezed off their land in part by expanding agribusiness and Green Revolution technology, only to go north for jobs—often on American farms.

Mexico was an early staging area for the Green Revolution, which has been introduced to several Asian countries since the Mexican program was developed. The first Green Revolution program was started by the Mexican government and the Rockefeller Foundation in 1943. Rather than being oriented toward helping the small farmer become more productive (as research and rural assistance under Cárdenas had done), the new program was capital- and energy-intensive, required the best land or land served by large irrigation projects, and concentrated on high-yielding varieties of wheat that depended on expensive new materials such as fertilizer and pesticides. It is a technology better suited to large landholders than to small farmers. Some *ejidatarios* were nevertheless required to purchase the materials at full cost (while the large farmers could obtain them at a discount), but were given no instruction in their use. Small subsistence farmers were completely excluded from the Green Revolution process.

The Green Revolution in Mexico was subject to all the problems and disadvantages—ecological as well as social—that have appeared elsewhere. Government funds subsidized the importation of farm machinery and large irrigation projects. Newly developed land was sold to businessmen and bureaucrats. Although Mexican law limits each landowner to 250 irrigated acres, the average size of farms irrigated in the Green Revolution wheat region in the 1970s was 2,000 acres. When wheat production rose most rapidly, in the 1950s, about 80 percent of the increase came from three percent of the farms. One of the more interesting results is that many of these wealthy farmers, despite all the government credit and subsidization of mechanization and irrigation costs, were bankrupt by the 1970s! They had foolishly invested their profits in luxury goods and nonagricultural enterprises rather than in their farms' productivity.

The Rockefeller-style Green Revolution in Mexico thus facilitated a movement undermining the intent of Cárdenas, land-reform policies. Farming was to be practiced by wealthy, large (often absentee) landholders, using highly mechanized technology, which replaced farm workers. (Tractors, after all, seldom demand better wages or working conditions.) Government credit and subsidy policies have favored large farmers at the expense of small ones. Large farmers have been allowed to form storage cooperatives, so they could sell their grain when prices were highest. Small farmers have had to sell to the government at harvest time, when prices usually are low. Thus they generally have been at a competitive disadvantage all around. When subsistence farmers are bankrupted, their farms are bought up by neighboring *hacendados*. Many *ejidatarios*, who cannot sell their land, have been forced to rent it to large landowners or remain perpetually in debt. Peasant credit cooperatives, which might have given *ejidatarios* some political and economic leverage, were abolished in the 1950s.

Even though land redistribution has continued, the issue of land reform remains a source of violence in Mexican society. In the minds of some, it is a potential spark for another Mexican revolution. Violent takeovers of land still occur sporadically. For example, in October of 1978 in the states of Oaxaca and Veracruz a coordinated takeover of *hacienda* land by large numbers of Indian peasants occurred. Leading the peasant army was an avowed communist trained in China. The peasants took hostage men who worked for the landlords and threatened to kill them if the federal government intervened. The government was in quite a bind: to evict the Indians by force would be to sully its carefully developed image of favoring land reform; not to act would open the way for a bloody war between the private armies of the landlords and the squatters. This could almost make one believe that a persistent peasant legend is true. Perhaps Emiliano Zapata was not killed in a storm of bullets almost six decades ago, and he will live on ageless in the southern mountains, rallying the peasants until the land that is rightfully theirs is secure in their possession.

Along with the bias toward large farmers, there has been an accelerating growth in production of cash crops for export. Mexican production of cotton and coffee, for instance, rose almost three times as fast as that of staple grains between 1940 and 1962. An important part of this picture is the rapid increase in the last decade or two of U.S. agribusiness involvement in Mexican farming. Attracted by low wages, abundant labor, and a year-round growing season, American companies have moved their operations to Mexico, growing such varied crops as cucumbers, onions, asparagus, eggplants, squash, tomatoes, and strawberries. The

agribusiness technology—fertilizer application, pest-control procedures, irrigation systems—is essentially identical to that of
California's Imperial Valley and is largely based on materials
from the United States. The export crops are often grown on the
best land, and the growers monopolize government credit and
extension services at the expense of farmers who grow staple
crops for local consumption. As the subsistence growers have
been restricted to smaller and poorer farms, prices have risen for
their reduced production of staples, making even basic foods less
available to the poor.

The Mexican government, needing foreign exchange, encouraged the shift to export crops, but in reality most of the proceeds
have gone to the big corporations, which also control the marketing, processing, distribution, and most production decisions. Because the agribusiness companies are looking for low costs and
high returns in the short run, little or no effort is made to protect
the soil and the land from abuse. If the soil is depleted, the
company sells and moves elsewhere.

These operations also exploit workers, giving them part-time
seasonal work for below-minimum wages. In order to survive,
families put their children to work. Working conditions are
dreadful in fields and processing factories, and jobs are insecure.
Attempts to organize for better pay or conditions have sometimes
met with violence.

The result of Mexico's general neglect of the agricultural sector
of its economy, together with emphasis on export crops and the
inefficiency of many small holdings, has been a faltering of food
production for domestic markets. In the early 1970s, as growth in
production fell behind growth in demand, especially of corn,
Mexico became a substantial importer as well as exporter of food.
In 1974 the cost of imported food exceeded the return from food
exports.

This is not to say that there is no room for increasing Mexico's
food production further, even though the present situation is not
encouraging. Only about 36 percent of the nation's rugged land
area is level or nearly level enough to be cultivated. And, most of
the land, including much of the relatively level portion, is at least
moderately eroded already. Water is a serious limiting factor;
three-fourths of the nation is arid or semi-arid, while another 16
percent would be more productive with irrigation. Moreover,
yields of staple crops (other than wheat) are relatively low. Corn
yields in Mexico, for instance, average less than one-fourth those
in the United States, reflecting the inefficiency of the small farms
and the lack of effort put into helping subsistence farmers. Thus
opportunities do exist to increase food production substantially

through erosion-control programs, extension of high-yield agricultural methods (though not necessarily mechanization) to
small farmers, and judicious development of irrigation projects,
among other measures.

In view of conditions in rural Mexico, is it any wonder that so
many young people, squeezed off the land and unable to find
steady, adequate employment, have migrated north in search of a
better life? They are a part of Mexico's "reserve army of unemployed," available for exploitation by large-scale agricultural enterprises, including U.S. agribusiness. The army exists and is still
expanding because Mexico's agricultural work force has grown
far more rapidly than have employment opportunities.

A great many of these unemployed workers have migrated to
northern cities in Mexico, where pay is generally better and jobs
have been more available. They have been lured in part by the
even brighter prospect of being allowed to work in the United
States as *braceros*—temporary farm workers. Between 1940 and
1960, for example, Tijuana's population grew about eightfold
from some 20,000 to about 165,000; today it is over 600,000.
Similar growth has occurred in other border centers such as
Mexicali and Ciudad Juárez. When the *bracero* program was discontinued in 1964, partly under pressure from American unions,
more than 200,000 *braceros* were suddenly left without access to
jobs in the United States. Their only choice was to enter the U.S.
illegally or remain unemployed. Risky as it is, and poor as working
conditions for illegal migrants may be in the United States, the
prospects are more attractive than what they have left behind.

PRESENT U.S. INVOLVEMENT IN MEXICO

It should be clear by now that the historic relationships, both
economic and political, between the United States and Mexico are
far from simple. Nor have they been conducted as if the two were
equal partners—a consideration that could easily sour future
negotiations on any issue, including the migration from Mexico to
the U.S. Today, the economic relationship between the two countries is more complex than ever, and each nation is more than ever
dependent on the other in a variety of ways.

By the 1970s the United States accounted for over two-thirds of
Mexico's foreign trade and thus is far and away its largest trading
partner. In 1976, Mexico imported nearly $5 billion worth of U.S.
goods and exported $3.6 billion worth to the U.S. That volume of
trade is not negligible to the American economy either; Mexico is
the fifth largest trading partner of the United States.

Of the direct foreign investment in the Mexican economy, the

United States accounts for some 85 percent to the tune of $3 billion. Although this amounts to only about one-tenth of all direct investment in the Mexican economy, U.S. investment has been concentrated in manufacturing and tourism, the two sectors that have been growing most rapidly. About half of the richest firms and almost two-thirds of those producing capital goods are owned by foreigners, mostly Americans. In addition, there are loans and credits to Mexico amounting to $11.5 billion held by private American banks.

None of this should be terribly surprising in view of Mexico's need for capital for development and American businesses' need for low-cost labor, which happens to exist in abundance south of the border.

Los Maquiladoras

In the 1960s many American firms were feeling the pressure of competition from Japanese and European companies, so some of these companies sought to solve their problems by moving operations abroad to areas where labor was cheaper. In the past decade or so, hundreds of U.S. corporations have chosen Mexico for the establishment of factories to take advantage of the abundant pool of workers.

When the *bracero* program was closed down in the United States, the Mexican government, in collaboration with American advisors, developed a new plan to ameliorate Mexico's unemployment problems. Through the Border Industrialization Program, American corporations were encouraged to establish assembly plants in Mexico along the border. These *maquiladora* (runaway) shops would then be able to take advantage of the large pool of cheap labor just across America's southern boundary. As the North American Congress in Latin America (NACLA) put it in a report, "Rather than import workers the United States would export the industries."

The first companies to take advantage of the Border Industrialization Program were electronics firms and garment and toy producers. Such well-known firms as General Electric, Litton Industries, Motorola, Fairchild, and Hughes Aircraft soon were operating south of the border. From 72 authorized U.S. plants in 1967, the number grew to 665 in late 1974. By that year Mexico had become the largest foreign assembler of items for re-export to the United States—surpassing places like Hong Kong, Taiwan, and other Asian localities deemed less stable by American interests.

As the Mexican government hoped, the *maquiladoras* provided many new jobs. By the end of 1974, within a decade, they were employing some 80,000 workers, over 12 percent of the economically active population in the border area. But their value in terms of the economic development of the Mexican borderlands is open to serious question. They represent an extension of U.S. industry that primarily serves U.S. economic interests. They were not designed with the primary goal of promoting Mexican development. For example, in late 1974 and early 1975 when the U.S. had a recession, many runaway plants were closed or their operations cut back, leaving Mexicans jobless once again.

When Mattel Toys' Mexican subsidiary in Mexicali closed in 1975, about 3,000 workers became unemployed. The closing of the Mattel plant was largely the result of a long struggle with the Mexican union, indicating that the Mexican worker is not the legendary doormat that exists in the imagination of many American employers.

The growing organization of Mexican labor just south of the border has led many companies to consider running away again. Some have moved farther into Mexico, others are looking toward Asia (again), Central America, or the Caribbean in their search for docile cheap labor. As they depart, they leave behind them a Mexican population embittered by fly-by-night exploitation. And, of course, one wonders why those who control the corporations never seem capable of asking when the whole process will come to an end. For just as Earth's physical resources are finite and cannot be plundered forever, there clearly are limits to exploitable labor.

The Politics of Boxcars

At the same time that American manufacturers do not want to pay even the modest prevailing wages in their runaway plants south of the border, they want protection of the United States Government against competition from Mexican-manufactured goods at home. Over 40 percent of Mexican exports are manufactured goods, and many aspects of Mexican industry are well developed and sophisticated. One of the most important steps the United States could take in stemming the flow of illegal-alien workers would be to import more goods from Mexico, thus creating jobs there. Mexico produces a wide range of items such as the Volkswagen Beetle (some of which are exported to Germany since production of that model has been discontinued there) and railroad cars. The problems Mexican manufacturers have met in marketing their railroad cars in the United States are illustrative of the myopia and insensitivity that the U.S. Congress frequently shows in dealing with Mexico and other developing nations.

It is no secret that the United States has neglected its railroads, but this neglect goes beyond the simple deterioration of roadbeds and the decline in passenger service. It extends also to the railroad service industries and to the manufacture of railroad equipment, including railroad cars. In most years, the United States needs more railroad cars than it can produce (52,000 produced in 1977), and about 95 percent of those imported come from Mexico. Mexico and Canada are the only foreign countries that produce cars that meet United States specifications, and Canada cannot meet even its own demand. Hence Mexico is the only country in the world that can supply the U.S. railroads with what they need.

Starting in late 1977, the shortage of cars became very serious in the United States. A series of explosions in grain elevators in Galveston and New Orleans made it necessary for the railroads to transfer hundreds of carloads of wheat to other ports and to reroute shipments already on their way to the damaged elevators. In addition, the extremely harsh winter caused a sharp increase in railroad-equipment difficulties. Snow shorted out diesel-electric generators, and extreme cold caused metal parts to become brittle and break. Repairs had to be made in the open under severe weather conditions. In some parts of the country, railroad operations were slowed by 30 to 40 percent. During this slowdown, goods were piling up in warehouses, and these had to be shipped sooner or later. The situation was not yet straightened out by the early summer when the wheat harvest began. The problem was made still worse because many farmers, who had held back their wheat from the 1977 harvest because of low prices, started moving it onto the market when prices went up in 1978.

On June 15, 1978, the *Wall Street Journal* reported that

> What's already the worst grain hauling crunch in U.S. history will get worse before it gets better. . . . Railroads currently are running 25,000 rail cars a day short of customers' needs and some buyers have been waiting since April for wheat, corn, soybeans and other commodities.

On the same day, the Interstate Commerce Commission announced that civil fines totaling $2.7 million had been assessed against the Consolidated Rail Corporation and the Atchison, Topeka, and Santa Fe Railway for failure to respond to federal orders to move freight cars to sections of the country where they were critically needed. A spokesman for the Santa Fe said, "There's two years' harvest out there . . . and there's no way in the world the railroad can handle it." On June 27, 1978, Richard B. Klaff, a spokesman for the scrap-metal industry, stated that many of the cars supplied to scrap dealers by the railroads were unfit for service and that the dealers had to repair them at their own expense to make them serviceable. Klaff was quoted as saying, "We have received cars without floors and the railroads expect us to use them."

Since the 1978 crunch was regarded as a short-run problem, U.S. railcar manufacturers were not interested in permanently increasing their production capacity to meet the demand. In anticipation of this, the Missouri Pacific Railroad and the North American Car Corporation had signed a contract with a Mexican firm, the Constructura Nacional de Carros de Ferrocarril (CNCF), for 1978 delivery of 1,269 railroad cars, valued at $31.7 million.

The Mexican railroad cars had been included in the Generalized System of Preferences (GSP) which allows certain kinds of manufactured goods to enter the United States without duty from 126 developing countries. On March 1, 1978, however, the cars lost their GSP protection because of Section 504 of the Trade Act of 1974, and the Mexican railroad cars became subject to an 18 percent import duty. Section 504 provides that import duties will be levied on goods when one country reaches the point that it is supplying 50 percent of the item being imported. The intention of this action was to spread the business around and give all developing countries a chance. However, railroad cars are not typical, since Mexico is the only country with the ability to produce them in any sizable numbers beyond domestic needs and to U.S. specifications.

At this point CNCF, the Mexican railroad-car maker, retained Joseph H. Blatchford, a former director of the Peace Corps and now an attorney practicing in Washington, to represent them. Mr. Blatchford's firm, Berry, Epstein, Sandstrom, and Blatchford, specializes in problems of foreign trade, and Mr. Blatchford concentrates his attention on Latin American clients. This seemed like a particularly straightforward matter, and Mr. Blatchford prepared a short list of cogent points to inform members of Congress and their staffs of what was happening. Among these points were:

—Neither U.S. railroad-car manufacturers nor their employees were being threatened by the temporary suspension of the 18 percent duty because they could not supply the desperately needed cars;

—The U.S. trade balance would not be significantly affected because about half of the value of the cars manufactured in Mexico, both for export and for use within Mexico, is in components and materials imported to Mexico from the U.S. in the first place.
—Indeed, the shortage of freight cars was complicating the balance-of-payments situation because deliveries of U.S. commodities were behind schedule. Ironically, $850 million worth of these commodities are sold to Mexico each year.

Mr. Blatchford pointed out that the United States had three choices. It could stop importing the cars from Mexico and continue to sustain the tremendous injury to the economy in general and to the agricultural producers in particular that was arising from the car shortage. It could retain the 18 percent import duty on the cars and pass the cost on to the railroad users and ultimately to the American consumer in the form of higher prices, thus adding to the U.S. inflation problem. Finally, it could remedy a situation detrimental to both the United States and Mexico by suspending the duty on the Mexican railroad cars.

These arguments were accurate, to the point, and by and large well received. For a time everything went along smoothly. Appropriate legislation passed the Senate and seemed about to pass the House, but suddenly it died. The legislation of benefit to two countries somehow was just never voted on. The rumor was that the opposition came from a single congressman, the chairman of one of the more powerful committees in the House, who had been contacted by one of his constituents who was in the business of manufacturing railroad cars. When this congressman learned of his constituent's lack of enthusiasm for competing with the Mexican manufacturer's capacity for prompt delivery, he used his considerable influence to kill the bill. American railroads, farmers, and consumers could simply wait until some U.S. manufacturer could supply the cars in their own sweet time and meanwhile do without the shipment of goods.

In early 1979 the American boxcar situation was growing steadily worse. The *Journal of Commerce* reported that the back orders for railroad cars to American suppliers had tripled in the previous year, from 30,000 cars to about 90,000. The purchase of the cars from Mexico was overwhelmingly supported by agricultural groups—the American Farm Bureau Federation, the National Wheat Growers, the Fertilizer Institute, etc.—but to no avail. The issue reached "the highest levels of government" when it was placed on the list of items to be discussed between Presidents Carter and López Portillo during Carter's trip to Mexico in February 1979.

The concern of the Mexican government over the matter arose from several sources. Mexican manufacturers had gone to considerable lengths to meet the standards of the American Association of Railroads and had successfully negotiated the sale with U.S. railroad companies. Then the deal was blocked by what seemed to be the whimsical, certainly petty considerations of a single congressman. Mexicans have long been cynical about the willingness of the United States to do business with them, and for good reason. The boxcar deal, as well as other botched negotiations, has forced them also to wonder about the ability of the United States to negotiate a business deal. A final irony is that while all this was going on, $200 million worth of food purchased in the United States by Mexico was going undelivered because there were no railcars to carry the goods.

By the summer of 1979, when the backlog of railcar orders had topped 130,000 and a car ordered then could not be delivered until 1982, some positive things had begun to happen. Senators of both parties and of such diverse viewpoints as Lloyd Bentsen of Texas, Jacob Javits of New York, Robert Dole of Kansas, and Max Baucus of Montana had submitted legislation that would relieve the problem. Also, the Association of American Railroads was actively supporting the bill, and their lobbying efforts were expected to be successful. Still, the handful of car manufacturers were expected to repeat their performance of 1978 and attempt to kill the legislation by quickly pressuring key members of Congress. One close observer of the situation said of the manufacturers, "Their motto is 'let the grain rot in the silos until we can deliver the cars.' "

In the June 1978 issue of the United States–Mexico Chamber of Commerce's *Washington Letter* there were three important stories. The lead article was about the loss of GSP treatment for the Mexican railcars. On page three was a short notice that the Carter Administration was considering the creation of a "Border Control Agency" by transferring most of the enforcement activities of the Immigration and Naturalization Service out of the Justice Department to the Treasury Department and joining them with the Customs Service "to provide a more effective control policy of border problems, such as the illegal alien flow . . ." The third item was the report of the introduction into the Senate of a bill that would charge employers as much as a $1,000 civil penalty for each illegal alien hired.

These items represented two attempts to do something about the problem of the illegal-alien worker—one by governmental reorganization and another by holding the employer responsible if he encouraged law-breaking—and one failure to try something that might help—the buying of Mexican goods sorely needed in the United States that cannot be supplied by U.S. manufacturers and workers. No single act will solve the problem of the illegal-alien flow, but the purchases of the Mexican railroad cars would certainly have employed Mexican workers in Mexico who might otherwise have to look north for a chance for employment and survival. The Mexican reaction to all this may well be imagined.

The Promise and Problems of Mexican Oil

There is one new element in Mexico that potentially could have profound effects both on the emigration from that nation to the United States and on economic and political relations between the two countries. That factor is the huge deposit of petroleum that has been discovered in southern Mexico. The size of the reserve was completely unknown until very recently. As late as 1972 Mexican planners were still expecting their country to be a net importer of oil in the 1980s. On March 18, 1978, the fortieth anniversary of the nationalization of the oil fields in Mexico, the director of PEMEX (the national oil company), Jorge Díaz Serrano, referring to the recently discovered oil reserves, announced, "We are sitting on a sea of oil." By September 1978, President José López Portillo felt justified in telling the Mexican Congress that Mexican oil reserves were as large as those of Saudi Arabia. Others have estimated that the Mexican reserves are as large as those of the entire Near East.

Later, in May 1979, there were some voices suggesting that the reserves might be more modest, something of the size of those on Alaska's North Slope. According to the *Los Angeles Times,* the analysts who were expressing this view included "key U.S. government officials, American geologists who are experts on Mexico's oil, [and] former and current high-ranking Mexican oil-industry officials . . . ." The only person named by the *Times* was James W. Watson, senior vice-president of DeGolyer and MacNaughton, a Dallas, Texas, firm hired by Mexico to certify its oil discoveries. Watson did not specify any particular size for the reserves, but was quoted only as saying, "We've reminded (the Mexicans) over and over about the danger of losing credibility. We've been trying to hold them back." In any event, the prospect of oil and gas in abundance has opened a new debate in Mexico over pricing and export policies and ironically has provided a new source of potential conflict with the United States.

PEMEX does not yet know exactly how much oil is actually in the new reserve and is hesitant to admit everything it does know. It is extremely difficult to know precisely what is in an oil field.

There are three ways to calculate oil reserves: *proven*—oil whose location and quantity has been established by drilling, and which can be produced at a profit with current technology; *probable*—oil thought to exist in extensions of known fields, but not yet confirmed by drilling, and producible economically with current technology; and *potential*—oil in fields not yet discovered but whose presence is suggested by geological evidence, or in known fields but recoverable only with new technology and/or at higher prices. Changes in technology and prices can change both potential and probable reserves to proven ones. Thousands of wells and even whole fields abandoned 50 years ago in both Mexico and the United States are back in production today because, with the increase in the price of oil and new techniques, more of the oil can be recovered at a profit.

In late 1978 PEMEX announced that Mexico had proven reserves of 40.1 billion barrels (a barrel is equal to 42 gallons), and observers expect the estimates to be raised again. The current estimate puts Mexico ahead of both Venezuela and Nigeria, both members of the Organization of Petroleum Exporting Countries (OPEC), but still behind Saudi Arabia with a proven reserve of 160 billion barrels. When President López Portillo spoke of Mexican reserves exceeding those of Saudi Arabia, he was talking about the *potential* reserves. Mexico's deposit thus far has been much less exhaustively explored than that of Saudi Arabia.

No one knows how much Mexican oil will end up on the world market, but clearly there will be a large amount. In early 1979, Mexico's oil production was increasing faster than expected and had reached 1.3 million barrels a day. The United States was Mexico's biggest customer, importing about 30 percent of the production.

Because of the oil, many Mexicans believe at this moment that an end to their problems is at hand. The headline in Mexico City's *La Prensa* for October 30, 1978, was:

Trabajo Para Todos los Mexicanos
Puede lograrse con los recursos petroleros: LP
(Work for every Mexican
It can be done with the oil resources: López Portillo)

The same day, Dr. Victor Urquidi, president of the prestigious Colegio de Mexico, told us that the oil revenues, for the first time in Mexican history, would allow his country to pursue its plans for development without depending on foreign capital. Mexico would be free to chart its own course, and Dr. Urquidi seemed to feel that this alone would go far toward solving Mexico's present problems.

This optimism is not limited to Mexico. U.S. Immigration and Naturalization Commissioner Leonel Castillo told us in August 1978 that he saw the population pressure on the southern U.S. border as a temporary concern because of the drop in Mexican fertility rates and the developmental potential of the newly found oil. We hope this optimism will prove justified, but have our doubts.

Others have also expressed caution, even in Mexico. A reader who went past the jubilant headline of La Prensa's article would have seen that what President López Portillo actually said was, "If we have the wisdom to manage the oil resources properly, the possibility exists that there will be work for every Mexican *by the beginning of the next century*" (emphasis added). PEMEX director Jorge Díaz Serrano said, "It must be considered an absolute error for Mexicans to pin all their hopes for progress on the oil industry." Dr. Urquidi did not imply that, even with their own capital, Mexicans would find it easy to achieve their goals.

Still, optimism is contagious and not only in Mexico. Great Britain, where industrialism was invented, is looking out over the storm-wracked waters of the North Sea, expecting the oil there to solve the problems of its decrepit social and economic system. The North Sea oil reserves are trivial compared with those of Mexico and so difficult to recover that they would have been mapped and ignored a generation ago.

The history of Western civilization for the last 200 years has been largely a history of bonanzas, and these sudden booms of wealth have often done little for the people on and under whose land the resources were discovered. More gold has been taken from the mines of South Africa in this century than was previously extracted from all the Earth since the first man picked up a nugget, and the wealth of South African diamond mines is legendary. In spite of this, there are few in the world, other than the South Africans, who believe that their society will survive the closing years of this century. The South Africans admit that they can survive only through measures repugnant to the rest of the world and by relying on a set of religious views repudiated by all but a tiny number of the rest of the world Christian community. The South Africans did not have the wisdom to use their gold or diamonds to finance the construction of a racially harmonious society when it was clear to everyone else that racial disharmony would destroy them. They have used their wealth and are still using it to sow the seeds of their own destruction.

In a single generation at the end of the last century, the Chileans and Peruvians squandered deposits of organic phosphates that had been built up over thousands of years. This wealth was conspicuously consumed in lavish homes and extravagant life-styles for a few. When the phosphate deposits were gone, the homes fell into decay, and today the graceless extravagance is only dimly remembered.

When the world started riding bicycles and later driving automobiles, the need for pneumatic tires created a rubber boom. The wild rubber trees of the upper Amazon were one of the few sources. The city of Manaus flourished, and life there was very elegant. The great opera companies of Europe traveled across the sea and 1,000 kilometers up the Amazon to perform in the opera house, then the most opulent and up-to-date in the world. Then came the domesticated plantation production of natural rubber in Malaya and elsewhere and finally the petroleum-based synthetics. Now Manaus finds its elegant opera house an expensive burden to maintain, but too beautiful to tear down.

No country in the world has experienced mineral booms as numerous or as rich as Mexico's. The gold and silver that poured out of the Viceroyalty of New Spain revolutionized the economy of Europe, ornamented the Vatican, financed the Great Armada that Sir Francis Drake and the storms of the English Channel and the North Sea demolished, and allowed the Spanish to wage a war in Holland in such a way that, 400 years later, they are still hated there. Spain today is one of the most impoverished nations of Europe. For Mexico the gold only financed the arrogant *gachupin* bureaucrat of Church and state who, regardless of his motives, only repressed and exploited those under him. Porfirio Díaz saw the wealth of Mexico and wanted it developed. He sponsored the first oil boom by inviting in the foreigners to show the Mexicans how to develop it. By 1921 Mexico was the second largest oil-producing nation in the world, but the fields were exploited for the needs of the market and the profits of the oil companies, and none of the wealth seemed to stay in Mexico. It took 20 years, much diplomatic skill, and great courage by a succession of Mexican presidents to get the foreigners out.

"Development," in the sense of creating social and economic institutions that enrich the lives of a nation's people, requires money, and the Mexican oil will bring that. But it also requires knowledge and wisdom that none of the other oil-rich, third-world countries has seemed able to create from within or buy from abroad. Has oil made life simple and easy for Iranians?

A comparison of two Latin American republics is illustrative. Venezuela, a member of OPEC, has had a steady flow of oil revenue for 40 years and because of it in 1978 had a per-capita gross national product of $2,570, the highest in the region. Costa Rica has no oil and its 1978 per-capita GNP was only $1,040.

However, when a baby is born in Costa Rica, its life expectancy is 68 years, while one born in Venezuela has an expectancy of 65 years. Out of every 1,000 babies born, 38 will die during infancy in Costa Rica, but 49 will die in Venezuela. Which is the poorer country?

An immediate problem with oil wealth in developing countries is that there is very little need for untrained workers in the development of oil fields or the building or operation of petrochemical plants. Once the fields and plants are operating, even fewer people are needed to keep them running, and those few have to be highly trained. One observer, David Gordon, pointed out that a half-billion-dollar investment in a natural gas processing complex in Chiapas is supplying 5,000 workers with short-term employment during the construction period, but it will give permanent employment to only 2,000 when it is completed. Thus, this complex requires a quarter-million dollars to create a job for a single worker. Political scientist Wayne Cornelius has pointed out that in its initial phases the oil bonanza may actually slow down the process of job creation because the capital being invested in petroleum might otherwise have been spent in industries where the same amount would have created many more jobs.

Another problem with oil in developing countries is that these countries do not have capital of their own with which to develop their resources, so initially they have to borrow from foreign sources. Since foreign obligations must be paid back first, or there will be no more funds forthcoming, the initial revenues go into interest and principal payments. After a few years, of course, this is no problem, but it means that the money does not start rolling in when the first oil is sent out of the country.

Mexico expects to receive $8 billion a year from foreign sales of oil by 1980 and then to maintain production and foreign sales at that level indefinitely. This is enough, or so the planners calculate, to wipe out Mexico's foreign-trade deficit, owed mostly to the United States, to make interest and principal payments on the development loans, and to buy whatever is needed from outside Mexico to carry on an orderly program of development. It is intended that the rest of the oil and gas will just stay in the ground, where it has been for 130 million years, until Mexico needs it.

All third-world oil producers suffer from the problem of foreign meddling, and Mexico's long history as a victim of foreign interference, even when it was not an oil superpower, does not bode well for its future. In August 1978, Zbigniew Brzezinski, National Security Advisor to President Carter, wrote "Presidential Review Memorandum 41," which called for a general reconsideration of relations with Mexico, including "potential U.S.

inducements to influence PEMEX to expand production capacity." In the first two years of the Carter Administration, Vice President Mondale, Secretary of State Vance, Secretary of the Treasury Blumenthal, and UN Ambassador Young all visited Mexico, but little resulted in terms of settling issues between the two countries.

The first attempt by the Carter Administration to work out a purchase of Mexican energy ended in disaster. After long and careful negotiation between six natural-gas distributors in the United States and PEMEX, and after a pipeline from Chiapas to the U.S. border was nearing completion, Secretary of Energy James Schlesinger vetoed the deal. It seems that PEMEX, cheeky fellows that they are, wanted to be paid the going price in the world market. Secretary Schlesinger rejected the price as too high—partly because it would be embarrassing to pay Mexico more than is paid for Canadian gas. But Schlesinger publicly stated that Mexico "has to sell us the gas sooner or later," thus showing that, where Mexico is concerned, little had changed in Washington since the Taft and Wilson administrations. Schlesinger fanned the embers of anti-gringoism in Mexico and very nearly made himself useless for future dealings with the Mexican government or PEMEX.

As a potential big customer, the U.S. does have some bargaining power. The price the American distributors were willing to pay, $2.60 per thousand cubic feet, would have given PEMEX a net profit of $2.20. But if the Mexicans had to liquefy the gas and send it to European markets by ship, they would make only about 27 cents per thousand cubic feet. Thus Mexico could well afford to drop its price for the U.S. market. If this line had been pursued quietly and with the same courtesy normally paid to Japanese or European trading partners, something could probably have been worked out.

But since the negotiators were dealing with Mexicans, decorum and good manners were forgotten. As an article in *Forbes* described it:

> The State Department gratuitously reminded Mexican representatives of the problems the U.S. had with their country—illegal aliens coming over the U.S. border, marijuana coming into the U.S. Senator Adlai Stevenson (D-Ill.) stupidly blocked the Export-Import Bank credit for the pipeline. In all the U.S. acted more like a banana republic than the world's greatest democracy.

Stevenson was trying to put pressure on the Mexicans to give in to U.S. price demands; he thought no one else would lend the

Mexicans money if the United States would not. But Stevenson was wrong. In 1978 PEMEX was able to borrow $200 million from French banks, more than $104 million from Japanese banks, and $1 billion from an international consortium.

Schlesinger was wrong, too. Mexico does not have to sell the gas to the United States or to anyone else; it can consume a lot of it internally. The pipeline that was to take the Chiapas gas to the United States indeed has been diverted to take it to Mexican cities. Much of the gas can be left in the ground, and what is yielded as a by-product of oil production can be "flared off" in the fields—that is, simply piped off into the air and set afire. Every day 300 million cubic feet of gas is being flared off. This means that twice a month gas sufficient to supply the energy needs of the state of Vermont for an entire year is wasted. If this seems outrageous and unconscionable, remember that the United States Government frequently pays American farmers not to grow food while Mexican children go hungry.

In his speech on the fortieth anniversary of the nationalization of the oil companies in Mexico, Díaz Serrano said:

> We are exploring and finding reserves which will be used in the twenty-first century because we have already found the petroleum that Mexico will consume during the present century.

The date of this remark was not coincidental, for the battle cry of the struggle for nationalization was "El petroleo es nuestro (The oil is ours)."

In February 1979, President Carter went to Mexico with several important issues to discuss, primarily the purchase of oil and gas, the problem of illegal migration, and the problem of drug traffic. In their first luncheon together, President López Portillo expressed his country's feelings toward its powerful neighbor:

> Among permanent, not casual, neighbors, surprise moves and sudden deceit or abuse are poisonous fruits that sooner or later have a reverse effect. . . .
> Mexico has thus [because of the oil discovery] suddenly found itself the center of American attention—attention that is a surprising mixture of interest, disdain and fear, much like the recurring vague fears you yourselves inspire in certain areas of our national subconscious. . . .

Perhaps President Carter was taken aback by these reproachful remarks, perhaps he was just trying to lighten the serious mood, but his response was not altogether appropriate. In his toast, he explained that he had taken up jogging some years earlier in

Mexico City when he discovered he was "afflicted with Montezuma's revenge." Mexican newspapers greeted their president's comments with enthusiastic praise; American newspapers found their president's performance dismaying.

The meeting thereafter proceeded more smoothly but produced no concrete results: both sides announced plans for continued negotiations on the three important issues. Despite pressure from Washington to press Mexico to increase its oil-production capacity above planned levels, mainly because of the interrupted supply of oil from Iran, Carter only expressed his country's willingness to purchase more oil should it become available.

The Mexican oil bonanza is not going to make an immediate difference within the Mexican society and economy of a sort that will change the pattern of migration across the Mexican–U.S. border that now has endured for so long. Perhaps in five or ten years, there may be a noticeable change, but, in the words of President López Portillo, only "If we have the wisdom . . ." In order to solve its problems, Mexico will have to devise and execute a plan by which the oil wealth builds something valuable and enduring. No OPEC country has yet succeeded in doing this. If any of the populous OPEC countries, Nigeria, Venezuela, or Iran, for example, were cheek by jowl with the United States as Mexico is, there would be a problem with illegal aliens from those countries.

It is not at all clear now what kind of deal the United States may be able to strike with Mexico over its oil and gas. What is clear is that it will have to be a deal in which Mexico is a full partner and it will have to be done quickly before more damage is done to relations between the two countries. The U.S. will have to open its borders to Mexican products other than coffee and tomatoes (its leading exports today other than petroleum). Railroad cars are just one example. Mexico wants to produce high-quality manufactured goods that will be competitive on world markets in addition to commodities. For instance, Mexicans look forward to the day when Americans buy Chevrolets and Fords made in Mexico just as they now buy cars manufactured in Canada. Mexicans can be expected to demand new trade arrangements with the U.S. because they feel they *must* have them in order to develop their own industry.

On the other hand, the United States needs Mexico's oil. The United States now imports about nine million barrels of oil *a day*. If the U.S. gets the maximum expected from Mexico—60 percent of some two million exported barrels a day by around 1985—that would be roughly 15 percent of U.S. oil imports then. Even if

Mexico sold every drop of its 40 billion barrels of proven reserves to the U.S., that would keep the American economy going for about a dozen years at present consumption rates. If the potential reserves in Mexico were 200 billion barrels and if every drop proved recoverable and were sold to the U.S., it would keep the economy going at those rates 60 years. But no matter how much oil there is in Mexico or in the earth, it will give out, sooner or later. The most *any* oil bonanza can offer, regardless of its size, is an extension of time for overdeveloped countries like the United States to adjust to an industry and a society not based on oil as the primary energy source.

Whether the oil bonanza will prove a blessing or a disaster for Mexico remains to be seen. If the foreign meddling can be kept under control, and if the proceeds can be used for the benefit of the people, rather than to enrich a small elite, Mexican optimism may not be misplaced. If this happens, there may eventually be fewer Mexicans needing to go north just to find work and keep their families alive. On the other hand, if the hopes and promises are not fulfilled, the migrant flow will probably not be stemmed; indeed it might accelerate.

Viewed in a positive light, Mexico's oil reserve presents a splendid opportunity for both the United States and Mexico. Mexico needs much that America can produce: technology and hardware for development and agricultural commodities. Mexico also needs jobs. The United States can employ Mexicans either by admitting them within its borders or by admitting Mexican products and commodities on more favorable terms—or both. Whatever happens, though, the effects will not be immediate. Neither Mexico nor the United States can afford to wait for oil wealth to solve (or worsen) the migration problem.

[5]

THE "WETBACK MENACE"

THE basic preconception that shapes the usual view of American immigration history is that everyone wants to come to the U.S. and that everyone who comes wants to stay. This view is contradicted by official but little-known U.S. Government figures which show that about 40 percent of all immigrants who came to the United States between 1900 and 1940 chose to go back home or on to some other country, and that perhaps a third of today's immigrants do not stay here. Much as Americans would like to imagine the United States as the City on the Hill, the Beacon to the World, the facts indicate something much more modest.

FAIRY TALES AND FACTS

Myths cloud the historical vision necessary to evaluate the national experience and build sound and lasting policy. In regard to immigration from Mexico, the cloud of myth becomes an impenetrable fog, because the false view of immigration history becomes mixed up with *la leyenda negra*—ancient prejudice against Hispanic peoples. The blending of myth and prejudice does not lead to an historical perspective, but to a fairy tale in which Americans are snow-white princes and princesses while Mexicans are a nation of wicked witches.

An essential ingredient of any good fairy tale is the ill-defined evil against which the good folk must struggle. In the first part of the story, all is happy and the good folk are living in well-deserved harmony and comfort. Then wickedness and evil appear. This threat is powerful and ominous, and most of the tale is devoted to the innocent, good folk evading the awful force. Toward the end,

175

though, they turn on it and through pluck and purity destroy it. This scenario is comfortable because it is familiar, and it is repeated over and over—with John Wayne as the cavalry colonel or frontier sheriff, Robert Blake or Angie Dickinson as big-city cops, or the eternal Captain Kirk aboard the starship *Enterprise*. It was Oscar Wilde who pointed out that life imitates art—that is, people live out experiences and view the world in terms of the themes they have seen portrayed on the stage or in books.

The fairy-tale scenario appears on the page, screen, and television tube to form the American view of the world, past and present. It pretty well explains the popular view of the United States' participation in World War II, for instance, and shaped the view Americans had of themselves during the cold-war era of the 1950s. The scenario was acted out with grace and style by John and Robert Kennedy and reported by the press under the title "The Cuban Missile Crisis" and emerged again to form the story line of *All The President's Men*.

The impact of the motion picture on how people view the world is powerful, and nowhere is it more powerful than in shaping the American view of Mexico and Mexicans. At the turn of the last century, events on the South Texas border created the concept of the "good Mexican" and the "bad Mexican." This simple idea has been embraced by motion-picture writers and it has served them well.

For example, *The Magnificent Seven* was adapted from a Japanese film, *The Seven Samurai*, which was based on a Japanese folk tale. In this story a peasant village, which has been victimized for many years by the local outlaw chieftain, hires a group of warriors for protection. In *The Seven Samurai* the three basic character-types—victims, victimizers, and ambivalent saviors—are presented as products of Japanese culture. In the American adaptation, the saviors are from north of the border, and the victims and victimizers are Mexicans—good (read "weak") Mexicans and bad Mexicans. Of course, the good (read "strong") Americans do their job (with glorious carnage) and ride off, leaving the good Mexicans safe and secure.

The Greeks went to the theater to see themselves and their flaws laid out before them and to be reminded that failure to know one's self would ultimately lead to disaster for individuals and for peoples; good theater still has a sizable element of this. In contrast, much that is in the movies and on television is intended to help people avoid this kind of self-confrontation.

In fact, the success of Americans and industrial peoples in general does not arise from individuals and small groups bravely riding into the fray with courage and élan. The success of Americans and the rest of the industrial world in imposing their way on others stems in no small part from the compliance of faceless, corporate men fitting themselves into vast bureaucratic organizations and mindlessly executing directions that they seldom understand. The characterizations in movies set in the Mexican borderlands help people obscure from themselves just how dreary they are. Drama proceeds most smoothly through the use of stock characters—personalities already familiar to the viewer. Let a short, swarthy man carrying a guitar and wearing a serape walk up to a tall, fair-skinned man carrying a revolver and wearing a Stetson and say, "Are you the gringo we have been expecting?" and a good ten minutes of character development have been saved, and the action can proceed. Yet when life imitates art, and people begin to respond in everyday life and in governmental policy to others as if they were stock characters out of the movies, we enter a world of psychotic delusion. In the end incredible damage can be done and lives can even be lost.

Americans have long been under the delusion that Mexicans are a threat. No army has ever invaded us from Mexico, though armies from Canada have. Some incursions that took place from Mexico during the chaos of their Revolution were accidental, such as the shelling of Douglas, Arizona, and El Paso, Texas. Others were of only local significance, such as Villa at Columbus, New Mexico, or the raiders of the Plan of San Diego in South Texas. While there is no doubt that the behavior of the Mexicans was provocative, it certainly was not threatening.

While almost every major espionage case since the Second World War has uncovered evidence of laxness on the Canadian border and among Canadian authorities, not a single important Soviet agent is known to have entered the United States through Mexico. Still, Americans mistrust and feel threatened by the Mexicans.

The "threat" from Mexican immigration has two of the necessary characteristics of the classic, fairy-tale evil: it is of unknown size and unknown character. Consequently anyone who wants to can frighten himself or herself into pure delight, just as children do in enjoying the false fear of the fairy tale. In the fairy-tale land of government policy and administration, nothing is as welcome as public fright over an unspecified evil. Witches, Communists, gay teachers, poisoned pot, and invisible hordes of Mexicans give irresponsible politicians and bureaucrats unlimited opportunities for posturing and allow them to neglect thornier public problems of known magnitude and difficult solution.

*The Creation of the Tale**

In the mid-1970s, during the Nixon-Ford administration, the Immigration and Naturalization Service (INS) presented hypothetical—really invented—figures as fact. The usual spokesman was the Commissioner himself, Leonard F. Chapman Jr., a career Marine Corps officer who had retired as commandant. The following statements from an INS news release, dated December 8, 1975, were typical of what was being authoritatively presented around that time and is still too widely believed:

> Independent studies done for the Immigration and Naturalization Service indicate illegal aliens cost taxpayers about $13 billion or more annually, INS said today.
> Commissioner Leonard F. Chapman, Jr., said the cost to the United States of the illegal alien problem may run as high as $16 billion a year, and is increasing by $500 million each year.
> The cost figures are based upon findings in a policy analysis done for the Immigration Service by Richard G. Darman . . . a principal in ICF, Incorporated, a Washington D.C. firm which specializes in public policy development . . .
> The analysis also states that the number of illegal aliens is conservatively estimated to be increasing by about 250,000 per year or more . . .

Further on, the news release says:

> An earlier study done for INS by Lesko Associates, Inc. estimated the number of illegal aliens in the nation at 8 million. At least 80 per cent or more are adults, indicating an annual tax burden of $13 billion or higher.

What General Chapman and his Immigration Service did not tell the press and the public was that Mr. Darman, in a letter to the INS of December 4, 1975, upon which the news release was based, specifically stated that:

> Currently available statistics do not permit reliable determination of the number of illegal aliens in the country, or of the percent of these in the labor market or on welfare . . .
> As with the estimates of the number of illegal aliens, estimates of the costs of illegal aliens are, of course, highly uncertain.

---

*The problem of estimating the illegal population is very complex, and only part of the story is told in the text. Those interested in more details should refer to the extended discussion of some points included in the notes to this and the next section.

Few informed observers agree with Mr. Darman's assessment of the economic burden of illegals. He seemed to assume that every job done by an illegal was one that otherwise would be done by an unemployed citizen or lawful resident, completely ignoring the way the illegals subsidize the economy through their cheap labor and the taxes they pay for services they rarely receive. Still, it was not Mr. Darman who sensationalized his work and gave it to the newspapers. That was done by General Chapman and his subordinates. A member of the INS statistical section told us in 1978 that General Chapman asked him and others in the section to justify the numbers he was giving to the press only after they had been published. General Chapman was then told by his own subordinates that his figures were totally unjustifiable.

Why did General Chapman and others in the INS launch this propaganda campaign? One explanation that has been suggested—and it is not without merit—is that General Chapman perceived a growing problem in the INS, namely its inability to cope with the flow of illegals into the United States as well as the many other problems of the Service. Those problems simply could not be met with the existing budget. After trying unsuccessfully to get some attention from his boss, the Attorney General, and from the White House, he gave up in frustration and decided to make such a fuss that the problem could not be ignored. According to one well-informed student of immigration and the INS, there was wide agreement that the INS was underfunded and General Chapman determined to use "the undocumented aliens issue to crystallize that agreement into increased budget."

It is important to remember that in those days Attorneys General came and went like migrant farm laborers. Richard Nixon spent most of his time holed up in the White House not talking to anyone, and his successor, Gerald Ford, was preoccupied by the task of gaining election to the office he held. It was not an easy time to do business in Washington, and General Chapman had some business to do. The problem he was addressing in the INS was very real, but the higher authorities of government were ignoring it. Apprehensions of illegals had gone up from 400,000 to almost 800,000 per year between 1970 and 1974, and almost all of the increase was from the Mexican border. Because the INS was then, and remains, a low-prestige agency in the government, it was hard to get the attention of anyone important in the executive branch or in Congress. So General Chapman went to the press in order to get the attention that his problem deserved.

The real news about illegals was that no one knew much about the problem, but the media picked up on General Chapman's remarks, elaborated on them, and started pouring out nice round numbers. For instance, in early 1978 *Newsweek* assured its readers that "Texas . . . has perhaps 50,000 school-age illegal aliens . . ." While giving age-specific data on the illegal-alien population is remarkable enough, they also predicted the future, for elsewhere they asserted that "about 1.5 million Mexicans are expected to slip into the U.S. in 1978." A few months earlier, *Newsweek* declared that the number of illegal aliens who entered this country prior to 1970 and are still here "totals no more than 500,000 persons." Almost a year later, in January 1979, *Newsweek* was still mesmerized by big, round, inaccurate numbers. According to the magazine, "a fresh flow of about one million immigrants, legal and illegal," was entering the United States each year from Mexico. There was no indication of where this fanciful figure might have come from.

The next step in creating a fairy tale out of a real problem came when serious men and women, many of them concerned about population growth in the United States, were misled by what they thought were carefully calculated, authoritative figures. Melanie Wirken, director of the immigration program for Zero Population Growth in the mid-1970s, declared that 800,000 illegal immigrants per year were entering the country. Her source was General Chapman. Garrett Hardin, professor of Human Ecology at the University of California, Santa Barbara, wrote in the summer of 1977 that "numerous students of the problem (in government and out) estimate the true number of illegals [entering annually] is not less than 800,000 and may be more than 1,200,000." By the following December, Hardin had raised his estimate to 1.7 million, though qualifying it by saying that "hard data are hard to come by." Again, General Chapman was given as the source.

The promulgation of made-up numbers was not the only example of destructive carelessness. *Newsweek* headlined its article on the schooling of illegal-immigrant children in Texas thus: "Aliens: A Right to School?" It did not say "Illegal Aliens," it read just "Aliens." There are over four million aliens residing legally in the United States, most of them admitted on the basis of his or her capacity to benefit the United States. Surely the editors of *Newsweek* do not question the right of legal-resident alien children to go to the public schools.

The practice of issuing big round figures for the numbers of illegals in the country and for the estimates of their social cost soon infected state governments, particularly those with a history of animosity toward Hispanics. In 1978 it was reported that officials of the State of Texas were saying that the cost of educating illegal-alien children that year was $50 million. While the INS did not know how many illegal aliens there were in Texas or anywhere else, Texas officials were throwing around big numbers on how much they were costing. In Dallas the schools started turning away children who could not prove citizenship or legal-alien status, and to the east, in Tyler, school officials were charging $90 per month tuition to children who could not properly identify themselves (a practice that was finally suspended under a court challenge in 1979). In 1975 the Texas legislature forbade the paying of state aid to schools for students who could not establish their residential status. Unfortunately, there are places in Texas where no public official has ever been convinced of anything by anyone with a Spanish accent.

In 1975 over 11 percent of the aliens apprehended for being illegally in the United States—more than 85,000 persons—were subsequently found to have earned the right to remain. Do you suppose the school officials in Tyler refunded the $90-a-month tuition payments in these cases? Did the authorities in Austin pay the withheld state aid to the districts?

Needless to say, the State of Texas takes the taxes paid by illegal aliens, and their employers take the products of their labors. It is only education for the children that requires proof of citizenship or status of residence. It would be interesting to know how many of the students hounded out of school in Texas are native-born children of native-born parents whose skin color and manner of speech do not measure up to the standards of the Anglo policy-makers on who deserves schooling. The situation is only too reminiscent of the West Coast nonaliens (read United States citizens) of Japanese descent who were ousted from their homes and had their property stolen in 1942 at the whim of white policy-makers. Is it possible that in the term "illegal alien," the bigots in Texas and elsewhere in the Southwest have found a new way of yelling "Greaser"?

The illegal-immigrant problem is not a problem only of Mexicans, of course, although everyone agrees that Mexicans are by far the largest group in it. It is now customary to say that 60 to 80 percent of the illegals in the United States are Mexican and that the preponderance of the rest are from the Caribbean basin. Nor are illegal immigrants limited to the American Southwest. There is a large population of illegals in New York City, for example, some 80 percent of whom are thought to be from Peru, Colombia, Ecuador, and the Dominican Republic, and the remainder from other Caribbean countries. These Hispanic peoples are concentrated in the lower East Side and upper West Side of Manhattan, East Harlem, and other neighborhoods in Brooklyn and Queens. Like their Mexican counterparts in the Southwest, the Eastern illegals work in light manufacturing, wait on tables or bus dishes in restaurants, carry bags at hotels, and do other jobs that are relatively low-paying.

The other nationalities among the illegal-alien population are used, sometimes in ignorance and sometimes in cynicism, to mask the need for a special immigration policy toward Mexico because of its special relationship to the United States. That Mexico is one of the two nations that touch the U.S. and that well over half of the illegals are Mexicans seem overpowering arguments for a specific policy for immigration from Mexico. The argument is even stronger when one considers the degree of United States economic involvement in Mexico and its long tradition of sitting as moral judge and earthly corrector of Mexican political affairs.

COUNTING THE UNCOUNTABLE, OR HOW MANY ILLEGALS ARE THERE, ANYHOW?

The question of how many illegals there are in this country is really two questions. How many are coming in? And how many are present at any given moment? No one knows the answers to these questions and no one is very close to finding out. In studies of this kind, the number of illegals in the United States (or any other base population) is rather inelegantly called by demographers the "stock." The numbers coming in and going out are called the "flow." Obviously, when the inflow is greater than the outflow, the stock grows bigger, and when the outflow is greater, the stock grows smaller. Thus the two questions are distinct but related to one another.

The inflow is usually calculated some way or other from the only real piece of hard data available, the reports on apprehensions of deportable aliens as published in Table 23 of the *Annual Reports* of the INS. The numbers published there increased from 423,000 in 1971 to over a million in 1978. This might seem to mean that, in 1971, 423,000 individuals were picked up for being in the United States illegally and that, in 1978, the number was over a million. It does not. The figures actually refer to the number of INS Forms I-213, "Record of Deportable Alien," counted in Washington each year. An I-213 is not an arrest report; one may be filled out on suspicion, hearsay, or rumor. I-213s are filled out on the crewmen of foreign aircraft and ships who stay in the country longer than scheduled. Furthermore, a separate I-213 is filled out each time an illegal is apprehended.

A man sneaking into the country who is caught on the north bank of the Rio Grande at Brownsville, or the Black Bridge at El Paso, or in Travel Lodge Canyon near San Diego, will have an

I-213 filled out and be back in Mexico before breakfast, free to try again and perhaps be apprehended again the next night. One man was caught at El Paso and ejected five times in one day, accounting for five I-213s. The Chula Vista Border Patrol Station near San Diego apprehended 33,000 illegals in April of 1978. What this really means is that the agents at the station filled out 33,000 I-213s, which might, for example, indicate that 16,500 illegals were each caught an average of twice. Thus when someone says that the INS "caught" a million illegals last year, this does not meant that hands were laid on a million individual illegals.

Even if it did, however, what would the number caught indicate about the number who get through? It is usually argued that for every individual caught, thus-and-so-many get through. The multiplier is generally a matter of judgment by the person who is talking. The closer one is to the border, the higher the guess on the number who get through. Numbers as high as ten to one are mentioned, though the usual figure is two or three to one.

The stated job of the Border Patrol is to *prevent* the illegal entry of aliens into the United States, as well as to apprehend them after they get in. Of course, prompt apprehension of illegals and repatriation to their source countries is one method of prevention, but not the only one. In mid-1978 and continuing on into 1979, the Chula Vista Border Patrol Station shifted its emphasis from an "apprehension mode" of operation to a "prevention mode." In seeking to prevent entry, agents are deployed right along the line, keeping themselves highly visible in positions where a group of would-be illegals might try to cross. The object is to discourage them from trying. In apprehension mode, agents are placed some distance behind the line (though only a few hundred yards farther back, and seldom more than a mile) in order to maneuver in front of any group that has already crossed over. Once illegals are within the United States, they can be "apprehended."

Obviously, a Border Patrol unit working in apprehension mode would turn in many more I-213s than one operating in prevention mode, but this would not necessarily mean that they were doing a better or worse job of preventing the flow of illegal aliens into the United States. This is just one more reason to be very cautious in interpreting apprehension figures for their meaning in the overall picture of illegal immigration into the United States and the effectiveness of the INS enforcement effort.

The people who sneak across the border are not the entire flow. A considerable number of illegals pass fraudulently through regular ports of entry, though, again, no one knows how many. In 1975–76 the INS intensified its inspection at 10 major U.S. airports, which accounted for 85 percent of the alien air arrivals in

1974, and at 15 crossing points along the Mexican border, which handled 95 percent of the incoming traffic that year. The purpose of this was to find out how many fraudulent entries there were. According to Charles Keely, a demographer with the Population Council, the inspectors involved in the study "were free from the usual time pressures to expedite inspection and avoid traveler delay, and they inspected entrants carefully for fraudulent documents and intent to violate visa terms."

At the Roma, Texas, crossing point, regular inspectors normally discovered fraud in one inspection out of each 251,920. The inspectors involved in the special study, however, came up with the rate of one fraud out of every 642 inspections. Actually, the special inspectors made 1,284 inspections and found two cases of fraud. From this and experience elsewhere, the conclusion was drawn that half a million people were entering the country fraudulently each year. In a classic understatement, Keely allowed that "It is difficult to have much confidence in this estimate."

If very little is known about the inflow, so little is known about the outflow that we hesitate to quote any figures. Tentative work by Robert Warren at INS and Wayne Cornelius at the Massachusetts Institute of Technology suggests that it is surprisingly high.

The *net* flow, the number of illegals coming in minus the number leaving, has been estimated by Alexander Korns. He compared the *Current Population Survey* employment series of the Census Bureau with the Department of Labor's payroll survey and suggested that the differences could be explained by the presence on payrolls of illegals not taken into account by the Census Bureau. Given Korn's assumptions and his data, the indications are that the stock of illegals increased markedly from 1964 to 1969, but has not increased in the 1970s.

Keely points out that the flow of illegals from Mexico into the United States is related to the termination of the Bracero Program in 1964. He argues that the Bracero Program, which admitted millions of Mexican field workers to the United States from its beginning in 1942 as a wartime emergency measure until it was ended in 1964, established a pattern of workers coming north for employment. When the program ended, the numbers of illegals apprehended started to rise. Indeed, even before 1964, the numbers apprehended rose when the number of visas issued to *braceros* declined. In other words, the Mexican field hands keep coming whether the United States immigration law recognizes them or not, and the increase in the numbers caught simply means that the Border Patrol is doing a good job.

Keely sums up what is known of the flow of illegals by saying:

> . . . no reliable estimate exists regarding the flow of undocumented
> aliens whether a number of entries, number of entrants, or net
> permanent or long-term additions to the undocumented alien
> stock; and no evidence has been presented other than the increas-
> ing trend in the number of apprehensions to indicate new perma-
> nent additions to the population or an "out-of-control situation."

There is even less dependable knowledge of the size of the
stock—that is, the number of illegals living in the U.S. at any given
moment. General Chapman, however, did not hesitate to offer
opinions that were presented as fact. He gave wildly different
figures at different times, finally testifying to Congress in February 1975 that there were somewhere between four and twelve
million illegal aliens in the United States. Congress was understandably skeptical when the general could not give any basis for
these figures. Unable to get support from the statistical section of
INS for his numbers, General Chapman turned to Lesko Associates, a Washington consulting firm. Lesko was already doing
work for INS on another, related project when General Chapman
asked them to produce a "quick reaction study to reduce the wide
variance of the estimates."

The Lesko study concluded on remarkably tenuous grounds
that there were between 4.2 and 11 million illegal aliens in the
U.S. in 1975 with an "average" of 8.2 million. It further concluded that some 5.2 million of these were Mexican illegals.
Others who have examined the Lesko study are not impressed
with its validity. The Congressional Research Service's evaluation
was that the estimates were "based on weak and untenable assumptions and add very little to our knowledge of the size of the
illegal alien population."

The next attempt by the INS to come up with a number that
Congress would buy came from within the agency when its planning and evaluation section requested each of the four regional
INS offices to make an estimate of the illegals in its region. The
total of these estimates came to about six million people. INS
presented that number as authoritative and used it for about a
year.

General Chapman's attempt to get the INS budget increased
through his "public education campaign" was moderately successful. The annual increase in appropriations for the Service
between fiscal year 1974, when he began the campaign, and 1977,
when he was replaced by Leonel Castillo, averaged 16.4 percent.
About half of this increase was eaten up by inflation, but the other

half represented a real increase in the resources available to do
the job. Despite General Chapman's reputation as a commissioner who put enforcement first, the Border Patrol, the chief
enforcement arm of the INS, did not get even its fair share of
these increases. While the Service averaged a 16.4 percent annual
increase, the Border Patrol lagged behind with increases averag-
ing 15.5 percent.

In January 1977, Jimmy Carter became president. Despite a
heavy debt to organized labor for his election, the most strident
and powerful interest group calling for immediate and tough
action against the illegals, President Carter appointed Leonel
Castillo as Commissioner of Immigration and Naturalization.
Commissioner Castillo, grandson of an illegal alien (at least technically illegal), had been active in Democratic party affairs in
Texas and had become comptroller of the city of Houston, Texas.
His lifetime of service within the Mexican-American community
in the Southwest led his detractors to call him a "Latino activist,"
as if this vague label somehow meant that he would not do his job.

Commissioner Castillo undertook three programs as soon as he
became commissioner. First, he decided the most important task
before him was untangling the unbelievably fouled and snarled
bureaucratic mess he had inherited. Second, he tried to bring
some responsibility to official statements of the INS on the
illegal-alien question. He asked the planning and evaluation section to go back to the regional offices for the basis of their
estimates of the previous year. In the words of Charles Keely,

> No response gave a specific estimation procedure. Three referred
> to experience of officials and the fourth claimed no scientific basis
> existed at all for the estimate from that region.

On this basis, Mr. Castillo instructed INS employees to stop guess-
ing and limit their statements to official figures.

The third program was to bring a higher level of intellect to
bear on the illegal problem. This began under General Chapman,
who brought in demograapher Robert Warren from the Census
Bureau. Commissioner Castillo has since hired a Columbia-
trained sociologist from Johns Hopkins University, Guillermina
Jasso, as a special assistant to bring some order to the study of
illegals. Dr. Jasso, who grew up bilingual in Laredo, Texas, seems
both intelligent and sensitive to the complexities of the problem.

No attention was paid by the public or within the INS to either
Castillo's general housecleaning or the scientific effort to evaluate
the stock of illegals. Only the Commissioner's efforts to stop the
big-numbers game were noticed. Some people who mistrusted

Hispanics or who had not understood the budgetary games of General Chapman and had been frightened by his "public education campaign" felt that a cover-up was in progress. As distinguished and knowledgeable a person as Garrett Hardin characterized Mr. Castillo's efforts to bring order and responsibility to the discussion as clamping "a secrecy lid on all estimates."

Castillo, following the lead of President Carter and others in the Administration, hurt his own cause by ordering the INS to use the term "undocumented" in place of "illegal" in referring to those improperly in the United States. By this euphemistic shift, he gave the impression of trying to paper over the entire problem. But we have seen no evidence that this has actually been the case.

When Joe Sureck, head of the Los Angeles office of the INS, requested a transfer to the Hong Kong office to serve out his preretirement years, the *Los Angeles Times* quoted some anonymous functionary in the office as saying that Mr. Sureck "has been on INS Commissioner Leonel Castillo's 'hit list' of senior officials who oppose his 'liberal' immigration policies." The same functionary said that Sureck's successor would be required to speak fluent Spanish, and

> ... what that means to a lot of us is that Castillo wants to get a Latino activist like himself in here to head up our operations. Then we can forget completely about law enforcement and concentrate on serving the illegals. ...

The *Los Angeles Times* did not inform its readers that fluency in Spanish has long been a requirement for a Border Patrol agent and that it is absolutely essential to any serious enforcement effort in the Southwest.

Competent work on the illegal-alien problem is going on in the INS now, but it is unsung and underfinanced. A start in this direction was made under General Chapman with the Residential Survey. This effort was made possible in 1976 when Congress authorized $1 million for an INS study of illegals, with only the loosest instructions as to how it should proceed. INS rightly decided that the most important question to settle was the number of illegals in the country. In an attempt to answer this question, the Service adopted a Domestic Council Committee's recommendation to conduct a household survey in areas of heavy legal-immigrant residence in the twelve most populous states in order to find out how many illegals were present.

The survey was carefully designed. Confidentiality was to be guaranteed, interviewers from the same neighborhoods were to be used by the private firm that would actually conduct the survey, and every possible effort was planned to reassure the person being interviewed that it was not an enforcement effort. The pretest was very promising. Unfortunately, there was just not enough money to carry out the effort as planned. The INS made the mistake of awarding a contract to a firm that tried to carry out the original plan, rather than advising a cutback in the scope of the project. Numerous problems were encountered in the field work, and the quality of the work that did get done was questioned. In August 1978 the Residential Survey was canceled.

Because most of the $1 million had been spent and almost no data were forthcoming, Congress was perturbed. According to the *Los Angeles Times,* some congressmen were saying that the cancellation of the contract was part of a cover-up "to avoid alarming the country over the extent of its immigration problems." This is hard to believe since, six months after the cancellation, no one in the INS had seen any appreciable part of the data. The responses to the survey were being held by the private consulting firm that had gathered them because of problems of protecting the confidentiality of the respondents. We have talked repeatedly with individuals who were intimately connected with the project from its beginning under General Chapman to its cancellation under Commissioner Castillo, and every one of them insists that no one knows what the data might reveal. The private firm that did the survey has not suggested that the cancellation of the project had anything to do with what it was revealing, even though people in the firm were very disturbed by the cancellation. The furor over the aborted project was summed up by an anonymous congressional aide, who said, "Chalk it up as another of those symbols of the country's frustrations with its immigration dilemma. Maybe next time around we'll get some good data on the problem—if there is a problem." The irony of the "cover-up" charge is that, from what we have seen, no one is trying harder to "get good data" than Commissioner Castillo, and no on orto get it before the public.

General Chapman's "public education program" at least had the virtue of stirring up interest in the problem, and government agencies other than INS have tried their hand at counting the uncountable. Clarice Lancaster of the Department of Health, Education and Welfare and Frederick Scheuern of the Social Security Administration have done the most generally accepted study of the subject. Their range for the number of illegals in the United States is between 2.9 and 5.7 million, with 3.9 million as their suggested, specific figure. These are the numbers most widely agreed upon today, and it seems that they will last for awhile as the basis for policy-making.

The mere fact that these figures are widely agreed upon, however, does not mean that they are right. The numbers were calculated by a very complex method that boiled down to subtracting an estimate of the size of the population without illegals from an estimate of the population including illegals (based on Social Security Administration and IRS data). Economist-demographer Don Leet, an outstanding student of the U.S. population, has expressed a reservation about this study, not on the expected grounds that the illegals really cannot be counted, but that estimates of the legal population are probably not accurate enough to spot a group of merely four million sloshing around in the melting pot. While four million is a lot of people, it is less than two percent of the estimated population. Leet suggests that there is no guarantee that U.S. population estimates have an accuracy of better than 98 percent.

Anything that attracts attention in Washington, particularly if it attracts public attention too, sooner or later attracts the attention of the Central Intelligence Agency. Not surprisingly, therefore, there is a secret CIA report on the illegal alien issue. The social analysis of the CIA is usually pretty good, not because their people are any better than those in other agencies, but because they have more people and virtually unlimited resources. Thus they can lavish manpower and money on a study beyond the wildest dreams of the people at INS or the Census Bureau or wherever. Often, though, their work does more harm than good to a public debate because they selectively distribute and selectively leak their results. This creates an "insider" mentality. The person who has seen the secret report says, "I know you do not agree with me, but I have seen the secret report and you haven't, and if you knew what was in it (of course, I cannot tell you what is in it), you would agree with me. But since you don't know what I know, why don't you shut up?"

The CIA often distributes its conclusions without revealing what information they are based on, so the conclusions cannot be criticized. If the conclusions cannot be evaluated, they cannot be fitted into the mosaic of information that forms the background of any significant social debate. Commissioner Castillo, who has tried unsuccessfully to get the CIA report released to the public, told us that it contains information that "would be of value to the public discussion," but that there is nothing in it that others have not noted. An article in *New Times* magazine, to which the report was apparently leaked, although referred to there as a National Security Council report, said that it proposed "U.S. pressure on Mexico to reorient its rural policies to promote small-scale industrialization in order to stem the flow of Mexicans over the border." If this is the most newsworthy morsel in the report, Commissioner Castillo is certainly right; there really is nothing in it that others have not noted.

Another contribution from the CIA has been alarmist statements from its former director, William Colby. Colby seems to think that he is the first to notice the population growth in Mexico and the first to see its implications for the United States. He told the *Los Angeles Times* that "the swelling population of Mexico, driving millions of illegal aliens over the border, is a greater threat to the United States than the Soviet Union." A number of persons in Washington who are familiar with both Colby's remarks and the CIA report have emphatically told us that they have nothing to do with one another and indeed that Mr. Colby's remarks often contradict the report.

Statements of some other government officials seem equally overdrawn. In regard to the flow of illegals Congressman Lester Wolff (D-NY) told *U.S. News and World Report* that:

> We really have a Maginot line. It is outflanked, overflown, and infiltrated. And you know what happened to the French.

Ray Marshall, Secretary of Labor, is quoted as saying:

> . . . the first generation of undocumented workers will endure their privations in relative silence. But you can rest assured that the children of these undocumented workers will be the focus of a civil rights movement of the 1980s.

Apparently a "civil rights movement" is some sort of grim specter to the Secretary of Labor.

Responsible demographers who are hard at work on the problem of counting the uncountable—and there are many—are rarely interviewed because their estimates are too low to sell newspapers and they are too quick to admit what they do not know. Charles Keely, Guillermina Jasso, Robert Warren, Jennifer Peck, J. Gregory Robinson, Frederick Scheuern, Clarice Lancaster, Alexander Korns, and David North are just a few of the people who are bringing their talent, training, and experience to bear on the problem.

HOW MUCH DO ILLEGALS COST?

It is obvious that if no one knows how many illegals there are in the country—and no one does—it is not possible to measure their economic impact with any accuracy. But this does not stop people from acting as if they could. Needless to say, the stories that appear in the press and on the air tell terrible tales of how much this "silent invasion" *costs* Americans. It seems to us that honest men and women who work hard for modest wages do not cost society anything but are a benefit.

Those who do worry about the "costs" of the illegals see those costs arising from several sources. They argue that the illegals take advantage of what are broadly defined as "welfare programs" without paying the taxes to support them. In short, they say the illegals are welfare bums. Another argument is that, while illegals may be employed and self-supporting, their very employment is an economic burden because they take jobs away from Americans and from legal immigrants. A third line of economic concern is that the portion of the illegal's wages sent home to support his family adversely affects the U.S. balance of payments. Each of these concerns deserves to be considered in turn.

Are the Illegals "Welfare Bums"?

The answer to this question is *No!* Few who have looked at the evidence even with a hostile eye argue this anymore. The bigoted, and there are many, still believe that Mexicans and Hispanics generally are shiftless and lazy and always will be. The need for bigots to justify their own inadequacies is too strong for mere evidence to matter. The information packet issued by the White House in February 1977 to explain the President's program on illegal immigration then before Congress succinctly stated the real situation by saying, "Through work, they [the illegals] contribute much and require little from the host society." The White House argument went on to say that when the illegals settle down and begin to have families, the cost of their presence increases, but not disproportionately. The burden presented by the presence of illegals is simply the burden of population growth.

Currently the best work on illegals and the welfare burden is that of David North and M. P. Houston for the Department of Labor in 1976 and of Jorge Bustamante of the Colegio de Mexico published in 1978. North and Houston showed that three-quarters of the illegals surveyed had income tax withheld and paid into Social Security. Of course, illegals, like everyone else, pay sales taxes and the like, which are collected at the moment of transaction. On the other hand, only one-half of one percent of the people interviewed by North and Houston were on "welfare," one and one-half percent received food stamps, four percent had unemployment compensation, and four and one-half percent took advantage of public health and medical programs.

These numbers correspond well with those collected by Bustamante in Mexico. Three-quarters of returning illegals he interviewed paid income taxes, and two-thirds had Social Security withheld, while only about three percent ever received any sort of public assistance. Bustamante's study also revealed that fewer than one percent of the illegals had children in United States schools. The shortcoming of both the Houston-North study and Bustamante's is that they depended on illegals who had been apprehended. Political scientist Wayne Cornelius's study of illegals from selected communities in Jalisco, however, was not based on apprehended illegals, and it revealed an equally low rate of public-service utilization and showed that about two-thirds of the illegals were paying Social Security and income taxes. As a rule, the longer an illegal stays in the United States, the less chance he runs of getting caught and the better integrated he becomes. With that social integration comes a better job and even greater likelihood that he will be paying taxes of all sorts.

The real tax an illegal alien pays is in the form of the substandard wages he or she receives. This extra margin is passed into the economy in the form of reduced prices for his employer's customers and greater profits for the employer. It is out of his gross profits, of course, that the farmer, manufacturer, or businessman who employs the illegal pays *his* taxes. If an illegal filed an income-tax return, complete with W-2 forms and lists of dependents, he or she would usually be found to owe no taxes and indeed to be entitled to a refund of what had been withheld. Finally, and this is a point too often overlooked, the illegal is seldom in this country long enough to get anything back from Social Security.

Do Illegals Take Jobs from Americans?

Answering this question is by no means as easy as the "welfare" issue. The simple-minded assumption here is that every illegal employed in this country is taking a job that would otherwise be held by a legal resident. General Chapman presented this view to Congress in September 1974, when he entered into this exchange:

> General Chapman: . . . I believe if we [the INS] had the Rodino bill [providing penalties against employers who hired illegals] and we had some increases in the Service and had some dollars to move the people, and could implement this card [the forge-proof work card], we could create a million jobs in this country at least, and practically overnight—I shouldn't say create; I mean open up.
> Mr. Randall (D-MO): Make available?

General Chapman: So that Americans could occupy them.
Mr. Randall: Make them available for our citizens?
General Chapman: I think we could open up at least a million jobs,
and practically right away.

Although his own statistical section within the INS could not back
him up with solid data even on the number of illegals in the U.S.,
and the outside consultant he had hired told him there was no way
to measure the economic impact of the illegal-alien population,
General Chapman was not only prepared to tell Congress how
many jobs were being gobbled up, he even submitted "estimates"
of what kind of jobs they were. Of the estimated total of one
million, one-third were each in agriculture and service industries,
and the remaining third was about equally divided between heavy
and light industry. In February 1977, the Public Affairs Office of
the INS put out another set of "estimates" showing that the
number of jobs taken away from legal residents was up to a
remarkably specific 3,666,000, with about the same breakdown in
the various sectors of employment.

While General Chapman and others maintain that for every
employed illegal there is an unemployed American or legal immigrant, there are people who hold the opposite view. They
argue that the availability of low-paying jobs causes the flow of
illegals. They claim that, if the illegals were not economically
needed in the work force, they would not be here in the numbers
they are, and they would not have been here for so long. It does
seem that, when times are good in this country, workers from
Mexico find work here in one way or another as farm laborers or
factory workers, whether they are illegal or legal immigrants. One
advocate of this position is economist Michael Piore of the Massachusetts Institute of Technology. Similar views among the
mayors of border towns were reported by Peter Nye in an article
in Nation's Cities. Nye reported that "illegal Mexicans are a way of
life along the southern border" and that the mayors are "tired of
easy solutions given to complex emotional problems stemming
from the economic disparity between the U.S. and Mexico." Alexander O. Campillo, the mayor of Calexico, California, which is
across the line from Mexicali, Baja California, said the unemployment in his town ran 20 percent, but denied that this was
caused by the illegals. Campillo attributed the unemployment to
"local farmers replacing laborers with machines."

Historically, there has always been a large part of the American
work force that could be pushed around. Immigration in the
nineteenth century brought such numbers of people that labor
was cheap and a given workman easily replaced. When that

source dried up in the 1920s, American employers turned to the Mexican, the black, and the poor Southern white. The latter two became migrants in their own land, going north to make tanks for the Second World War and finding intermittent employment in the 1950s making cars for those participating more fully in the postwar prosperity. The perennial Country-Western song, *Detroit City,* tells the story of a Southern boy who has gone north for a job, and, while writing home that he is getting along just fine, he complains of the loneliness and of spending his nights in bars. This Southern boy is as foreign to Detroit as the immigrant from Salerno or the plains of Poland.

In the 1960s, however, the blacks began asserting themselves, and industrial employment became available in the South to both blacks and whites. This loss of a source of easily exploitable labor in the North was compensated to some degree by the permanent entry of women into the job market. Even in the early 1970s women were paid less than their male coworkers for doing the same job, women were systematically denied advancement or the opportunity to work in the better-paying jobs, and they were not given the same job security as men. Although it is now against federal law and the law of most of the states to discriminate on the basis of sex, it is still done. Women are still recruited for dead-end jobs and for the occasional peak-season jobs.

Mexicans and other immigrants are used in the same way, by and large. Occasionally the INS picks up an illegal alien who has managed to work his way into a solid, middle-class income. These few cases are played up in the press, but they are just too few to worry about. If one goes through the I-213s—the form filled out when a deportable alien is located—at an INS office, an illegal is seldom found to be making over $3.50 an hour. In our conversations with illegals, we never found one earning over $5,000 a year. The illegals from the Mexican communities studied by Cornelius earned about $480 per month.

The farmers in the Southwest who employ illegals say they cannot get their crops in without them because they cannot afford to pay enough to attract the unemployed from the cities. Farmers often talk like this; they are a profoundly pessimistic and conservative lot. They will almost always maintain that any change, except a rise in crop prices or a government subsidy, will spell disaster for American agriculture. On the other hand, agricultural economics is very tricky, and most changes *have* been damaging to agriculture as practiced. In 1954, when the illegals were systematically thrown out of the Southwest in "Operation Wetback" and other INS enforcement efforts, the government did not begin the drive to get rid of them until legally admitted

Mexican workers were lined up to take their places. No one then argued that ousting these Mexicans from the fields would open up employment opportunities for Americans.

The statements that have been made to date are no more than speculation. Some honest and very promising work is now being done on the question of "job displacement;" that is, illegals displacing legal residents from employment. That work, though, is limited, preliminary, and exploratory. Its results do not describe the "real world" any more than did the old INS estimates, and those doing the work would not claim that it does.

There are three major arguments for the premise that exclusion of illegal workers would not add appreciably to the number of jobs available to Americans. One is that the jobs held by illegals would disappear due to mechanization or automation. If the employers had to hire Americans, they would find it to their advantage to invest in machines instead of people. The goods would still be produced, but the jobs would disappear. Another argument is that the jobs would follow the workers; if the United States successfully ousted the illegals, their employers would relocate in Mexico, the Dominican Republic, Haiti, or wherever there is cheap labor. The success of the *maquiladoras,* or runaway shops, in the Border Industrial Zone in Mexico seems to indicate that there is something in this position. Zenith, Motorola, Memorex, Burroughs, and North American Rockwell are some familiar American firms that have gone south of the border in search of low-cost workers.

The argument that expelling the illegals would actually *increase unemployment* among Americans is intriguing. Certainly it should be examined by anyone who earns a good middle-class living from a firm that uses illegals. The argument runs like this. There are many enterprises, especially companies that are marginal or in declining industries, that can make it competitively only if they have the advantage of cheap labor. In businesses using illegal workers, the administrators, foremen, salesmen, accountants, and the like are pulling down the usual middle-class wages. They are the proud superstructure of a vessel sailing the commercial seas, resting on a hull of sturdy, but inexpensive illegals. Take away the hull, or even punch a very sizable hole in it, and the comfortable fellows on top will sink into the sea of unemployment.

There is a lot more to cheap labor than a low hourly wage. Indeed, from reading INS I-213 forms and interviewing illegal workers, we have found that illegals get about the same wages per hour as legal workers in the same jobs. Cornelius's study of illegal immigrants showed that, outside of agriculture (where even many legal workers do not receive the minimum wage), 70 to 80 percent of the illegals were receiving the minimum wage or more. The source of the savings to employers comes from other sources: illegals can easily be laid off and readily rehired as the employer's needs grow or shrink, they do not get fringe benefits, and safety and health safeguards are usually ignored.

No one knows exactly what the situation is relative to job displacement, but the simplistic view that each illegal displaces an American is utter nonsense.

Dollars into Pesos

The work of Houston and North, Bustamante, and Cornelius, and our own interviews demonstrate over and over that illegal migrants are here not only so they themselves can work, but so they can send money home. The amount of money sent home from their meager annual wages is astounding. These people love their families, and they are here so they can provide for them. The pain of separation is less than the pain of deprivation. One of the illegals we talked with, a maid in a middle-class home, made less than $40 a week, but in 18 weeks she had sent $280 home. Most illegals make more than $40 a week, and they send about half of their money home.

It has been estimated, though the accuracy of the estimate is surely open to question, that Mexicans residing in the United States send home about $3 billion annually. How many illegal Mexican workers are in the U.S. is unknown, but there are many of them and they do send a sizable amount of money back to Mexico. Whether or not this is a matter for concern is another question. Mexico now runs a foreign-trade deficit to the United States, and any dollars that go into Mexico come back promptly to buy American goods, thus giving employment to American workers.

Although no ones knows, it is probable that the money sent home by Mexican immigrants does not add perceptibly to Mexican "capital formation"; that is, very little of it is invested in commerce or industry, thereby creating jobs and otherwise expanding and deepening the economic structure of the country in the conventional sense. The money goes to buy clothes and groceries, pay the rent, and buy the firewood that keeps people alive. Of course, it does create jobs for the clothier and grocer, justify the landlord's investment, and provide a livelihood for the *leñero* who cuts and sells the firewood. Most important, though, the money keeps people alive. If sheer humanity is not enough to keep the United States from meddling with the unknown, how about American self-interest? Interruption of these remittances would certainly increase the suffering of several million Mexican families, and it must be assumed that the resulting hardship and discontent would destabilize Mexican society. In the next 20 years, the Mexican nation will have to accommodate at least 40 million more people. Doing this while maintaining an orderly government and society will be a tremendous challenge, and Mexico will need all the help she can get. As usual, no one knows how much destabilization would result from the loss of income from the United States, but no possible benefit to Americans could come from any destabilization within Mexico.

If the American people were really concerned about the nation's balance of payments, it would be much more effective to undertake a reduction in the consumption of petroleum products. Each *day*, the United States imports an average of 9 million barrels of oil, and in summer of 1979 the price was edging toward $20 per barrel. If the United States set out to achieve an energy-use pattern like that of the European industrial nations or Japan, the balance-of-payments problems would diminish considerably and there would be no need for concern about dollars being sent to Mexico. The entire argument that hard-working men and women are threatening the American economy by sending pittances home to feed their families rings hollow when one looks at the extravagance with which Americans continue to manage their public and private affairs.

LEGAL MEXICAN IMMIGRATION TO THE UNITED STATES: A COMPARISON WITH CANADA

While most of the controversy today is over *illegal* Mexican immigration, about which little is known but the suppositions of press and bureaucrats, there is hardly any discussion of *legal* immigration from Mexico, about which there is solid data that may be the most useful indicator of what is really going on. The forces pushing people from Mexico and pulling them to the United States presumably operate on those who enter properly much as they do on those who come in illegally. Since there is good data on legal immigration, the general pattern of flow and counterflow are readily evident.

A discussion of the immigration pattern from a single country is unrevealing, however, because there is no way of discovering what is singular and significant about it. A lot of Mexicans have come to the United States, but so have many people of other nationalities. Thousands of Mexican immigrants went home (or

were ejected) during the Great Depression, but so did large numbers of people from other countries. What, then, is special about
Mexican immigration?

Mexico and Canada are the only two nations to share borders
with the United States. They are the only countries from which an
immigrant can easily come by bus or might even hitchhike without much trouble. A very important difference between the im-
migrations from Canada and Mexico is that so many, perhaps
even a majority, who have come from Canada were born somewhere else, while almost all who have come from Mexico were
native Mexicans. From one point of view, this should not matter
because, regardless of where they were born, until 1968 they were
admitted because they were "from Canada" just as if they had
been born there.

Another reason that comparison with Canada is valuable is the
very different way in which Americans view Canadians and Mexicans. While most Americans know no more about Canada than
they do about Mexico—few could tell the British North America
Act from René Levesque—they have a positive feeling toward
Canadians and do not see them as threatening.

Americans think Canadians are almost like themselves. They
speak the same language with an almost identical accent. They
tend to go to war against the same peoples, sometimes a bit earlier.
Canadians belong to the North Atlantic Treaty Organization with
which Americans fight Communism, but they have stayed out of
the Organization of American States through which the U.S.
controls Latin America. Americans are vaguely aware that some
Canadians speak French, though most are surprised to learn that
it is almost a third and that most of these "francophones" do not
speak a word of English. Then there are the Mounties beloved of
all American movie fans, and besides, Canadian water is safe to
drink.

The United States is very proud of its relationship with Canada.
It never tires of pointing to the U.S.–Canadian border as the
"longest unfortified international frontier in the world." But
Americans hardly ever point to Mexico and say, "There is the
second-longest unfortified international frontier in the world."
The lack of fortifications on both borders is summed up by the
standard Canadian joke, "Of course it isn't fortified. We can't and
they don't need to."

The Canadians' attitude toward the United States, on the other
hand, is about like the Mexicans'. Being right next door to the
United States is an uncomfortable fact of life from which, now
and then, some benefit can be derived. The United States is
politically meddlesome and economically exploitive. Both coun-

tries want American tourists, and U.S. currency is accepted in the remotest hamlets of either nation. Neither Canadians nor Mexicans really care for the annoying American habit of not converting currency, but they need the bucks and assuage national pride by gypping the tourists a little on the exchange rate. In either country, one is very well advised to go to the bank to change money. Finally, Canada and Mexico are commonly distinguished from the United States by having clean subways.

Historically, Canada has legally exported about twice as many people to the United States as has Mexico, four million compared with about two million, and native-born Canadians have always outnumbered native-born Mexicans in U.S. Census statistics. The ratio was about 800,000 to 750,000. respectively in the 1970 Census. Canadians entered the U.S. at a much higher rate than Mexicans in every decade through 1960, and at almost the same rate in the decade 1961–1970.

Why, then, has there never been any concern about the hordes of Canadians threatening American jobs, lowering the standard of living, and soaking up welfare dollars? Why have there been no articles in national newsmagazines or television programs describing the wretchedness of conditions, political or economic, in America's neighbor to the north that explains this exodus? If the forces pushing people out of the two countries were roughly the same, why would not Mexico, with two and a half times the population, have produced two and a half times the number of immigrants? It was only in 1972 that the proportional number of legal immigrants from Mexico surpassed the number from Canada.

Both Canada and Mexico have had phenomenal population increases in this century. While the United States population has grown 185 percent since 1900, that of Canada has grown 300 percent, and Mexico, 380 percent. Indeed, had the United States absorbed no immigrants from either country, the Canadian growth rate for the first three-quarters of the twentieth century would have been considerably greater than that of Mexico.

Once in the United States, immigrants from both Mexico and Canada seek naturalization in far smaller proportions than other immigrants do. They tend to go home, or at least elsewhere, in considerable numbers. Usually five years of residence in the United States are required before an immigrant can be naturalized. Altogether, about one million immigrants came to the United States from 1966 through 1970, and almost a third of this number were naturalized in the following five-year period, 1971–75. Among these immigrants were about 225,000 Mexicans, but only about an eighth of that number were subsequently naturalized. While 170,000 people came from Canada in 1966–1970, only one-seventh of that number of Canadians were naturalized during the following five years. In contrast, the number of naturalizations of Germans from 1971 through 1975 was almost half as many as the 70,000 German immigrants who arrived in 1966–1970.

The reluctance of Mexicans and Canadians to transfer allegiance formally to the United States suggests a degree of uncertainty about remaining. After all, a Mexican or Canadian can hop on a bus and go back home inexpensively; he or she can go home for Christmas, to take care of family affairs or just to see old friends. When a good job opens up back home, he or she is more likely to hear about it than the European, African, or Asian immigrant, and can go home to look it over without much trouble.

A very important force in encouraging Mexicans and all Latin Americans to return home is their distaste for American-style family life. While these people like nice homes in the suburbs, easy credit, and inexpensive television and stereo sets, they do not like what they see as negligent child-rearing and the ease with which Americans contract and dissolve marriages and break up families. Our personal experience in Latin America has been that this is the number-one reason for Latins returning home. Moreover, those who have gone back from the United States typically have made a considerable economic sacrifice in doing so.

Impressions gained from friends among whom we have lived in Canada are that Canadians who have returned from long residence in the United States were drawn back for a number of reasons, the two most important being the improved economic situation in Canada, particularly for the middle class, and the development of a distinct sense of Canadian identity. While wages are generally lower and most things still cost more in Canada than in the United States, the situation is better than it used to be, and the economic sacrifice of returning home is less. Few Americans realize the profound impact on the Canadian national consciousness of the observances of the centennial in 1969 of the British North America Act, the act of the British Parliament that fused the colonies of New Brunswick, Nova Scotia, and Canada into the Dominion of Canada and established a constitution for that Dominion. The thoroughgoing national discussion of the meaning of "Canadian" that was stimulated by that centennial did more to develop a sense of Canadian nationalism and patriotism than anything since the assault on Vimy Ridge in World War I and the raid on Dieppe in World War II in which Canadian troops suffered especially heavy casualties.

A precise analysis of the push and pull factors dictating the flow of peoples between nations is difficult, but an improved economic situation and an increasing national pride would surely pull Canadians back. Factors that push Canadians back home from the United States are what is perceived as a hectic and grasping way of life, the physical dirtiness of American cities, and, particularly during the Vietnam War, a desire not to be associated with U.S. foreign policy.

Immigrants have come to the United States from both Canada and Mexico in two waves, the first cresting in the mid-1920s and the second still swelling. The first wave washed highest from both countries in 1924 when 90,000 immigrants entered from Mexico and 200,000 from Canada. By 1929, the last year of prosperity before the Great Depression, immigration was down to 66,000 from Canada and 40,000 from Mexico, and the numbers from each country bottomed out in 1935 with 8,000 from Canada and 1,500 from Mexico.

Immigration figures by themselves give a distorted view of what is going on because they do not show the numbers who go back home. The government kept figures on the number of immigrants who left this country permanently between 1908 and 1957, and these reveal that just over 30 percent of the 15.7 million who came to the U.S. later went home or elsewhere. Demographer Robert Warren of the INS estimates that a similar percentage of the 3.3 million immigrants who arrived in the decade of the 1960s also departed.

Estimating the counterflow for specific nationalities is more difficult, but a comparison of INS immigration figures and census counts of the various foreign-born nationalities in the country provide some enlightenment. While the Immigration Service states that 460,000 Mexicans entered the United States as immigrants in the 1920s, a comparison of the 1920 and 1930 censuses shows an increase in the number of native-born Mexicans in the population of only slightly over 150,000, from 490,000 to 640,000. Even when 70,000 are added to the population increase to account for the Mexican-born who died during the decade, there were still over 225,000 who went somewhere else, presumably back to Mexico. During the 1930s, the number of native-born Mexicans in the U.S. population dropped by 40 percent and did not return to the 1930 level until the early 1960s.

The pattern of Mexican immigration in the 1940s as reflected in the official figures can only be described in the words of the King of Siam: a puzzlement. A comparison of the census of 1950 with that of 1940 shows an increase of almost 120,000 in the number of native-born Mexicans in the United States, but Immigration data indicate that only some 61,000 came into the country. Either some illegals were surfacing in the census or there was some really bad counting along the border.

In the 1950s and 1960s about three-quarters of a million immigrants came into the United States from Mexico, and the 1960 and 1970 censuses indicate that the increase in native-born Mexicans in the United States was a little less than 60 percent of that total. The remaining 40 percent had presumably returned to Mexico.

It is also important to realize that there are native-born Americans who emigrate from these shores: 385,000 in the 1960s, of whom 40 percent went to Canada and over 15 percent to Australia. Indeed the most recent research shows that in the mid-1970s Canada gained about 20,000 people per year in net migration to and from the United States. Very few U.S. emigrants go to Mexico.

This brief sketch of legal immigration from Mexico and Canada highlights a few details about people coming here from Mexico that have been obscured for too long. First, immigration from Mexico has not been extraordinarily heavy compared with the flow of peoples from other countries.

Canada, the other immediately neighboring country, has sent many more people here than has Mexico, even though Canada has only 40 percent of Mexico's population. Still, there has never been a public clamor about the Canadian influx.

Second, the flow of people across the U.S. southern border is not one way. At the very time that some Mexicans are filing their applications for immigration visas, others who are already residents of the United States are packing their things and preparing to go back. It is an assault on the American consciousness to think that anyone would not want to stay here if he or she could, but it happens frequently, nonetheless. Not everyone wants to be an American as much as most Americans do.

The Great Depression led to a decline in the number of Mexican-born residents, which continued through World War II. It was not until 1943 that the number of immigrants from Mexico was high enough even to compensate the mortality rate among the Mexican-born residents who had remained. It was another 20 years before the number of Mexican-born people in the United States returned to the level of the early 1930s. Even in the most recent years, the counterflow of Mexican-born residents of the United States has equaled over 40 percent of the number coming in.

ILLEGAL IMMIGRATION FROM MEXICO

The existence of the counterflow of legal immigrants raises a very important question about illegal immigration from Mexico.

If a substantial portion of those Mexicans who are admitted legally to the United States for permanent residence each year choose to go home, why should it be assumed that those Mexicans who are here illegally wish more fervently to stay? After all, they have no chance at the better jobs. And their lives are not very comfortable or secure. Any contact with federal, state, or local officialdom risks discovery, so they dare not apply for the social services that their labor and taxes have earned them. The fear of being "returned" is always present. Many illegal immigrants are turned into the INS by employers who wish to cheat workers out of their wages or by personal enemies. Some shop only at night, dealing mostly in cash because the use of checks or credit cards and the presentation of identification all increase the chances of detection. If they are laid off, even an application for unemployment compensation is a risk. The credit check involved in the purchase of a house or a car is another risk. If they are cheated, to whom can they go?

These people live in a world of shut-off opportunity, denial, and risk. If 40 percent of their compatriots who can live and work openly and securely choose to go back to Mexico, why should anyone assume that the illegal migrant wants anything except to do whatever work he can find, collect his wages, and go home as soon as he can?

There is no fairy-tale fright in the story of legal immigration from Mexico; that story is knowable and clear. But is there some way that the fright can be removed from the *illegal*-immigration story? How does one go about proving that there are *not* a quarter-million, or 800,000 or 1.7 million illegals, almost all Mexicans, entering the United States each year? After all, they are undetected, so who knows how many Mexicans or other aliens might be out there? How does anyone *know* there are not 1.7 million Albanians coming to our shores each year, every one illegal, every one undetected, every one a threat?

Basically, the official evidence about the illegal-alien population in the United States is limited to the number that are caught. Almost everything else has been learned from what they say about themselves. This information, in turn, is presented in about a dozen different ways in the *Annual Reports* of the INS, and these *Reports* can be purchased for $1.75 each from the Superintendent of Documents, Washington, D.C. 20402. Where else can one become a student of an important issue for $1.75?

The record shows that the number of deportable aliens apprehended is increasing dramatically. The problem is one of figuring out what the increase means. General Chapman and those who quoted him interpreted it to mean that, since more illegals are being caught than before, there must be still more to catch. There is a certain logic in this, but thinking about it very long raises some uneasiness. Why not argue that if more illegal migrants are being caught, there are not as many left to catch?

Obviously, an increase in arrests does not necessarily mean that the number of offenses has increased. An increase in arrests for prostitution can result from an increase in prostitution; but it can also mean that some motel owners have complained to the city council, or the lieutenant in charge of vice thinks he is close to becoming a captain and the vice squad is being leaned on to increase arrests, or it can mean simply that more people have been assigned to the vice squad.

If the job done by the Immigration and Naturalization Service is to be measured by the number of illegal aliens it apprehends, the figures must be examined carefully because every apprehension is not the same. There were 875,000 apprehensions of deportable aliens in 1976, but only about 3 percent of this number were deported. Lest you think that this means 97 percent are still running around the country scot-free, be assured that 87 percent of the number apprehended were "required to depart." The difference between a required departure and a deportation is considerable. A required departure boils down to an INS agent saying to the person, "Listen, we've got you dead to rights, and if you make us go through the deportation process, we'll throw the book at you and you may end up in the pokey. If you go quietly, though, we'll forget the whole thing."

The great bulk of required departures are "under safeguards," which means that they are put on the bus for Tijuana or the plane for Guadalajara under the watchful eye of an INS agent. In 1976, though, 35,000 deportable aliens were allowed to leave without supervision. They were usually told that they had 14 days to get out and they did—or it is assumed that they did. Another 10,000 of these deportable aliens were "unwilling crewmen violators"— sailors and the occasional airman who were stranded in the country when their ships or planes could not leave on schedule for some reason or other.

Still, in 1976, 875,000 people were deliberately in the country when they were not supposed to be, and they were thrown out. That is a lot of people, but, contrary to popular belief, *it is no larger than it has been at earlier times.* In 1954, 900,000 illegal aliens were expelled and, in 1955, an all-time high of 1.1 million. Moreover, this was done when the Border Patrol had about half the number of agents it has today. Under these circumstances, the large numbers being expelled now lose much of their impressiveness.

The rapid increase in the numbers is not so frightening when it is broken down. Between 1971 and 1976, the number of illegals apprehended annually increased by 450,000. But 75 percent of this increase were illegals who had been in the country less than 72 hours. The *visible* increase thus has been in hapless Mexicans who are nailed at the border, and it is very hard to see a big threat in a collection of people who cannot last even three days in the promised land. It seems at least as logical to argue that an increasingly vigilant and efficient Border Patrol is successfully stopping an increasing flow at the border as to buy the story that, if more illegals are being caught, then there must be even more illegals left to catch.

This is not to argue that illegal aliens are not a problem in the United States. What is argued is that no one knows how many illegals there really are and that the logic behind the estimates is faulty.

A View from the INS

The lack of solid information and conflicting attitudes toward the problem of illegal immigration that have prevailed at the top levels of the INS unavoidably create problems for the people in the field who deal most directly with the situation. In an effort to learn what an INS agent's problems in the field actually are, we interviewed one of them in March 1978.

INS Agent Bob Park sits in his office in the Federal Building in Fresno, California, and entertains his guest with war stories from his thirteen years in the Service. The stories have the reassuring ring of coming from a man who is not frightened by his job or the possibility of being hurt. Most of his stories are funny. He tells of scuffles and fistfights with illegals on the Mexican border when he was a Border Patrol agent. He gave as good as he got and is rather proud of that. He also has stories of bureaucratic screw-ups. Once, for instance, he and another agent went out to a ranch in the San Joaquin Valley, knowing that it employed a lot of illegals. When they got there, they found more illegals than expected and they had to turn half of them loose, because there was not enough room in the two buses they had brought along and the Service had no money to hire more. He emphasizes that this is not a unique experience. Such operations frequently yield more illegals than the agents can handle.

Some of the stories are serious. Park complains bitterly about apprehending illegals who are criminals and who are not tried for their crimes but simply deported. Once when he was assigned to the Canadian border, he apprehended a back-street abortionist who came "wet" (illegal) from Canada and was guilty of murderous medical malpractice in both the United States and Canada.

He had West German, Argentine, and Canadian citizenships and
a working knowledge of U.S. deportation law. When the higher-
ups decided that this crook should be deported instead of tried,
he manipulated it so he was deported not to Canada but to
Argentina at the expense of the American taxpayer.

Park's attitude toward illegals reflects a compassion born of
understanding. He thinks there are a lot more of them around
than there used to be, but he is glad that Commissioner Castillo
has sent out the word that agents should talk only when they know
what they are talking about. Park says that most of the estimates of
migration rates came out of Washington anyhow, and since a part
of his job was public relations, the old policy put him in an
awkward position. He often had to point out that numbers in the
newspapers were just estimates and that no one really knew how
many illegals there were or what they were doing.

According to Park, the big problem under the Carter Administration has been to clarify what has changed and what has not.
Park has just returned from Mendota, a little town on the west
side of the San Joaquin Valley that really booms during the
cantaloupe harvest. There are a lot of immigrants, legal and
illegal, in that part of the valley, and he has been at a community
forum trying to explain what is going on. Many members of the
audience were illegals, and a lot of questions were in Spanish, but
everyone was answered fully and courteously. Park will not bust
people who want information. Indeed, it is INS policy not to
apprehend anyone who comes into the office and asks questions,
no matter how suspiciously the questioner might behave. It is the
job of the INS to help immigrants and facilitate the immigration
process, as well as to apprehend the illegals. In addition, the INS
wants aliens, legal or illegal, to know what is going on, so the
agents try to keep the lines of communication open.

Bob Park thinks the flow of illegals is a problem, that their
presence in this country is a problem, and that something ought
to be done. But daily contact with that problem has not blinded
him to the basic overriding reality. He says it this way: "Hell yes,
we could stop them. We could stop them if they were dogs. If they
were dogs we could kill them. But they are not dogs, they are
human beings."

MEXICAN LABOR IN AMERICAN FIELDS

A casual reader of recent discussions of the illegal-immigrant
"problem" might easily draw the conclusion that the United States
has always opposed a flow of Mexicans across the border—that
the job has always been to "stop them." Nothing could be further

from the truth. As Ernesto Galarzo, a specialist in farm labor, put it, the Treaty of Guadalupe-Hidalgo, which ended the Mexican-American War in 1848 and established American hegemony over much of what had been Mexico, "left the toilers on one side of the border, the capital and the best land on the other. This mistake migration undertook to correct."

The roots of the problem are not found solely in the maldistribution of capital and good land between Mexican and U.S. territory. The land left in Mexico after the U.S. conquest was itself maldistributed; the revolutionary struggles of Mexico are largely a saga of efforts to resolve this maldistribution. The gross abuses and brutalization of *peones*, though now largely a thing of the past, provided part of the initial push that sent Mexican farm workers north in search of a better life. When the Revolution of 1910–1920 failed to bring rapid land reform, large numbers of peasants began leaving Mexico. Between 1910 and 1930, the number of Mexican-born residents of the United States increased by over 400,000.

The danger and disorder of the years of struggle and the chaos that followed them are long past, but it was in those years that the pattern of large-scale migration north from Mexico became established. Today the push factors are almost completely economic—the inability to find work in Mexico, either in factory or field. The great "pull" factor is the availability of jobs in the north and the willingness of Americans to profit from this pool of cheap, readily available labor.

Pull from the United States

Cheap labor was most welcome in the United States in the 1920s, particularly cheap labor willing to do jobs found unattractive by Anglos. The welcome was especially warm once the immediate post–World War I slump in U.S. agriculture had ended. Spokesmen for large growers in California praised the Mexican who "has no political ambitions; he does not aspire to dominate the political affairs of the community in which he lives," and who "likes the sunshine against an adobe wall with a few tortillas and in the off time he drifts across the border where he may have these things." A member of the Los Angeles Chamber of Commerce explained that

> No labor that has ever come to the United States is more satisfactory under righteous treatment. The Mexican, as the result of years of servitude, has always looked upon his employer as his patron, and upon himself as part of the establishment.

During this period there was a burst of concern among sociologists and social workers and other "subsidized sympathizers" over the life-style, health, diet, and politics of Mexican immigrants. As Carey McWilliams put it, "do-gooders subjected the Mexican population to a relentless barrage of surveys, investigations, and clinical conferences."

But the welcome mat for the immigrant who looked "upon himself as a member of the establishment" was quickly rolled up when the Great Depression of the 1930s hit. Suddenly Anglos were out of work and willing even to do the wretched stoop labor that had been the sole preserve of the Mexicans in the late 1920s. Mexican immigrants were suddenly both competitors for scarce jobs and potential welfare burdens; official approval and academic solicitude abruptly evaporated. By 1930 the problem was to get rid of the Mexicans. One possibility was mass deportation, but this involved a slight snag; a fair portion of the Mexican population consisted of youngsters who had been born in the United States and thus, embarrassingly, were American citizens. Furthermore, if the expulsion was to be based on illegal entry, federal regulations required a public hearing and a formal deportation order. Clearly, legal deportation could not be used efficiently to expel the large numbers of now superfluous Mexicans.

The solution suggested by social workers was to persuade them to leave voluntarily. Reportedly, numerous Mexicans on relief were "willing" to go back home. The ever civic-minded Southern Pacific Railroad determined that it could arrange shipment of Mexicans en masse to Mexico City for less than $15 apiece. This was less than a week of welfare payments, so the great expulsion was begun early in 1931. By April 1932, the *Los Angeles Times* was able to report that the U.S. had gotten rid of more than 200,000 Mexicans and that between 50,000 and 75,000 were removed from California, more than 35,000 from Los Angeles County alone.

The whole program was considered a fiscal triumph. The county spent a little over $77,000 to send a shipment of 6,024 *repatriados;* the welfare payments to which the group was entitled would have added up to nearly $425,000. The county saved more than 80 percent. No one asked who had created the wealth that was so proudly being saved.

That so many Mexican immigrants left the United States quietly added to the myth of the docile, almost subhuman labor pool that American agricultural and industrial employers assumed could be exploited perpetually on the employer's terms. Attitudes toward the Mexican labor force are exemplified by a famous quote from a Kern County, California, deputy sheriff:

". . . the Mexicans are trash. They have no standard of living. We herd them like pigs."

But in truth, Mexican farm laborers were anything but servile workers. Mexicans and Mexican-Americans have a long history of involvement in attempts to organize agricultural labor in the United States. Indeed, the first attempt of agricultural workers to organize in the United States came in 1883 when a group of cowboys went on strike in the Texas Panhandle. The call to strike was signed by one Juan Gómez.

Traditionally, Mexican immigrant labor was heavily employed in the sugar-beet industry. In that industry, conditions for those working in the fields were marginal at best—whether they were working in California, Colorado, or the north central states. Just after the turn of the century, these conditions led to a strike of Mexican and Japanese sugar-beet workers at Ventura, California. The strike lasted two months and involved some violence. The workers were victorious, winning the right to negotiate directly with growers rather than with a labor contractor.

A strike by Mexican streetcar workers in Los Angeles in 1910 led to the dynamiting of the *Los Angeles Times* offices, and in the 1920s there were repeated efforts to organize Mexican workers in California. Finally, in 1927 the CUOM (*Confederación de Uniones Obreras Mexicanas*—Confederation of Mexican Workers' Unions) was formed. The CUOM was modeled on the main labor union in Mexico, the CROM (*Confederación Regional Obrera Mexicana*). It had some 3,000 members in twenty locals. In 1928 when the CUOM called its first strike, it was against melon growers in the rich Imperial Valley. The growers broke the strike by a combination of threats and coercion. The local sheriff, one Charles Gilbert, carried out large-scale arrests in support of the growers, and there were threats of deportation and of importing scabs from Texas. Although the workers lost, efforts to organize in the area actually increased after the strike.

A second strike was called in the Imperial Valley in 1930. Five thousand field workers walked off the job. The surprised growers made some concessions to get the Mexican workers back in the fields, but later, when the cantaloupe harvest was about to begin, they arranged 103 arrests and extensive coercion to prevent another strike.

These strikes were only the beginning. During the depression, Mexican-American agricultural workers, like many other American workers, were attracted to radical labor groups. In the Southwest one of the most prominent was the Trade Union Unity League (TUUL): another, the Cannery and Agricultural Workers Industrial Union (CAWIU). Strikes inspired by these left-wing unions allowed many growers to claim that labor-organizing was a Communist plot. Whether or not the Communists were involved, however, the real source of labor unrest was wages. Not even in 1933 could a man live on the nine cents an hour some workers received. In 1933 large agricultural strikes were called in California by the CAWIU. Seventy-five percent of the strikers were Mexicans. Their action can be accounted for by the miserable wages, appalling working and living conditions, and the racial injustice they were subjected to—not by the philosophy of the union.

Strikes were often met with violence in the 1930s, as they have been in the 1960s and 1970s. Those in which Mexicans were involved were certainly not exceptions. When the CAWIU called out cotton pickers in the San Joaquin Valley in October 1933, the strikers eventually numbered 18,000. The growers evicted the strikers from their camps, and eventually a strike headquarters was set up near Corcoran on a rented farm. The workers tried to picket over a 100-mile-long perimeter and were harassed continually by the growers' vigilante groups. The vigilantes shot up the union hall at Pixley, killing two strikers and wounding others, and the same day killed another striker at Arvin.

The growers, supported by the California Chamber of Commerce, formed the Associated Farmers of California, a group dedicated to preventing the organization of farm laborers. In spite of the Association's activities, Mexicans continued to organize effective agricultural unions and to wrest concessions from growers despite the harassment and violence to which they were subjected. César Chávez and the United Farm Workers come from a long and noble tradition.

Before and during the depression, agricultural workers were not the only Mexicans who attempted to improve their lot by striking. Mexican miners provided leadership in copper-mine strikes going back to the turn of the century, and Mexican coal miners were involved in a major lengthy strike against the Gallup-American Company in New Mexico in 1935. Much of the unrest among Mexican-American miners and other nonagricultural workers was caused by discriminatory wage practices, with Anglo workers being paid more money for the same work.

By the end of the depression, it should have been clear to any reasonable observer that potential Mexican immigrants could not be viewed as a pool of robotlike workers who would put up indefinitely with hard labor under wretched conditions without complaint. They were not the "good Mexicans" of movie fame or of the imaginations of racist civic leaders in Los Angeles. Mexican leaders had shown great initiative in organizing their fellows.

Even with small, poor unions operating against growers and owners who were supported by local power structures, they had had some success in ameliorating the worst conditions. And they did it in spite of what Robert Cleland described as the customary weapons of California's industrial agriculture: "Gas, goon squads, propaganda, bribery."

The Bracero Program

The onset of the Second World War changed the Mexican-American labor situation dramatically. Those Mexicans who had remained in the U.S. after the mass expulsion at the beginning of the depression, along with various workers of various origins—constituted a sufficient farm-labor pool for the country in times of economic hardship. But now the demands of an industrial establishment tooling up for a global war were draining labor from the farm pool by offering decent wages and working conditions. Furthermore, in 1942 the wartime agricultural effort was dealt a telling and needless blow by the forced resettlement of Japanese-Americans from the West Coast. One of the side effects of that disgraceful episode was to remove some of the most skilled and industrious farmers from the area.

As a result of all this, and much to the distress of the growers, the gap between agricultural and industrial wages began to close. This trend was arrested with the help of the government through the imposition of wage ceilings. But the ceilings naturally did not solve the problem of labor shortage. The obvious place to turn to refill the pool of cheap labor was Mexico. The move was not, however, without potential shortcomings from the point of view of agribusiness. The speed and scale of operations required by the wartime emergency meant that the federal government would have to be an active participant in the planned migration. With the government involved, standards for wages and conditions of transport, housing, and work would probably be set up for the foreign workers. There might later be demands that the protection of such standards be extended to domestic workers—a distasteful notion to those accustomed to exploiting agricultural labor on their own terms.

Nonetheless, the appeal of government-planned and -managed migration of Mexican workers was overwhelming. A nonunion labor force of appropriate size would be formed that could not be lured to booming war industries, and much of the financial burden of assembling and maintaining the pool of workers could be shifted to the shoulders of the taxpayer.

The pressures for controlled migration began to build in 1941, but the U.S. Government resisted them that year. With the start of the war, however, official policy shifted rapidly. Negotiations were started in the spring of 1942 with the Mexican government, which would not permit unregulated hiring of its citizens—it had been sensitized by the mass expulsion of Mexicans and Mexican-Americans at the beginning of the depression.

By mid-summer 1942, after Mexico had joined the Allied side of the war, a U.S.–Mexican executive agreement to import Mexican labor legally was signed. It was agreed that the Mexican workers, *braceros* as they became known, were not to be used to displace Americans, but only to fill in where there were genuine shortages. Mexicans could not be used to depress wages. The immigrant workers were guaranteed full transport to and from their homes and free subsistence en route. Working conditions were specified and pay guaranteed at prevailing rates for a minimum of 75 percent of the contract period. A *bracero* had the right to terminate his contract at any time.

The train carrying the first *bracero* shipment, some 1,500 Mexican workers, pulled into Stockton, California, on September 29, 1942. Chalked on the railroad cars was the slogan, *"De Las Democracias Será La Victoria"* (Victory will come from the democracies). The program was initially under the control of a New Deal agency, the Farm Security Administration (FSA), which administered it in an exemplary fashion. Each *bracero* signed an individual agreement with the FSA which contained the guarantees of the U.S.–Mexico executive agreement, and the agreements the FSA signed with the growers' organizations also contained the guarantees. Mexican consular and labor officials were allowed to police the agreements. The FSA even arranged welcoming ceremonies for the *braceros* and had educational and recreational programs planned for them. The FSA had the notion that *braceros*, on their return, could be ambassadors of goodwill for the U.S. in Mexico.

The growers were interested in cheap labor, not in goodwill. They attacked the FSA from the start, and soon after the *bracero* program began, they brought political pressure to bear to get the migrant workers out from under FSA jurisdiction. One Mr. C.C. Teague of the citrus industry, representing Governor Earl Warren, testified before a U.S. Senate committee that the FSA was not the right agency to administer the program—and that the FSA was making relations between employers and *braceros* difficult (presumably by trying to make the growers live up to the executive agreement). Grower pressure was sufficient to get the program transferred to the War Food Administration, which appears to have been more concerned with keeping agribusiness profits high than with creating ambassadors of goodwill or prosecuting the war.

The *bracero* program was a bonanza for the growers. Between 1943 and 1947, some $120 million in federal funds were appropriated for the program, a massive subsidy for an industry already blessed with high prices and skyrocketing demand for its products. The agreement between Mexico and the U.S. expired at the end of 1947, but the era of the *bracero* was far from over. In January 1948, the U.S. Department of Labor became the agency responsible for dealing with Mexican migrant labor.

From 1948 on, the provision of *braceros* became a matter of direct contracting between growers and *braceros* (backed in part by the Mexican government), without agreements between the two governments. *Braceros* were generally favored as farm labor, especially in California, but the growers were not sure how well they could work things out with the Mexican government, which showed that distressing tendency to insist on a living wage for its nationals. Other restrictions on the use of *braceros*, such as a minimum four-month contract, which did not lend itself to short-term harvesting, added to the growers' tendency to use illegal immigrants, then known as "wetbacks," as an alternative labor supply while trying to shape the postwar *bracero* program more and more in their favor. Almost all students of the present illegal-alien problem trace its origins back to the years immediately after the Second World War when the agricultural community of the Southwest was adjusting its labor practices to a peacetime economy while trying to maintain the benefits of a wartime emergency measure.

Because they had been *braceros*, the new illegal migrants knew how to get to Harlingen or Casa Grande or Bakersfield, and they knew how to get out to the farms where the jobs were. They also knew they would be welcomed by their wartime employers. And getting across the border was no trick at all. The wetbacks were as glad to have the employment as the growers were to have them as employees. By Mexican wage standards, the pay was good and, after all, they were simply doing the same work for the same bosses they had been doing for the previous five years. By 1948 wetbacks made up a substantial portion of the farm-labor force in the Southwest. In California alone there were estimated to be more than 40,000 in 1948, and by 1951 the tomato harvest was done by about an equal mix of wetbacks and *braceros*, with American citizens and permanent residents running a poor third.

Some idea of the scale of the wetback immigration can be seen in INS statistics on deportations of Mexicans, almost all of whom had "entered without inspection." In 1944 the number was over 29,000; in 1945 it jumped to over 69,000; in 1948 it had tripled again, and then it increased steadily to a peak of 1.1 million in 1954.

Even with this wave of illegal immigration, pressure from Western growers for *bracero* labor pushed the U.S. Government into renewed negotiations with Mexico in 1951. The Mexicans then insisted on supervision of any labor contracting by a U.S. Government agency. The result was Public Law 78, which provided for the recruitment of Mexican agricultural workers under the supervision of the Secretary of Labor.

The "Repatriation" of 1954 and "Operation Wetback"

By 1954 the new, postwar *bracero* program was functioning, and, with over 300,000 Mexican workers brought in under it that year, no one needed the wetbacks anymore. Consequently, there was a campaign to round up Mexicans who had entered the country illegally and to expel them—or "repatriate" them, as the U.S. Government chose to call it. The effort was a massive one with operations reaching from California to the Gulf Coast. According to a story still told in the INS, it was President Eisenhower's original intention to use regular army troops for the project, but when he approached his West Point classmate General Joseph Swing, a World War II airborne division commander, the general tried to persuade the President that this would be an inappropriate use of federal troops. Eisenhower was still convinced that military-style operations were called for and prevailed on General Swing to become commissioner of the Immigration and Naturalization Service to oversee them. One such operation was mounted, inelegantly called "Operation Wetback," of which the 1954 INS *Annual Report* says:

> . . . the Attorney General announced on June 9, 1954 that the Border Patrol would begin an operation on June 17 to rid Southern California and Western Arizona of "wetbacks." . . . a band of roadblocks and railroad blocks was established and manned some distance from the border to prevent the escape of those who might flee toward the North. . . .
> On June 17 a special force of approximately 800 officers from all Border Patrol Sectors was assembled at El Centro and Chula Vista, California. The operation was divided into task forces which, in turn, were divided into command units, consisting of 12 men headed by a Senior Patrol Inspector and equipped with trucks, jeeps, and automobiles. . . .
> When the task force went into action they used a system of blocking off an area and mopping it up. Gradually they enlarged the operation until it embraced the industrial and agricultural areas of the entire State of California.

Despite its military jargon—task force, command unit, mopping up—the INS report could not come up with anything that showed the operation had been much of a success. The effort apprehended over 32,000 illegals during its 17 days in the month of June, which sounds impressive until one realizes that this averages less than three illegals per patrol officer per day. What the INS could not prove with numbers it tried to demonstrate with rhetoric:

> These aliens who entered the United States illegally are responsible for 75 percent of all crimes committed in some Southern California and Texas counties. Jails are frequently filled to capacity by illegal entrants committed for crimes ranging from theft and vagrancy to murder.

The *Report* fails to specify which counties bore the brunt of this scourge, nor does it give figures for the drop in violent crime in those counties that must have resulted from the ousting of so many miscreants. Finally, the INS used the ultimate threat of the early 1950s to justify their effort: "Even more serious is the possibility that among the 'wetbacks' who seek employment there may be those whose entry would be detrimental to our national security." Of course, no evidence is presented that there was any threat "to our national security" from this quarter, but no one knows how many Soviet or Chinese spies might have been out in those fields gaining invaluable information on how Americans pick tomatoes, prune grape vines, and otherwise maintain their agricultural power.

One claim for the success of the operation is as remarkable as it is shameful. The *Report* says:

> . . . As the drive progressed the results showed that approximately 10 percent of the "wetbacks" who had been discovered were employed in industry. Their forced departure resulted in a drop in weekly unemployment claims in the State amounting to some $325,000.

Could the writer of the *Report* really have been unaware that unemployment compensation is something that a worker, regardless of his status of residence, *earns* from his labor? A certain percentage of the employee's wages or the employer's profits is skimmed off and put in a fund to provide for that rainy day when the employer does not need the employee anymore. Unemployment is a part of the cost of the American way of doing business. Through "Operation Wetback," the United States kept part of the product of a man's labor, but exported his unemployment to Mexico, and an agency of the United States Government bragged about it.

The illegals expelled in 1954 were not just dumped out on the other side of the fence at Tijuana or Juárez, but were sent deep into Mexico with the "invaluable cooperation and assistance" of the Mexican government:

> . . . the aliens were placed aboard special trains and conveyed, under Mexican escort and at the expense of the Mexican government, to points deep in the interior . . . far removed from the temptation to return. . . .

Over 20,000 illegals were shipped back to Mexico aboard ships from Port Isabel, Texas. One of the ships was ironically named the *SS Emancipation*.

All this effort increased the number of apprehensions by less than 20 percent over the previous year when routine methods had been used. But it was subsequently declared a success because apprehensions dropped from a high of slightly over a million in 1954 to 72,000 in 1956 and 30,000 in 1959.

While the INS was very proud of "ridding the country of wetbacks," it did not mean an end to Mexican labor in American fields. As a part of Operation Wetback, "employers were urged to arrange for contract labor, and most of them did." The *bracero* simply replaced the illegal. In the period 1955–59, about one-quarter of the hired farm workers in California, Arizona, New Mexico, and Texas were legal *braceros*. In 1957 roughly 10 percent of all those over the age of fourteen who worked for wages on farms in the 48 states were *braceros*.

The Bracero Program continued into the early 1960s when a combination of forces conspired to close it down. With its discontinuance, the number of apprehensions of illegals started to climb again. In 1965 it was over 100,000 and reached nearly 350,000 in 1970. By 1978 it had topped a million again, the first time since 1954. One way or another, the Mexicans are still finding their way into the fields of the Southwest, just as they have ever since modern agriculture was introduced there.

Thus it is clear that at various times since 1920, Mexican immigrants, both legal and illegal, have been welcomed into the United States—mostly because of their value as agricultural laborers. After the passage of restrictive immigration policies in 1917–24, Mexico replaced Eastern and Southern Europe as the prime source of cheap labor—resulting in a legal and illegal flow that was only temporarily stemmed by the depression.

But what kind of welcome did Mexican immigrants find? When the depression started, the "welcome mat" was retracted with lightning speed, and close examination seems to indicate that, even in the best of times, the welcome mat was thin indeed. To understand this, it is necessary to examine "racial" prejudice against Mexicans in general, and in particular the so-called *Leyenda Negra*—a complex of pejorative notions about the qualities and habits of Hispanic peoples.

LA LEYENDA NEGRA

Recently it has become clear that variation in human characteristics is so complex that no biological units can be identified as distinct races. Instead it is now recognized that human "races" are socially defined entities, and the definitions are based on a mixture of real and imaginary characteristics. The swarthy, lazy, stupid Mexican with "no standard of living" is just such a socially defined race—defined by (on the average) lighter-skinned, not-too-bright Anglos too lazy to become familiar with Mexican culture and looking for an excuse to feel superior.

The origins of Anglo prejudice against Mexican-Americans may never be completely understood. The prejudice could be rooted in the xenophobia that probably characterized most groups of human beings in the distant past. It could be related to the complex problem of prejudice against darker-skinned people by lighter-skinned ones, a brand of nonsense not limited to insecure WASPs. Japanese, for example, had a strong preference for white skin and prejudices against those with dark complexions long before they had contact with the West. Curiously, however, it is not the white skin of the European that they admire, as can be seen in the following quote from a modern Japanese.

> This may be completely unscientific but I feel when I look at the skin of a Japanese woman I see the whiteness of her skin, when I observe Caucasian skin, what I see is the whiteness of the fat underneath the skin, not the whiteness of the skin itself.

In *A Passage to India,* E.M. Forster called Caucasians "pinkogreys" rather than "whites."

A large part of the Anglo prejudice against the "greaser" and the reciprocal Mexican prejudice against the "gringo" can be explained by historical events. These events occurred long before affairs in Texas and the Mexican War further inflamed mutual hatreds; they can be traced all the way back to the sixteenth century.

Elizabethan England gave William Shakespeare to Western civilization and Protestantism to North America. It also gave North America *la Leyenda Negra*—the Black Legend of the

Spanish. A massive campaign of anti-Spanish propaganda was fueled mostly by stories of Spanish treatment of the native inhabitants of the New World. The English public eagerly accepted the horror stories because they gave moral justification to English piracy, a principal weapon in the fierce struggle between England and Spain for control of the New World. The Spanish debate over the proper way to treat the Indians supplied most of the basic ammunition, particularly the writings of a Dominican brother, Bartolomé de las Casas, Bishop of Chiapas, a leading opponent of official Spanish policy. His *History of the Destruction of the Indies* vividly described the cruel exploitation of the Indians. The treatment of Protestant English sailors who fell into the hands of the Spanish Inquisition, a royal police and court system manned by churchmen and aimed at guaranteeing the purity of political and religious thought in Spanish lands, further fanned the flames. Finally, the atrocities committed by the Spanish against the Protestant Dutch during the Dutch War for Independence supplied the rest of the stories needed to keep English hatred of the Spanish going.

Anti-Spanish, anti-Catholic attitudes were transplanted to North America along with English colonists. These took hold especially strongly in New England, where colonists tended to be Calvinists dedicated to the notion that hard work meant not only success in this life but indicated salvation in the next; labor, not birthright, was the key to success.

The Spanish and the English also took different views of the American Indians. The reasons for this obviously were many. The Spanish had had long and intimate contact with Moorish civilization during the *reconquista,* the expulsion of the Moors from the Iberian Peninsula. The English had much less experience with people of dark complexion; what little they had tended to be with the miserable slaves torn from their cultural context in Africa. The English first came into contact with Indians who did not live in permanent settlements; the *conquistadores* had to deal with the highly civilized Aztecs.

The Spanish held the Indians they conquered in *encomienda* or trust—that is, in servitude. They were, of course, prejudiced against the Indians, but sexual relations between Spanish men and Indian women were accepted if not approved. Many Spaniards maintained an Indian mistress in a *casa chica* (little house). The conversion of Mexico to a *mestizo* (white-Indian hybrid) nation began early.

The English attitude toward the native inhabitants of the Western Hemisphere quickly became that of the American frontiersman—"the only good Indian is a dead Indian." Shove them out of the way or exterminate them and get on with settling the continent is a fair view of U.S. Government policy from 1776 to around 1900, and elements of that attitude toward Native Americans persist in high places today.

When Americans of Anglo background first made contact with the Spanish culture in the Southwest and California, they were charmed in some ways but appalled in others. The Spanish founders of New World colonies were aristocrats interested both in finding wealth for themselves and in propagating the teachings of their Christian faith. The system of *conquistadores,* priests, and *encomienderos* that they had established was dramatically different from the social system that had been established by English colonists on the East Coast of North America.

It is not surprising, therefore, that relations between Mexicans and Anglos were generally bad from the time of first contact. The Anglos tended to extend their attitudes about Indians to include "Indians and Mexicans" and to look down on anyone without light complexions and unaffected by the Protestant ethic. These attitudes and the reciprocal distrust by Mexicans of the aggressive gringos contributed to the many Anglo-Mexican conflicts in the borderlands and to the ferocity of the Mexican War in the 1840s. The *Leyenda Negra* also became part of the excuse for the vile treatment of Mexican-Americans—especially the expropriation of their lands—in the conquered areas after the Mexican War. It is one of the ironies of history that an attitude based in part on the dislike of early English capitalists for the way Spanish noblemen treated Indians has persisted as prejudice against the descendants of those Indians.

In the century between the Mexican War and World War II, Mexican-Americans were generally pressed into the position of second-class citizens throughout the Southwest. The provisions for their protection built into the Treaty of Guadalupe Hidalgo which ended the Mexican War were generally ignored. The first large-scale conflicts between the two communities came immediately after the war, with the discovery of gold in California, newly acquired by the United States. Some 100,000 new immigrants, mostly Anglos, poured into the state in 1849 hoping to strike it rich. Spanish-speaking miners were subjected to violent harassment and in many areas were excluded from the diggings.

When it became clear that not everyone was going to get rich in the gold fields, Anglos began to grab land from the huge *ranchos* of the *Californios* (old-time Mexican inhabitants of California—as distinguished, for example, from the Sonoran miners who moved into California during the gold rush). The *ranchos,* held under poorly defined Spanish land grants, were difficult to defend in the face of a concerted attack by a wide variety of Anglo scoundrels who included legislators, judges, and attorneys. Public opinion had become increasingly anti-Hispanic and supported the reduction of the *ranchos*.

In 1850 and 1851 the land conflicts gave rise to a period of banditry from which was generated, among others, the legend of Joaquín Murieta. Although fable would have it that *Californio* road agents of the period were Robin Hood-type characters who stole from rich Anglos and gave to poor Mexicans, there is reason to believe that they generally stole from the rich and kept it themselves. Whatever the truth of the matter, the Anglos used Mexican banditry as an excuse to abuse all Mexicans, a phenomenon of cultural generalization frequently encountered among bigots even today.

In both California and Texas, but especially in California, there also developed among the Anglos a nostalgia for the old Hispanic culture—or at least for what they imagined it had been. The image of Spanish dons and their beautiful wives in combination with kindly mission priests turning California into a land of milk and honey is treasured even today by many Anglos in California. It is a myth that was nurtured in part by early *Californios* (and in parallel in Texas by the original *tejanos*) who looked down upon more recently arrived Mexicans. Some of the early Hispanics intermarried with Anglos, and many identified with their interests. For example, while New Mexico was a territory (it did not become a state until 1912), wealthy Hispanic elements, sometimes known as *ricos*, collaborated with their Anglo counterparts in dominating the politics and economics of the territory—and in exploiting more recently arrived Mexicans. Although in California and Texas, Mexican immigrants from various periods became reasonably well integrated, in New Mexico the descendants of the early Hispanics kept their distance from the Mexicans and treated them as the Anglos did.

In the first part of the twentieth century, the efforts of Anglos and rich Hispanics to denigrate the average Mexican received support from racists in the scientific community. One of the most eminent psychologists of the day, Lewis Terman of Stanford University, wrote in 1916 that "high grade moronity" or "borderline" mental deficiency was very common among Mexican families. He used this "observation" as part of the basis for his suggestion that Mexicans were an inferior race, and that the inferiority was genetic and not correctable by education. Terman was upset by the reluctance of society to stop such people from breeding since their children would be ". . . uneducable beyond the merest rudiments of training. No amount of school instruc-

tion will ever make them intelligent voters or capable citizens . . ."
Such nonsense has kept the *Leyenda Negra* going for 400 years.

On the eve of the Second World War in California, the status of
the Mexican-American was clear to all. In a state where every
other street and landscape feature had a Spanish name, where
Santa Barbara had an annual "fiesta" for which everyone dressed
up like *caballeros* and Spanish ladies, where Los Angeles celebrated the Mexican holiday of *Cinco de Mayo,* the Mexican-
American was a thoroughly second-class citizen. He, or his cousin
from Mexico, was welcome as a cheap laborer as long as there was
work—and instantly unwanted when there were no more jobs.
Ironically, although pictured as lazy (or thieving) in the *Leyenda
Negra,* it was only for his or her willingness to work harder for less
that the Mexican was tolerated.

The war should have greatly altered the Anglo's view of the
Mexican. Not only did a disproportionately large number of
Mexican-Americans serve in the armed forces, but many Mexican
nationals living in the United States enlisted. Service in the armed
forces provided an easy route to naturalization for Mexicans who
were not yet citizens. In addition, many Mexican-American
youths clearly saw military service as a route to better jobs and
better treatment. Of course, the high percentage of Mexican-
Americans in the armed forces was partly due to the high proportion of draft-age men in the Mexican-American population and
to the small percentage of those men whose jobs qualified them
for deferments. Even beyond their heavy representation in the
armed forces, Mexican-Americans had a higher proportion of
men serving in combat divisions of the army than any other ethnic
group, and they were heavily represented in the marines and
paratroops. There is little doubt that a combination of a genuine
desire to participate and a tradition of machismo caused these
young men to select such hazardous duty.

Considering all this, it is not surprising that Mexican-American
soldiers both suffered heavy casualties and were heavily decorated. It is little known that about one-quarter of the U.S. combat
troops defending Bataan were Mexican-American—a consequence of the transfer to the Philippines shortly before the war of
two units of the New Mexico National Guard. As a result, many
Chicano soldiers died on the infamous Bataan Death March after
General Wainright surrendered Bataan and Corregidor. The
largest state building in Santa Fe is called Bataan Hall in their
honor.

Mexican-American troops served with great distinction from
North Africa, Italy, and France to the China-Burma-India theater and the Aleutians. Seventeen won Congressional Medals of

Honor—indeed five of 14 Texans who won the medal were members of *la Raza*. One of them, José López from Brownsville, not only received the highest decoration of the United States but also the highest military honor of Mexico. President Miguel Alemán awarded him the Aztec Eagle.

The exploits of Mexican-American combat troops, like those of the gallant Japanese-Americans of the 442nd Regimental Combat team, were little publicized during the War. And, sadly, prejudice dogged Mexican-American soldiers even into the grave. In 1948 when Félix Longoria returned in a coffin from the Philippines to Three Rivers, Texas, the local mortician refused to hold services for him in his chapel. Most Texans were apparently horrified by the resulting uproar, and a then relatively obscure senator from Texas, Lyndon Baines Johnson, arranged for Longoria to be buried in Arlington National Cemetery.

Unfortunately for the Mexican-American community, the Second World War was a time of increased xenophobia in the United States. The nation was fighting the "treacherous little yellow men in the Pacific," and much of American wartime propaganda was openly racist. The treatment received by Japanese-Americans on the West Coast and the refusal of the government to allow black and white soldiers to fight and die together were symptomatic of deep-seated feelings in the U.S. about "people of color." In contrast, white Americans of German and Italian descent suffered virtually no discrimination during World War II.

The valor and dedication of Mexican-American troops were not a sufficient antidote for the *Leyenda Negra*. The worst outbreak of anti-Mexican racial violence in this century occurred in Los Angeles in 1943. It has been claimed that the city of Los Angeles was shocked to discover that all its problems did not disappear with the removal of the Japanese-Americans from the West Coast. The Los Angeles press, in search of another scapegoat, began a campaign focused on "Mexican" crime.

The "Zoot Suit" Riots

An incident that fired passions in both Mexican and Anglo communities in 1942 was the so-called Sleepy Lagoon Case—a reporter's after-the-fact name for a little pond in a gravel pit that Mexican youths used as a swimming hole. Members of rival gangs had "rumbled" in the vicinity on August 1, 1942, and the next day one youth, José Díaz, was picked up unconscious on a nearby dirt road. He died from a fracture at the base of his skull without regaining consciousness. From scratches and bruises it appeared that he had been in a fight. The results of an autopsy were inconclusive: Díaz could have died from being clubbed in a fight, from a fall or falls on the road, or having been hit by a car.

The papers leaped upon the incident and blew it up into a major mystery. On August 3, the *Los Angeles Times* carried a front-page story headlined "One Killed and 10 Hurt in Boy 'Wars' " and devoted 24 column inches to what was a tragic, but basically still a trivial story.

The police, eager to please the press and the Southern California establishment it represented, rounded up more than 20 members of a rival gang and charged them with murder. The story of the roundup on August 4 was headlined "Gangs Warned 'Kid Gloves Off,' " and the gangs described as "closely organized groups of youths, mostly Mexican" and "terror groups." On August 5, the front-page headline was "Jury Delves into Boy Gang Terror Wave." The *Times* contributed an inflammatory editorial excoriating "professional mollycoddlers" of gangs and calling for a "get tough" policy. It is another irony that less than two months later the first group of Mexican *braceros* were enthusiastically welcomed to Stockton, California.

The Sleepy Lagoon affair, meanwhile, quickly turned into an example of the legal system gone awry. Some of the youths were beaten by the police, and the judge, Charles W. Fricke, was later found by an appellate court to be biased and prejudiced. During the trial, Fricke did not allow the defendants to have haircuts or fresh clothes, and the gang members quickly started to look like the "dirty Mexican" of the stereotype.

Something of the atmosphere in which the trial was held can be gained from a related event. In response to the death of Díaz and the anti-Mexican frenzy of the Los Angeles press, a special committee of the Los Angeles Grand Jury was appointed to look into the "awful problem of Mexican juvenile delinquency." Two weeks after the gang members were arrested, a report was made to the committee by the head of the "Foreign Relations Bureau" of the Los Angeles sheriff's office. The author of the report was one Captain E. Duran Ayres, who first described the conditions under which Mexicans lived in Los Angeles County, and then proceeded to ascribe the involvement of Chicanos in delinquency to an inborn desire to "kill, or at least let blood." Not surprisingly, Radio Berlin, Radio Madrid, and Radio Tokyo all quoted passages from the report to show that the views of red-blooded Americans were just like those of Hitler after all!

There is little question that Ayres' views represented the official position of a major segment of the law-enforcement community of Los Angeles at that time. There is no question that law-enforcement agencies in Southern California *behaved* as if each

Mexican-American youth had an innate tendency to violence. In August of 1942 massive raids were carried out in blockaded Mexican-American districts, and many hundreds of citizens were detained or arrested, some for having an "implement that might have been used in assault cases . . ." In other words, anyone who had a dark skin or Latin name and had a jack handle in his car was out of luck. The newspaper coverage continued to be sensational.

Needless to say, the Mexican-American defendants in the Díaz trial were convicted on various charges early in 1943. Carey McWilliams and others promptly formed a defense committee and raised funds for an appeal. The committee was subjected to harassment and "Red-baiting" (McWilliams and others were subpoenaed and interrogated by the Committee on Un-American Activities in California), but it persisted and was finally victorious. In an unanimous decision on October 4, 1944, the Second District Court of Appeals reversed the convictions, noting that the members of the gang had had their constitutional rights violated, that the case had been mishandled by the judge, and that there was no evidence connecting the defendants with the death of Díaz.

But in the course of its successful struggle for justice, the committee further inflamed Anglo bigots and the yellow press. In 1943 attention began to be focused by the Los Angeles papers on the terms "*pachuco*" (for a Mexican-American teenager) and "zoot suit," which referred to the outlandish (to the establishment) style of dress affected by male *pachucos*.

In retrospect the *pachuco* gangs seem little different from teenagers of different periods and different ethnic origins. During the war there was a sizable second-generation population of Mexican-American teenagers in the Southwest. The boys doubtless felt great pressure to express their manhood in an era when virtually all of their immediate seniors were bearing arms in the defense of the nation. They also felt the sting of prejudice. In Los Angeles in 1943 a Mexican-American youth faced a series of restrictions and taboos that would be difficult for those under 35 years old to comprehend today. Numerous public places barred them or made it clear they were not wanted. Certainly such restrictions were not limited to Los Angeles. We well remember a restaurant in Topeka, Kansas, that, as late as 1954, had a sign proclaiming "Mexicans and Negroes served in bags only"! But in Los Angeles such ungrammatical insults were directed at a very large population of Mexican teenagers, creating the potential for large-scale trouble.

The *pachucos* expressed their alienation in part through their dress, in the time-honored manner of teenagers. They wore the "zoot suits" of the jitterbugger—flat, broad-brimmed hats, a long "draped" coat, and baggy pants with pegged cuffs and a high waist. Ornamentation was provided by a fancy key chain and a "duck's-ass" haircut. Although zoot suits were worn by boys of all ethnic groups at that time, "zoot-suiter" became a code word for Mexican-American delinquent in the Los Angeles press, even though the vast majority who wore the uniform were law-abiding citizens.

The inflammatory press and inflamed police produced a situation that saner heads warned would soon lead to violence if there were no attempt to cool things down. The Los Angeles area had another population of teenagers and post-teens with easily stirred passions—servicemen, mostly sailors, on leave and looking for action.

In April and May of 1943 the prediction began to be borne out. Clashes between young men in uniform attempting to pick up Mexican-American girls and the girls' *pachuco* escorts began to occur. In early June these clashes developed into full-scale race riots. After some preliminary skirmishing on June 4, about 200 sailors crowded into 20 taxis and set out to show the *pachucos* their own brand of law and order—to "clean up the situation." Four zoot-suiters were beaten, but the Los Angeles police showed an astonishing inability to intercept the 20-cab caravan. The *Los Angeles Herald-Express* approvingly headlined its front-page story, "Sailor Task Force Hits L.A. Zooters."

On the nights of June 5 and 6, the sailors and marines repeated their rampage, while the L.A. cops followed them around, arresting their beaten and bleeding victims. On June 7, the *Los Angeles Times* headline read "Zoot Suiters Learn Lesson in Fights with Servicemen." The story began:

> Those gamin dandies, the zoot suiters, having learned a great moral lesson from servicemen, mostly sailors, who took over their instruction three days ago, are staying home nights.

The front-page picture shows "zoot-suiters" who were "stripped of clothing by servicemen" lined up for booking at the county jail. But this was just a prologue to the serious rioting on the nights of June 7 and 8, all carefully orchestrated by the Los Angeles press, which had boldly announced that the *pachucos* would no longer submit to being beaten but would retaliate.

Whipped up by the press, a mob of several thousand Anglo service personnel and civilians rioted in downtown Los Angeles on the night of June 7, stripping and beating every Mexican they could find and some blacks and Filipinos for good measure. Theater managers were required to turn on the house lights, and patrons of the wrong complexion were dragged out and assaulted. The police, anxious to show that brutality was a necessary adjunct to law enforcement because one of their number was on trial at the time for kicking a drunk to death, pitched in with beatings of their own. *Pachucos* were arrested on sight and clobbered if they did not submit immediately. In one oft-cited incident, a young Mexican-American man with a wooden leg was clubbed to the pavement by a police officer and kicked in the face. But the police made no move to interfere with the rioting Anglos.

Military police finally intervened to do the job that the city police were unwilling to do, in part because Washington felt pressure from the Mexican government with whom it was allied in the war and upon whom it was dependent for the functioning of the *bracero* program. By June 11, the papers had turned "responsible." The *Times* had a front-page editorial called "Time for Sanity," appealing to people not to condemn all Mexican-Americans because "some irresponsibles were causing trouble." That the *Times* was a major "irresponsible" was not mentioned. Westbrook Pegler contributed his inimitable analysis in a column on June 14, placing the blame on the zoot-suiters because "American soldiers and sailors are almost always well-behaved." By mid-June the rioting was over in Los Angeles, but a summer of race riots had been sparked in Detroit, Harlem, and Beaumont, Texas. Those in Detroit on June 19 and 20 resulted in the deaths of 25 blacks and nine whites and hundreds of injuries.

Reaction to the zoot-suit riots in the United States included a statement by Eleanor Roosevelt that riots could be traced to long-standing discrimination against Chicanos. "For a long time," she said, "I've worried about the attitude toward Mexicans in California and the states along the border." The California Chamber of Commerce quickly counterattacked. Its president, Preston Hotchkis, declared that Mrs. Roosevelt was dead wrong—that the zoot-suit riots

> have never been and are not now in the nature of race riots. . . .
> The statement that the citizens of California have discriminated against persons of Mexican origin is untrue, unjust and provocative of disunion among people who have lived for years in harmony.

In an editorial published the same day as the Hotchkis story, the *Los Angeles Times* agreed with him. Mrs. Roosevelt's statement was "as untrue as it is dangerous." It followed "Communist party line propaganda." Part of the editorial statement deserves reprinting—and reading to the sound of soft violins:

As for "long-standing discrimination" Mrs. Roosevelt ignores history, fact and happy tradition. California is a State that grew out of Spanish and Mexican civilization and it has always been rather ostentatiously proud of it. We have bragged of our Spanish and Mexican missions. We have paid homage and honor to the Californians of Mexican descent among us. Probably the most popular public official in Southern California is Sheriff Eugene Biscalluz, proud scion of a California family. The most beloved entertainment group in California's famous fiestas is the José Arias musical family, worthy Mexican descendants. We have the largest Mexican colony in the United States here and we enjoy fraternizing with them. We have been solicitous for their welfare in times of depression. We proudly maintain Olivera Street—a bit of Old Mexico—as a constant reminder of our affection for and our cordial relations with our sister republic.

In Mexico, *El Nacional,* the official government newspaper, in its first comment on the riots on June 17 expressed confidence that U.S. investigations would "yield a just decision." Harking back to the Ayres report, however, it noted that the Los Angeles Police Department had "entered the regions of Nazi biology" by saying that Mexicans were criminally inclined.

An investigating committee appointed by Governor Warren and headed by Bishop (later Archbishop) Joseph McGucken of Los Angeles lived up to *El Nacional's* high expectations. The committee determined that, contrary to the statements of the California Chamber of Commerce, the Los Angeles city government, and the *Los Angeles Times,* the riots had been race riots. It further found that the newspapers themselves and the police had to bear the major responsibility for the riots. The report stands in sharp contrast to the asininity of the Los Angeles City Council which, shortly after the riots, considered passing an ordinance that would have made wearing a zoot suit a crime! One pathetic consequence of these occurrences was the conversion of Sleepy Lagoon to a paid recreation area, effectively barring Mexican-American youths from one of the few swimming holes accessible to them. "Zoot Suiters to Lose one of Hangouts," bragged the *Times.* "Now in the near future Sleepy Lagoon will be fenced, there will be husky guards on duty, and zooters will have to go elsewhere to have their battles."

The Chicanos and Hispanics

A lot of things have changed since the Second World War, but the changes have come very slowly. Mexican-American soldiers shed their blood disproportionately in the Vietnam War, for

much the same reasons that they did in World War II. Some
Mexican-American families have been in the Southwestern
United States longer than the Anglos, and many have been there
for two or three generations. But they are only now beginning to
enter the mainstream of society.

The American public discovered the Chicanos and other citizens of Hispanic origin again in 1978. In October, *Time* did a
cover story on them, and in January 1979, *Newsweek* devoted five
pages to the Chicanos. News features in the press and on television abounded. Their discovery is something like the overnight
success of a movie star who has been in the business for 30 years. It
is not that they just arrived, it is just that someone started noticing.
It was customary to say that there were 12 million Hispanics in the
United States in 1978, or four times as many as reported in the
1960 Census, and that about 60 percent were "Chicano." Other
than the 1.8 million Puerto Ricans, the Chicanos are the only part
of the Hispanic population who are numerous enough or have
been here long enough to have a clearly recognized place in
American society. While Puerto Ricans are certainly Hispanic and
in many respects are "immigrants," they are, of course, native-
born American citizens.

Chicano is a word of disputed origin that is applied to Americans of Mexican descent who have retained at least some of the
Spanish language and participate in a distinctive U.S. subculture.
Even within the Mexican-American community, the word is controversial. While it is a source of pride and distinctive identity to
many Americans of Mexican descent and heritage, it is offensive
to many others because it seems a barrier to acceptance. Many
Anglos find it offensive, although why is not clear. Some feel the
term is fading from use, and it does seem that more and more
Chicanos are simply calling themselves "Mexicans." We use the
word here because it is convenient.

One of the great problems of the Chicano has been asserting his
or her cultural identity. In the United States he is regarded as
Mexican, and by the Mexicans he is regarded as *pocho*, a derogatory term meaning literally blemished or tainted and used to
describe an Americanized Mexican. His culture is not truly Mexican and not truly Anglo. The attempt to define it has led to a
self-conscious effort at literary and artistic expression. Best
known are the wall paintings that enliven the East Los Angeles
barrio, and there is a remarkably vital community of Chicano
poets and writers throughout the Southwest.

Currently, the best-known Chicano literary figure is Luis Valdez, whose play *Zoot Suit* is based on the 1943 riots in Los Angeles.
For many years Valdez has been the driving force in *El Teatro*

Campesino, a Chicano theater group based in San Juan Bautista, California, which originally grew out of the activities of the United Farm Workers. Váldez and *El Teatro* have a long and distinctive record of bold, innovative productions performed in Spanish and unabashedly intended to raise the political and social consciousness of Chicanos. For example, Valdez brought *El Teatro* into the fields to help César Chávez in the 1960s. That Valdez can now address the greater society in a play that is Chicano in theme, writing, acting, and production, and achieve financial and critical success is testimony not only to the power of his artistry but to the vitality of the Chicano emergence.

A remarkable increase in the size and affluence of the Hispanic community explains the sudden attention paid it by Americans. As is the case with some other population statistics in this book, no one really knows how many Hispanics there are, and the number of Chicanos is even harder to establish. Ethnic identity in the United States census is "self-ascriptive"; that is, the individual filling out the form defines himself. Thus a person who was Frank Torres in the phone book in 1960 and identified himself as white on the census form that year may have called himself Francisco Torres and counted himself as an Hispanic in 1970. A great many young people, children of Hispanics who used to declare themselves part of the majority, are now openly declaring themselves as Hispanics and Chicanos. Another reason for not knowing how many Hispanics there are is that so many of them, especially Chicanos and Puerto Ricans, are very poor; and all of the poor—black, Hispanic, Anglo, or whatever—are undercounted. The Census Bureau is making a special effort in its 1980 Census to come up with a better count of Hispanics.

The pattern of migration back and forth across the U.S.–Mexican border has already been described. Although some Chicanos can trace their ancestry in the U.S. back to the seventeenth century when most of the Southwest was part of Mexico, Mexican immigrants started coming in large numbers only in this century, the first wave during and immediately after the 1910–1917 Revolution and another starting in the 1960s. Those who stayed despite the "repatriations" of the 1930s are now grandparents, and the earlier arrivals from even the current wave have been here long enough to be established.

One has always been able to hear Spanish spoken in the southern half of California and in much of the rest of the Southwest, but a decade ago, even five years ago, one had to go to the "Mexican" part of town to hear it. Now it is out where the Anglos live. When one goes into the stores, and not only the cheap discount houses, the sign reads *"Calzados para Caballeros"* in the same size print as it says "Shoes for men." This is not just government-mandated bilingualism, it is simply good business. An increasing number of expensive shops keep at least one Spanish-speaking clerk on hand. No one knows how many Americans speak only Spanish or are more comfortable in Spanish than English, but it is a great many, and for the first time they have the money to buy the things that Anglos buy. The sight of an elderly Hispanic lady with her teenage granddaughter discussing a purchase, grandmother speaking Spanish and the youngster responding in English, is common. More and more members of *la Raza* are moving out of the *barrio*. In other words, Chicanos who strongly identify with their origins no longer feel their cultural identity threatened by having Anglo neighbors.

The reaction of the Anglo society has not always been gracious. Decades of propaganda and centuries of prejudice have conditioned Anglos to see Hispanics stereotypically, either as long-suffering peons or as brutal bandits. It is disturbing to many of them to see Chicanos selling life insurance or managing gas stations, though it would not be disturbing to see them *working* in a gas station. There is an attitude that, if they are going to hold entrepreneurial or managerial jobs, the least they could do is to speak English at home. Much of this reaction is simply "nativism."

Nowhere is American xenophobia seen more clearly than in attitudes toward foreign languages: "He don't even talk English" is the ultimate indictment of the immigrant. The gringo tourist in Mexico City who gets upset and abusive when the street vendor or the shop girl does not understand English, or the American army officer in Germany who insists that, "If you yell loud enough they will understand English," are showing a xenophobia as American as pizza or Volkswagens. By all means, the situation in Canada where one finds French, the language of Quebec, and English, the language of success, should be avoided. But it is not concern for the economic opportunities of the Chicano that outrages so many Anglos when they see ballots and voting instructions in Spanish. These angry Anglos usually say they resent the added cost in preparing the materials. They never seem to realize that the non-English speaker is taxed so the information can be made available in English. There are dangers in bilingualism, but there are also dangers in arbitrarily shutting people out of the political system.

Some of the estrangement between Chicanos and Anglos is attributable to the Chicanos, particularly to the adolescents. These young people tend to be surly, sullen, and slovenly. In other words, they are exactly like Anglo adolescents. A very few tend to form tight cliques and dress in a distinctive manner sometimes calculated to upset Anglos. They walk down the high school corridors in groups of six or eight, spread out so that others have to wend their ways through their group. They glare at people, stride arrogantly, and generally indulge in menacing hostility displays traditionally characteristic of teenage gangs. This behavior is temporary in the youth's life, at least in the vast majority of cases. It is born of adolescent uncertainty and fear of rejection by the rest of society.

No discussion of Chicano youth is complete without mention of the "chopped-and-channeled low-riders." A low-rider is a modified car, usually a big one, frequently several years old, and immaculately restored. It has a shiny, acrylic paint job with metallic flakes. It has been modified so that the body sits down over the wheels and rides as low to the ground as possible. They are customarily driven around very slowly in order to be admired. Because they are usually unwieldy, have the turning radius of a Greyhound bus, and can clog a parking lot by the simple process of driving in, they are completely impractical as a means of transport; the delight is simply in their ownership. To the middle-class, middle-aged Anglo eye, low-riders are dreadful, but what could be more American than wasting money on outlandish automobiles?

The future of the Chicano subculture is the most pressing social question in the American Southwest. Historians could be of profound service if they carefully studied the process of acculturation of other large immigrant groups, particularly the Irish, the Italians, and the Russian Jews. Given the academic historians' unerring instinct for the trivial and irrelevant, it is safe to assume that they will not. If they choose a social topic instead of another biography of Jefferson, they typically prefer to study such pressing problems as crime rates in industrializing cities in Germany in the last century. As a result there is no systematic body of information about previous immigrants to help in evaluating the Chicano subculture.

Are Chicanos more tenacious in clinging to their language and their ways than other immigrant groups have been? This is impossible to answer unless it is first established how long it took other groups to make it in American society and by what avenues they made their ways. Dwight Eisenhower, elected in 1952, was the first German-surnamed president of the United States; John Kennedy, in 1960, the first Irish one. No politician with an Italian name or any Jew has even come close. Edmund Muskie, of Polish extraction, was a contender in 1972. As the 1980 presidential election approaches, the names of the front runners are ones commonly found in the London or Dublin telephone directories—Baker, Brown, Carter, Ford, Kennedy (again), and Reagan.

Seventy years after large-scale German migration to this country began, there were scores of German-language newspapers in the United States. They were closed down by the anti-German hysteria accompanying U.S. involvement in World War I, not by the normal abandonment of the language. The process of amalgamation into the alloy formed in the American melting pot has been a slow one for all the other immigrant groups, especially those speaking languages other than English. It will be slow for the Chicanos and other Hispanics, and while the process is continuing, the Chicanos will cling to their own language and subculture.

It is not true, as often claimed, that the Chicano community lacks political organization. It is not yet effectively organized, but in terms of would-be leaders it suffers an embarrassment of riches. Throughout the Southwest, there are many Chicano political and social-action organizations. So far they have contended with one another for the leadership of their minority far more than they have contended with the greater society in their minority's behalf. Effective interaction with the rest of society is only beginning.

In the 1970 congressional campaign in one of the districts in California's San Joaquin Valley, where over 30 percent of the residents were Spanish-speaking/Spanish-surnamed, one campaign manager, an old pro, said, "The voters are over 35 and white. We will not spend a nickel on anyone else." His candidate gained over 70 percent of the votes that year. The campaign manager was not a curmudgeon or a bigot; he simply wanted his candidate to win the election. Not one word of campaign material was prepared to appeal to the Chicano voter, not one minute of airtime was purchased on a Spanish-language radio station, and it did not make the least bit of difference. Things will not be appreciably different in the 1980 elections. Thirty percent of the Valley's residents might be Chicano, but so long as low registration and voting rates reduce them to less than five percent of the electorate, the Anglo politician will ignore them and a Chicano candidate will make it only with heavy Anglo support.

At last, however, Chicano candidates for major offices are emerging. Two Chicano state assemblymen are considering running for governor of California in 1982, and a Los Angeles businessman is a Republican candidate for President in 1980.

If there were no outside problems, the Chicano community could be expected gradually to become amalgamated with the dominant culture in a sort of mutual adjustment process, just as earlier immigrant groups have done. Amalgamation is neither absorption of the minority culture nor corruption of it. The Italian community, after all, has not lost all its identity, and many of its values and qualities have had influence on the original Anglo society. Similarly, if given a chance, the Chicano culture and the Anglo society would evolve toward one another, each adjusting and accommodating to the other until the blend was complete. The resulting society would be more varied, more inclusive, and more vital.

In situations where a still culturally distinct minority exists within a larger society, however, there is always danger of social conflict. There has long been tension between the Chicano community and the rest of American society, and hysteria over large numbers of illegal Mexican migrants in the country only makes things worse. This understandably increases the ambivalence of Mexican-Americans toward illegals. The illegals compete to some extent with them for jobs, and the Chicanos worry that publicity will increase the amount of attention that Chicanos receive from the INS.

The lives of other Hispanic citizens have also been influenced by the presence of illegals. There is a steady flow of people back and forth between New York and Puerto Rico. Puerto Rico has itself become a major entry point for illegals from the Caribbean and from Latin America, however. As a result, Puerto Ricans, who are citizens of the United States and have every right to travel to New York, have frequently been detained temporarily as suspected illegals. The Commonwealth of Puerto Rico maintains a migration office in New York, and for awhile that office found it necessary to issue identification cards to Puerto Rican workers who requested them. Without the cards, the workers were being mistaken for illegals and harassed.

The grimmest specter is of another massive "repatriation" that would sweep up whomever the authorities deemed to be illegal, including "non-alien" Mexicans, Puerto Ricans, or other Hispanics. Extreme action, including disregard for civil liberties and due process of law supposedly directed against illegal aliens, might be used against bona fide American citizens and legal immigrants of Hispanic heritage. There are historical precedents for this in the treatment of both Mexican- and Japanese-Americans. Chicanos are greatly concerned that it could happen again if public hysteria rises against illegals.

The current public controversy over illegal immigration has made it clear that Anglo attitudes toward Mexico and Mexicans are still clouded by the *Leyenda Negra*. The popular image is of a dusky-skinned horde pressing against the southern border of the

United States and, in spite of heroic efforts by the Border Patrol, penetrating it.

The Dusky Horde

If there is any legitimate basis for concern about Mexican immigration, it can be found in the demographic situation of Mexico. In the mid-1970s, the Mexican population was estimated to be growing at 3.4 percent per year—one of the highest growth rates in the world. That rate, if continued, would double the 1979 population of about 68 million in 20 years. The 1979 Mexican population was less than one-third the United States population (living on less than one-fifth the land area). But if the Mexican population continued to grow at that rate, Mexicans would out-number Americans by the year 2015. This prospect is a part of what so many Americans find alarming about the illegal immigration from Mexico.

Population growth in Mexico, like that of every other country, is the result of births minus deaths, plus or minus any net migration factor. From the early 1930s to the early 1970s, the Mexican birthrate was around 43–46 per 1,000 population. By comparison, the mid-1970s birthrate in the United States was only 15 per 1,000. From 1930 to 1975, the death rate in Mexico declined from 25 to a low (for a developing country) of 8 per 1,000. The American death rate in 1975 was 9—not because the American health system is not as good as Mexico's, but because the relatively slowly growing U.S. population has a considerably higher proportion of older people who have relatively high death rates.

Mexico's population growth has been accelerating for most of the last 50 years, ever since the armed struggle of the Revolution came to an end about 1920. The loss of life from the Revolution was so horrendous that Mexico is believed to have had about a million fewer people in 1920 than it had when the Revolution began a decade earlier. Despite this setback, the Mexican population has more than quintupled since the first Mexican census counted 12.6 million people in 1895. In that same period, the United States' population grew only about three-fold, even with the highest levels of immigration this country has ever seen. Virtually all of the Mexican growth has been from natural increase due to very high fertility rates. Death rates, especially among infants and young children, have declined much more recently in Mexico than in the United States. Average life expectancy at birth did not exceed 50 in Mexico until after 1950. Even by 1960, when the rate of natural increase had risen to over three percent, life expectancy was still below 60.

Mexico's high fertility can be traced to an unusually pronatalist cultural tradition. *Machismo* is a powerful influence; male domination and female submission are the rule, especially among peasants and the urban working class. Both men and women derive status from the number of children they have; motherhood is viewed as the essential purpose for woman's existence. Reinforcing this cultural tradition has been the Roman Catholic Church, which generally disapproves most means of birth control. Until the early 1970s, the Mexican government followed the tradition and firmly opposed attempts to establish an official family-planning program. Indeed, during the 1970 election campaign, Luis Echeverría (who became President) publicly advocated further population growth in Mexico and rejected the idea of birth control as a matter of national policy.

When Echeverría took office, the Mexican population was just over 50 million and growing at 3.5 percent. It even seemed to be accelerating as the death rate declined slightly (mainly among infants and young children) and the birthrate remained well over 40. Soon afterward, the government did an abrupt about-face on the population issue and established a very strong, nationwide family-planning program. By late 1978, some results of the progam had begun to show. The Mexican birthrate was estimated by the United Nations' World Fertility Survey to have declined from about 44 per 1,000 before 1970 to 41 by 1975. By 1978, the annual growth rate (by unofficial estimates) had dropped from 3.5 percent to 2.9. This is a small, but clearly encouraging beginning.

If the growth rates prevailing in 1972 had been maintained, barring disaster, Mexico would have reached 300 million around 2025. If the present growth rate were cut in half by around the turn of the century and held there, the projected population size for 2150 would be about that of India today—660 million. Disaster would certainly intervene long before that sombre number could be reached. Millions of Mexicans are inadequately fed and supported today; the country's ability to feed a population several times larger than today's is highly questionable. Indeed it is possible that rapidly rising death rates will be part of Mexico's demographic picture within a few decades.

Even if the family-planning program's goals are met, there will be 110 million Mexicans at the turn of the century, 42 million more than today, a number that will enormously exacerbate the most serious of that nation's many problems. Mexico has yet to absorb the major impact of the most recent spurt of growth—46 percent of the population, 30 million of the 68 million people, are children under 15 years old. Mexico City may well have 15 million people by 1980, and skyrocketing rural population growth portends an even greater flow of people toward what is already recognized as a disaster area.

Mexico is in one of the worst demographic situations of any nation—something that should worry any humane person regardless of Mexico's geographic position. That Mexico is an intimate neighbor of the United States is a legitimate reason for additional concern north of the border—concern unconnected to the *Leyenda Negra*. But because of the myths about Mexicans, in many people concern has taken the form of outright fear of an invasion. This fear is rooted in ignorance of our southern neighbors, their past, and our past involvement with them. Some knowledge of them as *people*, rather than caricatures, should help to calm that fear and allow legitimate concerns to be handled sensibly.

[6]

LOS MOJADOS AND THE PUSH
FROM THE SOUTH

JORGE watched the two teenaged boys sitting back to back on the old oildrum. The youngsters were watching a green Chevy pickup truck as it moved slowly in the late afternoon sun through the field across the shallow valley beyond the chain-link fence. Those goddam kids are going to make trouble, he said to himself. The same thought occurred to officer Tim Redmond of the Border Patrol as he maneuvered the Chevy pickup toward the gaping hole in the fence. The teenagers, now only 30 yards away and on higher ground, hopped off the oil drum and crouched. Here it comes, Redmond thought, wincing as the two youngsters straightened up and hurled large rocks toward his vehicle. The first volley fell short, but the second throw, by the taller boy, was a strike. Redmond ducked involuntarily, but today the rock did not come hurtling through the windshield and turn it into an instantly opaque, crazed mélange of glass and plastic. Instead, it ricocheted off the chain-link and window-screen "armor" that surrounded the Border Patrol vehicle.

The boys laughed, treated Redmond to some obscene gestures and shouts, and returned to their barrel. It was not as much fun as it used to be, but it was still fun. After all, where else in the world could juvenile delinquents have the pleasure of throwing rocks at a cop car with impunity—and at the same time strike a blow for their country's honor? For it was they who had forced *La Migra* to go to the trouble and expense of screening its vehicles.

Jorge watched with a growing feeling of anxiety as Redmond left the pickup and proceeded to the repair of the chain-link fence. He could see that the officer was keeping an eye on the boys and vice versa, but there seemed to be little tension. They did not want to hurt him and they wouldn't have tried if they had wanted

237

to. Only fools throw rocks at armed men only 30 feet away—even if they are separated by an international border.

Jorge turned and trudged back toward the center of Tijuana. He was sorry that he had wandered out to look at the border in order to kill time before meeting Humberto, the *coyote* who would lead him into the United States that night. He had crossed illegally nine times so far and been caught on three of the attempts. The wait before going across always seemed the worst of it. The first time, two full days at the Puente Negro at El Paso; the last time, at Tijuana, three full hours in the trunk of a car. The actual crossings had been quick and in a way exciting. He had been really scared on the first two, but once he had been captured and expelled by *La Migra* his terror of them faded. They could be gruff, but the results of being caught were mostly discomfort, boredom, and despair. The filthy holding facility, the filling out of forms, and the sinking feeling while being bussed back into Mexico were unpleasant, but not frightening.

But now Jorge was frightened. Recently *bandidos* had taken to preying on the *mojados,* who were simply trying to get into the United States to work. *Mojados* were being beaten, robbed, even murdered. The *bandidos* carried guns, and more than once had used them against San Diego policemen. The tension along the border was increasing, and Jorge could not help feeling that the kind of juvenile-delinquent mischief he had just seen, though not related to the problems of the *mojados,* could be contributing to that tension.

Humberto was less worried. As a *coyote,* he had been smuggling illegal aliens for five years. He knew *La Migra* like a book. He knew their tactics because he had learned the same tactics in Vietnam, where he had served in the U.S. Marines. He had been born in El Paso of Mexican parents and been taken back and forth across the border many times as his father struggled to find work. When he was five, his father had been killed in a bus accident in Sonora. When he was nine, his mother died. An aunt provided shelter, but could not really afford to feed him. He had taken to earning money on the streets of El Paso, first begging and then shining shoes. Finally he graduated to breaking and entering. The latter led to several arrests and a short stay in juvenile hall. At eighteen, seeing that his life was going nowhere, Humberto tossed in the sponge and signed up with the marines.

Vietnam had been a nightmare. He had a recurring feeling that he was on the wrong side. His sympathies were partly with the peasants in that land suffering under the cruel assault of the Anglos and partly with the blacks, Chicanos, and Anglos of his fire team: the camaraderie of infantrymen under fire together.

After his discharge in San Diego, he had found the available work both dull and menial. The pay for cooking hamburgers in a fast-food stand was lousy, and the level of excitement far below that of a helicopter-borne assault. Gradually, through friends in Tijuana, he began to help people cross the border. He found in the *coyote*'s role some of the excitement of war, but with less risk. He found satisfaction in helping people. He also found money.

Humberto spent time studying *La Migra*—their patrol routes, how they deployed their sensors, when their shifts changed. He also learned the habits of the *bandidos*, and many *bandidos* knew about him. He was a big man and had a reputation for being armed. He never actually carried a gun, but had once used his extensive unarmed combat training to good effect in a Tijuana brawl. The word spread. All in all, the $300 Jorge would pay him would be well invested. Humberto got his people across and preserved his reputation. Many *coyotes* were less scrupulous.

Humberto knew it was old-fashioned, but still did all the work himself. He struck his own bargain with the *pollos (mojados)*, selected the routes, guided them across the border, arranged the contacts on the other side, and did everything else that had to be done. Many of those he'd started in the business with four years ago had become members of the big rings. He had been invited to join, but even after splitting the fee with the contacts on the U.S. side, he still made more on his own than he could have working for others. What Humberto enjoyed most was actually taking people across. He was a good guide, but guides are the most poorly paid members of a ring. The big rings would take a *pollo* across for one-third down and the rest on monthly payments. This required a collection operation and knowing a lot of ranch foremen and labor contractors to be sure the *pollo* had a job and could keep up the payments. Humberto could have formed a ring himself, but he did not really know anything about the business in the U.S.

Humberto did have one problem: he was sure that the intelligence people in the Border Patrol's antismuggling unit had identified him.

It was about 10 P.M. when Humberto led his party of five *mojados* into the valley and under the fence. He was taking a favorite route, one successfully used just a week before. Besides Jorge, he was smuggling a young man, Francisco. He was from Xilitla, heading for Sacramento to join his brother, who worked in a garage. The brother had sent the money required for the journey and Humberto's fee.

Two other *mojados*, Emilio and Ramón, were young farmers

from Guanajuato who were planning to go first to Wenatchee, Washington, to pick apples. In the meantime their wives, elderly parents, and young children could keep their tiny farms going. How long they would stay in the United States would depend on how good the work was and how long they could stand to be away from their families. Good friends, they had "gone north" together five times before.

Maria completed the party. She was the youngest and the most scared. At 16 she had been married to 24-year-old Roberto in their home town of Culiacán in Sinaloa. Two years later Roberto had somehow gotten involved in the heroin business centered in that small city—an estimated $6 million worth of the deadly white powder passed through every day. Murder had become a daily occurrence in Culiacán; in 1976 there were 300 killings in the city of fewer than 200,000—a rate 15 times higher than that of an American city of equivalent size, seven times that of New York, and three times that of Detroit—astonishing for a nation where the over-all murder rate is lower than that of the United States.

Somehow Roberto had gotten on the wrong side of one of the gangs, and the *pistoleros* had come after him. He had no choice but to flee, finally ending up in Los Angeles. He had found work as a janitor for a small company making desalinization membranes and had managed to save enough money to send for Maria. Now at the age of 20, she was stumbling across a rocky, dark field, nervous about running into cactuses, rattlesnakes and, above all, *bandidos*.

It was about then that X Unit Border Patrolmen Jack Mauk and Phil Dekkert, about to return to Chula Vista Station, received a radio call. A magnetic point sensor had alerted the system to the movement of a small group less than one-half mile from their vehicle. Humberto's luck had run out; the sensor had not been there the week before. Phil gunned the Ram-charger down the dirt road, switching on its spotlights. Humberto heard the powerful vehicle coming and, pulling Maria with him, told the others to scatter and take cover. They ran toward some low bushes 40 yards away, ignoring the chance of a broken leg as they fled over the rough terrain.

Dekkert's adrenaline level rose as he caught a glimpse of movement in his spotlights. "There they are, let's get 'em."

He swerved the Ram-charger toward the movement. A few more poor bastards just trying to find work, he thought. He wondered what was going through Mauk's mind—after all *he* was married to a *chicana*. But Mauk was, as usual, silent until the brakes were slammed on. Then he leaped from the truck, hand on holster, and shouted at what he could now see was a fleeing couple:

"Pare! Arriba los manos!"

Humberto and Maria fled on, Humberto cursing his luck and dragging the terrified Maria. Mauk rushed after them while Dekkert called for a chopper. What a way to make a living, Mauk thought. "The girl could be Christina ten years ago . . ."

The people in this based-on-fact story represent the main actors in today's border drama: *los mojados,* the illegal immigrants trying to enter the U.S.; *los coyotes,* the professional smugglers trying to help them; and *La Migra,* the agents trying to stop them, the Border Patrol (illegals also use the term to refer to the entire U.S. Immigration and Naturalization Service). They are all people trying to get jobs done, jobs whose roots go back in time to the treaty of Guadalupe Hidalgo and as far away in space as the poor Indian villages of Chiapas, congressional hearing rooms in Washington, and bean fields in Michigan.

LOS MOJADOS

Most of the illegal immigrants who are apprehended are Mexicans "entering without inspection." These EWIs (in INS parlance) just walk across the border wherever they can. Jorge and his friends were EWIs. When an EWI is a Mexican national, he or she is called a *mojado,* the Spanish word for "wet",* the idea being that they arrived in this country by having swum the Rio Grande. Hence the pejorative term "wetback." In the INS the term "wet" has come to mean any EWI; one hears inspectors and agents speak of having caught a "wet German" or a "wet Canadian." Another synonym for an EWI is "tonk," which probably goes back to the early years of this century when the Chinese benevolent societies, called Tongs, allegedly sponsored the smuggling of Chinese into the country.

Coyotes, the smugglers who bring *mojados* across the border, refer to them as *pollos* (chickens). Another term for *coyote* is *pollero*—chicken herder. The term *coyote* derives not from the doglike animal, but from a Spanish idiom for shyster lawyer or illegal broker.

In order to gain some insight into the lives and motives of the *mojados,* we approached several of them directly through an interviewer well known to them. It is not at all difficult to find illegals willing to talk, but it is difficult to get reliable information

---

*Mojado was originally used only in Texas, but now is generally used. Another term used in the Western states was *alambrista*—wire (or fence) jumper.

from them. The following interviews took place in the Fresno
area of California's central valley. Our interviewer, Aggie Rose,
grew up around farm workers. She summed it up this way:

> Illegals live in a world of lies. They are not liars, but theirs is a
> world of lies. They have to live—to eat—and to eat they have to say
> things that others want to hear. If a boss asks if they are here
> legally, they say they are. But they know that the boss knows they
> are lying and that the boss is lying when he acts like he believes
> them. When the boss asks for a Social Security number, they give
> him one. It may be someone else's number or it may be their own or
> it may be just a made-up number. The boss doesn't care; he just
> wants a number. The *mojados* do care. They would like to escape
> the deceit and they would like the Social Security benefits. But
> that's a luxury that comes way after salary. They need the work.
> When they use someone else's Social Security card, they may also
> use that person's name, so they are frequently known by a half-
> dozen or more names to the people they work for and the people
> they work with. I was in a bar once with a bunch of people, and
> there was one guy at the table who knew everyone there, but they
> all called him by a different name.
>
> The immigration rules are so crazy that nobody can understand
> them. Those who are working here and are trying to [immigrate
> legally] are not even supposed to be here when they apply. They go
> down to somewhere in Mexico and apply, and then they come back
> here to work. If they [are admitted], they have to go back to
> Mexico, get their papers, and come in legally. But then they just
> come back to the same job and the same house—the same every-
> thing. Nothing has changed, but everything has changed. Now
> they're [in legally] and they don't run or hide when the *Migra*
> comes. They just show their papers and they don't have to leave.
> When the boss asks for a *mica**, you may show him a phony one or
> one that belongs to someone else. All he wants is to be able to say to
> the *Migra* that he has seen a *mica* for everyone working there. He
> doesn't care whose *mica* it is or where it came from.

In conducting the interviews, we had two major concerns:
whether we could obtain honest answers to rather personal questions about income and family situations, and whether this could
be done without violating the subjects' dignity. Accordingly, we
reviewed the questions with Aggie to make sure she felt they were
not offensive and would elicit straight answers. Among the first
set of questions, about the family situation, one was whether or

---

*In Mexican Spanish a *mica* is any laminated identification card. Along the
border, the word usually means a local border-crossing pass. But inside the United
States, among the Chicanos, the Mexican immigrants, and the illegals, it means the
"green card," the identification that the INS issues to those lawfully admitted to
permanent residence.

not the interviewee was married. This would lead to a certain amount of joking along the lines of "I'm not, but my wife is," and the like. When it got down to the interview situation, though, they talked about their families. In regard to the rectitude of their personal lives, Aggie was always very insistent about their straight living.

> You know, what you hear about these guys isn't true. They don't go out drinking and whoring and fighting. This is an image the media often present. Illegals simply come here to try and support their families when it becomes impossible in Mexico. But the media often play them up as criminals. I have not met any who would fit this image.
>
> In the first place, they don't have any money. When they get some money, they send it back to their families. That's why they came here—to support their families. In the second place, they are scared to death of getting caught. If they go into town or to the bars or anywhere like that, they are afraid of getting picked up. If they get picked up for anything and end up in jail, Immigration will get them for sure. They just can't take the risk.
>
> When I was doing these interviews [the pretest] it was a rainy Sunday afternoon. Ramón had arranged for me to talk to these guys. The house in the migrant workers' camp was just a shack with one room and a kitchen on one end of it. There was a privy, just a hole in the ground right out the back door, and you could smell it. Everyone in that shack used it and some of the guys from the other shacks, because not all of the houses had their own privies.
>
> The money from the interview was the first they'd had in a few weeks because the rain had kept them out of the fields. This is what they were doing on Sunday—six or eight guys sitting around all afternoon and all evening in a shithole of a house watching a small black-and-white TV on the Spanish station and watching it rain and talking about whether or not there was going to be any work. They kept interrupting my interview to point out the show, which was coming from their home area of Michoacán.

Aggie's parents were Portuguese immigrants who farmed their own and other people's land in the Central Valley of California. She speaks Spanish now because of her work with the United Farm Workers and her teaching. She said that her parents complained because her Portuguese now had a Spanish accent. She worked her way through California State University at Chico and earned an elementary teaching credentials. She taught for three years in a bilingual education program in South San Francisco, but quit to become an organizer for César Chávez's United Farm Workers. She stayed with that for five years and during that time gained a great deal of knowledge about the farm-labor situation.

On the basis of her organizing experience with the union, Aggie estimates that 20 to 30 percent of the agricultural workers in the Central Valley of California are not documented. She adamantly asserts that the legal work force could not fill the gap if the illegals stopped coming. First of all, the work these people do in the fields requires experience and skill. One cannot just walk into a field or orchard and start pruning vines, weeding onions, topping asparagus, or picking peaches. The worker has to know what he is doing. Second, the wages are not good enough to attract legal workers even if they did have the experience and the skills. A substantial portion of the United States' food supply comes from the Central Valley, the Imperial Valley, and the other great irrigation projects of the Southwest. In all of them illegals are an important part of the labor force.

No one knows exactly what the impact of removing these men and women from the fields would be. What would be the effect of removing 20 to 30 percent of the work force from automobile assembly lines, or oil refineries, or any other industry? Anyone advocating closing the border and expelling the illegals should consider that higher food prices, a less varied diet, or greater dependence on foreign sources for food would be likely results. Ironically, the United States would probably turn to the great irrigated fields of Sonora and other regions of Mexico, which would not greatly please the farmers and landowners in the United States.

Mojados do not work only in the fields. Border Patrol Agent Richard Jones of the Chula Vista Sector Headquarters tells the story of a Mexican upholsterer friend from Tijuana who came to him complaining that an American upholsterer had been in Tijuana actively recruiting his workmen, offering to reimburse the Mexicans the cost of getting to Los Angeles (including the *coyote*'s fee, of course) and to pay them $3.50 per hour for all the hours they wanted to work. The Mexican upholsterer wanted something done about it, but Agent Jones was forced to explain to his friend that probably nothing could be.

It is not against federal law to hire an illegal alien. California is one of the few states that has a law—the Dixon-Arnett Act—against knowingly hiring illegals, but it simply is not enforced. The act does not define what "knowingly" means, does not require the employer to make any investigation, and makes no provision for enforcement. Finally, the law is of questionable constitutionality because the determination of who is and is not in the United States legally is a federal matter.

It is ironic that while the Dixon-Arnett Act makes it against the law to hire illegal immigrants, the California Agricultural Labor

Relations Act allows them to belong to unions, arguing that the status of residence of a worker does not affect his or her rights as a member of the bargaining unit. Thus an illegal can vote in representational elections, hold office in the union, and enjoy all the benefits of union representation.

Judge James L. Rose of the National Labor Relations Board feels that the protections given the illegal worker in California agriculture represent the federal courts' direction of thinking on labor matters. He cites the decision of the U.S. Court of Appeals, Seventh Circuit, in *National Labor Relations Board vs Sure-Tan, Inc.* In this case the seven employees of Sure-Tan, a small leather-tanning company, voted unanimously for unionization. The company went to court to have the election invalidated on a number of grounds, one of which was that six of the seven employees were illegals. Strange as it may seem, those six were picked up by the INS shortly after the union election and expelled from the United States. Sure-Tan argued not only that the illegals should not have union representation, but also that, because six out of seven of the workers were suddenly removed from the United States and therefore from their jobs, the newly created bargaining unit had ceased to exist. The court did not agree. It said, in essence, that if a man or woman is on the payroll at the time of the election, he or she has the right to vote and that the vote of the group is binding until another election changes it. The reason for the worker leaving the job does not matter. The decision further noted, ". . . no immigration statute prohibits an illegal alien from working and voting in a Board election."

Many states are attempting to deny illegals unemployment compensation to which they would be entitled if they were not illegals. The states claim that a person who is not a lawful resident of the United States is ineligible. But this is not a matter of federal or state law, rather an administrative practice of the unemployment compensation boards and offices of some states. Thus the bureaucrats have moved into an area of federal jurisdiction and taken over. Their technique works very well: if a worker protests that he is being unjustly denied his benefits because he is an illegal, a simple telephone call to the neighborhood INS office guarantees that the aggrieved party will not be around to press his or her case. The bureaucrats help keep the unemployment compensation funds solvent by collecting contributions from workers to whom the authorities have no intention of providing benefits.

The same kind of thinking led Texas school districts to deny schooling to the children of illegal aliens, even though the districts collect school taxes from these people. Similarly, though without the cynicism, the Social Security Administration shows a profit by taking the money of illegals whom they know—or certainly could know—will never be around to receive benefits. What do the Social Security computers in Washington "think" when they record contributions from five or six employers into the same account? It is strange that the people who command the computers do not program them to bring these curious cases to the attention of someone who would look into them.

All of this is a part of what Aggie Rose called "the world of lies" in which the *mojados* and all other illegal immigrants live. The State of California says that it is against the law to hire an illegal but that it is all right for a union to accept an illegal's membership; the owners of Sure-Tan say that they want the workers here, but not if they organize; the Texas school districts, the boards of unemployment compensation, and Social Security collect taxes and contributions knowing that benefits are not going to be furnished. Border Patrol Agent C.V. Hunter summed it up: "Everyone makes money out of this but Old Joe Wet. He just comes up here and works and gets sent back to Mexico."

What sort of person is "Old Joe Wet"? The stories recorded here are not from a scientifically selected sample; they should not be construed as representative of all illegals or even of all *mojados*. They are simply the personal histories of a handful of people upon whom inexorable forces have operated to bring them where they are today.

Ramón. One of our interviewees, Ramón V., has been in the United States on and off since 1966. He is 39 and has held various jobs to make a living, but for the past few years he has been a field hand on a vast agribusiness ranch complex in the Central Valley of California. He has had no formal schooling; he is self-taught and semiliterate. His wife and nine children, one of whom was born in the United States, live in his home town, a tiny, rural *rancho* in the Mexican state of Michoacán.

When there is work to do, Ramón and the other *mojados* on the ranch work a 53-hour week, nine hours per day Monday through Friday and eight hours on Saturday. As is usual on the ranches in California, the work force in the fields is segregated into three groups, the U.S. citizens, the Mexicans who are here legally, and the *mojados*. The hourly wages are more or less the same for all three groups, but the *mojados* work an hour longer each day and their quotas are higher than those for the other two groups. The most important difference, though, is that the *mojados* are the last to have work assigned, and if there is no work they just go back to their shacks on the ranch and wait, hoping that there will be work the next day.

Ramón takes home about $450 a month after deductions, and

he sends $300 of this home to Mexico. By contrast, a farm worker in central Mexico averages about $2.35 per day, less than $70 a month.

Ramón is a born leader and the other *mojados* defer to him. When César Chávez's United Farm Workers were trying to organize the field hands on the ranch, Ramón was instrumental in keeping the *mojados* loyal to the union. Now he is a member of the negotiating team that meets regularly with ranch management to iron out differences. One reason he is devoted to the union is that during the organizational struggle a union organizer helped him in a very special way. His youngest daughter, the one born in the U.S., spilled kerosene on herself and it ignited. If he and his wife had taken her to the rural health clinic, *la Migra* might have found them and sent them back to Mexico. When the union organizer learned of the problem, he got the child into the clinic without identifying her parents.

Another of Ramón's children was not growing properly because of earlier malnutrition. Ramón had simply been unable to afford adequate food in Mexico.

Ramón's adventures in getting into the United States are best told in his own words:

In 1963 or 1964 I decided I wanted to immigrate to the United States. I spent everything I had and I borrowed all I could, and my father invested all his money in getting letters and lawyers and such. My father said he would help me to the very end, but finally I had spent everything of mine and his, too. Then I went to the U.S. Embassy in Mexico City and paid more for an application form. I had some very good letters from Washington, D.C. They were from a lawyer who said they were from a grower who needed workers, but the embassy said that the letters were not any good because the workers in the United States didn't approve the Form 320*. I had to pay the lawyer in Washington for the letters, anyhow.

At this time we still had about 20 animals—goats and pigs and a cow—which we sold so I could get the money to make it to somewhere on the border—anywhere on the border. We had to do something because we had lost so much trying to get into the United States legally. People had fooled us by taking our money and I got no permit. This was in 1965, and I arrived first at Reynosa, Tamaulipas, across the border from McAllen, Texas. I went to the Mexican authorities and applied for a Form 13

---

*Ramón has a remarkable memory. A Form 320 was a Labor Department "Application for Alien Employment Certification," since replaced by another form.

passport. If you can get a Form 13 Mexican passport, then the Americans will give you a local border-crossing pass and you can get into the United States. The Mexicans turned me down because you have to be a resident of the Border Zone for at least six months before they will give you a Form 13. Then I went to Mexicali where I had some relatives I could stay with, and I tried for a Form 13 again at Algodones, across from Yuma, Arizona, but they turned me down there, too. Finally, I went to Tijuana, where I had more relatives. I worked in a liquor store for more than six months and then applied again for my Form 13 passport. After 51 days I got it and then went to the Americans and got my local border-crossing pass, and with this I came to the United States in hopes of getting back all I had lost.*

I got my first job in the United States in the Disneyland Hotel in Anaheim, where I worked for about six months and started saving a little. All the time I went back to Mexico and came back to the U.S. with the local pass, but in 1974 it was lifted when I tried to come back in. Someone told me that a false permit was just as good, so I paid $100 for one and entered again. Then in San Clemente *la Migra* got us and I got thrown back to Mexico. This time I got reported, and the Mexican authorities took my Form 13 away from me.

When I lost out this way, I tried again to come here because I had a place to come to work and all this. This time a *coyote* brought me. The *coyote* was a friend who had brought some relatives of mine in. I crossed on the beach at Tijuana with six or seven other guys, all friends. We did not walk very long, maybe two hours, but then we waited in a lemon grove for three days. We ate only once a day. We were waiting for a chance to get through when there weren't any *migrantes* around. The third day, about one o'clock in the morning, the *coyote*'s guide came for us. We split in a car, real fast, "as fast as a rooster crows." That's how I got to the ranch here.

I remember that when I got here I was so in debt that even though it was 115° and I was picking peaches, I wouldn't buy a 69-cent hat because I couldn't afford it.

In early 1975 I sent for my wife who managed to get through, and we had a baby on purpose to try to get us all immigrated. We are still waiting.

Ramón and his family will probably make it. Immediate relatives of United States citizens are eligible for immigration from any-place in the world without numeric restriction, and the birth of the child was duly recorded. It is only a matter of grinding through the paper and not getting caught in the United States. The so-called baby clause was used as a route to citizenship by

*A local border crossing pass entitles the bearer to enter the United States for a period of 72 hours and to travel freely within 25 miles of the point of entry. It does not entitle the bearer to work.

many immigrants. The catch was that citizenship could be denied
if the parents were caught living in the U.S. illegally. Since January 1, 1976, the immediate relatives of a child born in this country
when the parents were here illegally are not entitled to immigration, so this loophole is now closed. Ramón has his foot in the
door; whether he and his wife get through will depend on how
lucky and careful they are.

Ramón's Brother. Many illegals come to the United States to join
family members already there, and Ramón's brother is one of
those. And like Ramón (but unlike many other illegals), he wants
to become a permanent resident. Ramón's brother thinks he is 37
years old, and, like Ramón, he is totally uneducated. He is married and has seven children back in Michoacán. He has entered
the United States four times and goes back to Mexico "only when
la Migra catches me." He says of himself and his situation:

> You can't make a living down there. The government buys your
> crops at the price they want to pay, and you just can't live on what
> they give. When I first left Michoacán I went to the San Quintín
> Valley in Baja California where I herded sheep for a rancher and
> sometimes worked in the tomatoes. I came up here the first time in
> 1973 at Tijuana. My brother had been coming for years, but I was
> too scared. I was scared I would be caught. But by 1973 I was
> making enough just to live on myself, and that just barely. I had
> nothing to send home, so Ramón sent this *coyote* to get me and some
> other guys. He charged me $325 and I paid him, over time, after I
> got up here. I paid him every cent. The *coyote* brought us up—there
> were five of us—by walking through the hills north of Tijuana. We
> walked for about three hours to where a car was. The car took us to
> hide in a place near San Clemente. It was a clump of little trees on a
> hill. We stayed there a day and a night. We ate once when the *coyote*
> brought us some food. The *Migra* came by once, but we were very
> quiet and they did not see us, and finally a guy working for the
> *coyote* came and brought us up here.
>
> I have been sent back three times, twice to Mexicali and once to
> Nogales. The last time was in Tucson, and that time I went back to
> visit the family, but the other times I just came right back in. I
> always use the same *coyote,* and he always charges me $325 and I
> always pay him. Altogether that is $1,300, and that is a lot, but
> things have gone pretty well for me up here, and for me it is worth
> it. If it weren't for the *coyotes,* we just could not make it through.
> They take risks for us, so we all have to chip in.
>
> My first job up here was with a boss named K. who contracted
> labor for a Japanese rancher. My brother (Ramón) knew the fore-
> man and got me on. Recently I have been working with the hoe and
> the shovel in the irrigation ditches and I get $2.80 an hour. We

work nine hours a day, eight on Saturday, but this spring there has been so much rain that there has not been much work. I sure hope it dries up.

One time up in Oregon a guy ripped me and the others off for a whole week's pay. He just didn't want to pay us so he held out, and we were scared to do anything about it because that is how you get caught. We had been weeding cucumbers near Salem, and he just didn't come out to the field to pay us. We thought something was wrong because we knew the work was about over and he would not need us anymore. One of us had papers, and we sent him into town to get our money, and the boss—he was a Texan—paid him, all right but said that he wouldn't give him the money for the rest of us. If we wanted to be paid, we would have to come to town and see him. When we heard that, we just said *Ay muere* (that's where it dies) and gave up. We would have been picked up for sure.

What I want to do is live here. I want to bring my family up and then be able to go home to see my parents. It is possible that I will get immigrated because of a baby my wife had up here in 1974.

El Bracero. More typical, perhaps, is El Bracero, who only seeks work, not residence, in the United States. We called him El Bracero because he had once come north under the *bracero* program. He is one of 13 children, 11 of whom had survived to adulthood, and he now has a wife and five children in the tiny town of La Piedad in Michoacán. He has entered the United States illegally many times and in many places and has never used a *coyote*. He had arrived for his current stay the day before we interviewed him. He did not have a job but was confident that he would make a connection with a labor contractor or that friends would find him something. He was a friend of Ramón's, whom he had known in Mexico, and in a few days he did have a job as a field hand on the same ranch. He tells his own story:

My dad came as a *bracero* once a long time ago, and he came another time, even longer ago, before he was even married. That time he was immigrated, but he let his papers go. He's not immigrated anymore and lives back in Mexico. I have a brother here who is immigrated.

The first time I came here I came as a *bracero*. I was 18, and I worked in the strawberries and cauliflower around Watsonville. I stayed for eight months. That was in 1958 and 1959. I didn't try to stay then, I didn't want to. It is harder to get in than it used to be, and this time I am going to stay. I am going to stay, that is, if *la Migra* doesn't get me. You know, the guys with the pistols. I have only been picked up once, although I have come in many times. The time I was picked up was near El Centro. I was walking with a bunch of other guys, and we were trying to find a train, but we had been walking a long time and we were tired so we sat down to rest.

This one *Migra* guy came up, and everyone started to run, but I was tired and I was hungry, so why run? He caught three of us and took us into Calexico, and then they sent us to Mexicali. Then we went up to Tijuana and got through there. That was a couple of years ago.

In 1968 I started going into Texas, but those Texans pay so little I stopped going there. Now I come here, to California. The most I ever made in :ne season was $600. I have gone to other places in Mexico, but one place is like another there. Last time I tried Mexico City and came up here from there. What I want to do here is work. I want to work so I can get something to eat and to send some money home. . . . Everything costs so much in Mexico. I can't make more than 300 or 400 pesos a week there, and a pair of pants costs 300 pesos. If that's all you can make, then all you can do that week is buy a pair of pants, but you've got to eat, too.

Armando S. Our sample of *mojados* in the Fresno area illustrates the threads of family and friendship that often bind local groups of illegals. Armando is from La Piedad in Michoacán, the same town as El Bracero and works on the same Ranch as Ramón and the others. He was one of eight children, two of whom died in childhood, and he is the father of 11 children who live with their mother in La Piedad. He claims to have had seven years of schooling and is literate, but "it wasn't much of a school and they only taught us a little." He says of his coming to the United States:

Well, over there I could not support myself. First I went to Sonora but I only stayed about four months. That was when I was 18. I went back to La Piedad, but later I went to Mexicali where I picked cotton. I never tried to come in then, but I thought about it and I walked along the border a lot. I could earn more in Mexicali than I could in La Piedad, but I really don't earn much anywhere. My family lives in the same house I grew up in, just one room. I don't have any land.

I go back and forth across the border a lot. I usually go back to La Piedad to see the kids, especially the little kids. I don't want them to forget me. Crossing the border isn't easy. I have been stopped there twice, and once I was picked up inside the country after I had made it. This time I took the bus from La Piedad to Yuma and the train from Yuma to Tijuana. I couldn't get through at Tijuana the first time, so I went back to Yuma but couldn't make it there either and finally got through at Tijuana the second time. One time when *la Migra* lifted me—that was at Tijuana—I spent fifteen days in the San Diego jail because I refused to tell *la Migra* who my *coyote* was. Everyone thought I was bold, but to tell the truth, I didn't know his name. I wouldn't have told anyhow. I made the mistake of paying the *coyote* in advance, and when I got out I couldn't find him so I lost my money that time. After they let me out, I went to San Quintín and worked there for awhile. Then I came back into the United States. Then I went back, last November, to see the kids. This time I would really like to stay, but I think I might get returned. Really, I think I will be returned.

Last year I was able to send $600 home. I had a good job packing sweet potatoes. I worked eight or nine hours per day and got $25 after the deductions. I used Ramón's Social Security card.

It is really getting expensive to get in. Just to get to the border costs 600 pesos and the *coyotes* want $300. I promised that much, but here is what happened. This *coyote* got a bunch of us together, and we were all paying him $300 each. We had to walk for two nights and hide during the day, and the *coyote* didn't bring anything to eat like he said he would. The second day we were so hungry we gave him some money, and he said he would go back to Tijuana and get something. He came back the next day—the third day—but he didn't have anything for us to eat. He said Tijuana cops robbed him, and they might have, but I think he took the money and got drunk. He didn't help much, and he left us out there where we could have been caught. If he comes around to collect, he isn't going to get anything. He got us through those hills, though. I could come over a million times and never learn how to get through those hills without getting caught.

The Nurse from Guerrero. Women come north, too. We had a difficult time finding one who had "her own story," since most of the women we contacted had come to join their husbands. Woman on their own usually look for jobs in cities. The one we did find and interview at length wanted to go to Los Angeles, where she thought she could find a better job. Ampara S. was 29 years old, widowed, and the mother of three children who live with her parents in Rodesia, a small town in the state of Guerrero about two hours by bus from Acapulco. When Ampara was a child, there was no school in Rodesia, but her parents were able to hire a *maestro particular,* a state-licensed private tutor to help her prepare for the high school entrance exams. Ampara is intelligent, the tutor was good, and she was admitted to the high school in Tecpan de Galiano, about 30 minutes by bus from Rodesia. After two years of high school, she completed an 18-month training program for practical nurses. She supported herself as a seamstress in Tecpan and volunteered at the local clinic in order to learn hospital procedures. She married and had her children in Tecpan, but when her husband died she took the children to Acapulco where she took a job as a seamstress. In her own words:

I worked as a seamstress in Acapulco for four years, but then the tourists stopped coming, and in Acapulco there is nothing without the tourists, so I was laid off. I went back to live with my parents in

Rodesia, but the next December (1977) someone stole my father's five cows, and then we were very poor. You see, so long as we had the cows we could drink the milk and sell some, and even if there wasn't anything else there was that. My mother still cries about this. She says we sacrificed so much to get the cows and then someone stole them. . . .

This is when I decided to go north. I had enough money to get to Tijuana on the bus and to hire a *coyote*. First I stayed with some relatives who were waiting to come in, but they had some other relatives here in the United States who were helping them get in. When the word came from their relatives, there was no room for me, and so they left me. I waited alone in the hotel in Tijuana for ten days, and the *coyote* finally came to get me. It was raining very hard and it was cold. There were about ten of us, and we had to go through canyons and over hills, and the mud was terrible and I kept falling down. The guide told me I had better take off my wristwatch, and he said he would carry it for me. Later he offered to carry my suitcase. After about four hours in the rain and the mud he left us, and he took my watch and suitcase, and I never saw him again. Another guide came with a car and took us to a house in San Diego.

The guide who brought me across said he would take me to Los Angeles, but the one who took me to the house in San Diego said that if I wanted to go on I had to pay another $100. I had already paid $200. I called my uncle in Fresno, and he said he would pay them when they got me to Fresno. They finally took me to Fresno, but the *coyote* never came to my uncle for the rest of the money. Altogether there were four guides, the one who took me from the hotel, the one who took me through the canyons and stole from me, another who took me to the house in San Diego, and the one who took me to Fresno. They all worked together.

I had been a seamstress in Tecpan, and I wanted to get a job as a seamstress in Los Angeles, but I did not know anyone except my uncle in Fresno. I could make a lot of money in the fields, but that is where *la Migra* gets you. If you want a profession, you have to have papers. I work now in a home as a maid. They pay me $40 per week, but there are deductions for social security and I have to give some back for room and board. I have only been here for four months, but I have sent money back two times; once I sent $130 and the other time I sent $150. I don't know what I would do if I got caught. I spent everything to get here, and I haven't saved anything, and the *coyotes* will not help you without money. I just can't get caught. That's why I don't go to the fields.

Crossing must be a much greater ordeal for a woman, especially a Mexican woman, than for a man. *Machismo* is still a way of life in Mexico, and groups of male *mojados* may not easily accept the presence of a woman during a crossing. And *coyotes* may, as in Ampara's case, be more willing to take advantage of a female *pollo* than a male. Furthermore, women, unlike men, always run the risk of rape when illegals are attacked by the bandits or roving gangs of armed Mexican or American teenagers.

In one case a party of three, two men and a woman, were apprehended by a border patrolman. The two men were summarily ordered back to Mexico. The patrolman then raped the woman, said "I hope you do not have any disease," and sent her back to Mexico. She had the guts to report the incident, and the patrolman was cashiered and prosecuted. Such incidents are probably inevitable wherever a primarily male law-enforcement agency is apprehending females. The Border Patrol's record is generally excellent, but one must still admire the courage of women who risk not only the consequences of being caught by them, but of encountering some of the army of criminals that preys on honest *mojados,* who want only to go north to find work or join loved ones.

Not all *mojados* are from the countryside. Ampara S. grew up in a small town and lived several years in Acapulco before coming north. Forty percent of the 10,000 repatriated *mojados* interviewed in a project directed by Dr. Jorge Bustamante in Mexico indicated that they came from towns or cities. There is very substantial migration from the countryside to cities in Mexico. From the standpoint of the illegal immigration, however, this means only that some of the "push" forces may be changing; it does not mean they are diminishing. Migrants with urban backgrounds, however, tend to be better educated and may be generally better equipped for life in the United States.

The Student. He is 23 years old, unmarried, and from León, Guanajuato. He graduated from high school there and went to the university for one semester. He tells his story:

> I had to quit the university when my father died. Even though I am not the oldest son, it fell to me to support the family. I went to Mexico City and got a job in a pharmacy, but when the peso was devalued,* I just couldn't make it anymore. I took the bus to Matamoros and swam the river to Brownsville. I had arranged for a friend to meet me on the other side. He had been in Texas for five or six years and knew his way around. He was a real friend. He didn't charge me, and he took risks—he's illegal too. He got me in and got me a job. When I got a little money, I came to California on the bus. The pay is better here. In Texas they don't pay you anything.

---

*In fall of 1976 the Mexican government devalued the peso from about 12.5 to about 22 to the U.S. dollar. This created great hardship in the short run, but stabilized the economy and dramatically slowed the rate of inflation.

I will probably end up going back to Mexico, or being caught.and sent back. I made about $3,000 last year, and when I work full time I send about $70 a week home. When I work less, I send less. I would really like to stay and have a family and support my parents and brothers and sisters in Mexico, but I will probably be sent back to Mexico. Immigration is impossible for me.*

I am going to night school now, as much as I can. I want to learn English. Someday I would like to study again.

The Fisherman. His story is remarkably revealing of the harsh conditions that push mojados north and the bit-by-bit, day-by-day manner in which the decision is made to leave. The fisherman is 40 years old and has had two or three years of schooling. He is semiliterate. He has four brothers and sisters and told us that his mother bore at least two other children who died in infancy. He has a wife and two children back home.

Where I come from you just can't make a living, and after awhile we were completely without money. In that situation, you have to leave your family and look for a living wherever you can find it. You look around Mexico first. A lot of people go to Mexico City. I went first to San Quintín in Baja California and worked in the fields for a couple of years, but I wasn't making anything, so I went up to Ensenada and was a fisherman. I was a fisherman for nine years, but finally I got scared that I would drown. A lot of the guys I worked with drowned. You go out in a big boat, and then you go out from it in a little one-man boat. You have to go in close to shore where the waves are big. That's where the fish are, and they pay you by how many fish you catch. The waves are dangerous because they can capsize the little boats, and when that happens you almost always drown because the water is so rough there. After nine years I had had enough.

You talk to people about going north. Some have been there and tell you how to do it. I first came in in 1968. I took the bus to Tijuana and started talking to people. I found a *coyote* who said he would pass me through for $250. All the other guys in the group had been there before. We walked for three nights and we hid in the daytime. Then a car brought me up here. I have gone back to Mexico twice since then—to see my family. I have always come back in the same way. Once the *migra* got me. I was in a group and they got all of us—five or six. The others just stood there, but I ran. I didn't want to go back. The *migrantes* chased me in their van and on foot, and when I got tired they caught me. One of them punched me and another kicked me when I was going into the van, but they just sent me back to Tijuana the next day. That night I tried again

---

* He is dating a Chicana who has made it clear that she would marry him, but he feels that he cannot assume the responsibilities of marriage, even though it would make him eligible for immigration.

with the *coyote*, and we made it with no trouble. That's the only time the *Migra* ever got me. They never got me up here.

I work pretty steady year round, and I make about $400 a month, every month. I send about $200 home. I work in grapes and peaches mostly. Really all kinds of fruit. I can do anything in fruit. I have been here a long time and people know me. Once I made $1,500 in just three months. A job lasts for two or three weeks, and then you're off for awhile, and then you get another job.

Things are really expensive in Mexico now. I haven't been back since the devaluation, but I couldn't make a living even before that, and everyone says it is a lot worse now. You can't really live on 100 pesos a day, and you can't make even that. The government does some things, but mostly in the cities. In the provinces none of the poor has ever seen the help the government gives.

What I would really like is to be able to come and go between here and Mexico openly. All I came here for was to make a little money so I could get by and my family could get by. To aspire to more is impossible under the conditions we come by.

Although our interviews were not from a scientifically chosen sample, the impression that comes through is similar to those elicited by others who have looked into the situation. These are not the voices of lazy, shiftless welfare bums looking for an easy life. Nor, clearly, do these people lead lives of drunken debauchery at the expense of the American taxpayer. On the contrary, these are courageous and enterprising individuals who, rather than starve or desert their families, have entered another country, with a language and customs entirely foreign to them, to find work for decent wages. While there, they work harder and for longer hours than many Americans would even consider doing, and every spare cent earned is faithfully sent home to their families.

Do They Come to Visit or Stay?

The lives of *mojados* are governed by questions of immediate possibility; we therefore were unable to get from the interviews a clear insight into the most pressing question about the *mojados*. That question is whether they are immigrants in the old sense of people who have made the essential break with home and resolved to start again in a new land, or whether they are just here temporarily for work. We asked this question directly, but did not get direct, yes-or-no responses. This we learned is because it is not a yes-or-no question. The answer depends on circumstances and possibilities. Will it be possible for them to remain? Will it be possible for them to return to Mexico and find a livelihood? Over and over we asked, "If you could make a decent living in Mexico, would you return?" The typical answer was, "I cannot make a decent living in Mexico." When asked, "Do you want to stay in the United States?," the response was likely to be, *"La Migra* will send me back." If they had been asked whether they wanted to go to the Moon, their answer probably would have been, "Can we make a living there? Is there work on the Moon?"

The United States Justice Department has stated, without showing any evidence, that "about one-third of the Mexicans who enter illegally take up permanent residence in the United States." In Mexico, Wayne Cornelius interviewed families of *mojados* and learned that less than 12 percent of the *mojados* had settled permanently in the U.S. and fewer than 20 percent would remain in the United States if they could. But no one really knows what the *mojados* would do if they were free from the tyranny of daily circumstance and could make free choices about where they lived and what they could do.

The objective of any public policy is to influence human behavior in desired directions, but a policy, if it is to be effective, must be built around the attitudes of those whose behavior it is supposed to influence. One of President Carter's ill-fated proposals sent to Congress in August 1977 was to create a new status of immigrant, the Temporary Resident Alien (TRA). Illegals who had entered the United States between January 1, 1970, and January 1, 1977, would be eligible for TRA status. This would guarantee them the legal privilege of residing and working in the United States for five years, but the Administration had no plan for them beyond the five-year period. Illegals would have to report their addresses annually and otherwise identify themselves in order to take advantage of their eligibility.

In his critique of the Carter proposals, Cornelius pointed out:

> As unidentified, nonregistered aliens, having escaped the border patrol and now holding jobs in the interior of the country, they would run relatively little risk of being apprehended and deported during the next five years. . . . Why should they choose to increase their future risk of deportation . . . by coming out of hiding and surrendering themselves to the INS?

In a press briefing on the Carter proposals, Attorney General Griffin Bell was asked, "How do you expect to get any sizable number of people to register?" His answer was, "Maybe they will trust us."

Similarly, there is a risk involved in tightening up the border. If it becomes harder to get in, perhaps those illegals who are already here but have not decided whether they are going to remain will be persuaded to do so. Once they leave, they will have lost their freedom of choice. Thus, the end result of tighter security could be *more*, not fewer illegals residing permanently in the country.

The immigration policy of the United States will be one more set of forces outside the control of the *mojados* that will determine the daily circumstances of their lives and thus determine what they do. At this time no one knows enough about the attitudes of the illegals to predict the consequences of any particular policy. And not enough is being done to find out.

From what we have been able to learn, it appears that the *mojados* are simply people who have been forced by circumstances to go where they go and do what they do. Their choices are extremely limited; they are "pushed" north by forces arising out of social conditions in Mexico. Among the most significant of these forces is the staggeringly rapid recent population growth of Mexico (as well as all of Latin America) and its consequences. In the coming years, like it or not, Americans will be made aware of their long-neglected southern neighbors as the sheer force of their growing numbers impinges on American daily life.

THE PUSH FROM THE SOUTH

During the 1960s and into the 1970s, economic growth and expansion, along with changing migration trends within the country, led to a phenomenal growth in cities in the southern part of the United States, a region popularly called the "Sunbelt." While many older Eastern cities such as Newark, Buffalo, and even New York City were losing population, and others such as Boston or the Midwest metropolis of Chicago were just holding their own, the cities of the South and Southwest grew by leaps and bounds. And the rapid increase in urban population was accompanied by a frenzy of building and other commercial activities. On the average, the populations of major U.S. cities increased by slightly over 20 percent between 1960 and 1975, but Sunbelt metropolises such as Albuquerque, El Paso, and Atlanta gained population by an average of over 40 percent.

On short trips for booze and good times, many Americans became vaguely aware that Mexican border towns like Tijuana, Mexicali, and Juárez were booming as well. For many one-day tourists, these towns were not only a window on Latin America, but represented their total knowledge of what is south of the border. The border towns were becoming border cities. In the same fifteen-year interval that saw the U.S. population shift to the Sunbelt, these three Mexican cities jumped in population by almost 800,000 inhabitants. That was an increase of over 125 percent, putting the growth rates of the Sunbelt to shame.

The border towns have long been known for their close relationships with sister cities across the line in the United States. Thousands of Mexicans cross the border every day from Mexico to work as domestics, factory employees, and in other unskilled or semiskilled capacities from California to Texas. At night the flow is the other way, bringing American tourists to the Mexican fun spots, in turn providing employment for thousands of Mexican nationals. Here is a socially accepted, symbiotic relationship that seems to work. Americans know they can drop their Protestant ethic at the border and properly raise hell in the context of a foreign culture. Mexicans know that there are enormous wage differentials between Mexico and the U.S., and almost as large differentials between the Mexican border towns and the interior of Mexico. This acts as a magnet, drawing people from all over the country to the Mexican border towns, and presumably accounts for the phenomenal growth of Tijuana, Mexicali, Juárez, Nuevo Laredo, Matamoros, and other such places.

Slightly to the south in the interior of Mexico are the cities of Hermosillo, Ciudad Obregón, Chihuahua, and Monterrey. The combined population of these four cities rose from slightly over 1.1 million in 1960 to 2.3 million by 1975. But one only has to examine Monterrey, the largest urban complex in this group, to find a reason for the growth. Monterrey has a rapidly expanding industrial base from which flow a diversity of products, including beer and steel. What seems to have attracted all those people to Monterrey is employment in industry.

Farther south are Guadalajara—the third largest Mexican city in population size after Mexico City and Los Angeles, California—and, in a west-to-east band, the urban complex of Irapuato–Celaya–Salamanca located in the fertile El Bajío valley region and the urban area of Tampico–Ciudad Madero located on the Gulf of Mexico. The populations of these three together increased by over 100 percent between 1960 and 1975. There is an expanding industrial base in these cities and a surrounding fertile agricultural region as well.

Located on the site of earlier capitals since the time of the Aztecs, over 700 years ago, Mexico City today is not only the political capital of Mexico, but its cultural, economic, and commercial center as well. Here a tremendous population increase has occurred, one that matches the general development the country has experienced in the last several decades under a period of political stability. As in ancient Greece, where everything of value flowed toward Athens, so in Mexico everything flows to *la capital*. What as recently as 1960 was a substantial city of 3.5 million, roughly the same number as currently live in the metropolitan area of Washington, D.C., became an urban

agglomeration of 5.6 million by 1960 and ten years later reached
8.6 million. By 1977 it was estimated to be approaching 13 million
inhabitants, and the city and its accumulated problems were being
referred to publicly and in a demographic context as "monstrous"
by José López Portillo, Mexico's president. By 1980 some 15
million persons may be trying to live in Mexico City.

Is it possible that one city can grow by over four million people
in just seven years? Mexico City did, and comparable or even
greater growth has occurred all across the republic of Mexico.
Virtually all of the 192 cities of the country—small, medium, and
large—have doubled in the brief space of 15 years, from 18
million city dwellers in 1960 to 35 million in 1975.

But this phenomenon is not limited to Mexico. The next country to the south is Guatemala, whose capital, Guatemala City, grew
from half a million people in 1960 to around 1.2 million in 1976.
San Salvador, Tegucigalpa, Managua, San José, and Panama
City, the Central American region's other capital cities, have each
more than doubled their populations during this period.

Reasons for this very rapid changeover from a rural to an
urban-based society can be found in the countryside. In Mexico,
agriculture has been losing importance within the national economy for several decades. The adherence to traditional horse-
and-plow methods of cultivation by many of Mexico's Indians,
poor soil conditions resulting from centuries of maize monoculture, the rugged topography of much of the interior, the
existence of thousands of small, subsistence-level holdings, the
fragmentation of other agricultural lands into widely separated
holdings reached only by hours of travel daily, and the lack of
agricultural credit and trade and commerce facilities are not
features to encourage rural development. They are particularly
disadvantageous in competition with the urban-based capital-
intensive investments made in Mexico in the postwar period
under import-substitution policies.

Mexico's *ejido* program has waxed and waned according to the
weather and vagaries of commercial prices, and the ever-present
urban bias took its toll in one form or another, ranging from low
prices paid by city dwellers for farm produce to the disproportionately small amount of government funds allocated to rural
districts. Integration into the national economy remains a very
difficult venture for a rural society spread over a mountainous
terrain in more than 90,000 isolated communities with fewer than
1,000 inhabitants apiece. The agricultural stagnation produced
no increase in rural employment to match the increase in the
rural population. For all these reasons, the cities and their attrac-
tions, real or imagined, are tempting to many rural Mexicans. In

the cities there seems some chance for employment, and no matter how bad the conditions there, wages are certainly higher than the bare subsistence rates paid to agricultural workers.

The story of the population explosion in Latin America and in the Caribbean is primarily an account of victories over communicable and especially infant-related diseases, which allowed the death rate to plummet in the postwar period. That victory, however, contained the seeds of disaster because the birthrate remained very high. One result of this explosive population growth is that the labor pool has far outstripped the increase in numbers of jobs. This leads to international migrants, legal or illegal, going to many countries, of which the United States is but one. Whether numbering in the thousands, tens of thousands, or millions, however, they represent but a small fraction of those who remain in their home countries.

At present, American attention is focused on the illegal migration of hundreds of thousands of people to the United States primarily from Mexico, Central America, and the Caribbean. But to the donor countries, including Mexico, illegal immigration into the United States has been at best a matter of peripheral importance. Those countries have the more immediate problems of trying to accommodate millions of people into delicately balanced social, economic, cultural, and political systems that, with few exceptions, have been dominated for centuries by tiny elites. The dominant elites are now aware that a redoubling of the population is in the works, even as the present population is pressing for equality and creating one crisis after another for their governments.

Not so very long ago, the term population explosion was an abstraction to most people in Latin America, having little to do with day-to-day public needs. Reproduction was a private family matter, and the expectations for the futures of six or seven children were contained within the family structure. But the private family matter has now become a public concern, as millions in overcrowded cities and in the impoverished countryside have pressed on poorly equipped systems for food, education, housing, health and sanitation services, and above all for employment. Throughout the Caribbean and Latin America, the explosion is now very real to decision-makers. Although they are not sure when or where it happened, authorities sense they have crossed that fine line between an economically expanding cheap-labor heaven and a resource-depleted, overpopulated hell.

Most Latin American governments have now gone beyond the earlier simplistic notion that "development is the best contraceptive," just as the equally simplistic argument that birth control alone would foster development has been rejected. The emerging synthesis seems to be that both reducing the birthrate and encouraging economic development are goals to be sought. Yet even this seems naive on at least two counts. In countries that have had a rapidly growing population over some period of time the "momentum" of population growth guarantees further very substantial growth for many years after the birthrate has been reduced. This is because a fast-growing population has a disproportionate number of young people who will become the next generation's parents. For instance, nearly half of Mexico's population today is under the age of 15. Even if these young people each have much smaller families than their parents did, the next generation will still outnumber the parent generation. Generally it takes three generations for a previously growing population to stop growing after replacement reproduction has been achieved because there are so many more young people just replacing themselves than there are senior citizens subject to the high rates of old age.

On the other side, economic development has relatively little effect as long as the fruits of development are concentrated in the hands of a few. Accordingly, questions of who benefits and discussions about patterns of income distribution and the desperate need to improve the employment situation, are in vogue today in Latin America as never before.

The Population Program in Mexico

The growing awareness of the population dimension to problems of development has produced a dramatic change of policy in the Mexican government since 1970. Most Americans are unaware of this change or of the tremendous effort that the Mexican government is now putting into its family-planning program.

As recently as ten or fifteen years ago most Latin American governments were "pronatalist" in their official policies, that is, an official policy or aim of government was the increase of population. The slogan, *gobernar es poblar* (to govern is to populate), was heard in political speeches all over the region, and nowhere was it heard more often or cheered more loudly than in Mexico. Until 1973 it was against the law in Mexico to advertise the sale of contraceptives. The 1947 General Law of Population directed the Secretary of the Interior, a quite different and more powerful post than the one that bears the same name in the United States, to take "measures to encourage marriage and to increase the birthrate." In 1962 the eminent Mexican demographer Gilberto Loyo stated that "Mexico can for the rest of this century concentrate on economic development without worrying about a policy to restrict births." A few years later, a survey of the opinions of the Mexican leadership revealed that over half saw their country's population growth as leading to greater national economic power and only 13 percent saw it as leading to economic impoverishment. Over half of those leaders interviewed also considered the world population explosion unimportant.

There were voices from the other side, however. In 1967 Victor Urquidi, one of Mexico's leading economists and demographers, wrote that the regulation of births "every day appears to be more necessary to economic and social advance." By 1970 even Loyo had modified his position and wrote, "The strong Mexican demographic growth is not by itself a factor favoring economic growth." He had also added the prestige of his name to the board of directors of a family-planning organization. Between 1950 and 1970, the Mexican population had increased almost 90 percent, from 26 to 49 million people. Yet economic expansion had been even greater, and average levels of economic well-being had improved according to several indicators.

Concern was voiced by those who noticed that the rate of population increase was speeding up and that the number of people was going to redouble in the next twenty years if something did not change. Development certainly was not functioning as a contraceptive! Mexico had apparently provided an increasing average standard of living for 26 million more people in the two decades between 1950 and 1970, but could it continue with a further increase of 50 million in the next two decades? Even with Mexico's growing wealth, some bad things were happening. In 1950 those on the lower half of the income scale received about 19 percent of the national income. This was not very good, but development was supposed to improve this. In 1970, though, the lower half got only 15 percent; the disparity was increasing. Mexicans were growing farther apart economically. Even if everyone might be a little better off, such a wide disparity between rich and poor is socially dangerous.

The problem that Mexico was facing can be illuminated by a look at the literacy figures. Between 1950 and 1970 the number of Mexican adults who could read and write increased from 11.8 to 27.5 million, but the number who were illiterate *also* rose, from 8.9 to 10.9 million. The educational system, like all other Mexican social systems, could be very proud of its accomplishment, but it was still falling behind in some respects. In general, the task of supplying social services and the amenities of life to the people was growing bigger every year; worse, it was growing bigger at a faster rate.

There had been family-planning programs in Mexico for a long time, mostly private and some foreign in direction and leadership. Margaret Sanger had started a short-lived clinic in Yucatán in the 1920s. Dr. Edris Rice-Wray, a United States citizen, started the Family Welfare Association in 1959. With financial backing from American drug companies she had expanded her organization, later called the Association for Maternal Health, to ten clinics. In 1967 an overzealous public-health official closed Dr. Rice-Wray's main clinic on a technicality after she had written a newspaper article urging Mexico to become active in family planning. In the mid- and late 1960s, many organizations were formed and other clinics were opened. The government even became quietly involved, and it has been estimated that in the late 1960s 15 percent of all contraceptives were distributed by the government. But there was still no national program, and official government policy remained pronatalist.

It seemed that a great step backward, from the standpoint of the family planners, had been taken when the Institutional Revolutionary Party (PRI) nominated Luis Echeverría Álvarez for the presidency. No one knows why, but Echeverría took a hard-line pronatalist stand, *gobernar es poblar,* in the campaign. In his September 1970 inaugural address, he continued this theme:

> To govern is to populate.... I do not know whether Mexican mothers understand the effectiveness of the contraceptive pill. What I do know is that we need to populate our country . . . we do not want to control our population.

Two years later, though, President Echeverría apparently had second thoughts. He said in his state-of-the union address:

> Mexico cannot call a halt when halfway along the road. . . . Population growth could win out over economic development. Failure to make an intense, sustained effort could condemn the country to frustration and dependency.

The wife of the president has a special position in Mexico as in the United States. Well before the official turnaround, Señora Echeverría, a mother of eight children, said publicly in reference to a series of family-planning lectures, "If in my day there had been talk of family planning, I would have taught courses in it."

In November 1973, the Mexican Congress voted *unanimously* to revise the General Law of Population, stating that an object of government was "To carry out programs of family planning . . . with the object of regulating rationally and stabilizing the growth of the population. . . ." In 1974 the Constitution of Mexico was revised to give equal rights to women (something the United States has not done), and part of the revision stated that "All persons have the right to decide in a free, responsible, and informed manner on the number and the spacing of their children." Up to that time, only Yugoslavia, and since then only the People's Republic of China, have made family planning a constitutional right.

Well before this, in December 1972, a collective pastoral letter of the 80 Mexican bishops had endorsed the family-planning program as a "humane measure, wholly consistent with the Church's belief in the primacy of conscience and its concern for the family unit." They had justified their position because of "what is the very real and excruciating emergency for most Mexican families: the population explosion." The political left, usually as hostile to family planning in Latin America as the Church, was ahead of the bishops. In July 1972, *Siempre,* the most widely read Mexican leftist magazine, ran an article saying that "too many children" was the fundamental problem in Mexico's schools and praising Echeverría for understanding the "limits of the problem."

No one will ever know all the reasons for the Mexican turnaround, which was really the Echeverría turnaround, on family planning. One explanation is that he was faking with his hardline pronatalism in the election and was simply courting the favor of the left wing of PRI. This theory has it that Echeverría had always depended on the left but had lost this support in 1968. Then, as Minister of the Interior, he had ordered troops to fire on demonstrating students, thus causing the "Tlatelolco Massacre" in which the government has admitted that 250 unarmed people were killed. Other sources have told us the number was as high as 1,500.

If his position in the campaign was sincere, perhaps the turnaround can be accounted for by the fact that in 1971 the Mexican economy failed to grow as fast as the population for the first time since the Great Depression of the 1930s. Another explanation is that President Echeverría became interested in the closing of Mexico's best-known family-planning program at the government's Women's Hospital. His concern over the program being closed down led to a discussion of why it had been started, which in turn led to a discussion of Mexico's population explosion. In the course of all this, perhaps Echeverría's eyes were opened for the first time. Only Echeverría really knows the reasons for his conversion, and he is not telling.

In any event, a truly massive effort was launched. Family-planning services were instituted in all government hospitals and those of PEMEX, the federal railroad agency, and the federal electricity commission; in short, in virtually all the hospitals of Mexico. A National Council on Population (CONAPO) was formed, composed of the most important cabinet officers and headed by the Minister of the Interior. This council not only pushed contraceptive-service delivery, but coordinated a massive public relations campaign aimed at guaranteeing a good reception for the new services. The propaganda line did not directly emphasize reduction of fertility, but pounded on the theme of "responsible parenthood."

When one of us drove the length of Mexico in 1975, family-planning slogans were as numerous as Coca-Cola signs used to be in the United States. The theme of thousands of billboards and messages painted on walls in red and yellow was "To love the child is to educate the child," or to nourish, or to clothe, or to house, or whatever. No mention was made in the beginning of numeric goals for either family size or the national population. The goals were declared to be improvement in the quality of life for all Mexicans and the extension of freedom to all, particularly women.

Besides the massive ad campaign on radio and television, the other major facet of the program has been the establishment of public clinics that provide access to family-planning services as well as infant and maternal care for those who cannot afford to visit private physicians. It is too early to evaluate the program's success in reaching all of the people. Yet there are indications that it has had some effect outside the urban areas that have been the focus of most of the program's first efforts. Reports from those who have recently visited rural areas of southern Mexico, for example, indicate that women under 30 in particular often express an interest in having smaller families than their mothers did, in part as a result of what they have heard on the radio. Until recently, their options were effectively limited to illegal abortions or the hormone injections given by many pharmacists to induce abortion. Now, they may make a trip to the clinic in the nearest provincial city or they may ask a local doctor, nurse, or pharmacist to provide them with reliable methods of birth control.

The revision of the Mexican Constitution to guarantee the legal and social equality of women was accompanied by a propaganda assault on *machismo*, the peculiarly Mexican brand of sexism. One ad was a cartoon showing one woman saying to another, "Don't stand in the corner like a shotgun." This was a direct reference to the Mexican sexist belief that every home needed two things, a shotgun and a woman, both loaded (pregnant). Remarkably, the Mexican government was pushing family planning by appealing to the deep respect in which Mexicans hold the family and at the same time trying to change traditional ideas about the family. And the new concern has shown up elsewhere besides in the family-planning effort; for example, demography, population issues, and responsible parenthood are now being taught in public schools. Rarely if ever in history has a long-established government put itself so rapidly and forcefully behind an effort to change basic attitudes and basic social relationships.

In 1976 José López Portillo was elected to the presidency. He was fully aware that there would be 14 million more Mexicans when his term ended in 1982 than on his inauguration day. He lent the prestige of his name and office to the family-planning effort even more generously than had Echeverría. A series of national and international conferences of demographers was held in Mexico City, and López Portillo personally delivered the inaugural address to the meeting of the International Union for the Scientific Study of Population. In his speech he made specific reference to the barriers to Mexican development represented by too-rapid population growth and to the problem of the illegal migration of Mexican workers to the United States.

On August 28, 1977, CONAPO formally presented the National Plan for Family Planning to the President. This plan, "the most comprehensive ever developed by a government," included a number of goals. The targets were population growth rates of 2.5 percent per year by 1982, 1.8 percent by 1988, 1.3 percent in 1994, and 1.0 percent in 2000. These are all presidential election years in Mexico. Their selection as target dates seems to be an attempt by PRI, which certainly intends to select all the presidents of Mexico through this century and beyond, to serve notice to all its members that fertility reduction is a long-range aim of the party and that presidential aspirants will be expected to support them. The Plan contains many other specific goals, such as how many "new acceptors," that is, women brought into the family-planning fold, are to be achieved by various service-delivery agencies at specified times and what percentages of "dropouts" would be acceptable.

The Plan received significant endorsement from the Mexican scientific community and from outside the government in April 1977 when Victor Urquidi, President of the Colegio de Mexico, speaking before the Japanese Scientific Society in Tokyo, addressed himself to the issue of what would have to be done to make the plan work, thereby implying that the plan was indeed workable. After noting that a significant drop in the population growth rate had been achieved by the efforts up to that time, he said:

> If these trends prevail and a well-coordinated and intensive program in family planning is followed . . . it would not be impossible to reach a total population of 110 million by the year 2000, instead of currently accepted projections of 126 to 140 million. . . .

There is no longer any justification for Americans to say that Mexico "ought to do something" about its growing population. The argument that American tolerance of illegal immigration creates a "safety valve" that allows other countries to ignore their problems of population growth does not apply to Mexico. At the very time when the U.S. was most tolerant, Mexico was formulating and putting into operation a program for the limitation of population growth more comprehensive and with a greater degree of commitment than that given any social program in the United States. It can certainly be argued that Mexico should have started sooner. But that has nothing to do with what can now be done, and Mexico now seems to be making every effort to make up for the lost time and is doing all that can reasonably be expected.

Dr. Urquidi sees the possibility of limiting the Mexican population in this century to 110 million. This is still 42 million more Mexicans than there are today. In a country where unemployment in 1975 was officially estimated at nearly 50 percent, the accommodation and social advance of that many more people is going to be extremely difficult to achieve, even if the oil revenues should have the effects on development that are most optimistically predicted. The results of Mexico's efforts to control its population growth will be felt in the long run. No significant difference is going to be felt in the next few years, and not much in the next decade. For the foreseeable future, the push from the south can be expected to continue, and the United States will have to base its actions on that reality.

THE MEXICAN VIEW OF THE MIGRATION

To find out what Mexicans think about the migration of their people in large numbers to the United States and of conditions in their country, one of us visited Mexico City in 1978. Mexico City is one of the great cities of the world. It is not merely very large, though with more than 12 million people it is now the third largest metropolitan complex in the world and, with its growth rate, it will soon be the largest. Not all very large cities are great ones, but Mexico City has magnificent architectural monuments reflecting the styles and events of over 400 years of history. The battles of half a dozen wars and revolutions have raged in its streets, and thousands of promises have issued from its offices and meeting chambers, some resulting in cowardly betrayal, others in heroic fulfillment. All of this is visible in the city and in the people who live there. The *ciudadanos* or *capitalinos,* as those who are born there are called, have the same arrogant parochialism one finds in New Yorkers or Parisians. They have heard that there are other great cities in the world, but they do not really believe it.

As with Paris or New York, visitors either love Mexico City or they hate it. Many gringos say it is dirty, but it is less littered than American cities and the garbage collection is as good. Everyone says it is crowded, and that is undeniable. The clean, new, efficient subways—*el Metro*—are marvels of *transporte collectivo.* But the rush hour, which begins around four and can last until after seven, puts one in closer contact with "the people" than one really wants to be. It is not as bad as in Tokyo, but worse than in New York. The smog competes with the worst in the world. The main entrance to the National Palace, from which all distances are marked in Mexico, is over 7,500 feet above sea level, but it is only in the few minutes immediately after sunrise that the clarity of air and sky are what would be expected at that altitude. As soon as the sun rises, a translucent, gray pall forms, and the sky disappears. On bad days it is necessary to turn on auto headlights.

No matter how entranced a visitor may be by other things, the realization that any moderately windy day produces a "fecal snow" can be dismaying. The rapid growth of the city has far outstripped its sewage disposal facilities, despite the best efforts of the municipal authorities. Improperly disposed of human waste dries in the arid air to be whipped up by the breeze and distributed over the city. The bustle and vitality of the downtown area and the working-class residential districts near the railroad station and elsewhere can make one forget that hundreds of thousands of people make their livelihood by "mining" the refuse heaps and garbage dumps on the edge of town; what is rejected and discarded by one class is the resource base of another.

Mexicans, like other Latin Americans, are resentful of gringos who chide them over these things. After all, they tell you, the United States did not worry about air quality and the purity of their rivers until well after it was an industrialized nation. They say (incorrectly) that, during its conversion from agriculture to industry, the U.S. population growth rate was even greater than

Mexico's today. It was very high, but it never doubled in only 20 years. Yet they have a legitimate argument. It is useless for the gringo to argue that when the United States was industrializing it had no cities of 12 million people and that much of the population growth was from immigration—a shift of people from one part of the world to another—rather than almost entirely from natural increase in the country itself. Likewise, it does no good to point out that the *entire world* has problems today that it did not have then and that the worldwide industrial capacity is already quite enough to handle and process the available resources. Their answer to all of this is that there will be plenty of time to clean up the smokestacks and put smog-control devices on the cars and trucks after *desarollo* (development) is complete.

In Mexico and throughout Latin America, *desarollo* is a vague, mystical concept that everyone pursues and no one can define. Political scientist Freeman Wright, who has lived and worked in Latin America as a student, a professor, and an AID functionary, defines it as the "Los Angelesization of the world." Like the concept of "defense" in the United States, *desarollo* is infinitely plastic. It can be molded to fit any motive and can justify the most dreadful of actions or inactions. But people need ideals to live by and goals to pursue, and *desarollo,* by and large, is a better thing to believe in and to pursue than "defense."

Much of the vigor and hope one sees in Mexico City is there because Mexicans, and particularly *capitalinos,* believe in *desarollo.* They believe that once Mexico is "developed," the smog will go away, the fecal snow will stop, and everyone will be well situated and comfortable. In the last few years, the promise of *desarollo* has been enhanced by the constant flow of encouraging news from the oil explorations in Chiapas, Tabasco, and in the Gulf off Campeche on the Yucatán peninsula. Mexico today is a country living on hope, hope that is based on the faith in *desarollo* and strengthened by the belief that oil wealth is just around the corner. With hope, anything can be endured, anything can be accepted.

Despite all the things that need to be done, Mexico cannot employ all its people. Some 40 percent of the work force are either unemployed or underemployed. As many as two million Mexicans—one out of every seven in the work force—have illegally gone to the United States in order to earn a livelihood, and more are going every day. This is sometimes even welcomed as relieving Mexico's horrendous unemployment problem; at most, the migration is considered a problem like the smog and the fecal snow. Once the country is "developed" and the oil money is in hand, it is expected that the problem will cease to exist.

One way to learn quickly what prevailing attitudes and problems are in a foreign country is to read the newspapers. Mexico City has at least five daily newspapers, which are read voraciously. *Secunda Ovaciones* is a sensational newspaper with lots of pictures of pretty girls and breezy stories about everything. A three-inch-high headline on October 28, 1978, read:

ESTAMPIDA
A EE. UU.
Mil Braceros Tratan de Pasar
Cada Noche por Tijuana
(STAMPEDE TO THE U.S.
A thousand *braceros* try to pass
every night at Tijuana.)

The occasion of the headline was the announcement by the United States Border Patrol that a few miles of new fence were to be installed in places along the U.S.–Mexican Border. Two days later the more reserved *Excelsior* ran two stories under the headline:

Un Millon de "Mojados" a EU Cada Ano
(A Million "Wets" to the U.S. Each Year).

The first story was about the fence, *la cortina tortilla* (the tortilla curtain), and the other on the illegal immigration problem in general. Both articles were thoroughly researched and relied on interviews at Tijuana/San Diego and Juárez/El Paso with INS officials, knowledgeable persons in Tijuana and Juárez, and with illegals themselves. They were better articles than we have ever seen in the U.S. press. Along with stories about the visit of President José López Portillo to the United States and a welterweight boxing match between Mexican and Puerto Rican contenders, the fence and the illegals were the news of the day.

Everyone in Mexico City seemed to be eager to talk to an American who actually knew some Border Patrolmen and was writing about the subject. Our driver, Ricardo Valdez, whose English business card declared him "An Excellent in Guidance" summed up the situation this way:

There is a very small group in this country—maybe 10 percent—who have far too much money and another group about the same size who don't have anything. They just have to go to wherever they can make a living. They are the ones who go to the United States. The rest of us are getting along okay.

We could have argued with Ricardo about his proportions of rich and poor, but we were in Mexico City to listen. Ricardo had worked in Los Angeles as a graphic artist in an advertising agency. He would have emigrated, but his mother became sick, and he had to come back to take care of her. He felt that he could live as well in Mexico City as in Los Angeles. He told us that if one had a skill or some capital, he or she could really do very well in Mexico City. He owned his car, an immaculate and well-running 1970 Chevrolet Impala, and charged us $30 for his day's services. He also made a little money at night doing graphic art work for a television station. He said that, with the lower cost of living, he was doing better than he could ever do in the United States.

In a bar in one of the more prosperous parts of Mexico City, we met a Mexican lawyer whose practice is limited to representing rich Mexicans with tax problems in the United States. When asked what the principal problems of his clients were, he said, "Having to pay your damned taxes." When he learned that we were writing a book on illegal migration, he was eager to give us his views. He said that there was no way that Mexico could employ "all those people" because they had no skills that the economy needed. He observed that all they knew was peasant agriculture and how to wash cars. He went on to say that he had often wondered how the United States, with its sophisticated, high-technology industry and its developed economy, could find work for all those unskilled people while Mexico could not. We agreed that the same question had occurred to us.

Mexican Research on Migrants

We also paid a visit to the Colegio de Mexico, which is devoted to advanced training and research on any topic relevant to understanding the society and culture of Mexico. There is nothing like it in the United States. Similarly, the building it occupies is unlike anything devoted to intellectual or cultural matters in the United States. It is very large and the architecture is stunning. Pre-stressed concrete walls pierced by large, tinted windows rise up three or four stories around the open central core. It is a perfect blending of modern architectural boldness and openness with the traditional Mexican concern for the inward-focusing orientation to the courtyard. In the United States, that kind of expense and care are usually reserved for the home offices of insurance companies. If such a building were built at public expense, it would be for the National Aeronautics and Space Agency or the CIA.

The president of the Colegio, Dr. Victor Urquidi, is an important man in Mexico, more so than any social scientist is in the

United States. He is also very busy, so we were pleased when he agreed to talk with us about the emigration. What he says as the president of the Colegio or just as an individual carries a semioffi-cial and certainly authoritative impact, and this reinforces his natural tendency as a responsible social scientist toward caution in his remarks. He was quite hesitant to discuss the nature of the problems leading to the emigration but very willing to talk about the work now underway to study it.

The work that Dr. Urquidi and his colleagues, Dr. Jorge Bus-tamante and Dr. Francisco Alba, told us about demonstrated a very real concern about the problem on the part of the Mexican government and the Mexican social science community. They were quick to admit that very little is known today. The main effort is being done under the title *Encuesta Nacional de Emigración a la Frontera Norte y a los Estados Unidos* (ENEFNEU)—the National Survey on Emigration to the Northern Border and to the United States. It was funded for $900,000 in 1977, and before it is completed, it will employ more than 500 persons. The funds come from the Mexican government through the Secretariat of Labor and the work will be done at the *Centro Nacional de Informa-ción y Estadisticas del Trabajo* (the equivalent of the Bureau of Labor Statistics in the U.S. Government). Personnel from the Colegio are deeply involved in the project.

One of those most deeply involved is Dr. Bustamante, whose interest in the illegal emigration began long before it became a fashionable topic. He worked on the problem in the early 1970s when he was a graduate student at Notre Dame, where he earned his doctorate and coauthored *Los Mojados,* one of the first books on the subject. As Dr. Bustamante outlined the present project in a paper before a joint symposium held by the Colegio and the Brookings Institution in Washington in June 1978, it would pro-ceed through a series of carefully planned phases.

The first part of the study, executed in 1977, amounted to interviewing 10,000 illegal migrants as they were repatriated to Mexico by the INS. This was done to find out what questions were relevant for the second part and where the second set of inter-views ought to be administered. In short, by talking to the people who had gone to the United States illegally and had been caught—the only group of illegals readily available for interviewing—the investigators could find out what kinds of households and what parts of Mexico they came from.

On the basis of these interviews, 60,000 households in 120 communities were selected as the kinds of homes most likely to produce workers who would go to the United States illegally. As projected, the next phase of the study was a census of the target households, covering as much as one percent of the total Mexican population, in order to establish precisely the characteristics of this subpopulation. With this knowledge the investigators then can proceed to select those individuals who will actually be interviewed.

The projected scale, care, and cost of this research effort far outstrips anything that has been undertaken in the United States. In 1978 the Select Committee on Population of the U.S. House of Representatives has recommended an expenditure of $10 million for research into the nature and impact of immigration, legal and illegal, on American society. If this recommendation is followed, surely some of these dollars could be spent on establishing communication and liaison with the social scientists in Mexico who, at this moment, are far ahead of their colleagues in the United States in thinking and working on the illegal migration. The roots of the problem are in Mexico, and any real solutions will also have to come from Mexico—although the United States, which has contributed so much to it, can either facilitate or hinder those solutions.

It should be clear by now that the Mexican illegal-immigrant "problem" is not simply a matter of poor people from a foreign nation crowding into the rich country next door to get a share of the wealth. As Dr. Bustamante said before the Colegio-Brookings symposium, the phenomenon of illegal migration between the United States and Mexico "represents a mark of shame in the history of both Mexico and the United States."

To one degree or another, the United States has been involved since Mexican independence in shaping the Mexican nation—and thus has had a considerable hand in creating the problem. American interests have repeatedly profited from the exploitation of Mexicans in Mexico, first supporting the feudal regime of Díaz and then the more compliant of his post-Revolutionary successors. An American ambassador played a key role in the downfall of Madero and the beginning of the period of turmoil that "pushed" the first wave of migrants across the border. American agricultural interests must bear some responsibility for the neglect of rural development in Mexico and therefore for much of the subsequent flood of wetbacks and *braceros* into the United States. American corporations, most recently the multinationals, have helped to create the conditions of "two-tiered" development that have hindered job creation in Mexico, while making the "pull" factors in the United States so strong. And American businesses at home are only too willing to employ Mexicans who cross the border, whether legally or not. As long as these conditions persist, immigrants will continue to arrive, and others will make a living by helping the illegals across, despite the efforts of U.S. Government agencies to stop them.

LOS COYOTES AND LA MIGRA

Two groups of people loom large in the life of a potential *mojado: la Migra*—"the guys with the pistols," as one illegal called them—and the *coyotes*—the professional smugglers, a relatively new addition to the scene. As the sophistication of the devices and procedures of *La Migra* have escalated, the *coyotes* have been called into existence by the inexorable laws of economics. The *coyotes* and *la Migra* are now engaged in what has been, but may not long remain, a largely bloodless war.

LOS COYOTES

The Pension Jalisco has about 30 rooms. It is really two buildings joined back to back, but subsequent remodelings have completely obscured what their original purposes might have been. Today the buildings afford shelter to 45 or 50 people, about a dozen and a half of whom are permanent residents and take their meals there. There is no hot water except what can be heated on hotplates in the two bathrooms, but there are a total of four toilets, and some sinks have been installed in alcoves in the halls. The place is scrupulously clean. The Jalisco is run by Romano and Emilia S., a middle-aged couple who live in an apartment near the center of the structure. Their living room contains the registration desk and serves for television viewing by anyone who wants to watch what Emilia has decided on for the evening. Everyone shows up for the soccer games, but most late afternoons a smaller crowd of about a dozen gathers in the sparsely furnished vestibule at the front, and not to watch television. They are there to wait for the guide who will start them on their way across the United States–Mexican border a quarter-mile north of the pension.

276

Colonia Libertad, where the Jalisco is located, is the largest section of Tijuana and the fastest growing. No one knows its population exactly, but it is in the hundreds of thousands. It is no shantytown. The streets, while unpaved, are broad, well laid out, and thick with gravel and cobblestones. The houses are supplied with electricity and water, and the sewage system is being extended into the section. It is east of downtown Tijuana and built on steep hills that continue northward into the United States.

Not all sections of Tijuana are hilly, however. Tijuana's worst slum was on the floodplain of the Tijuana River. It was wiped out during the heavy rains of the winter of 1977–78. Some of the hovels were washed away by the rising river, but most were demolished by government bulldozers because the government was afraid that the big Ramírez Dam upstream was going to collapse from the rains. Development of any kind on the floodplain was forbidden; the slum was built by squatters whom nobody had bothered to move out. When the rains began, the authorities began to worry about a disaster, but the squatters stayed despite explanations and warnings. Finally, the government sent in the bulldozers. Months later there were still thousands of people in the tent city set up by the army at the Tijuana airport.

Downtown Tijuana is jammed and just not big enough to handle the population. There were 62,000 people in Tijuana in 1950, there are at least 600,000 today, and by the turn of the century there may be over 1.5 million. A large area, perhaps a mile long and a half-mile wide, has been cleared for expansion of the commercial district, and there are wide, gracefully curving streets running through it. There are some attractive new high-rise office buildings, but construction has not even begun on most of the lots. Judging from the number of "for sale" signs, most of the lots are still in the hands of promoters and speculators.

What the Pension Jalisco is to Tijuana—a hastily rebuilt shelter for people who need a place to stay—Tijuana and most Mexican cities are to the entire country. But Tijuana is like the Jalisco in another respect—it is one of the principal marshaling grounds for Mexicans who want to enter the United States. The mayor of Tijuana has estimated that at any moment there are a quarter-million people in his city waiting to "go north."

In spring 1978, he ordered the Tijuana Police Department (TJPD) to cooperate with the U.S. Border Patrol in curbing the flow. One night in May 1978 the TJPD blocked the return route while a force of Border Patrol agents pushed over 70 would-be immigrants back against the fence. The whole scene was illuminated by a Border Patrol helicopter. The 70 meekly surrendered to a Border Patrol force not one-fifth their number. If the illegals had scattered and run, most would have gotten away. But without their *coyotes* they would have gotten lost and would have been picked up later. No one even entertained the thought of going back through the fence into the arms of the TJPD. In this operation, the two land groups and the helicopter were coordinated by a U.S. Border Patrolman working on the Mexican side of the border. The senior agent observed the next day that "it sure is easier when you have someone coming up from the south."

Almost everyone who tries to enter the United States illegally from Mexico has some kind of help and in the last few years that help has become increasingly professional. One ranking INS enforcement official summed it up by saying, "We have caused the smuggling problem." The increased enforcement effort all along the border has forced the would-be illegal immigrant to use the services of a smuggler, and this same effort has forced the smugglers to develop more careful plans, more sophisticated approaches, and more highly organized structures. A few years ago most smugglers were individual operators who, like Humberto, personally led their clients through the various routes across the border. Today the smuggler is more likely to be someone who never sees a client and is occupied with organizational problems and the coordination of a dozen or more subordinates. He has to worry about his guides being caught in the United States, the proper placing and timing of "load cars" to pick up clients, the location of new "safe houses," keeping abreast of changes in the Border Patrol watch schedule and other variations in Border Patrol practices, collecting from clients who have been successfully smuggled into the United States and are paying the fee on the installment plan, and a host of other daily problems that confront many businessmen.

At the watch briefing in the U.S. Border Patrol station at Chula Vista, before a new shift goes out on the line, the senior agent reads the intelligence report to the agents and gives them instructions. A brown Dodge van has been observed loading people out of a certain house between 4:00 and 4:30 each morning for the last three mornings. A unit is told to check out what is going on. An informant at the chicken ranch says that a red motorcycle has been going "right up to the wire," just sitting there, and then leaving at regular times. The chicken ranch is about a quarter-mile from the border, which is marked at that point only by a heavy steel cable—called "the wire"—installed several years ago to prevent trucks carrying marijuana from just turning off the paved road on the Mexican side and driving through the hayfield on the U.S. side.

Each of these announcements indicates some new problem for one of the smugglers in Tijuana. If the same load car is used in the same place too often, someone will notice and call the Border Patrol. This is equally true for a safe house. If a routine is used successfully a few times, that success is a reason for abandoning it. The Border Patrol faces a similar problem. If a given placement of electronic sensors and a given deployment pattern of agents succeeds in stopping a lot of illegals for two or three days, one can bet that the smugglers will stop using that route and shift to another. Changes in deployment catch some *coyotes* like Humberto, but the word on them quickly circulates.

The border is virtually unprotected for about an hour three times a day when the shifts are changing. The timing of the shifts is a matter of common knowledge among the smugglers. The agent in charge tried varying the shifts for awhile, but the smugglers had observers watching the Border Patrol vehicles and the headquarters, and they simply varied their own operations accordingly. The surprise change of shifts might work once, but it was not worth the effort and the grumbling it caused among the agents. Their hours are irregular enough without the shifts being changed all the time.

There are three basic avenues from Tijuana into the United States, with slight variations within each one. One is across the floodplain of the Tijuana River, west of Interstate Highway 5. The most common path here is to cross the road going out to the beaches, then slip through one of the cuts in the fence or go under it where it has been dug out.

Once through the fence, the illegal is in the United States. It is no more than a twenty-minute walk, even in the dark, to a new housing development three-quarters of a mile to the north. The only serious barrier is the Tijuana River, which usually can be waded.

During the heavy rains that led to the bulldozing of the upstream shantytown in 1978, a group of 14 illegals were stranded on an island by the rapidly rising water. A Border Patrol unit spotted them and had to call in a Coast Guard rescue helicopter. No one on the island could speak English and no one in the helicopter could speak Spanish, so a Border Patrolman had to be ferried to the island to organize the rescue effort. One at a time, the men were hoisted aboard the helicopter and carried across the river. The last man off the island was the Border Patrol agent. The whole episode was filmed by a television news team from Japan, and the men and women at the Chula Vista Border Patrol Station are proud of it and like to show it to visitors.

Except for the river, this path into the United States is straight, unobstructed, and short. There is also no cover, and when the INS helicopter comes over with its bright lights there is no place to go. The *pollero* and his *pollos* have their best chance when there is fog or bad weather.

Most of the traffic comes through the canyons west of I-5 because there are so many alternate routes and so much cover. These hills and canyons are the continuation of those on which Colonia Libertad is built. When the northernmost street of the colonia is crossed, the traveler is in the United States. The smugglers know that *la Migra* does not have enough agents to cover the maze of canyons, so getting through is like a game, a combination of chess and hide-and-go-seek. Guides are absolutely essential, for they know where the paths up the steep canyon walls are and the advantages and disadvantages of each of the various routes. They know where the Border Patrol agents and the electronic sensors have been, where they are most likely to be, and all the other lore that is needed to get a group of *mojados* through.

The third route is right down the middle, right under I-5. The street drainage systems of the city of Tijuana and of I-5 are interconnected, and they take the water into the Tijuana River. It is possible to enter a drainage conduit in Mexico, work one's way through the maze, and come out in the United States. There are only a few places one can come out, and these are watched carefully by agents and are laced with electronic sensors, particularly the infrared sensors that detect body heat. Nevertheless, there are some *coyotes* who specialize in this sector of the border.

The immediate crossing of the border presents one set of problems, and that is where the smuggler's plans are most likely to go awry. But even after the group is a mile or so into the country, the smuggler's job is not done. The next step is to get the *mojados* into vehicles. This might be done by meeting a car at a prearranged spot—a parking lot, a residential street, or along some stretch of country road. It might be done by herding them into a safe house and waiting for a van to take 20 or more of them on to East Los Angeles or to jobs in California's agricultural valleys.

One of the recommendations in the December 1978 *Report on Legal and Illegal Immigration* of the House Select Committee on Population was to empower the Border Patrol to seize vehicles used in smuggling operations, just as customs agents can now seize vehicles used in smuggling goods. One senior INS enforcement agent told us that the only effect of the new power would be to force the smuggler to start using clunkers that he could afford to lose or just to rent a car in downtown San Diego. But it would still complicate the smuggler's operations, and the more complicated it is to smuggle wets into the United States, the fewer are going to make it. This is the basic idea behind all antismuggling efforts—to complicate life for the smuggler. The enforcement people at INS have no illusions about being able to stop large-scale smuggling with the few men and paltry resources they have, but they can use what Congress gives them to make life difficult for both the smuggler and his clients. And, of course, the more difficult the job, the more the smuggler will charge for his services.

The going rate for being smuggled into the United States in 1978 was about $300. This would be a first-class job, with transportation into the interior and the promise that the smugglers will keep trying until the client gets through. If a smuggling ring could run four groups of six people each through every night, and if half of them succeeded, the ring would gross $3,600 per night. Even after the employees were paid and the costs of safe houses, cars, and such were met, it would still be a very profitable business.

As one might guess, the laws of economics that have attracted Mexicans into the smuggling game have also attracted U.S. citizens. For example, reporter Joshua Baer has told the story of Lukas, the son of a Greek immigrant, who took over his father's large vegetable-farming business based in Arizona. It took Lukas only three weeks of running the business to become convinced "that the amount of money to be made from the growing and selling of vegetables was a fixed quantity, but the amount of money to be made from illegal activities along the United States–Mexico border was an open-ended quantity limited only by his imagination."

Lukas branched out into the business of smuggling narcotics and *mojados*. His vegetable farms and his illegal activities dovetailed nicely. The former, for example, provided start-up capital for the latter. Some of his farms were in northern Sonora, Mexico, and Lukas found he could pay many of the people who had worked on those farms simply by smuggling them into the United States. That reduced the labor costs of growing vegetables in Mexico. He invested part of his income in bribing law-enforcement officers on both sides of the border—including some officers of *la Migra*. This helped him in smuggling wets across the border at Nogales in his vegetable trucks. Border Patrolmen on the take looked the other way; honest ones thought wets, when discovered, were stowaways. Once he had the illegals in the U.S., Lukas used his trucks to distribute workers throughout the Southwest. Lukas eventually gained the nickname of *El Pollero Supremo* in recognition of his ability to deliver 50 illegals to a farmer anywhere in the area with 48 hours' notice.

Baer goes on to describe Lukas's manipulation of a corrupt

Border Patrolman and his hiring of an illegal, who had fled Mexico after murdering his wife's lover, to kill another patrolman who was a sadist. The story is described as "not untypical," but our evidence indicates that it is *not* typical. As with any law-enforcement organization of its size, there undoubtedly is some corruption in the Border Patrol. This is especially to be expected when no positive acts are required for a payoff and no one gets hurt. All a patrolman wanting to make some extra cash has to do is look the other way while some honest Mexicans seeking work cross a border to join employers eager to hire them. Not exactly a situation to strain the morality of an underpaid peace officer.

In spite of these temptations, we found no evidence that bribe-taking was anything but very rare in the Patrol. Even those like Grace Halsell, who are not great fans of the Border Patrol, do not describe it as corrupt. We asked George Watson, senior agent in charge of the Chula Vista station, whether or not it had occurred to him and his men that they might make more money helping *mojados* to get in than keeping them out. He replied:

"Yeah, it's occurred to all of us at one time or another."

"Does it worry you?"

"No, not much."

Our general impression of the Patrol, its men, and its operations is very positive. Lacking evidence to the contrary, we assume that at present the Patrol is doing its job as best it can with a high degree of honesty. But, should U.S. policy move more in the direction of simply fencing wets out, then the situation could change. The *coyotes* will become even more highly organized, the stakes will go up, and the funds available for bribing will increase. Many in the Border Patrol have grown to know the people they pursue personally and to like them. Their sympathies will make them all the more vulnerable when they are approached to look the other way. When one can help people one likes *and* make money at it, technicalities of the law may not be much of a deterrent. *La Migra* is in a difficult position now; its position could potentially become much more difficult in the near future.

The relationship between *la Migra* and the *coyotes* is a constantly evolving one. By the summer of 1979 a new and ominous situation appeared to be forming. At about 2:15 in the morning of June 9, a Mexican man entered the United States just west of the San Ysidro crossing point at San Diego. He encountered border patrol agent Randall Graham, at whom he fired one shot from a .22 caliber pistol. Agent Graham fired two shots at the man as he ran back into Tijuana. Neither man was hit.

Senior border patrol agents felt that this was probably not a chance occurrence but represented use of a new smuggling tactic.

The purpose of the shooting may have been to draw agents out of position so that a group of illegals could be brought in. The use of firearms in any capacity is a new and dangerous departure from the tradition of restraint that has so long ruled the border. The area where this occurred had seen such a steady escalation of violence and threats of violence over the previous months that the agents had come to call in the "war zone." They did not enter it without riot helmets and shields to ward off rocks.

As a result of this incident, U.S. attorney Michael Walsh stated that he would urge INS Commissioner Lionel Castillo to send more agents to Chula Vista. Walsh had previously announced an agreement with Baja California governor Roberto de la Madrid by which the Mexican authorities would take a more active role in controlling the rock-throwing hooligans, the bandits who prey on the illegals, and the organised smugglers. Wash was quoted as saying, "I want the violence stopped, I want the border to be patrolled safely."

The melding of these three groups—the hooligans, the bandits, and the smugglers—does not promise that the border *can* be patrolled safely. At this writing (June 1979), it is impossible to foresee whether the traditional ways can endure.

LA MIGRA

The Immigration and Naturalization Service traces its origins back to March 3, 1891, when Congress provided for a Superintendent of Immigration who reported to the Secretary of the Treasury. This made good sense because the Treasury Department had customs agents on the docks and at the land ports to collect the taxes. Indeed, Treasury had been handling what little immigration supervision there had been since the government started counting the foreign arrivals and making periodic reports in 1820. As a matter of fact, the new superintendent did not do much more than count arrivals and make reports. As concern over the number and nature of the immigrants grew, the legislation concerning them increased and so did the bureaucracy. In 1903 a Bureau of Immigration was formed and placed in the newly created Department of Labor and Commerce. In 1906 it became the Bureau of Immigration and Naturalization, which remained in Labor and Commerce until 1913 when these were divided into separate departments. At this time, Immigration and Naturalization were divided into separate bureaus, and the new bureaus went into the Department of Labor. So it remained until 1933 when New Deal reorganization put Immigration and Naturalization together again under the current name, the Immigration and Naturalization Service (INS). But it was still in the Department of Labor. Finally, on June 14, 1940, in another New Deal reorganization, the INS was transferred to the Justice Department, where it has remained to this day.

There are a number of lessons in this tedious bit of administrative history. The first is how late it was before anyone decided that anything special need be done. Fifteen million people had already immigrated to the United States before Congress decided that anyone needed even to supervise the process. Then, having decided that something ought to be done, the government was not at all sure who ought to do it. For the first 40 years of this century, it was generally agreed that the flow of immigrants was primarily a part of the American labor scene, but since then immigration has been seen primarily as a matter for law enforcement. Yet to this day the Department of Labor has not been shut out. For many would-be immigrants, the U.S. Department of Labor, Manpower Administration form MA 7-50 A and B, "Application for Alien Employment Certification," is an absolutely crucial document, and its approval or denial is a turning point in their lives.

The function of the Immigration and Naturalization Service is divided into two contradictory parts—on the one hand, helping people come into the country and, in the case of immigrants, helping them through the naturalization process, and on the other hand, keeping people out and apprehending those who are here improperly. The INS is thus part social-service agency and part police force. Since there are more than 270 million legal entries into the United States each year, 90 percent of them by land from Mexico and Canada, and only about 11,000 people in all departments of the INS, actual inspection at border checkpoints is cursory. About 100 million of these entries are by U.S. citizens returning home who do not like to be delayed or asked a lot of silly questions. The usual extent of the inspection is to ask the entrants if they are citizens of the United States, where they live in the U.S., and how long they have been out of the country. The immigration inspector makes the necessary judgments almost completely on the demeanor and accent of the person seeking entry. If an entrant is an Anglo, middle-class American returning from an outing to Niagara Falls or Juárez, and if that is how he or she looks, acts, and sounds, the "inspection" will take only a few seconds. No borders in the world are more open than those of the United States to its own citizens. If, however, the entrant is a Chicano or a naturalized citizen who has not lost his or her foreign accent, it is advisable to have a birth certificate or naturalization papers along.

In addition to inspecting the millions who enter, the INS assists the nearly 400,000 people who each year are "Lawfully Admitted to Permanent Residence" (LAPRs), the technical term for immigrants. These are issued identity cards—the so-called green card, which is now bluish-white and has not been green since 1965—and assistance is arranged by INS for those preparing for naturalization. In the latter regard, the INS publishes a self-study guide for the English language, the United States Constitution, and the like. A command of English is not a requirement for naturalization, but the examination is in that language, so some knowledge is essential. Finally, the INS administers the examination. The proportion of LAPRs eligible for naturalization who actually apply has been decreasing for a quarter-century, but the number is still considerable. In 1976 almost a quarter-million immigrants applied for naturalization, and over 140,000 were naturalized.

The other aspect of the Service's work is the detection and prevention of attempts to enter the United States unlawfully and the apprehension of those who have done so. There are three basic ways that an alien finds himself illegally in the United States: he has "entered without inspection" (the most frequent situation); he has entered "with inspection" but through the use of fraudulent documents (a forged passport, for instance) or false claims of admissibility; he has entered properly yet finds himself with illegal status (the least frequent situation). Examples of the latter would be a foreign student who drops out of school for a semester and takes a job to earn enough money to go back to his home country, a young tourist who decides to prolong his stay here—or needs to earn money for his return ticket—or someone who simply overstays his visa.

It is a federal misdemeanor to be in the United States illegally, and there is no distinction in the law regarding how that happened. In 1976 the INS apprehended almost 900,000 deportable aliens. However, only about three percent of these were actually deported. A little less than 10 percent were allowed to remain because their illegality was of a purely technical nature or because of extenuating circumstances, and the remaining 87 percent were "required to depart." Deportation requires at least an administrative hearing and could end up in the law courts; it is expensive and a bother to everyone. In most cases the alien jumps at the chance to depart voluntarily. In some cases, the illegal is simply set free with the understanding that he or she will leave within two weeks, but over 90 percent of the voluntary departures are "under safeguards." If a person who has been deported or has admitted

his guilt and departed voluntarily returns to the United States, he
or she is guilty of a felony under federal law, although there are
few prosecutions.

The Border Patrol

"The Border Patrol, as the mobile, uniformed enforcement
arm of the Immigration and Naturalization Service, has as its
mission the detection and prevention of the smuggling and illegal
entry of aliens into the United States." Overwhelmingly, the efforts of the Border Patrol are directed against EWI's, and over
three-fourths of its manpower is concentrated on the Mexican
border. The patrol of the southern United States border began
on a haphazard basis in 1904 when the Commissioner-General of
Immigration assigned a small group of mounted inspectors, later
called mounted watchmen or mounted guards, to patrol its nearly
2,000 miles. Since this force never exceeded 75 men, the job they
did was not very thorough. Nor was there much need for a
thorough job, because the border between the United States and
Mexico was little more than a legal fiction in those days, and an
easy, casual coming and going across it was both traditional and
useful to all parties. For many years, the great social event of San
Antonio, Texas, was the semiannual arrival of the wagon train
from Saltillo, the capital of the Mexican state of Coahuila, for
purposes of trade. Even more than San Antonio, the border
towns of Brownsville, Laredo, and El Paso were oriented toward
Mexico socially, culturally, and economically. And the great cattle
ranches of South Texas and all along the border owed their
inspiration more to the Mexican *hacienda* than to any Anglo
enterprise. West of El Paso, where the border was only an imaginary line through the Sonoran Desert, no one lived near it and
few crossed for any reason. Moreover, the practice of appointing
mounted inspectors from the border areas went far to guarantee
that local custom would not be breached by any fastidious ideas of
formality emanating from Washington, D.C., or anywhere else.

In the years following 1900 things changed. The railroad was
extended to the border from San Antonio, and irrigation pumps
went into the Rio Grande. South Texas shifted from being cattle
country to the fruit and vegetable area it is today. The fortunes
that came out of these new fields and orchards far outstripped all
the wealth that ever flowed from the cattle ranches. The big-
cattle-ranch society, now largely passed away, has been roman-
ticized beyond any semblance of reality in song, story, and motion
picture; however, that society certainly surpassed in gentility and
humanity the one that followed. Big-scale fruit and vegetable

production required huge investments and, with careful management, yielded hefty profits. "Careful management" includes
control of the labor supply. Agribusiness, then and now, requires
a labor supply of considerable skill and great elasticity. The supply must stretch when needed and snap back when unneeded,
and the pool of poor Mexicans filled the bill to perfection. Because of the new wealth to the north and the old poverty to the
south, the border lost its casual character and took on a very real
significance.

While all this was happening in South Texas, the rest of the
country was beginning to worry about immigration, which averaged over a million persons per year for the five years before
World War I. First in 1917, and then in 1921 and 1924, Congress
did something about it. This legislation and, even more, the mood
of the country had its effect down along the border. Although
immigration from Latin America was left untouched by the quota
system, the manifold restrictions of the 1917 Act—particularly
the old Puritan concern about those likely to become public
charges—provided a legal basis for regulating the flow of people
coming north from Mexico. When agribusiness needed them,
they were workers and were permitted to enter. But when the
crops had been tended, each was "likely to become a public
charge." Then the border was closed, and the Mexicans north of
the river, whose casual entry had been winked at a few months
earlier, were forced to disappear south of the Rio Grande until
the crops were ready again.

The border was long and largely free of natural barriers. Some
mechanism was needed to regulate the human flow across it for
the benefit of the United States. That mechanism, the Border
Patrol, came into existence against the background of a changing
economy and society at the border and the hoopla of the immigration debate of the 1920s. Its origin does not stem from any of the
great pieces of immigration legislation of the day, but from a
simple passage in the Department of Labor Appropriations Act
of May 28, 1924, which provided that "at least $1,000,000" of the
appropriation "shall be expended for additional, land-border
patrol." In accordance with this terse mandate, the Border Patrol,
composed of 450 men, was set up in the Bureau of Immigration.
The initial force was appointed in 1924 from the same Civil
Service register used for the appointment of railway mail clerks.
One may well imagine the consternation of some young man, who
had set his hopes on a job sorting mail in a railroad car, when he
received an offer of federal employment if he would only strap on
a six-gun, mount a horse, and start detecting and preventing "the
unlawful entry of aliens into the United States." Not surprisingly,

the turnover of personnel ran about 25 percent in the early months.

The Mexican border (of course it was the Mexican border that got the lion's share of attention from the new force) was a wild and woolly place in 1924, far away and exotic. The turbulence of the Mexican Revolution had not fully subsided, and the great events of that upheaval were still vividly remembered. The inadvertent artillery bombardments of Douglas, Arizona, and El Paso, Texas, the Villa raid on Columbus, New Mexico, and the Pershing expedition into Mexico had all occurred fewer than ten years before. The Border Patrol quickly came to feel isolated, largely because it was. The pay was low, promotion came slowly, the work was hard, and there were too few men to cover a very long border. Furthermore, the Border Patrol was the victim of the contradictory forces and cross-currents that affected the determination of immigration policy. The forces that wanted the laws enforced were strong enough to create the Border Patrol and keep it functioning, but the forces that wanted lax enforcement were strong enough to ensure that the men along the border never got the support they needed to do a proper job. This was the way it was in the 1920s, this is the way it is in the 1970s, and this is the way it will remain until the American people and government decide what they really want done there.

This early history did much to form the character of the Border Patrol, a character that has served it well over the years. But when times change, old ways can become a problem. Richard L. Jones, assistant chief patrol agent, Chula Vista Sector, California, and a 23-year veteran of the Patrol, described the situation this way:

> We grew up in the tradition of the Texas Rangers. We thought we could handle anything that came at us. "One riot, one man." We didn't tell anybody anything, we didn't ask for anything, and we didn't expect anything. We were almost a secret service. After Oxford and Montgomery,* we could have written our own ticket, but it was decided in 'he Service and right here in the Border Patrol not to play up the fact that those "United States Marshals" were mostly Border Patrol agents. We just did the job and came back.

---

*This refers to the Universities of Mississippi and Alabama, which in the early 1960s refused to obey federal court orders to admit black students. In both cases, Attorney General Robert Kennedy hastily organized forces composed largely of Border Patrol agents, deputized them into the service of the federal court, and dispatched them to enforce the court orders. The court orders were enforced amid the most extreme provocation against the federal marshals, who earned the respect of all involved for their professionalism and failure to respond in kind to the jeering, rock-throwing, and physical abuse visited upon them.

About ten years ago things started coming at us we just could not handle, but nobody listened because we had never talked before. So we went out and talked to high schools and civic groups and anyone who would listen. General Chapman helped, too. He spoke out himself, and Commissioner Castillo has continued the openness. Now, people are beginning to listen, but we still talk to anyone. We don't always like what they write about us, but it's better than being ignored, and we need all the help we can get.

Like the INS as a whole, the Border Patrol was, and is today, undermanned, underfinanced, and isolated. Still, Congress gave it sweeping powers of arrest and investigation, and these have been maintained and expanded ever since. The Act of February 27, 1925, provided that any employee of the then Bureau of Immigration, authorized under regulations established by the Attorney General, under certain conditions and without a warrant could:

(1) arrest any alien who in his presence or view was entering or attempting to enter the United States illegally, and
(2) board and search for aliens any vessel within the territorial waters of the United States, or any railway car, conveyance, or vehicle in which he believed aliens were being brought illegally into the United States.

The power of the Border Patrol and other authorized agents of the INS is covered today by Sections 235 and 287 of the Immigration and Nationality Act of 1952, which provide that

. . . any officer or employee of the Service authorized under regulations prescribed by the Attorney General shall have power without warrant . . .
To interrogate any alien or person believed to be an alien as to his right to be or to remain in the United States;
To arrest any alien who in his presence or view is entering or attempting to enter the United States in violation of any law or regulation made in pursuance of law regulating the admission, exclusion or expulsion of aliens;
To arrest any alien in the United States if he has reason to believe that the alien so arrested is in the United States in violation of any such law or regulation, and is likely to escape before a warrant can be obtained for his arrest;
To make arrests for felonies which have been committed and which are cognizable under any law of the United States regulating the admission, exclusion or expulsion of aliens if he has reason to believe that the person so arrested is guilty of such felony and if there is likelihood of the person escaping before a warrant can be obtained for his arrest;

Within a reasonable distance from any external boundary of the United States, to board and search for aliens any vessel within the territorial waters of the United States and any railway car, aircraft, conveyance or vehicle;

Within a distance of twenty-five miles from any external boundary, to have access to private lands, but not dwellings, for the purpose of patrolling the border to prevent the illegal entry of aliens into the United States.

By their designation as customs agents, members of the Border Patrol have additional powers relating to search, seizure, and arrest in connection with violations of import and export laws.

These seemingly far-reaching powers are limited by restrictions on the use of force by Border Patrol agents. Firearms may be used only in self-defense, defense of a fellow agent, or defense of an innocent party. Like most policemen, the Border Patrol agent seldom fires his weapon in the field, and many complete whole careers without ever having unholstered their revolvers except for cleaning and target practice. In the Southwest the service revolver is primarily used against the ever-present rattlesnake, and many officers carry birdshot as the first round in their weapons to use against them. Birdshot would have no stopping power against a man at any appreciable distance, but easily destroys the snakes—which present no threat at all to a man who has already seen one. For enforcement of their very considerable legal powers, the agents depend on the legitimacy of their office—their legal authority to be where they are and to be doing what they are doing—and by the recognition and trust they engender even in those whom they are trying to apprehend.

None of this obscures a somewhat troubling point. There exists in the United States a police force that, on the basis of suspicion only and without warrant, can interrogate any citizen, arrest any alien or citizen believed to be an alien, stop and search any vehicle on land or water within the territory of the United States and, within 25 miles of the border, enter private land and buildings other than people's homes. These powers remain intact and largely unchallenged for two reasons. One is the tact, restraint, and good judgment with which the Border Patrol agent and others within the INS typically use them. The other reason, sadly, is that, when the powers have been improperly used, it has usually been against a poor brown-skinned U.S. citizen with a Spanish accent somewhere in the Southwest who was politically impotent. Now the poverty and powerlessness are waning, and so is the docility they inspire. Chicanos whose ancestors were born in the United States, sometimes as far back as the seventeenth century, are getting a bit testy about being asked where they belong, just as would a member of the Anglo middle class.

A Border Patrol officer, in making his decisions about possible illegal activities, depends only in part on ethnic stereotypes. He also depends on a kind of instinct born of training and experience. Throughout the Southwest, the Border Patrol maintains checkpoints on major highways. One of the busiest is at San Clemente, 90 miles north of the border on the California coast. An agent who has worked that checkpoint said that whether or not he stopped a given vehicle depended on how he "felt" about it as it approached him. He said that one tipoff was how heavily loaded it was, particularly if it was a van, and another was the behavior of the driver. He said that most people stare right at the agent out of curiosity, but a smuggler tends to stare straight ahead, appearing to take no note of what is happening. Often he slows down excessively. All these things count but there is much more. It is just the "feeling" the agent gets. When asked how often he had stopped a vehicle that was innocent, the agent said that this hardly ever happened, that it was at least embarrassing, and that if an agent did that too often he would get into trouble. References to the "feeling" were repeated over and over by the Border Patrol and INS agents, and they are insistent that if the strict application of the rules on "probable cause" and "articulable reasons" for stopping and talking to people were applied to them, they simply would not be able to do their jobs. (Of course, this is what the police officer usually says when the courts say "no" to the old way of doing things.)

There is a danger more serious to most of us than that of inadvertent harassment through an erroneous, even if well-intentioned, application of the powers of the Border Patrol. That danger is the deliberate, intentional misuse of those powers to limit civil liberties, instill fear in people, and tighten political control in the hands of a self-righteous few. During the Nixon years there was constant agitation for a "no-knock law," which would have allowed federal officers to kick anyone's door in whenever they felt like it and say afterward that they thought that person had some narcotics. It has now been amply demonstrated that that administration was more concerned with political regularity than the maintenance of law and order. Today there is agitation to "do something" about the illegal aliens, and legislation very nearly as sweeping as the no-knock law is already on the books. Much skulduggery can be done in the name of emergency and against a background of confusion and hysteria. If these laws were being implemented by less sensible and restrained people, or if events should erode sense and restraint, havoc could be visited throughout the Southwest or anywhere there was a person with a Spanish accent.

An effective restraint on the Border Patrol today is the lack of resources. Although for several years there has been talk of the need for someone to do something, the Border Patrol has been given precious little with which to do it. There have been some modest changes, but by no stretch of the imagination has any serious attempt been made to "close the border," and rightly so. No one in contact with the complex problems leading to illegal immigration, and particularly no one in INS, believes that they are fundamentally police problems.

This is reflected by the size of the Border Patrol. Its projected authorized strength for 1979 was 2,801 positions, which is remarkably small for a force expected to control movement over a 2,000-mile Mexican border, 3,000 miles of Canadian border, and another 2,500 miles along the Gulf Coast. Still, this is an increase of 300 positions over 1978 and an increase of 25 percent since 1975.

Note that this is *authorized* strength, the number of positions Congress says the Patrol can have. Because of low pay, lack of recognition, and slow promotion, the Border Patrol has a difficult time recruiting and retaining agents. Indeed, the Border Patrol is a happy hunting ground for recruiting by other federal law-enforcement agencies, particularly other branches of INS and Customs. In 1974 the Border Patrol's authorized strength was 2,122 positions, but the average number of persons on duty for the year was 1,655, only about three-quarters of the number authorized. Even if it is assured that the Border Patrol can recruit and hold the 300 additional people provided for in the 1979 budget, they can make only a marginal difference.

"Service" vs. "Enforcement" in the INS

The dual role of the INS, to assist the legal entry of qualified aliens into the United States while trying to prevent and detect the illegal entry of other aliens, is partially contradictory and causes confusion in the organization. When INS officials are helping someone enter or gain naturalization, their function is referred to as "service." When they are trying to prevent another alien from entering or remaining in the country, their function is called "enforcement." A clerk in an INS office helping an alien fill out his or her naturalization forms is clearly in the service column, whereas a Border Patrol agent filling out an I-213 on a *mojado* he has just caught sneaking into the country is an example of enforcement. Not all cases are so clear-cut. When an immigration officer at a border crossing point asks to see an alien's crossing pass, is this service or enforcement? If all is in order and a legal entry is facilitated, it is service. If the pass has expired and the officer refuses to admit the person, that official has crossed the line into enforcement.

INS Deputy Commissioner for Enforcement Charles Sava is aware of the confusion growing out of this dual role. In our discussion with him over enforcement problems, he stated quite strongly that "enforcement *is* service." He went on to point out that everyone in INS is carrying out the will of the American people as legally expressed in the laws and regulations under which the Service operates. There is a tendency to look upon those whose duties require them to prevent people from doing what they wish, namely from entering or remaining in the country contrary to law, as "bad guys," while those who help people to come in and to stay are "good guys." We had the feeling that Sava was tired of being the bad guy all the time.

After all, the enforcement operations of the INS are just the other side of the service coin. The objective of U.S. immigration law is to help some people enter the country; inevitably some others will not be helped, but must be told either they cannot come in or they must leave. Helping people enter is much easier and cheaper than trying to keep people out; 80 percent of the INS budget is earmarked for "enforcement."

The distinction between enforcement and service is deeply ingrained in most INS officials, and this inevitably leads to some bureaucratic feuding, which sometimes hinders the INS in doing its work. The *Los Angeles Times* quoted an angry INS enforcement official as saying that, if Commissioner Castillo's leadership were followed, "we can forget completely about law enforcement and concentrate more of our efforts on serving the illegals—and I'll be damned if I'll call them 'undocumented workers.' "

Commissioner Castillo's concern for service, as reflected in his public statements and our conversation with him, has nothing to do with "serving illegals"; it had to do largely with improving the flow of paper through the organization, a flow that was very nearly clogged when he took over. Visa and naturalization applications, as well as other documents crucial to the lives of people, had simply been lost in the archaic filing system of the Service and by the underpaid and overworked staff. An accomplishment of which Commissioner Castillo seemed particularly proud when we talked with him in August 1978 was his successful effort to upgrade the civil-service classification of clerical workers in the visa section. Many of these were GS-1s, the lowest pay category in the government. Their monthly paychecks kept them barely above the official poverty level. He was also proud of getting the visa section into INS headquarters and out of a converted warehouse where there were holes in the floor so big that desks had to be turned upside-down over them so no one would fall through. A similar attempt to get a reclassification and a pay increase for Border Patrol agents was turned down by the Civil Service Commission.

Commissioner Castillo's attempts to make some small progress toward bringing the INS's detention facilities, which hold hundreds of thousands of federal prisoners in the course of a year, up to the minimum standards of the Federal Bureau of Prisons has been cited repeatedly as proof of his "softness" on enforcement. His support of the idea of a "forgery-proof" identification card for aliens lawfully admitted to permanent residence, however, and his hope of making such a card available through the Service at a citizen's request, suggest no softness on enforcement. He told us that one of his top priorities in the Service had been to increase the production of the new cards and that the service was now able to manufacture 2,500 cards per day, up from 400 when he took charge.

There are many people, and we are among them, who have grave doubts about the overall wisdom of an official government-issued ID card. How easy it would be to change it from a voluntary convenience to a mandatory document, or even to convert it from a simple device for identification to a government-issued work permit, which any petty bureaucrat could take away. Some of the types of identification cards we have heard talked about in Washington sound too much like the passbooks that blacks have to carry in South Africa. There, losing the pass or having it taken away by an official can mean starvation. Commissioner Castillo's strong advocacy of the forgery-proof ID card, though, certainly indicates that he is not soft on enforcement.

Still, many people do not feel comfortable with Castillo as head of the INS, and there are two reasons for this. The first is that he is an American of Mexican heritage and he makes no apologies for it. In two generations, Castillo and other members of his family have risen from the most modest of circumstances to positions of prominence. They have done this through their own ability and through participation in the social, economic, and political institutions of American society. Yet we have seen on bulletin boards in INS offices cartoons depicting Mexicans according to the degrading stereotype—slovenly, wearing sombrero and serape, with cartridge belts crossed over the chest, the whole works—and the caption, "Castillo's Cousins." We assume that these cartoons are put up by the tiny handful of bigots one encounters anywhere, but it would be reassuring if members of the majority could find the courage to tear them down. Tolerance of racism is utterly unacceptable in any office of any agency of the

United States Government, and it is particularly offensive in an agency that must deal with Mexican nationals and Americans of Mexican descent. The mission of the INS is too important and too delicate for this sort of impropriety.

The second problem Mr. Castillo has is that too often and for too long the office of INS Commissioner has been perceived as filled by men who had less interest in doing their job than in using it as a stepping-stone to something bigger and better. The noteworthy exception to this was General Leonard Chapman, Castillo's immediate predecessor. General Chapman had a long and distinguished career as an officer in the Marines culminating in his last assignment, that of Commandant of the Corps. In the fine tradition of American citizen-soldiers from George Washington to George Marshall, General Chapman interrupted his retirement to serve again. He devoted himself tirelessly to the INS, its mission, and to the interests of the men and women who make it up. To bring attention to the very serious problems of the Service, he used the only issue available to him—the rapidly rising figures on the apprehension of illegal aliens. He misused these and other figures, thus inadvertently leading the public to a mistaken view of the scope and nature of the problem. But he did it because of the real urgency he perceived in the situation of the agency for which he was responsible. Within the Service, he was unquestionably the most popular commissioner the INS ever had, and he was the first commissioner to become well known to the public in many years. People within the INS still speak glowingly of him, and none more so than Commissioner Castillo.

It is difficult to imagine anyone who could measure up to General Chapman in the eyes of Service personnel. Mr. Castillo's relative youth, energy, and general attitude suggest a man who intends to continue in public service at the highest levels he can attain. But this, in turn, suggests to some that he is simply an office-seeker. His background in electoral politics and in the Democratic party in Texas marks him as a "politician." A built-in animosity exists between civil-service administrators and elected or appointed officials. In the most extreme cases, civil servants tend to view themselves as career specialists and see elected or appointed officials as here-today, gone-tomorrow opportunists who neither know nor care about anything except the next rung on the ladder or the next election. In contrast, the elected official frequently views the civil servant as an entrenched and intransigent bureaucrat bent on substituting his own values for the expressed will of the people.

Relations between Commissioner Castillo and some INS personnel, particularly those in enforcement, have suffered from these differences in viewpoint. The most cogent analysis of the present situation that we have seen came from two INS agents in the field. One was quoted as saying, "I don't see any difference in morale because of Castillo's administration. It is just a hopeless, frustrating job." When asked for the solution to the problem, his colleague responded, "For Congress to get off its ass . . ."

The morale problems of the INS are serious, and they will remain so until the American government and people decide what they want, clarify the policies the enforcement people have to work under, and vote them the resources to do the job however it is defined. In the meantime, every day and every night, several thousand men and women of the INS do their best with existing resources and within existing policy to "prevent the illegal entry of aliens into the United States."

Down on the Line at Chula

Chula Vista Border Patrol Station, which is not in the town of Chula Vista but a few miles south in the San Ysidro section of San Diego, is the biggest, busiest, and best-equipped station of the Patrol. The station is responsible for about 17 miles of border running from the Pacific Ocean to the Otay Mountains. As many as 250 agents are sometimes assigned to it, more than 10 percent of the whole Border Patrol. The station's equipment includes fixed-wing aircraft, two helicopters, and the most elaborate array of electronic sensing equipment on the border.

Consequently, Chula Vista apprehends more *mojados* than any other station. In the month of April 1978, the men and women on the line at Chula apprehended 33,120 aliens seeking to enter the United States illegally. Among these were 30,322 adult Mexican males, 2,583 Mexican women and children, 137 Salvadorans, 58 Guatemalans, 9 Colombians, and 11 others.

At that time, the line watch was divided into five units: West Unit, which covers the border from the ocean to Interstate 5, a distance of about five and a half miles; Central Unit, which covers San Ysidro, the urban strip along I-5, and liaison with the San Diego Police Department, hospitals, etc.; and East Unit, which covers the 12 miles from I-5 to the Otay Mountains. East Unit concentrates on the maze of canyons running about three miles east of San Ysidro and a mile or mile and a half northward from the border. The canyons abut the city of Tijuana, and one of them runs directly into the Colonia Libertad section of Tijuana, providing a thoroughfare from Mexico into San Ysidro, a couple of miles away. One of the canyon routes ends within 50 feet of the San Ysidro Greyhound Bus Station.

The five units are rounded out by two X units for the night shift, who work wherever they feel they can do the most good, although one usually works west of I-5 and the other to the east.

The West, Central, and East units each have 12 agents at full strength, and the X Units have 18 each. This means that the seventeen miles of border are watched by 36 men for 18 hours per day and by 72 during eight of the nighttime hours. However, the units are seldom at full strength, and when one of us visited them on May 19, 1978, East Unit on the 4 to 12 P.M. shift was staffed by a supervisor and seven men. In all there were fewer than 50 agents on line that night. In spring 1978, George Watson, agent in charge of the Chula Vista station, was instructed to draw up a plan that would close to illegal entry those 17 miles of border. His plan, which was generally accepted and certainly not criticized for being wasteful of resources, called for a force of over 600 agents. If all the new agents coming into the Border Patrol in 1979 were sent to Chula Vista, the station would still not be able to put into operation the plan, which sits on a shelf in Agent Watson's office.

In recent years, increasingly effective deployment of agents has been more important than rises in personnel in helping the Border Patrol do its job. A report done in 1975 for the Law Enforcement Assistance Administration by David North showed that there was little relation between where the agents had been stationed and where the wets were actually being apprehended. At Chula Vista in 1974 an agent on "line watch," one who was actually out patrolling the border, caught someone trying to sneak into the country every couple of hours, while the agent on the line at El Paso, Texas, was nabbing someone about half as often. Farther down the Rio Grande, at Brownsville, an agent had to wait an average of a day and a half between apprehensions. Moreover, North made the casual observation that, while most of the apprehensions were made at night, most of the agents were working in the daytime. Following the report there was some shifting of agents to put them where the apprehensions were taking place. The shifts of course had the effect of making even more apprehensions occur in those places.

There has also been an increased reliance on technology in the past few years. The Border Patrol has long relied on fixed-wing aircraft patrols and has about 30 planes in service, but these are of no use after dark when most of the wets cross the line. For night work at Chula Vista in 1978, the Border Patrol had two helicopters equipped with a battery of powerful lights. Hovering at 500 feet, one of them can illuminate a considerable area with startling brilliance. If the helicopter comes in low, the combination of the light, the noise, and the downdraft whipping up a dust storm is enough to make anyone give up or at least run back to Tijuana. Because of pilot fatigue, a crew can remain aloft only for two hours, hence the need for two machines to maintain constant surveillance. In April 1978 a little over 25 percent of the 33,000 apprehensions made by the agents at Chula Vista involved the use of aircraft.

Electronic sensors are also being used, although not as elaborately as the news media and popular writers sometimes indicate. In 1978 Chula Vista Station had the most elaborate array of electronic sensing equipment on the border and the greatest experience in using it. Forty-three sensors of seven different kinds were in place there. The first and most numerous device was the seismic point sensor, which senses vibrations through the ground caused by anything passing by. It can be set for varying degrees of sensitivity, such as a single footstep within five meters. It can also be set to register an alarm only after the twentieth footstep or the fiftieth or whatever. Second is the magnetic point sensor, which notes changes in the local magnetic field caused by movement within it. The nails in Humberto's shoes coming within a distance of several feet were enough to register an alarm and end his string of undetected crossings. This too can be set for varying levels of sensitivity. Third is the magnetic vehicle direction sensor, which is similar to the magnetic point sensor, except that this one operates in sets of two planted near roadways and not only senses vehicles but also gives their direction of travel. Fourth is the active infrared sensor, which resembles the common electric-eye device but operates with an invisible infrared beam. It can monitor an area up to 100 feet in width. Fifth, the passive infrared sensor responds to the infrared wavelengths generated by the human body. Sixth, the point contact sensor responds to the pressure of a footstep or any other pressure directly on it. Seventh, the buried line intrusion detector responds to pressure on a buried line which can be up to 100 feet in length.

When any of these devices is activated, a low-power radio signal is sent out. The signal is picked up and amplified by a nearby, more powerful radio, which sends the signal directly or through other relays to the communication center at Chula Vista Station. Here the signal is received by a computer which causes a red light to flash on a large map showing the location of the sensor, and a written description of the alarm appears on a cathode ray terminal, which looks like a television set. Three agents monitor these terminals 24 hours per day, seven days per week. The monitoring agent decides whether to feed the alarm into the computer for a permanent record and whether to alert a unit in the field as to the possible intrusion. These sensors are laid out in patterns and are so adjusted that the size and direction of a passing group of people can be monitored. Most of the sensors are laid out in the labyrinth of canyons east of San Ysidro, and knowledge of the terrain and thoroughfares used by the illegals allows a field unit to place itself ahead of the group and apprehend them—at least that is the way it is supposed to work.

This technology was developed during the Vietnam War to reveal movement through the McNamara Line in the De-militarized Zone of Vietnam and along the Ho Chi Minh Trail in Cambodia and Laos. Indeed, the first devices installed along the Mexican border were military surplus, although those have since been replaced by more durable models. The Border Patrol's array of equipment is paltry by military or wartime standards. A former intelligence officer who had experience with this sort of hardware in Southeast Asia told of "strings" as large as 200 to 250 devices along a single, five-mile stretch of the Ho Chi Minh Trail. He expressed great reservations about the cost-effectiveness of the system in Southeast Asia or anywhere else. The basic problem there was the incredibly high cost of installing, maintaining, and operating a system that produced a high frequency of false or misleading alarms. Even when everything functioned well in Vietnam or Laos, the system simply piled up a lot of frivolous information that did not answer any useful questions. When the system did come up with something, the resources for an effective response frequently were not there. Accurate evaluation is dif-ficult because, when a lot of money has been spent on hardware, the people who spent it are usually reluctant to admit that it has failed to meet their expectations.

These observations apply to equipment used in another time and place, but similar problems seem to plague the sensor array at Chula Vista. In the month of April 1978, there were 3,443 sensor alarms, but because of a lack of manpower the station was able to respond only to about 60 percent of them. Of the alarms re-sponded to, 1,223 were either false or were set off by legitimate traffic. The remaining 832 alarms were followed by 6,160 ap-prehensions. This comes to about three apprehensions per re-sponse and 7.5 apprehensions for each response to a true alarm. These 6,160 apprehensions represent 18.6 percent of all ap-prehensions for the month of April 1978. In the first seven months of fiscal year 1978 (October 1977 through April 1978), Chula Vista Station apprehended over 120,000 illegals, twenty percent of whom were discovered by sensors.

On every shift there are three agents off the line monitoring the system. Considering this and the cost of its acquisition and main-tenance, one wonders if the men and funds thus employed might produce more apprehensions if used in other ways. But everyone at the Chula Vista station emphasizes that the electronic sensors are a useful aid and that their effectiveness should not be measured only by the 20 percent of apprehensions that they facilitate. They believe that the system allows a more effective deployment of men, which further increases the rate of apprehensions. Yet there is something mesmerizing about electronic technology, and more is usually expected from it than is received. The value of the electronic sensor equipment was perhaps best summarized by one agent who said, "No sensor ever apped (apprehended) a wet." It may help, but ultimately an agent has to be standing in the middle of the path to intercept the *mojados*. In April 1978 Chula Vista Station had to ignore 40 percent of the alarms because there were not enough agents to respond to them. The problem of the illegal flow of people into the United States cannot be solved by sowing the border with more little black boxes that go beep in the night.

In addition to the electronic sensors, there are two kinds of nighttime visual equipment at Chula Vista. One is a telescope that weighs six or seven pounds and electronically amplifies the available light. It gives a clear, greenish view of the landscape, but, used for 30 seconds or so, it completely, if momentarily, blinds the eye and then seriously impairs vision for fifteen or twenty minutes after use. The other nighttime equipment is an infrared spotting device which is large, cumbersome, and very expensive. These devices have to be set up each evening and cannot be moved, but when properly placed and adjusted they can survey great areas. It is said that they can spot a jackrabbit at three miles. The infrared gear detects the body heat of the person being observed, and this can be sensed even through foliage dense enough to hide a person in daylight.

It is ironic that the most primitive device available to the Border Patrol, the fence, is the most controversial. There have been fences of various kinds at various places along the border for decades; the only reason that fences became news in late 1978 is that anything that happened along the border then was news.

The old fences at El Paso, San Diego, and a few other places had become useless as deterrents to anyone who wanted to enter the United States. They had deteriorated beyond repair simply from the passage of time and from frequent cutting by the *mojados* and patching by *la Migra*. INS first asked Congress for funds to replace portions of the fences in 1974, but it was not until August 1978 that the prospect of getting the money was promising enough for detailed planning to begin. By that time, the appropriation that INS had asked for, two million dollars for about six miles of fence at El Paso and another six miles at San Diego, seemed reasonably certain of passage. No one had come forward to speak against the fence in hearings, and additional funds had been added by the Senate to replace the fence at Yuma, Arizona, with no request from the INS at all. Fence-building along the southern border was very popular in Washington in the late summer of 1978.

The routine announcement by the INS in October 1978 that funds had been appropriated and that construction of the fences would begin was met by a storm of criticism. Some Chicano groups and various organizations devoted to helping immigrants attacked the idea as inhumane and an affront to human dignity. On another level, the design of the fence was questioned. Rumors implying calculated cruelty were circulated and picked up by the press. It was said that the fence would cut off the toes of barefoot men and women who tried to climb it, and one report had it that portions would be electrified. The latter nonsense seems to have originated in a confusion of the electronic spying devices with electrification of the fence. Finally, the government of Mexico let its disapproval of the fence be known. In this instance, good fences were not making good neighbors.

In response to all this, none of which had surfaced in the four years that INS had lobbied and testified for the project, Commissioner Castillo ordered a review of the fence design, though not of the idea itself. The review, of course, brought construction planning to a halt. In his press conference of January 26, 1979, less than three weeks before his trip to Mexico, President Carter characterized the fence as "unnecessarily aggravating and ill-advised." It appeared that undoing the damage Energy Secretary Schlesinger, Senator Stevenson, and others had done in botching the Mexican pipeline and gas deal had a higher priority in the President's scheme of things than did 12 or so miles of fence along a 1,950-mile border—and rightly so.

A senior INS enforcement official regretfully told us in early 1979 that "the status of the fence . . . seems to be a political football with the field offices having little input." A few weeks later, Vern Jervis, of the INS public information office, said that the future of the fence was uncertain and that "the decision would be made at a higher level than the INS." Indeed, it certainly was made at a higher level. On April 24, 1979, at a special press conference, Attorney General Griffin Bell announced that replacement fences of conventional design would be installed at Chula Vista and El Paso. He further stated that the decision had been made by him and President Carter, but only after consultation with the Mexican government.

George Watson, whose Chula Vista Station is responsible for

the border south of San Diego, summed up the importance of the fence by saying that, like any other single enforcement tool, its presence or absence would not determine the total success or failure of the enforcement effort, but having it would make his job easier. The fence would channel the flow of illegals. They would have to go around it, over it, or through it. Having to decide which of these three choices to take and where to make the attempt would limit the paths open to the *mojado* and the *coyote* and allow *la Migra* to be more certain that they were standing on the right path to stop them.

The redeployment of agents and the increased use of technology—aircraft, sensors, and visual-assistance equipment—has had its impact. In fiscal year 1974 Chula Vista Station apprehended over 127,000 illegals. In the first seven months of fiscal year 1978, the station had already apprehended over 120,000 with the heaviest months of the year yet to come. No one knows what the total apprehensions for 1978 would have been if things had remained the same, because, as is usual in human affairs, things did not remain the same. In the summer, the Border Patrol changed its mode of operation from one that led to "apprehension" a few hundred yards inside the line to a mode that would *deter* the *mojado* from entering the United States at all. In fiscal year 1978, apprehensions by agents at the station almost doubled to just over a quarter-million. Can one conclude from this that the flow across the border doubled? Certainly not. There were only about 100 agents at the station in 1974; at times in 1978 there were as many as 250. In 1974 there were no helicopters for night patrol; in 1978 there were two. In 1974 there were no electronic sensors; in 1978 there were 43. In the judgment of the agents at Chula Vista, though, the concentrated effort in their sector worked, at least to the extent that it diverted some of the flow to less tightly patrolled stretches of the border. Another consequence of this increased effort may well be the escalation of violence in the sector as the smugglers increase their efforts to stay in business.

Although it is against Mexican law to leave that country and against United States law to enter this one without proper clearance, nothing much happens to most of those who try. When a *mojado* is apprehended, the agent fills out an INS Form I-213 on him, usually in the field, and calls for a van to pick him up. The illegal is then taken to the Staging Area (formerly called the Detention Facility) at the station, where he is held. In the overwhelming bulk of cases, the illegal is voluntarily repatriated—"VR'ed"—to Mexico within a few hours. In this event a statement is stamped onto the Form I-213 in which the *mojado* admits that he sought to enter the United States illegally, and the *mojado* signs it.

As many as possible are VR'ed to Mexicali, about 100 miles away, simply to put them that much farther from the border at San Ysidro. There are not enough buses to send them all, so most are VR'ed to Tijuana, about a mile and a quarter away. The bus stops at a gate leading from the United States to Mexico, and the people are let through. They are interrogated by a Mexican immigration official who turns back those whom he feels are not Mexican, and the rest are free to try to cross into the United States again that evening.

Record-keeping on the illegals is very skimpy because of the lack of clerical assistance at the station. The I-213 is a manifold form with three copies of the full report and two more copies of basic data on the illegal. The original is simply filed chronologically under the date of apprehension at the station. Another copy is sent to Sector Headquarters, and the third is thrown away. One copy of the smaller, basic-data form is sent to Washington, D.C., and the other is supposed to be filed alphabetically at the station. When the station found itself one and a half years behind in its alphabetical filing, it gave up and now maintains alphabetical files only on smugglers.

There is no computerized record-keeping except for the alarms from the sensors. The monthly totals of figures on apprehended illegals—age, sex, nationality, etc.—are broken out by hand by agents, again because there are no civilian support personnel. Tabulating even the little information that the station keeps is a tremendous job considering the thousands of I-213 forms that must be sorted through. This chore keeps a lot of agents off line watch.

With 10 percent of the Border Patrol, 5 aircraft, and 43 electronic sensors out to get them, why do more *mojados* pick this 17-mile strip of border than any other? There are three reasons. First, even with this formidable array of men and machines, the border is by no means sealed. Second, nowhere else on the border does a major Mexican city abut a major U.S. city with easy access to the interior. El Paso/Juárez abut one another, but El Paso is still a long way from anything else. Moreover, like almost everyone else, Mexicans want to come to California. Now it is incredibly easy to cross from Tijuana to San Diego, and as urbanization fills in the empty places between the two cities it will become even easier. There is still open country between Tijuana and the towns on the United States side, but it varies from a half-mile to two or three miles. Finally, the volume of persons trying to come in is simply too great for the Patrol agents to stop—a case of safety in numbers.

The Border Patrol at Chula Vista and every other station is proud of the low level of force they use in accomplishing their mission. They are aware that this low level of force is in everyone's interest, including that of the Patrol agents. They do not get tough, and in turn the *mojados* do not resist when apprehended. Occasionally one will run, like Jorge in the last chapter, but only rarely does he strike an agent. The *mojados* understand that they will not be beaten up or robbed. At Chula Vista they will merely be locked up for the night and repatriated in the morning. There is little to run from and less to fight over. An illegal does not pay his *coyote* unless the crossing is successful, and most have little chance of making it if separated from the smuggler. It is these attitudes on the part of the *mojados* that make it possible for less than 250 Patrol agents to apprehend 33,000 illegals in a single month.

In addition to offering no resistance, a captured *mojado* ordinarily does not take legal action, and consequently the legal niceties are often overlooked. An I-213 is filled out, a rubber-stamp admission of guilt is pressed into the appropriate box, the illegal signs it, and waits in the detention facility for the bus that will take him or her back to Mexico. However, this gentlemen's agreement has begun to break down in some respects.

In May 1978, the INS raided (or "surveyed," as they prefer to call it) the Sbicca shoe factory in the Los Angeles suburb of El Monte. The raid yielded 120 illegals, who were processed and put on the bus for Tijuana within a few hours. The Retail Clerks union, however, had recently won the right to represent the workers in the Sbicca factory, and the union was eager to show that it was on the job. A union functionary contacted the Legal Aid Foundation, the People's College of Law, the Los Angeles Center for Law and Justice, and the American Civil Liberties Union. Peter Schey, a lawyer with the alien's rights program of the Legal Aid Foundation, convinced a judge to issue a restraining order, and the buses were stopped. The inadmissibility in court of the "confessions" on the I-213s was so blatant that the Justice Department did not even bother to introduce them. The lawyers explained to the illegals that they did not have to say anything and that it was up to the government to prove that they were illegal.

About half of the group decided to go back to Mexico voluntarily, perhaps on the grounds that it was easier to continue playing the game by the old rules than to be involved with lawyers. The remaining 65 *mojados* decided to fight and asked for separate trials. It is not easy for the Justice Department to prove, through due process of law and beyond a reasonable doubt, that a given person is illegally in the United States. At the end of November 1978, 17 of the "Sbicca 65" cases had been dismissed, and the rest were still pending.

In the fall of 1978, the courts stopped issuing the warrants under which the INS had been conducting its "surveys." As it was explained to us, the INS had obtained warrants that allowed its agents to enter the premises of a place of employment and check everyone in sight. This practice was challenged, and thereafter the INS could only obtain warrants by naming specific persons they were seeking. Since the agents seldom knew precisely whom they were seeking, the decision in effect put an end to the factory raids.

Even though illegal immigrants are lawbreakers, surely they are entitled to the same rights and protections as any other suspected lawbreaker in the United States. Whether the INS calls them "detention facilities," "staging areas," or whatever, they are prisons, with bars on the windows and no doorknobs inside, and they are run by the federal government. But they do not begin to meet the government's own standards for federal prisons, and bringing them up to those standards would be prohibitively costly. The same is true of legitimizing procedures and providing due process, which would require enormously more time and paperwork and more personnel to deal with the problem just because of the huge numbers of people involved. In 1978 more than 800,000 people were put through the INS mill nationwide, and most of them were detained for some period of time. If the rights of *mojados* were observed as those of other accused persons are in the U.S., the federal criminal-justice system could quickly become hopelessly bogged down and snarled in red tape.

Today, Patrol agents, experienced *mojados* like Jorge, and *coyotes* like Humberto are concerned that the gentlemen's agreement may also be wearing thin with regard to violence. First of all, the danger of violence is increased by the sheer numbers of illegals the agents now encounter. The danger is further raised by the growing professionalism among smugglers and the gigantic profits that can be realized from smuggling. This is not to say that violence is a common occurrence at this time; just that there is concern and nervousness that it might become so.

On the evening of March 15, 1977, Supervisory Patrol Agent Jim Bradshaw was struck in the forehead by a hand-held rock and nearly killed. His assailant was a citizen of Mexico residing in Tijuana and a member of one of the bandit gangs then operating back and forth across the border, preying on the *mojados*. Agent Bradshaw's partner, Agent Lucio Aguilar, apprehended the assistant and turned him over to the Federal Bureau of Investigation. He was prosecuted under federal law for assault against a federal officer, convicted, and given a one-year sentence. It all happened in the dark, and perhaps there was no intent to kill, but it does not take many incidents like this to make reasonable men nervous. This incident was still vividly remembered two years later by the men and women in Chula Vista Sector—as was the remarkably light sentence the federal court handed down.

The first line of defense for police officers against the kind of assault Agent Bradshaw suffered is the authority carried by their uniforms and badges and the certainty in everyone's mind that force used against them while dispatching their lawful duties will meet with swift, firm, legal retribution. The second line of defense is weapons. When the first line is worn too thin, officers must resort to the second. It is easy to sit in a Washington office or in front of an audience at a university symposium and talk about "sealing the border." But if the discussion is to be honest, it has to include some consideration of how much the rate of violence might be increased. It should also be understood that "rate of violence" means how many Agent Bradshaws one is willing to risk and how many Humbertos and Jorges one is willing to kill. Such risks are a necessary part of law enforcement, but the society that authorizes their escalation should be certain that they are both unavoidable and well justified. The emergence of the "war zone" at Chula Vista and the shots fired at and by Agent Graham have made this consideration inescapable.

The *mojado* has reason to fear violence, though not primarily from the Border Patrol. Unlike Humberto, many smugglers are not honorable with their clients; they lead them into the canyons east of San Ysidro, rob them, and leave them for the Patrol to pick up. If the victims resist, they may be beaten up. Even more hazardous than double-crossing smugglers are the bandit gangs who work the canyons on both sides of the border, preying on the illegals. These are composed of vicious, gratuitously violent young toughs from Tijuana. According to Agent Watson of Chula Vista, brutal rape, near-fatal beatings, and murders came to his attention weekly in 1978.

The suppression of banditry has been successful though not easily achieved. The San Diego Police Department (the station's area of jurisdiction is within the city limits of San Diego) had a volunteer task force in the area trying to clean up the canyons on the American side in early spring 1978, but they gave up. Their method of operation was for officers to decoy the bandits into approaching them by posing as vulnerable groups of *mojados*. When the bandits approached a group, the police officers would attempt to arrest them. This led to a great deal of shooting. Members of the task force were wounded, as were a number of suspects. In one memorable incident, the task force inadvertently got into a shootout across the border with members of the Tijuana

Police Department, seriously wounding a Mexican officer. Ultimately, the task force was withdrawn on the quite reasonable grounds that a modern, metropolitan police force does not have the manpower, equipment, or training to deal with this kind of wild-west problem. The San Diego Police were replaced by the Border Patrol, who dealt with the problem as uniformed officers. By early 1979, the bandits had largely been forced to retreat into Mexico.

This turn of events highlights the absurdity of the United States Border Patrol policing the smuggling lanes it is supposed to be suppressing. Ridiculous as it may seem, it still reflects a proper order of values: the operation in this country of bandit gangs from Tijuana is an illegal intrusion far more loathsome than the honest *mojado* trying to enter in order to feed his family.

The increasing numbers of people trying to pass through the border, the questions of legality and constitutional rights, the increasing profitability and professionalism of the smuggling operations, and the rise of banditry all raise legitimate concern about the ability of the Patrol to carry out its work while maintaining its traditional code of restraint.

On Line Watch With East Unit

One can read the annual reports of the INS and go to Washington to talk to people about the "big picture," but the heart of the enforcement effort against those who seek to enter the United States illegally is in the daily routine of the units on line watch along the United States border with Mexico. Because of this, one of us went out with one of the units at San Ysidro in spring 1978. The notes from this experience give the flavor of the operation.

G. J. Watson, agent in charge of Chula Vista Station, had arranged for me to accompany the East Unit supervisor, A.M. "Skip" Voytush on his shift, 4 to 12 P.M. We met as scheduled and went out to the canyons east of San Ysidro. Skip was taking me to see "the buildup in Dead Man's Canyon." Along the way, he oriented me as to the topography and Patrol procedures. He stopped several times to show me the networks or paths up the canyon walls worn by illegals. Some of the walls looked like spiderwebs with the crossing and recrossing of trails.

We arrived at the overview of Dead Man's Canyon, and about a quarter-mile away, on the shoulder of the canyon, perhaps 100 or 150 yards inside the United States, was a group of about 75 or 100 people—would-be *mojados* waiting for dark. We were watching them through binoculars, and they waved at us and occasionally gave us the finger. While most of the group were men, there were women and children, too. They had built fires to keep warm or maybe to cook, and one of the fires had gotten out of control and was burning the grass. The grass was very thin and there was so much bare ground that it was no danger.

There were four Patrol vehicles with us, counting Skip's car. The others were two four-wheel-drive vehicles and a van used as a paddy wagon to transport those apprehended back to the Staging Area at the station. Two *mojados* were in the van, having been apprehended before we arrived.

About eight o'clock some of the people across the canyon started moving. Skip ordered the two four-wheel-drive vehicles—called "Ram Chargers"—into the canyon to block the path of the movement.

As the vehicles descended into the canyons, the people on the other side started moving back across the line into Mexico. Some were already in the canyon floor, but they went back, too. After the vehicles had withdrawn from this not-too-spectacular show of force by the world's most powerful nation in defense of its territorial integrity, I saw four men come out of a clump of brush well below where most of the people had been and run down the canyon. I pointed them out to Skip and followed them with binoculars for about a quarter-mile until they disappeared. He said that a unit was stationed down there and in addition the area was so full of sensors that they probably would not make it.

We then drove around the canyons in the dark for awhile as Skip explained what was going on in relation to what we were hearing over the radio. I listened as two units closed in on a big group in Travel Lodge Canyon, and we visited another couple of units just as they finished apprehending four *mojados*. The agents were still filling out the Form I-213's.

Then Skip took me across I-5 where the West Unit was working with the helicopter. The helicopter cruised and hovered at about 500 feet and illuminated one group at the fence that marks the border. After hovering for awhile, the spotter in the aircraft called down on the loudspeaker in Spanish, "Okay, you guys, run one way or the other." The Mexicans laughed and waved.

Then we drove back to the east side to an area called the "loading docks" because there used to be railroad loading platforms there. If an illegal can make it to the loading docks, he is home free because it is only a couple of hundred yards to the urbanized area of San Ysidro. If the *mojado* had made arrangements to meet a load car in the parking lot of the Safeway store, or if an accomplice had rented a room in one of the many motels in the area, he had it made.

At 11 o'clock, we went back to the station, and I waited while the watch commander filled out I-213's on some people who had been brought in. His big problem was with a Salvadoran lady who had been apprehended and had tried to pass herself off as a Mexican so she would be shipped back to Tijuana to try again. However, the

Mexican authorities had refused to let her in, and now she would be deported to El Salvador. She did not want that and was very upset. She had probably spent a lot of money to get to Tijuana and then blew the crossing. The watch commander did not like it too much either, because he had to fingerprint and photograph her and do all the paperwork for a deportation. Previously an agent had explained that "OTMs" (other than Mexicans) were a big pain because of the paperwork. This one was particularly so because she kept giving different names for herself. Everyone was tired.

By this time the agents from all the units were coming in with their I-213's, and problems and confusion reigned. East Unit had apprehended 28 *mojados,* and the count for the day at Chula Vista Station was a little over 500. It had been a slow night, and Skip apologized for not having had more action for me.

Skip then took me to the Staging Area, a fenced compound containing several austere buildings. Six or seven feet inside the door of the building we entered was a grate that ran from the floor to the ceiling, and there were a few small, barred windows. The holding area was about 30 feet wide and perhaps twice that long. The room was completely bare of furnishings except for a couple of exposed toilets in the back. The walls were completely lined with sitting men. The only person standing was a young man with classic Mexican good looks who was at the grate staring out the door. I had to cross his line of vision to get in, but he took no notice of me. I stood about three feet from him, and the scene and his presence embarrassed me. I tried to think of something appropriate to say, but could not come up with anything, even in English, much less in my meager Spanish. *Buenas noches* did not seem to fit the situation.

We went over to another building which was like the first except it was full of double-decker bunks. I did not see anyone in it. It was for people who were going to stay a little while, although no one stays at the station more than three or four days. We then returned to the building where the watch commander's office was to see the facilities for holding real criminals or smugglers. They were a series of rather grim cells, each containing only a toilet and a cot. Finally we went to a room off the watch commander's office which Skip said was for women who had been apprehended. It was a big room with eight or ten double-decker bunks like those below. Skip had not known about the Salvadoran lady who was there trying to sleep, and she looked up, confused. Skip apologized and we closed the door.

By this time the shift was over, and we went down to the coffee room where five or six agents were sitting around talking about their work.

Every stretch of the United States–Mexican border presents its own problems to the *mojados,* the smugglers who take them across, and to the Border Patrol agents whose job it is "to detect and prevent the unlawful entry of aliens into the United States." Each group responds to the other's initiatives and sometimes takes initiatives of its own. As long as there are people willing to pay for their entry and others who know the way, the game is likely to go on. Until now the game has gone on with relatively little friction between the main players. But, as the American public becomes more aware of the illegal traffic, there may be increased pressure on the Border Patrol to clamp down on it. The entire situation is potentially explosive, with important international implications.

[8]

MIGRATION IN THE FUTURE

Now it is time to consider what role migration might play in the future of the world and of the United States in particular. Our crystal ball, like everyone else's, is clouded (and perhaps a bit cracked), but nonetheless, desiring a better world for ourselves and our children, there is little choice but to gaze into it and ponder carefully what appears.

A fundamental choice now facing civilization is whether to follow the advice of the "Cornucopians" or the "neo-Malthusians."

The Cornucopians think that everything is going very well. Certainly, humanity is faced with a daunting array of global problems that include rapid population growth, resource depletion, environmental deterioration, and the danger of nuclear war. But Cornucopians feel that society will also be able to deal with those problems by the application of increasingly sophisticated technology. Population growth will be stopped if it ever *really* becomes a problem, economic growth will go on forever, and the excess capital supplied by that growth will be used to clean up pollution. The poor will be made rich, and the balance of terror (or some technological peacekeeping device) will keep us from blowing everyone to hell. In the view of the Cornucopians, everything will be all right as long as society continues to turn the same old crank a little faster all the time.

The neo-Malthusians, on the other hand, see Earth's resources as finite, its ecological systems as fragile, and the planet as a whole already overpopulated. They view with alarm *any* increase in population size, and are desperately concerned that the interactions of population growth, an ever more desperate struggle for diminishing resources, deteriorating environmental systems, and

311

overburdened sociopolitical systems will in the relatively near future lead to catastrophic consequences for civilization—quite possibly a thermonuclear war.

The neo-Malthusians do not want to turn the old crank faster—they want to design an entirely new machine. They not only want population growth brought to a halt as quickly as is humanely possible, they want to see the population size gradually reduced until human numbers are at a level where they can be supported more or less indefinitely by the ecological systems of the planet. The neo-Malthusians want to see the economic system transformed from one that puts emphasis almost entirely on economic growth, which turns natural resources into rubbish and pollution as rapidly as possible, to a "steady-state" economic system in which throughput is minimized by emphasizing the durability of physical capital and the quality of human capital. The neo-Malthusians consider the transition from the former "cowboy economy" to the latter "spaceship economy" to be absolutely essential to the survival of civilization.

Migration in the Future: the Business-as-Usual Scenario

If humanity continues to try to turn the old crank ever faster, migration is bound to become a major political issue very soon. For one thing, the quality-of-life gap between the rich and poor nations will continue to widen. Even the most optimistic demographers, for example, expect population growth rates in the poor nations to remain above 1.5 percent annually around the year 2000, more than three times the projected growth rate in the rich nations. Many of the poor nations will double their populations between 1978 and the turn of the century. This will greatly intensify the push factors in the global poor-toward-rich migrational trend.

Consider for a moment the implications of population doublings in less developed countries in 20 to 30 years. Somehow, if today's level of living is only to be maintained, all of the existing amenities of those nations must be duplicated. They must double their agricultural production, double their housing, double the number of work places, schools, teachers, hospitals, physicians, and nurses. The capacity of highways, rail systems, and port facilities must also be doubled, as must both imports and exports. Such a task would be well-nigh impossible in a rich nation such as the United States, even with its abundance of capital and resources, well-educated population, excellent communications and transport systems, and ample leverage for gaining resources abroad—leverage provided by an agricultural system producing food for export and a strong military establishment.

Poor nations, with few or none of these advantages, will be hard pressed to maintain their quality of life under the business-as-usual scenario. Many poor countries with "rising expectations" also have plummeting prospects. Indeed, even if they should manage to double their amenities, it would only mean that around 2000-2010 there would be twice as many impoverished people gazing enviously across the widening gap. And, if the Cornucopians have their way, the gap would still be widening, for if the Cornucopian scenario is followed, the rich will be even richer. Our guess, of course, is that the Cornucopians will fail—that environmental constraints will assert themselves, and the quality of life will decline in both rich and poor nations. The decline will likely have much greater impact on the poor, however, plunging many less-developed countries (if not the world) into chaos.

Under such conditions, the incentives for poor people to cross the widening gap will be enormous—as will be the incentives for the rich to prevent their crossing except as a temporary source of cheap labor, easily if brutally deported when the immediate need has been satisfied. Whether the rich will have the collective will (and the necessary brutality) to try to slam the door is a question raised allegorically in Jean Raspail's novel, *The Camp of the Saints*. He describes the reaction of the rich nations in general, and France in particular, to an unarmed invasion fleet of 99 rusting ships carrying nearly a million poor people from Calcutta.

Another factor that will increase tensions and pressures related to migration in the business-as-usual scenario will be rising tensions between racial and ethnic groups as the scramble for remaining resources becomes more frantic. As Canada finds it increasingly difficult and costly to have a bilingual society, the already high tensions between the Québecois and the English-speaking Canadians could grow even higher. There is currently a sharp debate on immigration policies in Canada, many of whose recent immigrants are non-Europeans from the Caribbean and South Asia, which could lead to further ethnic tension. If caught in an economic pinch, the already inadequate efforts of South African whites to improve the lot of South African blacks could be replaced by increasing oppression. Rising oil prices and a declining Israeli economy would make the search for permanent peace in the Middle East ever more difficult. Britain may find it an unacceptable strain to attempt to keep the peace in Northern Ireland; and the already high tensions between natives and non-European immigrants in England may become explosive.

All over the globe the story would be the same: the Ibos and the Hausas in Nigeria, the Walloons and Flemish in Belgium; natives and immigrant workers in Germany, Switzerland, and Sweden;

the Malays and Chinese in Malaysia and Indochina; blacks, Chicanos, and Anglos in the United States, and so on. All these will find competition increasing, and with it the chances of conflict will escalate. And when conflicts do erupt, there will once again be multitudes of refugees migrating or wishing to migrate.

The reasons for which people want to move from place to place in large numbers seem certain to multiply under a business-as-usual scenario. Poor people everywhere will have no trouble believing that things must be better somewhere else—especially where the rich now live. They already paper their hovels with rotogravure pictures of the promised lands of wealth; for many of them, in a decade or so, the urge to migrate to one of those places offering a better life will be overwhelming. And where the pull of rich areas does not produce migration pressures, the pushes of hunger and joblessness or of international, interracial, or internal political conflict may well do so.

If current trends indicate that the pressures toward migration will increase, what can be said about the future attitudes of the native-born toward immigrants? The easiest prediction is that immigrants everywhere will be increasingly resented and resisted. This indeed seems to be a universal trend, from European host countries with guest workers to traditional receiving countries like the United States. The frontiers of the world are now pretty much used up; nations that once saw strength in numbers now realize that there is, instead, weakness.

Australia, for example, is slowly beginning to appreciate that in many respects that nation is overpopulated, with serious overcrowding problems in the larger cities and a shortage of water over most of the continent. In addition, Australians know that the continent could easily be overwhelmed by immigrants moving to Australia—a single year's population increase in India alone would double the Australian population. Consequently, Australia has stopped subsidizing migration from Europe and North America (while opening the door a tiny crack for non-Europeans for the first time in this century) and has become relatively much stricter in accepting immigrants. Neighboring New Zealand has similarly begun discouraging immigration. Reportedly, the New Zealand policy has been so successful that in the mid- to late 1970s emigration (principally to Australia) exceeded immigration.

Canada, whose immigration rate on a per capita basis in recent years has been about three times as high as that of the United States, is in the process of revising its policies. The Canadian Immigration Act of 1952 permitted restriction by the government on essentially racist or ethnic grounds. More recent legislation would remove those criteria but would be potentially even more restrictive, basing decisions on "demographic goals." These goals include reunion of families, erasing discrimination, helping refugees, and promoting economic growth. To reduce problems and social friction that have resulted from immigrants settling mainly in a few large cities, the government will have the right to admit some newcomers only on the condition they settle for up to six months in designated, less densely populated areas.

At the same time, other developed countries that are not traditional receivers of immigrants but that have been accepting them during the past generation, primarily to fill labor shortages, have been tightening their immigration restrictions as well. Switzerland, where as much as a quarter of the work force has been made up by migrant workers, even held a referendum to expel all foreigners in 1974. Fortunately, it was defeated. Germany and other Common Market countries are closing the door to additional migrant workers even while encouraging those already in residence to stay permanently. And the United Kingdom is contemplating slamming the door in the faces of former colonials, even those who hold British passports.

Resistance to liberal immigration policies in all overdeveloped countries is likely to harden substantially over the next few decades as their economies are weakened by resource and environmental constraints on growth. As jobs become tighter in faltering growth-oriented industrial societies, the need for willing bodies to do unskilled, dirty jobs—one of the classic reasons for encouraging immigration—will tend to disappear. To some degree these jobs may be filled by locals, and to some degree they may be eliminated by automation.

In the overdeveloped nations there is the greatest awareness of the consequences of population growth, and they have gone furthest toward reducing their own natural growth. Most of them have reached or gone below replacement levels of reproduction, and some already actually have declining populations. Many people in overdeveloped countries are aware that further growth of their national populations is certain to mean a decrease in the quality of their lives. Many of them also perceive their own small families as personal sacrifices to the future. They have had fewer children so that those children may enjoy the benefits of a relatively uncrowded environment. It seems easy to predict their attitude toward the crowding of that environment by large numbers of immigrants—especially immigrants from strange cultures. The very success of the zero-population-growth movement seems to carry with it the seeds of a movement to restrict immigration.

The political will to institute strict policies against immigration can obviously be mustered. In the first quarter of this century, when immigration quotas were being established by Congress, Americans were having large families and no one seriously considered the country overpopulated. Since then there has been a dramatic increase in awareness of migration as a contributor to population growth, as well as other social and economic problems, as evidenced by the current uproar over illegal immigration from Mexico. What may have been an even higher level of illegal immigration in the 1950s caused no such stir because, among other things, few Americans then realized that the nation was already overpopulated. If attitudes are changing in the United States, a nation that for most of its history has had liberal policies on immigration, countries without a recent tradition of accepting immigrants in large numbers seem likely to close their borders even more tightly.

Of course, once draconian immigration laws are established, the question of successful enforcement inevitably rears its head. For insular nations such as Great Britain and Australia, the problems of enforcement may be relatively simple, although far from trivial. Long stretches of coastline must be guarded and internal checkpoints maintained to attempt to capture those who slip through. Host countries of Northwestern Europe do not generally share boundaries with the donor nations of their guest workers, and their regulations for admission and length of stay are relatively strict and carefully enforced. Yet these countries have problems with illegal aliens too; perhaps 200,000 were living in Europe in the mid-1970s. In situations where international land boundaries separate the rich from the poor, the problems of control are likely to be especially serious, and nowhere more serious than along the U.S.–Mexican Border.

Countries like the United States will have to undertake difficult cost-benefit analyses. Is it worth the effort to maintain barricades, patrols, and checkpoints in order to gain a certain percentage of captures out of a certain number of illegal crossings? Considering human ingenuity (and the effort required by the East German government to prevent its citizens from crossing to the West, for instance), it is quite clear that few nations will be able to seal their borders very effectively. Anti-immigrant activity would therefore involve a great deal of internal police work. The Soviet Union can handle the problem with little trouble, but for the democracies this immediately raises grave questions of civil liberties that would affect not only immigrants but citizens. What kinds of documents would have to be carried at all times? What sorts of questions would one have to answer before being granted a job? Would laws governing police search and seizure have to be relaxed? To what political purposes might their new police powers be put?

Obviously, the future of immigration in a business-as-usual world seems none too pleasant. There is every reason to believe that the numbers of people wanting to migrate will steadily rise, while the inhabitants of desirable areas will be increasingly resistant to the reception of immigrants. To the rich, the problem may seem like attempting to strengthen and increase the height of a leaky dam, backed by a lake with an ever-rising water level. Perhaps the greatest danger in the situation is that the rich may eventually decide that something has to be done about the streams feeding the lake.

Migration in a Sustainable World

What if the "business-as-usual" scenario could be avoided? Suppose that the expanding international population-control movement reduced birthrates rapidly enough that the world reached a population peak of around eight billion people and then started a gradual decline (a wildly optimistic supposition). Suppose further that a combination of shortages and minidisasters finally convinced everyone that trying to run the same collapsing economic machine ever faster will just not work. As a result, there might be a transition toward a steady-state or "spaceship" economy in which all nations adopted programs calling for highly efficient use of energy and materials, with energy supplies based mainly on the constant input of the sun. Programs would be instituted to maximize recycling of materials and minimize the depletion of resources, and ecological constraints would finally be recognized as placing fundamental boundaries on human activities. In short, humanity would decide to live with nature rather than attempt to conquer it.

Imagine further (as long as we are pipe-dreaming) that all of these developments contributed to a trend toward equity in the world, and overdeveloped nations like the United States started to de-develop. Laws could be passed to encourage high standards of durability in consumer goods, while automobile factories greatly reduced production and started making only small, long-lasting, fuel-efficient automobiles. The activities of the petrochemical industry would also be reduced as the production of plastic junk and synthetic pesticides declined.

As various antisocial activities such as freeway-building and purveying of junk food fell off, the United States might shift its human ingenuity and productivity toward conversion to a sustainable society. Huge numbers of jobs would open up for renovating cities, designing and installing efficient transport systems, and decentralizing energy systems—beginning with the installation of solar heating and cooling systems in virtually all structures within the country. A national dialogue might begin on gradual reduction of the work week so that in a few decades, when most conversion jobs were completed, every American would still have an opportunity to be involved in productive work.

Suppose that all other overdeveloped countries were to undergo similar transitions, with the scenario modified according to the special conditions of each nation, and that the less-developed countries adopted new development goals—that grass-roots development became the order of the day. There would be no attempt to compete with industrialized nations by instituting grandiose projects ranging from national airlines and Ford assembly plants to colossal dam projects that do little to solve the basic problems of the people. The LDCs would more wisely concentrate on ecologically sound agricultural development, giving special attention to improving the lot of the poorest segments of their populations. The "two-tiered" development now found in nations like Mexico and Brazil, where one relatively small part of the population becomes prosperous while as many as half of the people languish forgotten in hopeless poverty, would start to fade. Health standards would rise as population growth slackened and the distribution of food and other amenities became more equitable.

In such happy circumstances, what patterns of migration might be expected? One general conclusion seems obvious. The level would be much lower. In a sustainable world of increased equity and diminishing population growth (or even diminishing population size), many of the pressures that generate migration would be relaxed. As overdeveloped countries de-industrialized, the "pull" incentives to migrate would diminish. With the gap between rich and poor nations shrinking, and with the rich openly admitting that their previous course had been a wrongheaded one, the grass would no longer appear so green on the other side of the fence.

Obviously, the "push" factors would also be reduced. The brutal poverty in which so many of the world's citizens live today would begin to be alleviated, and the natives of less-developed countries would see some chance of realizing their rising expectations. People therefore would no longer have to look to new homelands to realize their hopes for a better life.

Similarly, the transition toward a sustainable society should remove some of those sources of international conflict that in the past have helped to generate refugee movements. It would be naive, however, to think that even such an ultra-optimistic program would entirely remove the threat of war. The sources of intergroup tension are much too complex and culturally ingrained to expect that even as great a revolution in human affairs as has just been described would completely solve the problems that often lead to armed conflict.

Nonetheless, if civilization were working toward a sustainable world and diminishing the differences in wealth and opportunity between rich and poor within and among countries, many of the sources of migration "problems" would dissolve. Mexicans would no longer flood across the United States border, because conditions in Mexico would be improving and the availability of jobs in the United States would be decreasing. Similarly, the movement of job-seekers from less-developed countries to industrial Europe—a movement that has already begun to decline—would come to an end. It is even conceivable that nearly everyone would stay put. With the exception of people who moved for reasons relating to health, business, or family commitments, nearly everyone would be satisfied with their present locations. There would be an end to mass movements of peoples.

Cultural Diversity Versus Cultural Homogeneity

What would be the costs of such a relatively static situation? One would be a loss of the talents and cultural inputs of immigrants to their new society. There is little doubt that past migrations have enriched the lives of both immigrants and natives in receiving countries. It is generally accepted that American culture has been greatly enriched by the traditions of its immigrants. The arts and sciences have bloomed under the impact of European immigration. The Hispanic tradition enlivens California and the Southwest in architecture, language, song, and cuisine. Black, Chinese, and Mexican labor, almost always exploited, helped build the general prosperity of the nation. For anyone interested in a diversity of ideas, cultural events, diet, or just plain people, the benefits derived from immigration are enormous.

The majority of people in the United States have benefited greatly from the most shameful migration episode in its history—the massive importation of slaves. Many white Americans profited (and many continue to profit) from the disgraceful treatment of black Americans long after their emancipation. Both American culture and the American economy have been vastly enriched by the presence of black citizens who would not be in the United States but for one of history's most painful forced migrations.

Other traditional recipient countries have enjoyed similar benefits. For example, until a decade or so ago, restaurant food in Australia was generally atrocious, in the English tradition. Today one can find well-prepared, tasty food in all the major cities, largely because immigrants from nations like Italy and Greece have opened restaurants. Indeed, an outstanding example of cultural enrichment is the cuisine that, along with their legendary industriousness, migrating Chinese have carried around the globe.

Not surprisingly, one of the things that make people nervous about the prospect of a sustainable, steady-state society is that it might be too monotonous—lacking in cultural variety, new ideas, and new perspectives. Migration has helped to overcome such stagnation in the past; would it not be sorely missed in a sustainable society? Some concern by Americans here may be reasonable, but not much. The United States is already a very diverse nation. It is also a very large nation, and its diversity can be maintained or increased by means more likely to be effective than an annual net immigration at current levels or below.

But there are also obvious costs to all of humanity as a result of the movement of peoples. The greatest of these might be the other side of the "enrichment" coin—cultural homogenization. The "Westernization" of the world is surely one of the most striking trends of the post–World War II era. Western technologies have penetrated to the four corners of Earth, as have Western ideas on political organization, economics, and religion. Knowledge of some Western language has become essential for elites almost everywhere outside of China, and even there the situation may be changing. American pop culture, from rock, jazz, and blue jeans to *Kojak*, Coca-Cola, and Kentucky Fried Chicken, has slowly engulfed the globe.

In the Western Hemisphere, the trend toward homogeneity started with Cortés in Mexico. In the Eastern Hemisphere, one might arbitrarily place the start at a small village in Bengal called Plassey. There, on June 23, 1757, Robert Clive, leading some 1,000 European and 2,000 Indian troops and equipped with only ten artillery pieces, defeated an army of 60,000 men with more than 50 heavy guns fielded by the Nawob of Bengal, Suraj-ud-Dowlah. The British suffered only about 65 casualties. The battle of Plassey brought Bengal under the hegemony of the East India Company and led directly to the conquest of India, the centerpiece of the British Empire for the next 190 years. Some 400 million people on the Indian subcontinent in 1947 were still subjects of George VI, and Britain could create two nations there, with all the accompanying horrors of partition.

It is incorrect, however, to view global cultural homogenization simply as a result of Western military prowess. It stems from a combination of socio-political-economic organization, technology, and chauvinistic attitudes. Evangelical Christianity and feelings of superiority, combined first with mercantilism and then with capitalism, gave impetus to the spread of Western colonialism. Central organization and purpose combined with superior technology permitted divide-and-conquer strategies to be used. A few Spaniards with Indian allies or a few Englishmen with the backing of local rajahs subjugated and held vast territories. Had the peoples of either Mexico or India been united, organized, and determined to throw them out, the Spaniards and English could not have stayed even if they had had machine guns.

Cortés began his conquest of Mexico with only 500 soldiers and destroyed the Aztecs with an army that never contained more than 1,000 Spaniards. He did it with cleverness, Roman Catholic religious zeal, a vision based on loyalty to a central authority (the king of Spain), a great deal of luck, and even more *chutzpah.*

That Spanish technical superiority alone could not hold in the face of determined opposition was demonstrated by the relative ease with which the Aztecs defeated Cortés when they got their dander up. After bloodlessly taking over the Aztec capital of Tenochtitlán, Cortés departed, and, in a fit of incredible stupidity, a lieutenant slaughtered thousands of defenseless Indians. When Cortés returned, the Aztecs attacked and drove the Spanish troops from the city, killing over half of them. Only with the help of smallpox and armies of Indian allies (who hated their former bloodthirsty Aztec overlords for sacrificing hundreds of thousands of prisoners and slaves) was Cortés able to return and destroy the Aztec empire.

In the more than 450 years since Cortés, the cultural diversity of humanity has been continuously worn away. When the British finally left India in 1948, they left in place the system that had been used to control that nation. The highest places in the once-British hierarchy were promptly occupied by Indians trained at Oxford, Cambridge, the London School of Economics, and other British institutions. The dominant western view was retained in most of the former subject lands, even after independence. In the New World the natives never had a chance—Western religion, economics, technology, and general attitudes dominated early and largely exterminated the indigenous cultures.

Even China, a holdout since 1949, now shows signs of conversion. The establishment of "normal relations" between China and the United States on January 1, 1979, was accompanied by sales of Boeing 747s, big tourist hotels, Coca-Cola, and Western technology in general. If China forsakes its traditional culture and revolutionary goals, the West will have made, in essence, a clean sweep.

If high levels of human movement continue, even the relatively minor differences between variants of Western culture might fade away. Isaac Asimov's "Global Village" will become more of a reality than he might wish; television and population-mixing could homogenize the world—a depressing, even frightening prospect. Human beings have not yet learned how to live nondestructively with each other or with the natural environment, and solutions to these problems may well not emerge from Western culture.

For cultural evolution, diversity may well be as indispensable as genetic variability is in biological evolution. Is it reasonable to claim that one world view is "better" than another; that, say, an American's way of structuring the world is superior to that of a Hopi Indian? The Hopis, after all, never created anything capable of exterminating humanity. Is a militant Christianity a better guide for living than, say, Zen Buddhism? Might we not learn something about dealing with our relatives from Australian aborigines, whose sense of kinship is much more refined than that of a jet-set sophisticate?

It seems clear that migration can provide enrichment only if enough isolation is maintained to promote cultural diversity. Finding a way to do this without also fostering intolerance and prejudice will be a major challenge for the future. Such policies will clearly not materialize except in the unlikely event that a much greater proportion of humanity begins to value cultural diversity. It would appear that almost all considerations make a steady but relatively small, multidirectional international migration the *ideal* future pattern. Total restriction would be both immoral and impossible, and might lead to cultural isolation, xenophobia, and hostility. But too heavy a flow would be both socially disruptive to the nations involved and culturally disastrous.

THE DEMOGRAPHIC FUTURE OF THE UNITED STATES

To understand where the United States fits into any scenario, it is necessary to have a grasp of its basic demographic situation. Many people are under the impression that the population of the United States has reached ZPG (zero population growth—a population that is neither growing nor shrinking), or that it would have reached ZPG if migration were not a factor. Neither of these views is correct. The source of the confusion is the attainment in the American population of what is sometimes called "replacement reproduction."

Replacement reproduction means that each female in the present generation will be replaced by exactly one female in the next generation. Each successive generation will be the same size. In the long run, if replacement reproduction is achieved and maintained in a previously growing population, it will lead to ZPG, *but it does not do so instantaneously.* There are two reasons for this. One is that in a growing population there is a much greater proportion of young people than of old people. The other is that in human societies several generations are living simultaneously.

In order for the population to stop growing (ignoring migration), the birthrate must be equal to the death rate. In the American population today there are many more young people, who contribute to the birthrate by having children, than there are old people, who are the major contributors to death rates. The babies produced by the large younger generation just replacing itself greatly outnumber the members of the small older generation who are dying. The present pattern in the U.S. of families having just under two children on the average will eventually lead to a reduction in the proportion of young reproducers and to an increase in the proportion of people in the older age classes. There will be a decline in the birthrate and a rise in the death rate. When the rising death rate meets the declining birthrate, ZPG will be achieved—input will balance output (remember, we are ignoring migration). But the end of natural increase occurs only 50 or more years after replacement reproduction is reached.

What all of this boils down to is that there is a "momentum" of population growth built into the youthful age composition of growing populations. In the United States it means that, should the reproductive rate remain around or just below the replacement level, where it is today, some 30 million people will be added to the American population by natural increase before natural increase ceases. Therefore, if there were no increase from immigration, the population of the United States would still grow from today's approximately 220 million to something like 250 million people before ZPG could be achieved.

The consequences of adding 30 million more people to the United States will not be trivial for either the nation or the world as a whole. For example, assume that current discrepancies persist between the behavior of American citizens and those of LDCs in their consumption of petroleum and other nonrenewable resources. If this happens, then the 30 million people added to the American population will have an impact on the environment and resources of the globe roughly equivalent to the addition of one to two *billion* people in poor countries like Ecuador, Nigeria, Malawi, India, Burma, and Indonesia.

The impact of 30 million additional Americans would not be trivial within the United States, either. While this would be slightly less than a 15-percent increase over the present American population size, it would be a mistake to assume that it would result in no more than a fifteen percent increase in problems of environmental deterioration and resource depletion. Population growth now has disproportionate effects on these. For example, the most accessible and highest grade mineral resources have already been depleted. Thus each additional person to be provided for by society requires ever more costly exploration, extraction, transport, and refining activities. All of these activities damage the environment.

Furthermore, in many cases additional people can push environmental systems across thresholds, causing breakdowns. For example, the natural systems of a lake may be able to absorb and purify the wastes of 100 families living along its shores without any problems. The addition of five more families may overwhelm the natural purification system, leading to a decrease in the quantity of fish and other resources taken from the lake. After a few years, the lake will not support even the 100 families it formerly did. Thus a critical five-percent increase in population size will not result in some small increase in environmental problems but in an ecological and social disaster for the lake dwellers. In scientific jargon, one would say the relationships between population growth and resource depletion or between population growth and environmental impact are "nonlinear." Adding a unit of population may result in much less than a unit increase in population-related problems at low population densities and in much more than a unit increase in population-related problems at high densities.

A thought experiment may help clarify the disproportionate environmental impact of further growth. The building of roads affects both resource depletion and environmental values. Picture a situation in which there are two cities each of 100,000 people, connected by ten miles of freeway. Suppose that the local population rose by another 100,000 people, and that these people established another city ten miles from each of the first two cities so that the three cities formed a triangle. Then assume that the new city is connected to each of the old ones by ten miles of freeway. In this case a 50-percent increase in the number of people will have caused a 200-percent increase in the mileage of freeways. Similar examples of the impact of population growth may be constructed in most areas—including many aspects of socioeconomic behavior.

It is of course impossible to predict precisely what the total consequences of adding 30 million people to the United States would be for the American resource-environment situation, but the impact will be highly disproportionate. This increment of natural growth could even double population-related problems.

Demography of Immigration

Immigration to the United States must be viewed in a similar context. Legal net immigration is estimated today to account for slightly less than 20 percent of the growth of the U.S. population. (The further contribution to growth of illegal immigration is unknown, though the 1980 census may shed light on that.) As an example of the difference immigration can make, if U.S. fertility remained at the present level and total net immigration (legal and illegal) were constant at 400,000 per year, growth would not end until 2025 and the population would peak at 269 million. If fertility stayed the same and total net immigration were as high as 900,000 per year, the population would pass 269 million in 2000 and continue growing indefinitely.

How immigrants behave is a matter of consequence also. If native Americans continue unrepentantly in their traditional "prosperity," that is, a resource-gobbling, environment-destroying life-style, then America will continue to attract immigrants, legal and illegal, who will strive to do the same. If the past is any guide, most immigrants will sooner or later achieve a standard of living that is not significantly different from that of the native-born. After all, this is what attracts most immigrants in the first place. Thus, adding people to the United States population by migration would increase the total American impact on global resources and environment, as well as contributing to domestic problems, just as adding people by natural increase would.

The patterns of impact from immigration and from natural increase are probably not as dissimilar as they might seem at first glance, considering the average lower economic status (hence lower environment-resource impact) of immigrants. Babies, after all, do not begin to have their full environmental impact until at least two decades after birth—when they begin to drive Cadillacs, build houses, eat steaks, or occupy seats on airliners. To compare the impact of an immigrant with the impact of a native birth, therefore, one must look not at the standard of living of the individual as he or she enters the country, but at the standard of living two or three decades after entry.

One area in which migrants may have a very different per capita effect is in their contribution to natural increase. For example, some experts have concluded that the population of recent immigrants has an age composition more conducive to a high birthrate than has the remainder of the population. What this means is that most immigrants are young adults in their 20s and 30s—the ages at which people are most likely to have children. Furthermore, recent immigrants from nations like Mexico may bring with them a culture in which large families are still the norm. For example, in the United States in 1970, women of Mexican origin between the ages of 40 and 44 had borne an average of 4.4 children. The national average for women of that age was 2.9.

The degree to which this difference would persist as the Mexican immigrant became socialized to American ways is difficult to predict, but in general, major differences in reproductive behavior usually disappear by the second generation. Those women of Mexican origin, it should also be pointed out, still had smaller families than did their counterparts who remained in Mexico. The average number of children born to each woman there until very recently was over six. And the large-family ethic in Mexico seems likely to change rapidly under the impact of the family-planning program; there are signs it has already begun to do so.

Another factor that influences the immigrants' reproductive contribution is that so many are men who have left their wives and children in Mexico. They obviously are not adding to U.S. population growth, unless their families join them, and they probably are contributing less to Mexico's because of their long absences than they would if they stayed home.

Like most aspects of human migration, predicting the consequences of different mixes of immigrants and native births for the future of America is obviously exceedingly complex. And this is especially true when the size and composition of the immigrant population is unknown, as it is for the illegals.

From another point of view, it could be argued that environmental and resource problems may not be dramatically increased by either natural increase or by immigration, because the resulting population growth may lead to a significant *decline* in the standard of living. Few people, however, would find this a compelling reason to promote population growth by either route.

Close examination of the probable consequences of further population growth in the United States should convince any sensible person that the sooner American population growth can be brought to a halt and a slow decline initiated, the better it will be not only for the citizens of the United States, but for everyone in the world. This means that the nation must strive for an annual total of births *plus* immigrants that is slightly *below* the annual total of deaths plus emigrants—the input must be brought slightly below the output.

Statistically, there are many ways that this can be accomplished, but methods that would mean raising American death rates or forcing people to flee the country cannot be considered morally reasonable options. This leaves some combination of further lowering birthrates and limiting immigration.

In a child-loving and xenophobic world, it is not surprising that most Americans appear to favor restriction of immigration over further reduction of birthrates. While there are manifest cultural advantages to the admission of immigrants, the present patterns of immigration do not optimize these. Rather, they fuel the fears of many Americans that, while they are limiting their own reproduction, they are permitting nations like Mexico to "solve" *their* population problems by exporting their surplus people to the United States. But, at the present time, such a "solution" for Mexico would involve a net annual influx of Mexicans of about 2.5 million, far beyond the most extreme estimates of actual migration. It would be closer to the truth to say that the United States is maintaining its "cowboy" life-style by exploiting Mexico and other developing countries. And Mexico is, after all, now addressing its population problem directly through its vigorous family-planning program. Nevertheless, this does not invalidate the concern of Americans who try to make the world better for their children by having fewer of them and who perceive that their children's chance for a better life is being threatened by the profligate reproduction of foreigners.

Potentially, there is a great deal of truth in their perception. It is obvious that nothing resembling the present American way of life can persist if the Mexican population continues to increase as it has for the last 20 years and the border between the United States and Mexico remains open. Nor can the American way of life persist in the face of present Mexican demographic patterns *regardless* of the state of the border; that way of life depends too much on heavy U.S. involvement in the affairs of Mexico and other "donor" countries.

WHAT ARE AMERICA'S OPTIONS?

In theory the United States can establish an immigration policy anywhere along a continuum. At one end would be an open door to the world—a policy of allowing anyone who so wishes to immigrate legally to the United States. Few Americans would favor such a policy, even those most concerned with the problems of the poor of the world. A flood of immigrants into the nation would be even more disruptive than the equivalent growth from natural increase. The opposite end of the continuum is almost equally unacceptable. Even the most dedicated of the nativist and "fortress America" crowd normally are willing to accept some immigration—refugees fleeing Communist tyranny, professionals and technicians with valued skills, close relatives of citizens and legal residents, etc. To construct the functional equivalent of the Berlin Wall around the United States would, in the view of almost all Americans, be immoral (in addition to being incredibly expensive).

A North American Economic Union

Perhaps the closest thing to an open-door policy that might ever come to pass is some kind of economic union between Canada, Mexico, and the United States. A North American Union would be a unique human experiment, joining as it would three of the largest (and two of the most populous) of the world's nations. It would make a geographically natural unit while bringing together peoples who are culturally diverse, although they share traditions of individual freedom.

These three countries are already more economically fused than most Americans know or are willing to admit. Recognizing the reality of this economic fusion would be greeted as heresy by virtually everyone concerned but would change remarkably little. The fears of many Americans of being swamped by Spanish-speaking people would actually be minor compared to the panic of Mexicans and Canadians over the prospect of being devoured by their colossal neighbor. On the other hand, it would solve many problems by reducing the significance of two of the world's longest international land borders. This process would provide the world with a laboratory experiment in how different cultures might work together to reconcile such problems as differential rates of population growth, the exploitation of one people by another, and the uneven distribution of natural resources. Indeed, these problems will cause at least as much trouble with North America divided into three traditional nations as they would if the continent were more openly unified economically. The maintenance of political independence while acknowledging economic union would be the most difficult problem.

North American economic integration will not come about as the result of some highly publicized summit conference or series of dramatic actions. It will come about as the result of a great many tiny steps all in the same direction. Indeed, the first of these steps was taken many years ago. The Canadian Auto Parts Agreement of 1965 provides for the free flow of spare car parts between the United States and Canada. This was a relatively easy agreement to obtain because, by and large, Canadians and Americans drive the same cars, the same models are manufactured in both countries by the same companies, and the workers who build them often belong to the same unions. The idea that two identical clutch assemblies or carburetors built under similar circumstances should have considerably different prices because one was manufactured in Detroit, Michigan, and the other five miles away in Windsor, Ontario, was so obviously absurd that something could be done.

In large part the agreement was successfully concluded due to the personal interest of President Lyndon B. Johnson and in spite of the spirited opposition of the smaller independent parts manufacturers in the United States who feared competition from Canada. After a decade and a half of operation under the agreement, the manufacturers are hard put to demonstrate that their economic position has been hurt, while the interests of American and Canadian consumers have certainly been well served by it. Similar agreements with Mexico would be more difficult to conclude, particularly if the Mexican goods are not produced by branches of American companies. Another problem is that Mexican labor unions, unlike those in Canada, are not closely connected to American unions.

While decisions on what items should flow freely across the borders should be made in terms of the overall economic welfare of all the countries involved, the decision, in fact, will be largely political. One case that bears careful watching as an indicator of the ability of the United States to negotiate wisely is that of the importation of railroad cars from Mexico. The continuing rise in energy prices means that the United States must shift to a greater reliance on more energy-efficient forms of transportation such as railroads, and obviously a dependable source of rolling stock is necessary for this. Mexican manufacturers can supply some of the railcars, so why not let them? U.S. railroads want to buy the Mexican cars, and the major shippers and agricultural groups endorse the free flow of the cars. The U.S. railcar manufacturers and the unions to which their employees belong, however, are less concerned about meeting U.S. transportation needs than in maintaining their own happy current situation. To these groups, the growing shortage of railroad cars simply means guaranteed sales and work for an indefinite period into the future.

A frustrating irony in all this is that the American companies, some of which have lobbied very actively against the importation of Mexican rolling stock, have divisions selling their rolling stock to Mexican railroads; they are only too happy to sell their products to Mexican railroads, but they do not want Mexican competition in the United States, an attitude sadly typical of American industry in the international trade scene.

In 1978, the "politics of boxcars" worked in favor of the American manufacturers and unions. A single congressman was able to sidetrack the bill to import Mexican boxcars after it had left committee and before it was brought to the floor. Blocking legislation on the subject will not be so easy in the future, however. The Mexican manufacturers continue to have their viewpoint represented by Attorney Joseph Blatchford, who is knowledgeable on the political, economic, and legal aspects of the problem, and the railroads and shippers are devoting more of their lobbying effort to the boxcar issue. There is now support for the idea of the free flow of rolling stock across the U.S.–Mexican border among staff members of the White House Special Trade Representative and of the Trade subcommittee of the House Ways and Means Committee. The issue is also under active study by the White House itself.

If the United States and Mexico succeed in building a free trade agreement for rolling-stock cars on the foundation laid many years ago with the Canadian Auto Parts Agreement, a crucial step will have been taken toward a free common market for North America. It would be a relatively simple matter to amend such an agreement to include other products in the years to come. Mexican President José López Portillo has said repeatedly that Mexico wishes to export goods, not workers. It is time that the United States realized that it will either import Mexican goods or it will have to accept the importation of Mexican workers.

Improving the Legal Aspects

Even with a steady, incremental movement toward North American economic integration, the United States ought to consider establishing a special immigration policy toward Mexico. The unique proximity of these two great countries, one rich and one poor, whose histories are so closely intertwined, cries out for special treatment. But the form of the special treatment will depend on the outcome of the current national debate on illegal immigration. Here we will merely point out the obvious; one way to clear up many of the worst aspects of the illegal immigrant "problem" is to convert illegal migrants into legal ones.

Indeed, the sheer volume of the problem may eventually force the United States Government into decriminalizing the illegal migration across the Mexican border. At present, aliens found illegally in the United States are generally regarded as criminals and are treated accordingly. Recently, the long-standing "gentlemen's agreement" between the Border Patrol and the illegals, whereby a captured *mojado* offers no resistance, but gives up quietly, has begun to break down. There is a growing danger of violence occurring in the process of apprehension as the stakes become higher and numbers of migrants increase. Perhaps even more of a potential problem is the unconstitutional way in which the legal aspects of apprehension, detention, and repatriation have been handled. The illegal signs a rubber-stamped admission of guilt, is detained in substandard facilities, and bussed back to Mexico.

There seem to be only two possible paths out of this dilemma. One would be for the U.S. Government to continue processing suspected illegal aliens in a totally unconstitutional manner, detaining most only briefly in inadequate facilities. The main difficulty of this approach is that, when constitutional safeguards are ignored in any one case or for any one group, their protection may, in effect, be removed from everyone.

Mark Twain once observed that law was scribbled in the sand and custom was carved in rock. What the United States is trying to do is take a rock-hard customary practice, one that is deeply ingrained in the illegals, their employers, and the *de facto* practices of the Justice Department itself, and change its shape by scribbling some laws in the sand. Small wonder the government has so much trouble when it tries to enforce the present laws on immigration. Those laws were enacted with no regard to reality. Most of the time it is easier and much wiser to adjust the law to common practice than it is to try to modify practice by passing laws.

Right now, when the entire situation is so poorly understood, however, the first path may be the best: do nothing dramatic, try to improve facilities and handling procedures, and simply cope pragmatically with migration problems as they arise. The United States could treat the "illegal problem" as a low-priority issue and stop the ill-informed scare-mongering, while working toward an informed consensus on policy. Surely this is preferable to the second path: going off half-cocked in a restrictionist direction, with more fences, a greatly strengthened Border Patrol, and the erosion of civil liberties. Unfortunately, the current public discussion, including much of the government's contribution, seems to be inspired by the old navy maxim:

> When in trouble or in doubt,
> Run in circles, scream and shout.

President Carter's Program

The growing concern about the "immigration problem" in the press and among the public began to stimulate interest in the government during the mid-1970s. On August 4, 1977, President Carter offered to Congress a program intended "to help markedly reduce the increasing flow" and "to regulate the presence of the millions of undocumented aliens already here." Although it came to nothing in Congress, the program is worth consideration because it is the only coherent set of proposals yet to emerge, and, as INS Commissioner Leonel Castillo said in early 1979, it still represents the thinking of the executive branch of government on the issue.

The centerpiece of the program was punishment of "employers who engage in a 'pattern and practice' " of hiring illegals by fining the employers $1,000 for each illegal hired. The program would also have imposed penalties against labor contractors who obtained jobs for illegals in return for remuneration.

The Immigration and Nationality Act of 1952 made it illegal to aid and abet an illegal alien who was entering the United States or to help one stay; however, that law included a specific section, called the Texas Proviso, according to which employment of an alien was not considered "aiding and abetting" his or her presence in the United States. The Carter program would have wiped out the Texas Proviso.

The new program would also have stepped up enforcement of existing laws, both by the INS and those agencies charged with administering the Fair Labor Standards Act and the Federal Farm Labor Contractor Registration Act. The President told Congress that "a minimum of 2,000 additional enforcement personnel will be placed on the Mexican border." An additional 265 inspectors were to be hired "and targeted to areas of heavy undocumented alien employment" to enforce the minimum-wage law.

For many illegals already in the United States, there was a proposal to offer an "adjustment of status." Those who could show continuous residency in this country since before January 1, 1970, would have been amnestied and could have applied for immigrant status. A new immigration category, Temporary Resident Alien (TRA), would have been created for those who could prove they had been here continuously since before January 1, 1977, allowing them to remain for five years, pending final determination.

Finally President Carter showed his awareness of the foreign-policy dimension of the immigration issue by proposing "continued cooperation" with the governments of donor countries "to improve their economies and their controls over alien-smuggling rings."

The idea of penalizing employers for chronically hiring illegals probably strikes at the heart of the issue; if there were no employment opportunities, there would not be considerable number of illegals. But the politics of the situation keeps the Texas Proviso in effect. In immigration legislation, the restrictionists are usually strong enough to get the law written their way, but the anti-restrictionists, particularly the employers, are strong enough to write the loopholes. Even if the Texas Proviso were wiped off the books, the anti-restrictionists would be strong enough to ensure that not enough money would be available for enforcement, and the United States does not need any more unenforced laws. With the idea that stricter enforcement of the Fair Labor Standards Act to insure equal pay for illegals would make a difference, the Carter Administration started going off the track. Our own observations and the studies that have been done, particularly those of Wayne Cornelius, indicate that illegals typically are not paid less than the minimum wage, except in agriculture where "substandard" wages are standard.

The spirit of the Texas Proviso permeates a great many federal laws and regulations and many of those of the states. The claim that knowingly employing an illegal-alien worker is not "aiding and abetting" his continued residence in the United States is so absurd that it need not be argued. However, inclusion of this absurdity was the political price of getting the law passed. In other words, certain forms of entry by an alien into the United States could be defined as a "crime" in terms acceptable to the authors of the law only at the cost of explicitly decriminalizing the employer's role. The employer is, of course, the primary beneficiary of the "crime" and one who, by the usual definition, was at the very least an accomplice.

The accomplices—that is, the employers—were not powerful enough to get the law written exactly the way they wanted it. Such a law would have allowed Mexicans to enter the U.S. freely when workers were needed and then be ejected at government expense when they were no longer needed. The employers, however, were powerful enough to get the next best thing: a law that decriminalized their complicity and kept the enforcement arm of the INS sufficiently impoverished that their workers would not be harassed on the job.

California and many other states have passed laws making it illegal knowingly to hire an illegal alien, but the spirit of the Texas Proviso is maintained by the usual practice of not enforcing these laws. This way everyone wins. The restrictionists—nativists, some labor unions, and people concerned about population growth— win in Washington or the state capitals; and the anti-restrictionists win where it really matters, in the fields, the factories, the restaurant kitchens, and wherever else illegal aliens are hired. The restrictionists get their victory in the press, and the employers get theirs on the balance sheet.

The handling of immigration law in this manner—passing the law and then not enforcing it—is typical of the way "fair employment" legislation is generally handled. Americans want to be proud of the legal protections that workers have under their laws, but they want cheap lettuce, neatly tended shrubs and lawns, clean floors, and inexpensive restaurant meals, too. They are simply unwilling to pay the higher prices, in dollars and cents, that the enforced laws would generate. In evaluating the coming immigration debate and the legislation it produces, it will be necessary to scrutinize not only the letter of the law, but also the appropriations that go to the various agencies—the Department of Labor, the INS, and other divisions of the Department of Justice—that carry out the law. In a day when reduction of government expenditures is in fashion, it is not likely that Congress will vote to raise taxes in order to ensure higher labor costs.

Quite apart from the question about the will of the American people to stop the flow of illegal-alien workers, there is the question of whether or not the flow *can* be stopped within any reasonable budget while preserving "due process of law" and other constitutional safeguards on the rights of the accused. The outrage that has been expressed against Commissioner Castillo's meager steps to bring INS detention facilities into compliance with the minimum standards set by the Federal Bureau of Prisons (he supplied the detainees with Spanish-language reading material and spent $400 on soccer equipment) is not promising. This complex of problems has no easy solution, though people far removed from the scene sometimes think it does. Usually, the further one gets from the border, the more faith one finds in enforcement as the solution to the problem.

The problems involved in the adjustment of status proposal are also not simple ones. How is an illegal alien, who has been trying to obscure his presence in this country for several years, expected to come up with the documentation that will demonstrate his "continuous residence" in the United States? Bureaucrats and lawyers will select some set of documents or affidavits that would be accepted, and a booming business in counterfeiting those documents and affidavits will spring into being. Many of the customers will be individuals who are lawfully entitled to admission to permanent residence or to the new TRA status, but need false documents in order to prove it. Furthermore, why should an illegal alien who is permanently employed and otherwise well settled come out of the closet to seek TRA status which would only target him for expulsion five years hence?

The final element of the President's 1977 program was action to "promote continued cooperation with the governments" of the countries that are major sources of illegal immigrants. To be sure, the proposed actions were limited to "an effort to improve their economies and their controls over alien smuggling rings," but the foreign-policy implications were recognized at least in part. The executive branch typically has been more sensitive to the impact of U.S. immigration policies on other governments than has Congress. We criticize the President's concern in this area because it seems to be based on some old and false thinking about American relations with other countries and fails to recognize the foreign-relations aspect in its entirety. If the United States is going to assist the economic development of foreign countries, particularly countries that send illegal aliens to the United States, it must revise its notions of what development is and what this country can do to facilitate that development. El Salvador, whose involvement in the Soccer War was discussed earlier, is the most rapidly "developing" country in Central America if judged by the increase in its per-capita gross national product, the usual yardstick for measuring "development." Yet, in 1969, El Salvador had exported ten percent of its population illegally to neighboring Honduras, a country with a *lower* per-capita GNP. Currently, more Salvadorans are apprehended as illegal aliens in the United States than any other Central American nationality.

The problem, which we have discussed primarily in relation to Mexico, is that of two-tiered development. The benefits of increased productivity are simply not evenly distributed among all segments of the population. In many Latin American countries, one group, larger and more inclusive but otherwise reminiscent of Porfirio Díaz's *científicos* on the eve of the Mexican Revolution, is prospering. This group includes not only the technical-managerial elite, but skilled workers, too. A steelworker in Mexico, or television repair man in the Dominican Republic, or someone who can reline brakes or repair automobile clutches in El Salvador is living in a manner vaguely reminiscent of his or her counterpart in the United States. There is another group, usually rural people, who are simply left behind as the society changes around them. They can only move to the city and wash cars or become squatters on land claimed by someone else and practice subsistence agriculture.

In between the relatively rich and the poor is another large but ill-defined group that is only marginally involved in the "developed" society. What little work has been done on the subject indicates that this middle group contributes most of the illegal immigrants to the United States. A problem of economic development is that it often prepares people for a role in the developed segment of the society before it can provide a place for them. These people do not want to go back to the farm—indeed the farm might well have been sold to some large land-owning neighbor, who has thrown himself lock, stock, and government subsidy into the Green Revolution.

Economic development, as it has been preached and encouraged by the United States and enthusiastically embraced by so many third-world countries, may just be a major cause of the immigration problem. New definitions and strategies of development are sorely needed, hard to come by, and harder to sell to the professional developers in the governments of the United States or in other affected countries. Some people in the Carter Administration have recognized some of this, albeit vaguely.

In the information packet subsequently issued to clarify the Presidential Message to Congress on illegal immigration, the economies of donor countries were characterized as "rapidly expanding but unable to provide adequate employment to meet even more rapid population growth." Certainly, rapid population growth is a part of the picture, but some types of development displace as many workers as they create jobs for. Mechanized agriculture, for instance, usually results in higher crop yields and fewer jobs. How much of the unemployment and underemployment in less-developed countries results from population pressure and how much of it is from development itself? It is now necessary to question the old maxim that the cure for the ills of development is more development, especially if development continues to be measured by economic expansion. It is time to ask how many people have been lifted from abject poverty, rather than how many goods have been produced. A development-of-accommodation program should be the primary aim of the United States, because those who are not being accommodated at home will seek accommodation somewhere else, and quite often that is going to be in the United States.

There was no suggestion in President Carter's message that the United States or its citizens abroad are in any way responsible for the illegal immigration. There was no mention of the significant, often determinative role that American investments and loans can play in the economies of these countries. Neither was there any hint that the capriciousness with which foreign products are admitted to U.S. markets makes any difference. This has been discussed elsewhere in relation to Mexico, but U.S. involvement in many of the Caribbean and Central American countries is far more potent there than in Mexico because their economies are smaller and weaker. But no regulation of American business practices abroad was suggested by the President.

There was one tiny suggestion that part of the solution might lie in "enhanced trade" and the implication that this would be done "with support from the United States." This is most encouraging. If the United States worked for a development of human accommodation instead of the old development of an expanding economy, it could probably do better by selectively opening its markets to the goods of the donor countries than by sending them money and machinery. Among the good ideas to be found in Adam Smith's *Wealth of Nations,* is the one that nations, like individuals, are better off doing what they do best and trading that for whatever else they need. Of course, to make this work, Americans will have to stop thinking they do everything best—Mexican boxcars being a good example.

In order to do any good, the accessibility of the American market to the new suppliers must be constant and sure. It cannot be cut off because some high-rolling constituent kicks $5,000 into some Congressman's campaign fund. Similarly, no one industry or small group of industries should be expected to absorb all the dislocations stemming from a new flow of foreign goods. Someone will have to sit down with the people from the affected industries and figure out how their problems can be shared. This will not be easy. It does seem, though, that this sort of work would be more challenging, rewarding, and ennobling than chasing Old Joe Wet through the brush.

The idea that the governments of donor countries will spend very much time and "effort to improve their . . . controls over alien-smuggling rings" is largely mistaken. This is basically an American law-enforcement problem, not a pressing problem for policemen in Mexico, Colombia, the Dominican Republic, El Salvador, or anywhere else. This is akin to the idea that, since the heroin sold on American streets comes from poppies grown in Turkey or Thailand, the Turks and the Thais ought to crack down on the poppy growers. The United States does not prosecute the American liquor manufacturers whose wares end up being sold in Moslem countries where alcoholic beverages are forbidden. Heroin is not widely used in Turkey or Thailand, nor is marijuana in Colombia, and those cultures do not define their use the way ours does. Insofar as the drug trade is a serious law-enforcement problem in those countries—and the killings among drug merchants in the Mexican state of Sinaloa certainly became a problem for Mexico—the problem is viewed as one caused by the United States. After all, it is the Americans who want those drugs and buy them. The attitude of the countries from which the illegal aliens come to the United States is much the same. If the Americans do not want them, why do they give them jobs? If they want something done about it, why don't they enforce their own laws?

One recently installed minister of public security in a third-world country told us that the biggest problem in his agency was "cutting the narcs down to size." The country was an exchange point for cocaine dealers, and his predecessor had taken so much equipment and money from the United States to fight the narcotics merchants that it had upset priorities for law enforcement in that country. With U.S. money, the narcotics unit had grown completely out of proportion to the size of the narcotics problem for that country. All the better police officers wanted transfers to where they could get their hands on all the shiny new equipment from the United States. This man told us that the principal crimes his country faced were petty thievery, pickpockets, and purse snatchers. He felt the problem should be approached through more manpower, more foot policemen on downtown streets, and more motor patrols in residential areas. When he took over his ministry, however, he found his force concerned with helicopter maintenance and figuring out how to run the elaborate communications gear. He thought he could use the communications gear, but he did not know what he was going to do with those helicopters.

The point here is that it is improper for the United States to think other countries are going to reorder their law-enforcement priorities to benefit the U.S. by attacking the groups that smuggle aliens. Moreover, it is damaging to those countries for the United States to try to induce them to change their priorities through coercion, blandishment, or gifts of money and equipment. Those are countries with horrendous problems of their own, and they have neither the time nor the talent to do for the United States what the United States cannot do for itself.

The most encouraging thing about President Carter's first-round attempt to do something about illegal immigration is that there is evidence that he and his Administration can learn. In his message to Congress dated August 4, 1977, the President said that the illegals "have breached our nation's immigration laws, displaced many American citizens from jobs, and placed an increased financial burden on many states and local governments." In the explanation packet issued by the Justice Department the following February, the Attorney General was still sure that illegals were taking jobs away from people who ought to have them, but there was a note of grudging respect in the acknowledgment that "they work 'scared and hard.' " There was even a hint of uncertainty about job displacement in the statement: "The precise degree to which undocumented workers are displacing native workers is not and may never be known."

The Justice Department's explanation package completely abandoned the position taken in the Message to Congress that the illegals are a terrible financial burden on society. By February the President was willing to admit that "they contribute much and require little. . . ." With doubt comes questioning, and questioning opens the door to reasonable debate.

On October 12, 1977, Congressman Peter Rodino, Chairman of the House Committee on the Judiciary, introduced the President's bill, which, if it had been passed, would have been the Alien Adjustment and Employment Act of 1977. It contained the formal proposals for the adjustment of status and for the elimination of the Texas Proviso. The bill never became law. The 2,000 additional enforcement personnel were not even hired for the southern border (although the Border Patrol did get 300 new positions), nor were any inspectors added to the federal payroll to ensure that employers were paying the minimum wage. One reason for this was that, while the President on one hand was suggesting the hiring of more people for enforcement of immigration and employment laws, he was on the other imposing a "hiring freeze" on all federal agencies. If Congress had felt strongly about the matter, however, it could have persuaded him to make an exception for these positions. Two years after President Carter's program was sent to Congress, the illegal-immigrant issue was still being addressed with the same laws and with about the same number of personnel as before.

The failure of the President's bill was a fate it deserved. Not all of the ideas in it were bad, but many of them were. It should be realized, however, that this legislative failure was only the beginning of a debate (or a squabble) that will go on until something comes out of it. If that something is to be of any value, a good many people will have to listen carefully and make up their minds slowly.

The Coming Debate

After President Carter's proposed legislation was defeated in Congress, an Inter-agency Task Force on Immigration was set up in late 1978 among the Departments of Justice, Labor, and State to evaluate current policy and its administration and to make recommendations on changing both. At the same time, the House Select Committee on Population was considering the same issues, and a Presidential Commission on Immigration was being formed, composed of over a score of persons inside government and out. There is concern in government, there is concern in the press, and there is concern among the people.

The current discussion is the third major public review of American immigration policy in this century. The first culminated in the Immigration Act of 1917 with its lists of exclusions and exceptions and the National Origins Act of 1924 with its elaborate sets of quotas. The second review produced the Immigration and Nationality Act of 1952, which reaffirmed the national-origins principle, and the 1965 amendment to that act, which junked it. In each case, what should have been a serious discussion of the national interest degenerated into a pointless squabble which led to an irrelevant immigration law. The same forces that prevented anything useful from happening on those occasions are still present and promise to make a shambles of the coming debate. An examination of these forces is in order.

A basic problem is that the legislative and executive branches of the government have fundamentally different views of the nature of immigration and of immigration problems. Some of the most important pieces of immigration legislation have been passed over presidential vetos, as were the 1917 and 1952 acts. In other cases, such as the 1924 Act, the president signed the legislation grudgingly because he feared that something worse would be forced down his throat if he did not. Throughout this century and earlier, Congress has forced on the executive branch immigration legislation that could not be administered and that was regarded by the men who had to make it work as not being in the national interest.

One element in this difference in viewpoint is that Congress steadfastly maintains that immigration is a domestic matter. It is argued that every nation has the right—indeed the duty—to safeguard its borders, and part of this is the responsibility to regulate what and who comes across those borders. If it is decided that this regulation requires the building of a fence along parts of the border, an increase in the Border Patrol, or even more stringent measures, so be it. The decision is the responsibility of Congress.

The president of the United States, on the other hand, is charged by the Constitution with the conduct of the country's relations with foreign nations. He knows—and if he does not his Secretary of State will soon tell him—that the flamboyant exercise of sovereign rights will complicate the orderly transaction of business with other countries. When Slavs and Italians are called morons by the invited witnesses of congressional committees and the Japanese are publicly declared unworthy of trust, as happened in the 1920s, the Slavic countries, Italy, and Japan can be counted on to take note and bring the matter up when the United States wants something from them. When the United States systematically subjects those citizens of other countries who wish to enter the U.S. to humiliating and degrading questioning, as was required by the 1952 act, our citizens abroad should expect little sympathy from foreign authorities. When Americans of Mexican heritage are insulted, scorned, and persecuted because of that heritage, and honest Mexican workmen who only want an honest day's work for half a day's pay are described as a "scourge," the United States should not expect favored treatment when it wants to buy Mexican oil. The President realizes this, but many in Congress still do not.

The politics of immigration present themselves quite differently to a congressman or a senator than they do to the president. A president is only vaguely responsible to any constituency; his responsibility is to all the people. Members of the House of Representatives, on the other hand, are immediately responsible to a small, specific electorate. Since their conduct is reviewed every two years, they are effectively running for re-election all the time, and their continuing capacity to serve the public depends completely on the attitudes of the people who live in the district, they represent. Senators, with their six-year terms and usually much larger constituencies, have a little more freedom. Nonetheless, they are apt to be as skittish in the presence of a powerful constituent as any member of the House.

The politics of immigration contains one of the elements most feared by elected officials, especially by Congressmen. It can create a "one-issue" voter. The one-issue voter irrationally reduces the complexities of the American political scene to some single issue and judges elected officials on that issue alone. Classic examples of one-issue voter blocs are those who believe that any restriction on the possession of handguns is a violation of the Constitution and a threat to their individual liberties or those who believe that abortion is not a matter for medical expertise and personal judgment, but needs restriction by the government. Whether there are certain problems that create blocs of one-issue voters or whether there is a certain type of voter who seeks some single issue to simplify the responsibilities of citizenship is a matter of dispute among students of voter behavior, but one thing is clear. Immigration can be one of those issues that blinds the voter to all others. If the congressman votes "wrong" on immigration, the rest of his record is forgotten, and there is nothing he can do to save himself.

Immigration issues are complex ones on which honest men can easily disagree. It is not easy to determine what is right for the United States in terms of obligations to people in other countries, in its relations with foreign governments, or even in terms of its own cultural and economic well-being. The complexity is lost as the argument deteriorates into a black-and-white, one-issue squabble between "restrictionists" and "anti-restrictionists"— between those who would slam the door tightly shut and those who would open it wide. Yet politics is "the art of the possible," and neither of these choices is possible. There is no way the United States could accommodate all "the poor, the tired, and the huddled masses" of the world, and indeed it never has.

Similarly, slamming the door completely shut is not an option. Could Americans deny immigration and citizenship to the husband or wife of a United States citizen? Their minor children? Their elderly parents? Not even in the 1920s, an age of rampant restrictionism, was it argued that families should be kept apart, and the principle that immigration law should allow and even foster the unification of families has been observed ever since. In 1976, 60 percent of the immigrants admitted from the Eastern Hemisphere were immediate relatives of United States citizens.

Is the United States going to deny itself the service and enrichment of scholars, scientists, artists, and craftsmen? Can it say "no" to future Albert Einsteins and Enrico Fermis? These men were refugees from oppression who needed the United States, but whom the United States needed much more.

Finally, can the United States turn its back on men and women who have become refugees from their own lands because of faithful service to American foreign-policy objectives? That would not only be callous, it would be stupid. The United States will surely continue to be active in the arena of international affairs and will need not only alliances with governments but alliances with individuals. People hesitate, however, to ally themselves with those who turn away when things go badly. Stripped of the formal and legalistic language in which laws are written, it is mainly people with special U.S. connections who are now lawfully admitted to permanent residence.

It is not known exactly what *net* legal immigration into the United States is, but the best work indicates that it is not more than 320,000 per year. When someone says that this is too many people, he or she should feel the responsibility to indicate just what category presently admitted should be excluded.

So many people react so strongly to immigration issues because immigration touches Americans in two very tender areas of insecurity, the psychological and the economic. Discussion of immigration brings out our "nativism," the U.S. brand of xenophobia. Then the fear of the foreigner becomes connected with fears over individual economic well-being. These ideas coalesce into the single idea that the feared, by now hated, "others" represent some heavy economic burden or threat. *Parade,* a magazine supplement included in many Sunday newspapers, ran an item in its June 4, 1978, number on Proposition 13, the California initiative to limit property taxes which was on the ballot in the following Tuesday's election. One of the reasons *Parade* cited for the overwhelming support for the initiative revealed the blend of these two touchy issues. It reported, in part:

> Some Californians say their state is becoming "Mexicanized," that Hispanics constitute the largest single group of public-school students in their districts. They resent booming taxes to educate kids "whose folks are probably illegal immigrants."

There is not the slightest basis for the belief that California schools are clogged with the offspring of illegal aliens, but many people believe they are. None of the half-dozen or so fragmentary studies on the subject indicates that more than seven percent of the illegals have children in the public schools, and one study indicated less than one percent. The House Select Committee on Population, which reviewed the studies and heard testimony from authorities, reported in 1978:

> Despite popular belief, illegal immigrants do not appear to be a heavy burden on Government social service programs. Undocumented aliens appear to be more likely to pay taxes than to use tax-supported programs. Nevertheless, the most current research in this area is concerned with illegal immigration. This emphasis may reflect the frustration of public officials faced with rapidly increasing social service costs and their attempts to limit these costs.

This passage seems to mean that, when public officials cannot figure out why things cost so much, they blame Old Joe Wet, who in fact is paying for other people's benefits. Somehow the American public cannot admit that illegal immigrants are in many respects an economic benefit.

Nor are *legal* immigrants an economic burden on the nation. A Government Accounting Office study of immigrants who had been in the United States less than five years revealed that only about three percent of them were receiving Supplemental Security Income from the Social Security Administration and that over 20 percent of the money paid out to immigrants went to individuals who had entered the country as refugees and were admitted with the full knowledge that they might require substantial assistance.

The other half of the economic fear is that the immigrant, particularly the illegal immigrant, depresses wages and displaces legal workers. There is a beautiful contradiction in these fears. On the one hand, the illegal is a freeloader; on the other, he is so diligent a worker and requires so little to stay alive that Americans cannot compete with him in the job market.

There is one new element in the developing immigration debate: concern about the consequences of an increasing U.S. population to natural resources, the environment, and the quality of life for all Americans living now and still to be born. In the great immigration debates of the 1920s and the 1950s, no concern was expressed over the ultimate size of the population in this country.

Today there is widespread agreement that there are "limits to growth," that the environment is endangered, and that there is some size that the population of the United States should not exceed. These concerns spawned a number of organizations that a decade ago devoted themselves to energetic grass-roots activity. Their goal was to spread the word about overpopulation and environmental deterioration. Today many of these organizations have shrunk in membership or disappeared. But some of them, such as Zero Population Growth (ZPG) and Friends of the Earth (FOE), have survived. They have offices in Washington, they lobby, and their lobbyists have contacts among congressmen, staff members of congressional committees, and relevant government agencies. They have matured to the point that their personnel quit their lobbying jobs to take positions in the government agencies and congressional committees they formerly lobbied. These organizations still do not have much money, but insofar as possible they try to operate just like the United Mine Workers, the oil companies, and the National Rifle Association. They have to make up for their meager resources by hard work, and often they are remarkably effective in delivering their message.

Among other things, these organizations feel that the U.S. population should be stabilized, and they rightly view current immigration practices as destabilizing. They believe that there should be a national population policy, spelled out and written down, and they realize that there can be no coherent population policy that does not include an immigration policy. Eventually, the number of people who enter the United States must be balanced by the number leaving or by a reduction in fertility. The sooner this is achieved, the better. The population of the United States has already exceeded the optimum if not the maximum for maintaining the kind of life Americans expect.

This is an important message, one that must be delivered to and accepted by those in the executive and legislative branches who will determine what the new U.S. immigration policy will be. But it is much more difficult to deliver a complex message than a simple one, and what must be done in the area of immigration is complex. The great danger facing the population/environmental organizations is that they will slip into the strict restrictionist, slam-the-door camp.

Any intelligent move to reduce the level of illegal immigration in particular presents some thorny problems and equally inelegant choices. The economic role of illegals in the United States is unknown; they may well be a net economic plus. Current evidence indicates that illegals are not costing the United States anything, and, to the extent that they are only transient residents, their effect on America's overall population growth is negligible. In regard to illegal immigration, particularly that from Mexico, the United States is simply reaping what it has sown. A tradition of importing labor from and exporting unemployment to Mexico began early in this century. The Mexican society and economy have adjusted to the reality, not to the legality of U.S. immigration policies. The current heavy involvement of United States business firms and banks in the Mexican economic scene and the inconsistency with which Mexican products are admitted or excluded from American markets mean that "the Colossus to the North" has much to do with determining what happens in Mexico. With such power must go some responsibility for the consequences.

Much more information is needed now about the problems that immigration encompasses. The *Report on Legal and Illegal Immigration* of the House Select Committee on Population recommended an "expenditure of up to $10 million earmarked for research on the dimensions and impact of immigration to the United States and the development of accurate data on legal and illegal immigrants." This is a large amount of money compared to usual government practice in social policy development; but, even if it is spent, there is no guarantee that it will result in a wise immigration policy. Nevertheless, whatever emerges could hardly be worse than earlier legislation. Once the facts on the immigration situation are known, the real problem will be for legislators and the American public to accept them and put their irrational, unfounded fears behind them. The burden of adjusting law to reality and policy to practice will fall unequally on different parts of the country and different segments of the population; therefore any sensible immigration policy will have to try to adjust these inequities.

An excellent example of how easily a debate on immigration can degenerate into a squabble is the events accompanying the publication of the *Report on Legal and Illegal Immigration* mentioned above. The report is excellent, by far the best summation of immigration issues available today. It does a remarkable and efficient job of informing the reader of the various attitudes toward the problem and conveying much of what is known and not known about immigration into the United States. The Chairman of the House Select Committee on Population (the committee unfortunately was dissolved in 1979) which issued it was Congressman James H. Scheuer. Scheuer is one of the best-informed and most vocal members of Congress on the subject of the United States population and the need to establish a population policy for the country. He has pursued the public interest in this regard, often in the face of political expediency. Congressman Scheuer's seriousness about the subject was demonstrated by his appointment of Michael Teitelbaum, a Rhodes scholar and a well-trained sociologist/demographer, as staff director for the Committee. The excellence of the report is largely attributable to the dedication of these two men.

The press coverage of the report's publication, however, completely obscured its excellence because the publication produced a far juicier story—dissension within the Select Committee. Congressman Scheuer used the December 20, 1978, press conference announcing the report to state his own opinion about enforcement along the Mexican border. According to the *Washington Post,* he said:

> We advocate a firm, hard sealing of the border. . . . We consider it a quintessential precondition in our emerging new relationship with Mexico that the integrity of our borders be protected.

The next day Baltasar Corrada, a Resident Commissioner from Puerto Rico* said, "I'm vehemently opposed to sealing the Mexican–U.S. border on practical and humanitarian grounds." Another member of the Committee, Congressman Paul M. Simon, appearing with Corrada, also noted the impracticality of "sealing the border."

---

*Puerto Rico is represented in Congress by resident commissioners who sit in the House of Representatives as full members in every respect except the vote.

In fact, less than one of the report's 63 pages focuses directly on border enforcement, and only one of the 15 recommendations deals with it. There is no talk of "sealing" the border anywhere in the report. It seems that Congressman Scheuer is profoundly concerned about the damage being done the United States by its failure to frame a population policy, and he recognizes that the illegal immigration from Mexico is a serious problem in this context. But he did not move the country toward facing this problem with his ill-chosen words.

A belief in democracy includes the belief that good policy comes out of a good debate, and a good debate requires sound information, the patience to listen carefully and speak precisely, and the courage to defer action until its consequences are understood. When the United States has discovered what the current migration situation is and has established some demographic goals, then it will be in a position to begin considering appropriate policies to meet its goals. We suspect that the national decision will be to attempt to restrict immigration to a level below what is now prevailing (whatever that level should actually prove to be). The main reasons for this will be a combination of a desire to end population growth as rapidly as possible and a wish to have most of the population input to be from births rather than immigrants.

Presumably, whatever level of migration is permitted should be legal migration allowed under a sound and humane immigration law. It should be designed, as far as possible, to meet the needs of potential immigrants as well as those of United States citizens. This will involve significant changes in both U.S. domestic and foreign policies, the exact nature of which will depend, of course, on the outcome of the informed national dialogue.

U.S. Domestic Policy

One of the first goals of America's domestic policy will probably be to discourage illegal immigration in order to gain rational control of the inflow. At present, pressures in this direction seem to be toward fortification of the Mexican border. This seems to us precisely the wrong approach to the problem, since it does not even attempt to attack its roots. Some of the roots, of course, are to be found in the donor countries, and there is relatively little that domestic policy can do to influence those. But the pull factors exerted by conditions in the United States are another matter.

To the degree that the United States does wish to create a barrier at its borders, however, that barrier should be deployed so that it can achieve the greatest restriction of the total illegal flow, not the flow of illegals with a given skin color or from a particular country. If the Border Patrol is to be increased, it should at the same time be reinforced along the Canadian border in order to provide information on the illegal flow from the north (are we really faced with an Albanian invasion?).

Dealing with the complex problem of restricting illegal flow would probably be made easier if the immigration-related functions of the Labor, State, and Justice departments were redistributed somewhat. Consideration of placing immigration-law enforcement in the Treasury Department and combining it with Customs to form a single border police force is well along. We do not know if this is a good idea—government reorganizations usually promise much and produce little—but it shows that at least some thinking is going on.

Beyond these measures, the most effective domestic options would seem to be measures to reduce the "pull" factors that attract illegals. According to one group of economists, the way to do this would be to make jobs in agriculture and other sectors that are now often filled by illegals more attractive to native workers. Supposedly, this would have the additional benefit of helping to reduce unemployment. But how can this be done in practice? One possibility would be through legislation to facilitate the unionization of job categories where illegals are common, thus generating higher wage-benefit rewards and attracting unemployed citizens. However, as in the case of the "Sbicca 65," this might simply bring the labor unions into the anti-restrictionist camp. In any event, facilitating unionization is more easily said than done. Unions with a high proportion of unskilled workers, many of whom do not speak English and are afraid to contact authorities, would be easy victims of corruption. Furthermore, the economic effects could be very undesirable. Although many illegals make prevailing wages, employers (and taxpayers) benefit because illegals get very much less in the way of fringe benefits (and social services). And consumers benefit from lower prices, especially for food and clothing.

It is all too easy to say that these benefits to Americans are immoral—the result of "exploitation" of illegals. But the response is, "If they're so exploited, why do they keep sneaking back to be exploited some more?" The answer, of course, lies in the international rich–poor gap. As long as that gap remains as wide as it is now, or continues to widen, people will attempt to slip into the United States so that they can be "exploited."

The "cure" of reducing pull factors by filling jobs now occupied by illegals with native-born workers, if successful, would almost certainly result in both inflation and increased, not decreased, unemployment. Where workers cost more, the costs will be passed on to consumers or the jobs will be eliminated either by automation, by simple foregoing of services, or by transferring the jobs to wherever there is cheap labor. The results would be similar to those achieved when the government increases the minimum wage.

In short, government attempts to manipulate domestic job availability cannot have results that everyone will consider desirable or that anyone will find desirable in all respects. There is no sign, for example, that large numbers of unemployed Americans would be available to fill, say, jobs picking fruit or vegetables in California or Texas, even if wages for those jobs went up and benefit packages were attractive. The heaviest unemployment in the United States is among black teenagers, who are unlikely to leave the ghettos of Watts and Harlem to go to Salinas or Harlingen. Who takes what jobs and in what places is more than a matter of simple economic cost and benefit; it involves complex social arrangements and cultural traditions that are slow to change.

Other domestic options involve a high, and in our opinion undesirable, level of government involvement and policing. Employment of illegals *could* be much reduced by extracting heavy penalties from any employers caught hiring them. This, however, makes the employer a *de facto* enforcer for the INS. How, for example, is the employer to identify an illegal? Is each employer to become an expert on forged documents? Is each suspicious (read "brown-skinned and Spanish-speaking") applicant for a position to be subjected to a police check? Must the United States move to nearly forgery-proof internal passports that everyone will be required to carry at all times?

Few Americans would show enthusiasm for these steps, which would take the United States further down the road toward becoming a police state. Fortunately, the courts have recently become reluctant to issue the warrants or honor the procedures that allow mass police action in the search for illegals—the Sbicca factory incident being a case in point.

There has also been a trend toward informing illegals of their legal rights, which include the option of taking the Fifth Amendment when asked if they are aliens. Should every detainee choose that option, the criminal justice system could become hopelessly bogged down in the process of attempting to prove that each illegal *was* illegal and then subjecting them to prison or legal deportation.

In addition to (or instead of) stronger internal policing, the government could become involved in the importation and supervision of alien labor, much as it did in the early *bracero* program, which was administered humanely in 1942 by the Farm Security Administration. This system has worked reasonably well for European countries. It certainly has not prevented exploitation of migrant workers there, but preventing serious abuses would certainly be easier with a supervised, legal program. Nor has Europe been totally free of illegal entrants, but their numbers have been kept relatively low.

Unquestionably, installing a "guest worker" system would create another array of problems. It would be opposed by many unions for fear that jobs would be taken from native workers. It would be opposed by business interests afraid, as in the past, that government supervision would mean higher labor costs and smaller profits—and that it would set dangerous precedents. It would be opposed by Chicano groups, who would claim it was racist and immoral to bring in Mexicans to do work that Anglos consider too menial.

Of course, the unions could be told that legal aliens would be no greater threat (and possibly a lesser one) than the illegals. Businessmen could be lectured on the immorality of exploiting illegals. The Chicanos could be told that the use of legal labor would help illegals, many of whom could change their status. But if the past is any guide, these arguments would fall on deaf ears. The AFL-CIO is a major restrictionist force in U.S. policy-making circles. Businessmen have historically worked to maximize profits, and most have opposed all efforts to improve the lot of migrant workers. And image-building is a common and understandable concern of activists among minorities. One positive suggestion for legalizing Mexican migrant workers while ensuring that their tour in the United States is temporary has been put forward by Senator S. I. Hayakawa of California. He suggested that each worker deposit $250 with the Mexican government, which would be held in interest-bearing government bonds. In exchange for the deposit, the worker would receive a travel document entitling him or her to a six-month visa issued by the United States at the border. In order to reclaim the deposit, the worker would have to return to Mexico within the six-month period, but he or she would be guaranteed another visa the following year if desired.

In presenting his proposal, Hayakawa cited a number of problems in both countries that his idea would help to solve. These included Mexico's serious unemployment problem and its—

apparently contradictory—need for a pool of skilled workers for industrialization; the need for workers in the U.S. willing to take low-paying jobs; the preference of most Mexican workers to take jobs in the U.S. only temporarily, leaving their families in Mexico and returning for frequent reunions; the apparent futility of stopping the illegal flow with increased instrictions and the risks to human and civil rights inherent in the present situation, to say nothing of what would follow stricter enforcement measures. Finally, Hayakawa pointed out that this approach had the advantage of being administered cooperatively by both Mexico and the United States to solve a problem that affects both nations. Reportedly, the Mexican government was very receptive to the idea. Hayakawa's suggestion has considerable merit, and, once the illegal immigration situation has been carefully analyzed, something like it may prove the best way to go.

A final area of domestic policy has to do with the "brain drain"—the pull that the American educational system and job opportunities have for students and professionals from LDCs. Students come from all over the world to attend universities in the United States; they become physicians, engineers, and other kinds of technicians and professionals. Once trained, they very often do not return home. In addition, many professional people—scientists, engineers, doctors, lawyers, teachers, and so on—whose degrees were earned elsewhere are welcomed in the United States. Some impact on the job market for native-born Americans seeking to enter similar professions can be guessed from one set of statistics. In 1970 there were only about 6,000 black doctors practicing in the United States. In that year alone, 770 physicians entered the U.S. from the Philippines, 242 from India, 228 from Korea, 130 from Egypt, and 127 from Iran. *Some 7,000 Filipino doctors were licensed to practice in the U.S., or more than roughly 1,000 the number of black doctors.*

The labor-certification program is supposed to ensure that immigrants do not compete with native-born workers. Unfortunately, however, only a small fraction of immigrants are required to be certified. It is hard to believe that this influx of physicians does not work to the disadvantage of blacks, women, and other disadvantaged Americans wishing to become physicians. Problems in other professions may well be similar. At first glance it would seem to be to the benefit of both the United States and donor nations to refuse entry to professionals from less-developed countries and to require their students to return home immediately after completion of their degrees. In many cases, however, there are no jobs in the donor countries. Therefore, unless jobs can be created there, the potential immigrants would lose, and the United States as a whole would also lose, although some disadvantaged Americans would gain.

WHAT SHOULD BE DONE?

In writing about policy issues, authors always face a moment of truth: having examined the background of the problem and a series of possible courses of action, what do *they* think should be done? Having explored with us the complexities of the migration situation, however, the reader might well be sympathetic if we chose to make no recommendations at all, except perhaps merely to call for national and international dialogues on the topic. But it is evident that some steps toward dealing with the problem should be taken immediately. Beyond those, the sensible options for further action can, given basic assumptions, be narrowed down. We will turn first to the actions that are self-evidently required.

First and foremost, the United States must adopt an *explicit* population policy designed to lower American birthrates further, bring population growth to a halt in the United States as soon as possible, and begin a slow decline. The policy should set as a preliminary goal target sizes for the population of the United States at various times in the future. One, for example, might be a size no larger than 220 million (approximately today's population size) by the year 2025.

The point of having target sizes is simply to allow for rational planning within the society. If, to make an analogy, an aeronautical engineer is asked to design an airliner, one of the first questions that he would have to ask is, "How many people should it be able to carry, in what degree of luxury, and with how much baggage?" If someone asked him to design a transport airplane for an ever-growing number of passengers, that person would quite promptly and properly be thrown out on the street. But somehow, many of the people concerned with the future of our nation and our planet see nothing wrong with attempting to plan for an ever-increasing passenger list.

Once mutually compatible goals of number of passengers and standards of living are established, then the question of how those goals might be achieved can be addressed. As noted earlier, this requires an input-output analysis, in which births and immigration are the inputs and deaths and emigration are the outputs. When the calculations were done, they might lead to some revision of goals. For example, it might be found that a return to 220 million people by 2025 would imply either a total stoppage of immigration, or so sharp a reduction in the birthrate that either or both would cause an unacceptable level of social disruption. It might be, then, that the achievement of that goal should be postponed to 2035. On the other hand, careful analysis might show that a small lowering of birthrates in combination with some dampening of immigration and encouragement of emigration might meet the target easily. We are fully aware that the techniques for this sort of "social engineering" need considerable refinement, to say the least. The point is that, once society sets some goals, then intelligent questions can be asked about how those goals are to be achieved.

How can a program moving toward such explicit goals be implemented? It seems to us that the gathering debate on immigration, combined with the general conclusions of the United States Commission on Population Growth and the American Future provide excellent bases for the required consensus. In 1972 the Commission concluded that:

> . . . in the long run, no substantial benefits will result from further growth of the Nation's population, rather that the gradual stabilization of our population would contribute significantly to the Nation's ability to solve its problems. We have looked for, and have not found, any convincing economic argument for continued population growth. The health of our country does not depend on it, nor does the vitality of business nor the welfare of the average person.

It is true there are some people who are still not alerted to the need to bring population growth to a halt; they presumably are not alertable. Those people have little cause to be concerned about immigration. After all, immigrants generally make positive economic and cultural contributions to society. For those who have become aware of the dangers of further population growth, however, the immigration situation poses a serious problem, and part of the problem is that no one knows exactly how serious it is. In order to have any chance of dealing rationally with the immigration issue, accurate information must be obtained.

This brings us to our second recommendation, which is that a substantial effort be made immediately to clarify the migration situation of the United States. Accurate data are needed on how many people are entering legally and illegally, from where, and for what reasons. The characteristics of the immigrant population must also be determined: age composition, reproductive behavior, education, skills, and so on. So must its impact—kinds of jobs occupied, social services used, taxes paid, and so forth. Information must also become available on the counterflow—the number of legal and illegal aliens who are departing and the number of American citizens who choose to move elsewhere to live. Information similar to that accumulated for the immigrant population must be assembled for emigrants if reasonable estimates of the net effects of migration are to be made. Gathering such information would require considerable effort, but reasonably accurate figures could be obtained if the effort were made. The techniques are reasonably well established, and the Census Bureau and INS, with appropriate support, could get the job done. Without such information, the United States will be in the preposterous situation of conducting a public debate about population and immigration policy with no solid information on what obviously are major factors influencing the size of its population.

Our third recommendation is that the President immediately set up and seek adequate funding for a government population task force. The job of the task force would be to work out the demographics and socioeconomic consequences of various population "trajectories" for a remaining period until zero population growth is achieved, and then for the beginning of a decline—for instance, as far as a return to present population levels. The output of the task force could be a series of scenarios similar to those for energy growth that were developed by the Committee on Nuclear and Alternate Energy Sources (CONAES). These scenarios could be based on a series of different assumptions about when ZPG would be reached and about the mix of vital rates and migration rates that would give the desired result. Each scenario could include a rather detailed look at the social, economic, and environmental consequences of following each trajectory. Based on the history of the CONAES study, and assuming rather more competent leadership for the task force, the basic information necessary for national policy-making could be gathered in a couple of years at a cost of about $2 million— roughly the amount of money required to build the 13 miles of new fence along the Mexican border authorized in 1978 for the INS.

We might note here that a lack of even the most elementary data required for making policy decisions critical to the lives of all Americans in the future is not unique to the migration question. This lack may be traced directly to the absence of coordinated planning within the United States Government. We and others have suggested elsewhere the need for a revision of the Constitution so that, among other things, a "planning branch" of the federal government can be established. The government already "plans," but, as long as the nation continues to be reluctant to institutionalize planning, the government will rely on ineffectual *ad hoc* commissions and task forces that work at cross-purposes with one another. All too often these are convened too late, and all too often their results do not even enter the national dialogue, much less get implemented. The fate of the *Report of the U.S. Commission on Population Growth and the American Future*, utterly ignored by Richard Nixon, is a prime example.

Foreign Policy

Although the prospects for doing much that is sensible about the immigration situation through changes in domestic policy do not seem terribly encouraging, perhaps something can be done through foreign policy. For example, projections of future unemployment in less-developed countries make it obvious that one of the goals of foreign-aid and foreign-trade policies should be job creation for potential migrants. One possible way to help technically trained potential immigrants is by specifically putting effort into creating jobs within their own countries for physicians, scientists, engineers, and so on. If it were successful, the United States could count the foregoing of the talents of highly trained LDC citizens as one part of its foreign-aid program.

Foreign economic policy designed to create jobs and improve living conditions for targeted subgroups within a nation's population rather than brute "development" (as measured by per-capita GNP increase) is slowly becoming recognized as the best way to go. Among other things, it is seen as the best means of avoiding "two-tiered" development, in which a part of a poor nation's population becomes wealthy, while the rest is bypassed by modernization and left in poverty. In Mexico in 1969 the richest 20 percent of the population controlled 60 percent of the wealth. In developed countries, by contrast, the richest 20 percent controlled, on the average, about 40 percent of the wealth. Mexico and other developing nations would do well to adopt this characteristic of the industrial world as a developmental goal along with the simple increase of goods and services. The Mexican Revolution may be "institutionalized," but it has a long way to go before the majority of Mexicans reap the benefits they have struggled for since the bloody days of Madero, Zapata, Carranza, and Villa.

We cannot go into detail on the intricacies of development here, but some key points can be made. For example, one of the best forms of "foreign aid" might be the relaxation of trade restrictions for commodities and other goods coming from less-developed countries. Jobs could be created in Mexico by giving Mexico trade preferences and lowering tariffs on goods imported from that country. But here again, things are not so simple. In many poor countries, a large portion of exports are produced by giant multinational corporations. Sometimes measures to make it easier for LDCs to export to the U.S. simply help the multinationals and have little impact on the supply of jobs for potential migrants. For instance, U.S.-backed agricultural operations in northern Mexico aimed at U.S. markets have tended to *promote* illegal Mexican migration, not retard it.

Programs of aid that will generate jobs for the poor—especially the rural poor—can be designed and supported, however. It is noteworthy that Mexico now has underway two pioneering programs designed to do just that. One, called PRODESCH, now supported by the United Nations and the World Bank, was initiated by the governor of Chiapas in that state in 1970. The objective is to help the local people, who are mostly Indians, help themselves. The program uses a radio station, local organizations and clubs, special education for village leaders, and so forth, to disseminate information on better farming methods and the availability of social and health services (including birth control). Among other successes, by 1978 maize yields under the program had been tripled. A second local program has been started in the state of Oaxaca, and a third is planned for Quintana Roo.

The other program, PIDER, is a nationwide rural development program that was started in 1968, also partly supported by the World Bank, with some contribution from the Inter-American Development Bank. This program is concentrating its efforts on the poorest, least-developed areas of the country. Rather than being an agency itself, PIDER coordinates the activities of existing agencies—to ensure that the new road goes to the new dam, for instance. Besides helping farmers improve their land and raise yields, the program tries to stimulate village-level industry and development of general improvements such as roads, schools, water-supply systems, electricity, health services, better housing, etc. Although they as yet reach only a small fraction of the people, the mere existence and apparent success of these projects gives us some hope that such well-designed foreign-aid projects in the future might help undo the harm that more exploitive activities have done in the past.

Unfortunately, the past history of foreign aid and the general unconcern of Americans (and the people of other rich countries) make us believe that this type of assistance may be offered only on a limited scale. But if the rich countries are unwilling to help poor countries on the scale needed, the least they can do is refrain from self-serving meddling in the affairs of the poor countries. They could stop exporting their pollution—for example, using combinations of economic leverage and lies to persuade LDCs to permit the siting of oil refineries and petrochemical complexes that would be environmentally unacceptable in rich countries. They could stop interfering in the internal politics of LCDs and attempting to maintain in power governments that welcome the exploitive activities of multinational corporations.

But this, too, is easier said than done. To a very great degree, the multinationals are independent of the governments of all countries, rich or poor. They are often as effective in corrupting—or at least influencing—officials in the United States, Japan, or the Netherlands as they are in Honduras, Chile, or Iran. Yet, in spite of this, in the view of many observers, they can be and often are a positive force in the healthy development of LDCs. The workers they employ may be exploited, but those who migrate to rich countries—the U.S. or Europe—are also exploited. And there is no reason to believe that rich countries will respond to escalating migration by being less exploitive. It seems likely to us that the rich will attempt to continue maintaining their borders as differential barriers and control flows of people and products across them for their own exclusive benefit.

A final foreign-policy option of rich countries is to help LDCs establish population control. Again, this is an enormously complex problem, made all the more difficult in much of Latin America by the contradictions within Roman Catholicism on the birth-control issue. The Party of the Institutionalized Revolution (PRI) in Mexico has long been anticlerical but only lately has become committed to population control. But American involvement will have to be unobtrusive. Should gringos appear to be trying to decrease the number of Mexican babies, the traditional Mexican distrust of the United States would surely be reinforced. In general, the United States will never be in a strong position to advocate population control in poor nations until a strong, explicit population-control policy is established at home.

One place where U.S. foreign policy might be able to do some good is in relations with the Vatican. The U.S. Government could well learn something from the governments of Catholic countries like Mexico and Italy (the latter has recently liberalized contraceptive and abortion laws), namely, that having a difference of opinion with the clerical hierarchy is not automatically anti-Catholicism. As part of the establishment of a national population policy, the government could express formal disapproval of the activities of any nation, person, or organization that promoted pronatalism—just as it would disapprove of the promotion of pollution, crime, war, or any other dangerous or antisocial activity.

The government should emphasize the difference between the

policies promoted by the Vatican and the reproductive performance of Catholics, emphasizing that religious belief *per se* has
little to do with reproductive behavior or family-size goals. It
should be pointed out that vital rates in Catholic nations tend to be
very similar to those of non-Catholic nations at about the same
level of economic development. For example, Catholic Italy's
birth and death rates are very close to those of Communist Yugoslavia; in fact, Italy's birthrate is slightly lower.

Differentiating between the anachronistic stand on birth control of many members of the hierarchy and the behavior of
Catholics could have two beneficial results. One might be to lessen
the prejudice against Hispanic immigrants in the U.S., which is
now partly based on the attitude, "They're Catholics, they'll breed
like flies." While it is true that Mexican–Americans have tended to
have higher fertility than Anglos, there is no reason to believe that
Catholicism is the major reason for this. Indeed, in a study of the
fertility of Mexican–Americans in the early 1970s, it was found
that 86 percent of couples had used contraceptives. In 1969
proportionally almost twice as many Mexican–American couples
had used the pill as had all white American couples in 1965.

A second beneficial effect might be to speed the moment when
the Church, in its time-honored way, enunciates a clear, formal,
and consistent policy on birth control. We hope that it would be
along the lines of the Mexican bishops' collective pastoral letter of
December 1972. This would enlist the organization of the Church
into the battle to save humanity from a population-related disaster. Nearly as important, it would end the confusion of hundreds
of millions of devout Catholics who now, because of their concern
for themselves, their children, and humanity, are ignoring their
Church's contradictory teachings at a considerable cost to individual conscience.

A final foreign-policy option would be to work through the
United Nations or through multilateral negotiations to develop
international agreements on the acceptance of refugees. If such
negotiations are not successful, then such horrors as the drown-
ings of hundreds of Vietnamese boat people will become more
commonplace, and the world will be an even less humane place in
which to live.

Conclusions

As should be obvious from the foregoing discussion, there are
no easy solutions to migration problems. Even though this may
not be as serious and acute a problem today as it has sometimes
been presented, it promises to become so in the near future if
humanity continues to play out the terminal "business-as-usual"

scenario. For the United States (and other receiving countries), most of the possible steps that might reduce the flow of illegal migrants involve serious questions about civil liberties on the domestic front and about politics and ethics in foreign affairs.

The immediate course for the United States should be to establish an explicit population policy, determine the actual number, flow, and socioeconomic impact of migrants, and develop demographic scenarios that would achieve the goal of ending population growth and beginning a gradual reduction. When that has been done, it may turn out that current levels of migration will prove acceptable. If not, relatively minor *ad hoc* measures might be sufficient to adjust the flow to desired levels. We suspect the latter might well be the case and that illegal migration could be removed from the crisis list while the nation gets on with the really serious job of making its transition to a sustainable society.

What You Can Do

Two environmental organizations are concerned about migration policy and are worthy of support. One is Zero Population Growth (ZPG), the original American population-control organization. ZPG (1346 Connecticut Avenue, N.W., Washington, D.C. 20036) is the leader in the campaign for a sound American population policy, of which a sound migration policy, of course, would be an essential part.

A new organization, the Federation for American Immigration Reform (FAIR), has been formed to deal exclusively with migration policy (2957 Atkins Road, Petoskey, Michigan 49770). This organization is also based in the population-control movement and is dedicated to developing restrictionist policies that are humane and consistent with modern democratic values. If you are interested in the immigration issue, join FAIR and help it toward that hard-to-reach goal.

How much these organizations contribute to the migration debate will depend on how well informed and active their members are. Joining ZPG has the additional advantage of supporting an organization that is playing an important role in attempting to move humanity toward a sustainable society. In our opinion, the help of every human being is desperately needed in that task. Unless that transition is achieved in the next few decades, illegal immigrants will quickly become among the least of our problems.

IN SUMMARY

As should by now be evident, the subjects of human migration in general and of U.S. immigration policy in particular are almost

incomprehensibly complex. We would therefore like to emphasize what we feel are the major "take-home" points emerging
from our investigations.

First of all, the United States has never offered an unqualified
welcome to the world's "wretched refuse." The flow of immigrants into the United States has been governed very largely by
American self-interest, racial prejudice, and political expediency,
with the occasional leavening of genuine compassion. Despite
this, the United States is more a "nation of immigrants" than
most—the result of both historic accident and more liberal immigration policies than those of the majority of nations.

Second, the popular view of the Mexican immigration "crisis" is
largely fallacious. There is no firm evidence that there has recently been a rapid increase of permanent illegal residents from
Mexico, nor even that the level of illegals entering temporarily
has exceeded levels that were previously found acceptable. There
is also little reason to believe that illegal aliens are taking jobs away
from Americans in significant numbers or are placing stress on
welfare systems. Indeed, to the contrary, there is evidence that
illegals generally pay for more services than they receive, and to
that extent are a net economic benefit. Money sent home to
Mexico by illegal aliens represents a trivial part of the U.S.
balance-of-payments problem and is compensated, at least in
part, by Mexican purchases made in the United States.

Third, part of the public concern over illegal immigration from
Mexico can be traced directly to the scare tactics of bigots and
bureaucrats, and the *Leyenda Negra,* the historic ethno-racial
prejudice against Hispanics. It is noteworthy that many Americans see a "wetback menace," whereas larger-scale immigration
from Canada has never generated a counterbalancing "Canuck
menace."

Fourth, part of the problem of American attitudes toward
Mexican immigration is the failure of Americans to understand
and appreciate Mexican culture and history in general or American involvement in Mexican affairs past and present. There is
every reason to think that the patterns of immigration seen today
are in considerable part a direct continuation of a pattern of
exploitation of the Mexican labor pool by American interests
traceable to the early years of this century. Many Americans seem
to want a Mexican border that allows the free northward flow of
American profits from ventures in Mexico, and a flow of goods
(including fresh vegetables and petroleum) and workers that is
available when Americans want it and cut off when Americans do
not need it. They seem to want a relationship that is based on the
needs of Americans with no regard for the needs of Mexico and

Mexicans. In large measure, this is exactly what the United States has had in the past with Mexico. It must now be realized that those days are over.

Fifth, whatever the current illegal-immigrant situation, there is legitimate cause for concern over the continuing explosive growth of the Mexican population projected for the next few decades. This in itself seems certain, all else being equal, to cause a great increase in the number of illegal aliens from Mexico, even though the majority of them may only be entering the country on a temporary basis. The belated but heroic effort of the Mexican family-planning program holds only a long-term promise of alleviating the pressure. Mexico itself must not only press that program but also strive to distribute economic benefits—especially those expected to come from the oil bonanza—more equitably. A great part of the problem has its source in Mexico. As Americans, we have concentrated on what needs to be done north of the border; knowledgeable Mexicans know full well what is required to the south.

Sixth, in spite of the assertions of numerous politicians, bureaucrats, and others, there is no real evidence that the United States, now or in the recent past, has ever served as a "safety valve" for the population growth of any less-developed country. Even the most cursory examination of the world's population statistics shows that any attempt to do so would be a disaster for all parties concerned.

Seventh, it is essential that the United States re-examine its immigration policy in the context of both an explicit national population policy and a much more complete knowledge of what the immigration-emigration flows actually are and the roles played by immigrants in our culture and our economy. Without these preconditions, the debate on immigration policy would be both fruitless and disruptive in a nation that badly needs to consider its future in a spirit of unity.

NOTES

Chapter 1

2   For details on extinctions of large mammals in the New World by early hunters, see Paul S. Martin and H.E. Wright, eds., *Pleistocene Extinctions,* Yale University Press, 1967.

2   Some of the information on prehistoric and early historical movements of people comes from Kingsley Davis, "The Migrations of Human Populations," *Scientific American,* September 1974, pp. 93–105; and Leon F. Bouvier, with Henry S. Shyrock and Harry W. Henderson, "International Migration: Yesterday, Today, and Tomorrow," *Population Bulletin,* vol. 32, no. 4 (Population Reference Bureau, Inc., Washington, D.C., 1977).

2   For information on Germanic tribes, see John Wallace-Hadrill in *The Barbarian West,* Harper Torchbook, 1975; Data on their numbers is from Dopsch, Alfons, *Wirtschaftliche und Soziale Grundlagen der Europäische Kulturentwicklung . . . ,* Vienna, 1923–24.

4   A basic source on the Arab expansion is Philip R. Hitti, *The Arabs,* Princeton University Press, 1943.

4   The discussion of the Huns, Avars, Genghis Khan, and Tamerlane follows that of René Grousset, *The Empire of the Steppes: A History of Central Asia,* Naomi Walford, translator, Rutgers University Press, New Brunswick, New Jersey, 1970; and the articles "Genghis Khan," "Tamerlane," and "Mongols" in the eleventh edition of the *Encyclopedia Brittanica.* The quotes from Genghis are found in Grousset, p. 249; Grousset's quote on artisans sent to Samarkand, p. 445.

7   For information on the Crusades, see Sir Stephen Runciman, *History of the Crusades,* Cambridge, 1951–54, 3 vols; Dana C. Munro, *The Kingdom of the Crusaders,* New York, 1935; Joshua Prawer, *The Crusader's Kingdom, European Colonialism in the Middle Ages,* New York, Praeger, 1972.

8   Figures on the slave trade are from Kingsley Davis, "The Migrations of Human Populations."

10   The definition of migration and the following description of the "theory of migration" is drawn from Everett S. Lee, "A Theory of Migration," *Demography,* vol. 3, pp. 47–57 (1966). A great deal has been written on the subject, a lot of it speculative, a lot of it analyzing various isolated economic aspects of migration. This paper is the most readable and concise treatment that we have seen. For those who wish to delve into the rather turgid literature, a useful entrée is P. Neal Ritchey, "Explanations of Migration," *Annual Review of Sociology,* 1976.

362

12 The discussion of the Boers and Bantus is based upon Leonard Thompson and Monica Wilson, eds., *Oxford History of South Africa*, Oxford University Press, New York, 1969–71; J.D. Omer-Cooper, *The Zulu Aftermath*, Northwestern University Press, Evanston, Ill., 1966; Roland Oliver, "The Problem of Bantu Expansion," *Journal of African History*, vol. III, no. 3, 1966, 361ff; and "South Africa," "Bantu," "Zulu," and "Boer," *Encyclopedia Brittanica*, 11th ed. The story of the British fight with the Zulus is beautifully told in Donald R. Morris's *The Washing of the Spears*, Simon & Schuster, New York, 1965.

17 Information on potato cultivation is from Donald Ugent, "The Potato," *Science* 170:1161–1166, 1970.

17 The source for the plant-disease aspects of the potato famine is a superb book, *Famine on the Wind: Man's Battle Against Plant Disease*, by G.L. Carefoot and E.R. Sprott. (Rand McNally, Chicago, 1967)

19 The garrison quote and much of the information on the potato famine is from Cecil Woodham-Smith, *The Great Hunger, Ireland 1845–9*, Hamish Hamilton, London, 1962, p. 18. The other major source is R. Dudley Edwards and T. Desmond Williams (eds.), *The Great Famine; Studies in Irish History 1845–52*, New York University Press, 1957.

19 The figure of five million is from K.H. Connell, *The Population of Ireland, 1750–1854* (Oxford, 1950).

20 Irish population growth and pre-famine emigration figures from R.B. McDowell, "Ireland on the eve of the famine," in Edwards and Williams, *The Great Famine*.

20 Woodham-Smith quote from p. 32.

21 Woodham-Smith quote from pp. 71–72.

22 McKennedy story from T.P. O'Neill, "The organization and administration of relief, 1845–52," in Edwards & Williams.

22 *Illustrated London News* quote from January 1847 issue.

22 Wynne quoted in Woodham-Smith, p. 155.

23 Cummins' report from Woodham-Smith, pp. 162–163.

23 Profit statement from Woodham-Smith, p. 132.

23 Starvation quotes and information from Woodham-Smith, p. 182.

24 For an Irish scholar's view, see O'Neill's chapter in Edwards & Williams.

24 Statistics and discussion on immigration from Oliver MacDonagh, "Irish immigration to the United States of America and the British colonies during the famine," Chapter 6 in Edwards & Williams.

24 Clanricarde quoted by MacDonagh, p. 320.

25 Quote on emigrants from Woodham-Smith, p. 277.

25 Landlord emigration from Woodham-Smith pp. 227–230.

27 A superb popular book about the partitioning of the Indian subcontinent can be found in L. Collins and D. Lapierre, *Freedom at Midnight* (Avon Books, New York, 1975). Rarely is history so interestingly presented, and some of this section is based on their account.

28 *Freedom at Midnight* quote from p. 26.

29 Radcliffe is quoted in Kuldip Nayar, *Distant Neighbors: A Tale of the Subcontinent* (Vikas, Delhi, 1972), p. 45.

30 The people of Punjab quote is from *Freedom at Midnight*, p. 330.

30 The Ramgarh quote is from Judge Gopal Das Khosla, *Stern Reckoning* (Bhawnani, New Delhi, 1949), p. 131–132.

31 The hospital quote is also from *Stern Reckoning*, p. 181.

31 Figures on the train massacre are from H.V. Hodson, *The Great Divide*, Hutchinson, London, 1964. p. 412.

31 The Punjabi and Bengali quote is from *Freedom at Midnight*, p. 126.

33 The nutrition estimate for Central American children by The Institute of Nutrition of Central America and Panama is from William Durham, *Scarcity and Survival in Central America: Ecological Origins of the Soccer War*. Stanford University Press, Stanford, California, 1979.

34 A recent report on the repression in El Salvador is Robert F. Drinan, John J. McAward, and Thomas P. Anderson, *Human Rights in El Salvador—1978: Report of Findings of an Investigatory Mission*, Unitarian Universalist Service Committee, Boston, Mass., 1978.

35 Report on Durham's field studies and the general treatment of the Soccer War can be found in William H. Durham's excellent *Scarcity and Survival*.

39 Information on Africa and Latin America is from the United Nations Economic and Social Council, "The Welfare of Migrant Workers and their Families." . . . *Report of the Secretary-General*, E/CN5/515, 14 October 1974.

40 Information on guest workers in Europe is from several sources, including the UN ECOSOC, "The Welfare of Migrant Workers"; Reinhard Lohrmann, "European Migration: Recent Developments and Future Prospects," *International Migration*, vol. 14, no. 3, pp. 229–240, 1976; W.R. Bohning, "Immigration Policies of Western European Countries," *International Migration Review*, vol. VIII, no. 2, Summer 1974. An excellent brief summary of recent developments can be found in Thomas T. Kane, "Social Problems and Ethnic Change: Europe's Guest Workers," *Intercom* (Population Reference Bureau), January 1978, pp. 7–9. A more detailed recent source is Bernard Kayser, "European Migration: The New Pattern," *International Migration Review*, vol. XI, no. 2, Summer 1977. For a general view of migration in the twentieth century, especially since World War II, including useful discussions of causes and consequences, see the chapter on "Migration" in United Nations, *The Determinants and Consequences of Population Trends*, vol. 1, ST/SOA/SER.A/50, 1973.

40 Complete statistical information on where Europe's guest workers were and where they came from in 1975 can be found in Thomas T. Kane, "Social Problems and Ethnic Change: Europe's 'Guest Workers,'" *Intercom* (Population Reference Bureau), January 1978.

42 Information on violence is from Kurt Mayer, "Intra-European

Migration During the Past Twenty Years," *International Migration Review,* vol. 9, no. 4, Winter 1975.

42 Case history of Mohammed is from Peter Chappell, "People Don't Respect Us Here," *New Internationalist,* May 1976, pp. 24-25.

44 Report of Britain's virginity tests is from an AP wire story, *Palo Alto Times,* February 3, 1979.

44-45 Recent information on Britain's immigration policies is from "Immigration Hot Topic in Britain," *Intercom* (Population Reference Bureau), May 1978, p. 3; and "Now We Need You Now We Don't," *New Internationalist,* January 1978.

45 Information on recent immigration policies in Northwestern Europe comes from Kayser, "European Migration."

46 Information on effects on donor countries of worker migration can be found in the UN ECOSOC, "The Welfare of Migrant Workers and their Families"; and Reinhard Lormann, "European Migration: Recent Developments and Future Prospects."

47 Transfer of funds by migrant workers from "On the Move," *New Internationalist,* May 1976.

48 Problems of African donor countries are vividly described in the UN, ECOSOC, "The Welfare of Migrant Workers . . ."

Chapter 2

50 Here are further figures on the number and percentage of immigrants and their offspring in the U.S. population. The highest proportion of foreign-born recorded in a Census was in that of 1890 which recorded 9,249,560 residents of foreign birth, or 14.7 percent of the entire population of 62,979,766. The largest proportion of foreign-born plus offspring with at least one foreign-born parent was reported in the 1910 Census which showed 13,515,886 foreign-born in a population of 118,107,855 and 18,897,837 offspring, or 13.2 percent and 18.5 percent respectively. The largest numbers of both foreign-born and their offspring were in the 1930 Census when a population of 138,439,069 was recorded, with 14,204,149 foreign-born and 25,902,383 offspring. The source is U.S. Bureau of the Census, *Historical Statistics of the United States, Colonial Times to 1957,* Washington, D.C., 1960, Series A 4–16, p. 7; Series C 185–217, p. 65; and, Series C 218–283, p. 66; hereafter cited as *Historical Statistics,* 1960.

50 The estimate of what the U.S. population would be today without post-1789 immigration is from Richard A. Easterlin, "The American Population," *An Economist's History of the United States,* 1972, p. 128; and Warren S. Thompson, and P.K. Whelpton, *Population Trends in the United States,* New York, 1933, 303 ff.

50 The INS *Annual Report, 1976* shows 47,601,208 immigrants since official records began in 1820; hereafter cited as INS *Annual Report,* with date.

50-51 The Malthus quote is from *An Essay on the Principle of Population . . . ,* London, 1798 (The First Essay), Chapter X.

51   The figures on immigration in this chapter are from INS *Annual Report, 1976*, Table 13, unless otherwise indicated.

52   The origin of official U.S. immigration records and their general discussion can be found in U.S. Bureau of the Census, *Historical Statistics of the United States, Colonial Times to 1970*, Bicentennial Edition, Part 1, Washington, D.C., 1975, p. 97; hereafter cited as *Historical Statistics, 1975*.

52   The pre-1820 immigration estimate is from Thompson & Whelpton, p. 303.

53   For the discussion of the "Know-Nothings" and the general reaction to the Old Immigration, see Richard Hofstadter, *et al.*, *The United States: A History of a Republic*, Prentice-Hall, Englewood Cliffs, New Jersey, 1960, pp. 345 ff.

53   For the view of Winthrop and the other Puritan leaders, see Samuel Eliot Morison, *The Oxford History of the American People*, Oxford University Press, New York, 1965, p. 65.

54   U.S. population figures for 1860 and 1900 are from *Historical Statistics, 1975*, Series A1–5, p. 8.

54   For the discussion of Turner and his frontier thesis as well as the "extraordinary fertility" quote, see John David Hicks, *The American Nation*, Cambridge, Mass., 1946, 280ff.

55   The figures on Oriental immigration are also derived from the INS *Annual Report, 1976*, Table 13.

56   The description of the Chinese as an inferior race is from Frank Soule, John H. Gibson, and James Nesbet, *The Annals of San Francisco*, Appleton and Company, New York, 1855, p. 530. The John Chinaman quote is from Herbert Asbury, *The Barbary Coast*, Alfred A. Knopf, New York, 1933, p. 143. This "Informal History of the San Francisco Underworld" makes interesting reading today. The following material on the Chinese in California is from this source.

57   The following material on Chinese exclusion is based on Marion T. Bennett, *American Immigration Policies: A History*, Public Affairs Press, Washington, D.C., 1963, p. 36ff. Like all who write on immigration policy, we are deeply indebted to this work and its author. (hereafter cited as Bennett).

58   Information on Japanese population at the turn of the century is from "Japan," *Encyclopedia Brittanica*, 11th edition, 1911, vol. XV. Between 1891 and 1907 the annual population growth rate averaged less than 1.25 percent.

58   This discussion of the special problems of Japanese immigrants has been greatly enriched by conversations over many years with Professor Izumi Taniguchi, Department of Economics, California State University, Fresno. As a youth in 1942, Professor Taniguchi, along with his family, was placed in an internment camp from which he volunteered for service in the United States Army. Discussion of the Gentlemen's Agreement is from Bennett, p. 36ff.

60   Kemp Tolley's *Yangtze River Patrol*, (Naval Institute Press, Annapolis, Maryland, 1966) is an excellent and readable history on this subject by one of the Patrol's veterans. Another veteran of the

Patrol, Richard McKenna, has preserved the spirit and interpreted the meaning of the patrol in his novel *The Sand Pebbles.*

62 Casualty-rate and further information about the 442d Regimental Combat Team is in "Go For Broke," *Soldiers,* Vol. 33, no. 11, November 1978. Senator Inouye's account of the haircut incident is in Daniel K. Inouye, with Lawrence Elliot, *Journey to Washington,* Prentice-Hall, Englewood Cliffs, N.J., 1967; information on his military decorations was supplied by his office.

63 The 1639 immigration law based on Bennett, p. 2.

63 The Franklin quotations are from M. Grant and C.S. Davidson, *The Founders of the Republic on Immigration, Naturalization, and Aliens,* New York, 1928, p. 26.

64 For the significance of the Alien and Sedition Acts and the early history of restriction, see Bennett pp. 10ff.

64 The figures on deportation and on those turned away are from *Historical Statistics, 1975,* Series C 158-161, p. 114.

64-65 For the Immigration Act of 1917, see Bennett, pp. 26ff.

66 The discussion of the various pieces of quota legislation is based on Bennett, p. 47ff. The national immigration quotas under the systems set up in 1921, 1924, 1929, and 1952 may be found in a table in Bennett, p. 160.

66 The actual patterns of immigration by country were not as laid out in the law because of various exceptions in the laws themselves, which worked in favor of the Southern and Eastern European countries. The patterns of European immigration under the various systems for the first 40 years of this century may be found in Bennett on pp. 68f.

67 The role of psychologist Henry Goddard in building the restrictionist argument on the basis of the mental incompetence of the immigrants is from Paul R. Ehrlich and Shirley S. Feldman, *The Race Bomb,* Ballantine, New York, 1977.

68 The House vote on the National Origins Act was 323 yeas, 71 nays, and 38 not voting. In the Senate, the vote was 62 yeas, 6 nays, and 38 not voting.

68 The official wording on the term "quota immigrant" is from Bennett, p. 56.

70 Nonfulfillment of quotas and the wartime decline in European immigration are from *Historical Statistics, 1975,* Series C 89–119, p. 105, and information on emigration by immigrants is from *Historical Statistics, 1960,* Series 156–157, p. 164.

71 Truman's directive is from Bennett, p. 89. The mortgaging of the quotas is from the same, pp. 77 and 202.

72 On the deaths of the Russian repatriates, see Nikolai Tolstoy, *The Secret Betrayal,* Charles Scribners and Sons, New York, 1977.

73 This discussion of the McCarran-Walter Act and the quotes are based on Bennett, pp. 133ff.

79 The pattern of admission of Hungarians and their numbers are from Bennett, p. 204ff.

79 The discussion of the Cuban Revolution is from Hugh Thomas,

Cuba: The Pursuit of Freedom, Harper & Row, New York, 1971; Robert Taber, *M-26, Biography of a Revolution,* New York, 1961; and, Herbert Matthews, *The Cuban Story,* G. Braziller, New York, 1961. Taber was one of the CBS newsmen who interviewed Castro in the Sierra Maestra. He later left journalism to become executive director of the Fair Play for Cuba Committee. Thomas's massive and masterly work contains the best account of the Cuban Revolution and the best biography of Fidel Castro in English. We are particularly indebted to Professor Richard Fagen, Department of Political Science, Stanford University, for his personal comments on our treatments of the Cuban Revolution and the Cuban refugee issue.

81 The 1,600-per-week figure for the flow of Cuban refugees in 1960 is from Bennett, p. 235. It is impossible to establish from printed sources the pattern of flow of Cuban refugees or even their total number. They entered the United States in all sorts of categories, including illegal. Even the published figures in the INS *Annual Reports* are contradictory. Part of this confusion arises from the complexity of the problem, but it appears to us that part is also contrived.

82 Thomas, pp. 1355ff. contains the best account in English of the Bay of Pigs fiasco and the ransom.

82 No one has, as yet, even attempted to piece together a coherent account of what went on in Cuba, Florida, and Washington relative to the Cuban refugees and the attempted subversion of the Cuban government by the United States. It is a task of great public service crying out to be done. Many government officials who were deeply involved in the various aspects of the matter were not then aware, and are still not aware, of what was going on around them or the significance of their actions in the overall context. What we say here has been pieced together from many fragmentary sources and admittedly contains a great deal of conjecture. The admission of a large body of foreign nationals, their concentration in one part of the country, and their use as agents for illegal activities in the pursuit of foreign-policy objectives has significance far beyond the abuse of immigration policy, and we hope our brief treatment will renew interest in these events which began over two decades ago.

83 Total numbers of Cubans and airlift statistics are from INS *Annual Report,* 1976, Table 35, p. 143 and the same, 1972, p. 3. Figures on Cuban-born residents of the U.S. are from *Historical Statistics,* 1975 Series C 228–295, p. 117. Cuban "adjustments of status" are from INS *Annual Report,* 1976, p. 3 and Table 39, p. 149.

84 The quotation on the fading political settlement is from INS *Annual Report,* 1975, p. 7, which contains the general discussion of the Vietnamese refugee effort centered in Guam on which this is based. Other material is from Gail Kelly's *From Viet Nam to America,* Westview Press, Boulder, Colorado, 1977. The total number of Vietnamese refugees is from INS *Annual Report,* 1976, p. 9.

86 Information on the continuing problem of Indochinese refugees is

from Iver Peterson, " 'Boat People' Find Hardship in U.S., but also Hope," *New York Times,* February 13, 1979.

87 The total number of persons admitted to the United States under the designation "refugee" by country and by particular laws can be found in INS *Annual Report, 1976,* Table 6E, p. 52. It is well worth studying. It should be remembered, however, that many hundreds of thousands of refugees, particularly Cubans and Vietnamese, were admitted under other categories and are not included in this table.

87 For more on the Azores and Netherlands Relief Act of 1958, see Bennett, pp. 207, 209, 232, 267, and 338. For the number admitted under it, see INS *Annual Report, 1976,* Table 6E, p. 52.

88 Refugees admitted under the 1965 Act are from INS *Annual Report, 1969,* pp. 3ff. Current legislative initiatives of the Carter Administration are from Graham Hovey, "A Bill that Would Allow More Refugees into the U.S.," *New York Times,* February 13, 1979.

88 Details of the numeric restrictions of the 1965 Act are from INS *Annual Report, 1966,* pp. 3ff; 1976 figures from the same, p. 6 and Table 6, p. 44. The comparisons of total gross immigration 1961–65 with 1972–76 are from the same, Table 1, p. 39.

88-90 Data in the discussion of "dates" are from INS *Visa Bulletin,* July 1978.

90 The impact of Public Law 89–236 on European and Asian immigrants is from INS *Annual Report, 1976,* Table 6, p. 47 and the same, *1968* and *1976* Tables 14, p. 61 and p. 89, respectively.

90 Figures on occupational preferences are from INS *Annual Report, 1976* Table 8a, p. 57.

Chapter 3

95 Description of Spanish superiority based in part on Charles Gibson, *Spain in America,* Harper and Row, New York, 1966.

95 The material on the demographic holocaust is based on the work of Sherburne F. Cook and Woodrow Borah, two scholars associated with the interdisciplinary study of the past begun by Carl O. Sauer and A.L. Kroeber at the University of California at Berkeley in the 1930s. Their work is summarized in *Essays in Population History, I,* University of California Press, Berkeley, 1971, pp. v–xiv.

96 McWilliams quotation is from his classic *North from Mexico,* Greenwood Press, New York, 1968, p. 29.

96 Description of Spanish frontiersman in Charles J. Bishko, "The Castilian as Plainsman: The Medieval Ranching Frontier in La Mancha and Extremadura," in Archibald E. Lewis and Thomas F. McGann, eds., *The New World Looks at Its History,* University of Texas Press, Austin, 1963.

96 McWilliams quotation from p. 30. During the *reconquista,* the *encomenderos* were Christian Knights given jurisdiction over people and territory captured from the Moors.

98 Quote about Malinche from Daniel James, *Mexico and the Americans,*

Praeger, New York, 1963, p. 14. The foregoing discussion owes much to this excellent and highly recommended overview of Mexico and its relationship to the United States.

99 Description of Hidalgo's execution from Hugh M. Hamill, Jr., *The Hidalgo Revolt, Prelude to Mexican Independence,* University of Florida Press, Gainesville, 1966, pp. 216.

99 For details of the "loan"—actually the compulsory redemption of certain mortgages, see Jan Bazant's excellent *A Concise History of Mexico,* Cambridge University Press, Cambridge, 1977, pp. 5–7.

99 Quote of *Grito* from James, pp. 27–28, and Hamill, p. 23.

100 Much of the material on Hidalgo is from Hamill.

101 Morelos's recommendation is quoted in Bazant, p. 22.

101 Much of the material on Morelos is based on W.H. Timmons, *Morelos: Priest, Soldier, Statesman of Mexico,* Texas Western Press, El Paso, 1963.

102 The quote on the *caudillo* is from James, p. 34.

102 There is considerable argument about the actual authorship of the Plan of Iguala; but it seems reasonable to assume that it was largely Iturbide's, with some suggestions and emendations from others. See W.S. Robertson, *Iturbide of Mexico,* Duke University Press, 1952, Durham.

103 Material on the "troubled years" is based in part on Bazant and Henry Bamford Parkes, *A History of Mexico* (3rd ed. Houghton Mifflin, Boston, 1969), both of which provide basic historical background on Mexico.

105 Material on migration into Texas largely based on accounts in Parkes and Bazant.

106 Much of the material on Santa Anna is from W.H. Callcott, *Santa Anna: the Story of an Enigma who Once Was Mexico,* University Oklahoma Press, Norman, 1936; and O.L. Jones, Jr., *Santa Anna,* Twayne Publishers, New York, 1968.

108 Description of Polk from Parke, p. 212. General background on the Mexican War can be found in Samuel Eliot Morison, *Oxford History of the American People,* Oxford University Press, New York, 1965.

109 Material on Buena Vista is largely from Justin H. Smith, *The War with Mexico,* Macmillan Co., 1919. Scott was also a Whig. Polk could not find a suitable Democrat general, so he tried to dilute Taylor's popularity.

110 Quotations from Scott and Meade are from McWilliams, pp. 102–103.

110 Details on San Patricio from B. Kimball Baker, "The St. Patricks fought for their skins, and Mexico," *Smithsonian Magazine,* March 1978.

111 Population statistics are from *Statistics of the Population of the United States at the Tenth Census* (June 1, 1880), Washington, 1883, Tables II and III. Hereafter cited as 1880 Census.

115 Material on Texas-Mexican tensions and incidents is based largely on Carey McWilliams, *North from Mexico,* Greenwood Press, 1968.

115 Goliad quote from Paul S. Taylor, *An American-Mexican Frontier* (1934), quoted in McWilliams p. 106.

115 Quote on lack of justice from John L. Linn, *Reminiscences of Fifty Years in Texas,* University of Texas Press, Austin, 1935, pp. 352–354—quoted in David J. Weber, ed., *Foreigners in their Native Land,* University of New Mexico Press, Albuquerque, 1973, p. 153.

116 Cortina quote from U.S. House of Representatives, *Difficulties on the Southwestern Frontier,* 36th Congress, 1st session, 1860, House Executive Document 52, pp. 70–82.

116 A detailed look at border problems can be found in Robert D. Gregg, "The influence of border troubles on relations between the United States and Mexico, 1876–1910," *The Johns Hopkins University Studies in Historical and Political Science,* series LV, no. 3, 1937, pp. 1–200.

117 Gregg quote is pp. 15–16.

117-18 Text of Order of June 1 from Gregg, p. 51, as is the description of the Mexican reaction to the order.

119 Quote from 1882 agreement from Gregg, p. 157.

119 Material on Apache from Gregg and Clarence C. Clendenen, *The United States and Pancho Villa,* Cornell University Press, Ithaca, 1971.

120 The Creelman interview, "President Diaz, Hero of the Americas," was in the March 1908 issue of *Pearson's Magazine.* The quoted material is followed by a further paragraph of flattering physical description: ". . . crisp white hair . . . dark brown eyes that search your soul . . . huge virile jaws . . . deep chest . . . sensitive spread nostrils . . . ," etc.

120 For discussion of Díaz's motives in giving the Creelman interview, see S.R. Ross, *Francisco I. Madero, Apostle of Mexican Democracy,* Columbia University Press, New York, 1955, pp. 46–47.

121 Cumberland quote from his *Mexican Revolution, Genesis under Madero,* University of Texas Press, Austin, 1952, p. 55.

121 Quote on elections from T. R. Fehrenbach, *Fire and Blood, A History of Mexico,* Macmillan, New York, 1973, p. 490.

121 For details on the Flores Magon brothers and the Liberal Revolution, see L.L. Blaisdell, *The Desert Revolution, Baja California, 1911,* University of Wisconsin Press, 1962.

122 "Pancho" is the common Spanish nickname for Francisco. The life of Pancho Villa is so clouded by myth that there is no really satisfactory biography of him. For further information on this fascinating man, see Martin Luis Guzman's *Memoirs of Pancho Villa* (University of Texas Press, Austin, 1965) and *The Eagle and the Serpent* (originally published in 1928 under the title *El Aguila y la Serpiente,* by Companía General de Ediciones, S.A.; latest English edition by Peter Smith Pub., Gloucester, Mass., 1969), remembering always to keep a salt shaker near at hand. John Reed's *Insurgent Mexico* (International Publishers, New York, 1969) gives fascinating vignettes of the Mexican people living through the horror of the revolution and of their leaders, including some sympathetic

glimpses of Villa. *The* novel of the Revolution is Mariano Azuela's *The Underdogs (Los de Abajo)*, trans. E. Munguía, Jr., Signet Classic edition, 1963. It found its way into print in a small Spanish-language newspaper in El Paso, Texas, in 1915. Azuela, a doctor who treated and traveled with the troops, had been part of the medical staff of the famed Division del Norte when Villa was at his most powerful. Vivid imagery and a sensitivity toward *campesinos* make unforgettable this tale of the rise of a poor, unlettered peasant to revolutionary general and his subsequent corruption by power.

124 Womack's book is *Zapata and the Mexican Revolution*, Alfred A. Knopf, New York, 1968. For Meyer's general conclusions in English see *The Cristero Rebellion*, translated by Richard Southern, Cambridge, 1976. For his more detailed argument, the Spanish-language version is essential: *La Cristiada*, translated by Aurelio Garzón del Camino, 3 vols. (México, 1974).

124 The role of northern money in subverting Orozco appears to have been overrated. In *Mexican Rebel: Pascual Orozco and the Mexican Revolution, 1910–1915* (University of Nebraska, Lincoln, 1967), historian Michael C. Meyer argues convincingly that Orozco's disappointment was the overriding reason.

125 Material on Madero's assassination is largely from Ross, Cumberland, and Parkes.

125 The conventional wisdom that Huerta's drinking hurt his administration appears to be wrong—see Michael C. Meyer, *Huerta: A Political Portrait* (University of Nebraska, Lincoln, 1972), pp. 131–132.

127 Figures on Celaya from J.W.F. Dulles, *Yesterday in Mexico*, University of Texas Press, Austin, 1961.

127 Our material on the Plan of San Diego is based on the work of historian James A. Sandos. His "The Plan of San Diego: War and Diplomacy on the Texas Border, 1915–1916," *Arizona and the West* XIV (Spring 1972), pp. 5–24, presented the first comprehensive argument that Venustiano Carranza used the Plan to secure American diplomatic recognition. Sandos's research in the National Archives and the Library of Congress in Washington, D.C., encompassed only the United States sources. His argument has recently been restated by Charles Harris and Louis Sadler in "The Plan of San Diego and the Mexican–United States War Crisis of 1916: A reexamination," *Hispanic American Historical Review*, LVIII (August, 1978) pp. 381–408. However, in the interim, Dr. Sandos has reformulated his views based upon extensive research in Mexican archives. Most recently, he argues that, irrespective of Venustiano Carranza's wishes in the matter, Carranza lacked the physical control to manipulate the Plan to his ends and in fact worked diligently to extirpate it upon receiving pressure from Washington. See "The Mexican Revolution and the United States, 1915–1917: The Impact of Culture Conflict in the Tamaulipas–Texas Frontier upon the Emergence of Revolutionary Government in

Mexico," (unpublished Ph.D. dissertation, University of California, Berkeley, 1978), pp. 178–336.

131 López quote from *Literary Digest,* January 22, 1916, quoted in Clendenen, p. 225.

132 Material on German machinations from James A. Sandos, "German involvement in northern Mexico, 1915–1916: a new look at the Columbus raid," *The Hispanic American Historical Review,* vol. 50 (1970), pp. 70–88.

133 Although a popular and romantic figure of the Revolution, Villa proved less of a revolutionary than, say, Carranza or Zapata. Villa never issued a Plan as the other two did, and apparently had no coherent view of social change. His reactions generally were against what he saw as abuse rather than for reform. Friedrich Katz, who is working on a biography of Villa, has recently advanced the curious thesis that Villa's attack on Columbus, New Mexico, was motivated by patriotic nationalism. It appears to at least one student of the Revolution that Katz can advance such an argument only by ignoring the evidence, and the article may presage the publication of a hagiography. See Friedrich Katz, "Pancho Villa and the Attack on Columbus, New Mexico," *American Historical Review* LXXXIII (February 1978), and the comments by James A. Sandos to be published in a forthcoming issue.

Chapter 4

136 Much of the historical material in this chapter is based on Daniel James, *Mexico and the Americans,* Praeger, New York, 1963 (López Mateo's quote is from James); Jan Bazant, *A Concise History of Mexico,* Cambridge University Press, New York, 1977; and Henry Bamford Parkes, *A History of Mexico,* 3rd ed., Houghton Mifflin, Boston, 1969.

136-37 Details of Poinsett's role can be found in Gene M. Brack, *Mexico Views Manifest Destiny, 1821–1846,* University of New Mexico Press, Albuquerque.

137 Sierra quote is from *The Political Evolution of the Mexican People,* University of Texas Press, Austin, 1969, p. 292.

138 Figures on industrialization are from C.C. Cumberland, *Mexican Revolution: Genesis under Madero,* University of Texas Press, Austin, 1952, p. 6.

138 Demographic history here and elsewhere is mainly from John S. Nagle, "Mexico's Population Policy Turnaround," *Population Bulletin,* vol. 33, no. 5, December 1978, Population Reference Bureau.

138 The quote is from Cumberland, p. 26.

138 The quote on *hacendados* and peasants is from Stanley R. Ross, *Francisco I. Madero: Apostle of Mexican Democracy,* Columbia University Press, New York, 1955, p. 24; information from Ross; and Charles C. Cumberland, *Mexico: The Struggle for Modernity,* Oxford University Press, New York, 1968.

139 NACLA quote from *Latin America and Empire Report,* vol. 10, no. 6,

July–August 1976, p. 5. In spite of its openly political slant, NACLA is respected by social scientists for the detail and accuracy of the information it gathers. For information on Díaz's land policies, see also Bazant, *A Concise History of Mexico,* and Thomas G. Sanders, "Mexico's Food Problem," *Common Ground,* vol. 1, no. 3, July 1975 (American Universities Field Staff).

139   Data on land concentration in Jalisco and Veracruz from Ernest Gruening's *Mexico and its Heritage,* Century, New York, 1928, pp. 129–131. The section following these pages describing *haciendas* is well worth reading and is the basis for the material on hacienda life. Gruening eventually served as U.S. Senator from Alaska.

139   Statistics on Terrazas holdings from Ernesto Galarza, *Merchants of Labor, The Mexican Bracero Story,* McNally and Laftin, Charlotte, 1964.

139   Quote on treatment of peones is from Gruening, p. 138, based on Andres Molina Enriquez, *Los Grandes Problemas Nacionales,* Imprenta de A. Corranza e Hijos, Mexico City, 1909.

140   Material on colonizing companies from NACLA, pp. 5–6.

140   For Díaz's program and attitudes, see, in addition to NACLA, Cumberland, Chapter 8; a telling description of wealth and privilege in the Soviet Union can be found in Hedrick Smith's *The Russians.*

141   Ross quote is from *Francisco I. Madero.*

141   Quote is from "Criminal Classes," James, p. 152.

142   For a discussion of the responsibility for the murders, see Cumberland, *Mexican Revolution: Genesis under Madero,* pp. 241–242, footnote 53, and Ross, *Francisco I. Madero,* pp. 328–329.

142   Statistics on foreign holdings from James, pp. 118–119, and James D. Cockroft, "Mexico," in R.H. Chilcote and J.C. Edelstein, eds., *Latin America: The Struggle with Dependency and Beyond,* p. 248. NACLA estimates that the Hearst holdings in all of northern Mexico were seven million hectares—an area about a fifth the size of California.

142   The quote about Henry Lane Wilson is from James, p. 163.

143   The account of the *Dolphin* incident is from K.J. Grieb, *The United States and Huerta,* University of Nebraska Press, Lincoln, 1969.

143   A detailed description of the Veracruz battle can be found in Robert E. Quirk, *An Affair of Honor: Woodrow Wilson and the Occupation of Vera Cruz,* University of Kentucky Press, 1962. Don't miss the description of conditions in Veracruz in this fascinating book. Note also Quirk's statement, on p. 155, after describing the occupation troops' efforts to clean up the city, that "the record of the military government was in the highest tradition of American service to mankind"(!)

144   The anti-American reaction is detailed by Quirk, pp. 107ff.

144   The quote is from Article 27, from H.N. Branch, *The Mexican Constitution of 1917 Compared with the Constitution of 1857,* American Academy of Political Science, Philadelphia.

146   Material on oil-company behavior is based largely on Cumberland, *Mexico: the Struggle for Modernity,* chapter 10.

146 The Bucareli Conferences are described in some detail by J.W.F. Dulles, *Yesterday in Mexico: A Chronicle of the Revolution,* University of Texas Press, Austin, 1961. See also H.F. Cline, *The United States and Mexico,* Harvard University Press, Cambridge, 1963. Material on the oil companies' deviance based in part on James, chapter 10.

147 Hearst's quote is from James, p. 219.

147 Coolidge speech at United Press dinner, April 25, 1927, quoted in James, p. 238.

148 Cardenas was elected for six years because in 1928 the term of the president was increased from four to six years with no possibility of re-election.

149 The statistics on wages are from James, p. 281. Some of the material on the expropriation is from Cline, Chapter 11.

150 The legislation under which the Board of Conciliation and Arbitration acted was the Labor Code of 1931, which required government arbitration to settle "economic conflicts."

151 The description of U.S. response is largely from James, Chapter 12, and Cline, Chapter 11.

151 For a thorough account of the Hay-Hull debate, see James, pp. 295 ff.

152-53 Stories of Mares and Murillo from Manuel Gamio, *The Life Story of the Mexican Immigrant,* University of Chicago Press, 1931; reprinted by Dover Publications, New York, 1971.

153 Information on Cárdenas's agrarian reforms is from various sources, including Jan Bazant, *A Concise History of Mexico;* Thomas G. Sanders, "Mexico's Food Problem," and David Gordon, "Mexico, a Survey," *The Economist,* April 22, 1978.

153-54 Some of the information on agricultural policies comes from Lappé and Collins, *Food First,* Houghton Mifflin, Boston, 1977; NACLA; and Cynthia Hewitt de Alcantera, "The Green Revolution as History: the Mexican Experience," *Development and Change,* vol. V, no. 2, 1973–74.

155 The material on the two-tiered society is from Gordon, "Mexico, a Survey."

155 Data on days worked by farm laborers and nutrition are from Sanders, "Mexico's Food Problem," and Hewitt de Alcantera, "The Green Revolution."

156 See Hewitt de Alcantera, "The Green Revolution," for a full discussion of the effects of the Green Revolution on Mexico's rural social structure.

156 See P.R. Ehrlich, A. H. Ehrlich, and J.P. Holdren, *Ecoscience: Population, Resources, Environment,* W.H. Freeman and Co., San Francisco, 1977, Chapter 7, for more on social and ecological side effects of the Green Revolution.

157 Information on the 1978 land takeover is from NBC *News,* October 9, 1978.

157-58 Information on U.S. agribusiness operations in Mexico is taken from Lappé and Collins, *Food First.*

158 Information on food imports and exports is from Thomas G. Sanders, "Mexico's Food Problem," *Fieldstaff Reports* (American

Universities Field Staff) North America Series, vol. III, no. 1, 1975.

160 Statistics on U.S. investment are from Stanley R. Ross, "Introduction" in S.R. Ross, *ed., Views Across the Border,* University of New Mexico Press, Albuquerque, 1978, p. 11; and Martin Tolchin, "Washington Seeking to Repair Schism with Now Powerful, Oil-Rich Mexico," *New York Times,* February 11, 1979.

160 Material on the runaway shops based on NACLA's *Latin American and Empire Report,* vol. IX, no. 5, July–August 1975.

162 This account of the Mexican railcar story has been taken from many sources. Much valuable background is from private communications with Joseph Blatchford. Development of the railcar shortage in the United States is from the *Washington Letter* (United States–Mexico Chamber of Commerce), June 1978, Vol. IV, no. 5. The fining of Conrail and Santa Fe Railroad and the Santa Fe spokesman's response are from "Conrail, Santa Fe Fined . . ." *New York Times,* June 16, 1978. Quote from Mr. Klaff is from "Rail Car Shortages . . ." *Journal of Commerce,* June 27, 1978. The story of the killing of legislation to restore GSP protection to the Mexican railcars from private sources in the United States and Mexico who declined to be named. For that reason we have not given the name of the congressman.

166 Unless otherwise indicated, this section is based on William D. Mertz, "Mexico: The Premier Oil Discovery in the Western Hemisphere," *Science,* vol. 202, pp. 1261ff, 22 December 1978; "Mexico Joins Oil's Big Leagues," *Time,* December 25, 1978; and Anthony J. Parisi, "Economic and Political Concerns Could Slow Tide of Mexican Oil," *New York Times,* February 13, 1979.

167 Information on Mexican oil production is from Richard Halloran, "Mexico Oil Output Is Called 2 Years Ahead of Plan," *New York Times,* February 18, 1979. Doubts about the vastness of the Mexican oil reserve are from the *Los Angeles Times,* reprinted in the *Fresno Bee,* May 18, 1979, p. A2.

169-70 Comparative data on Costa Rica and Venezuela from *1978 World Population Data Sheet* of the Population Reference Bureau.

170 David Gordon quote from his article, "Mexico, a Survey."

171 The "banana republic" quote is from James Flanigan, "Mexican Oil: the U.S. is most Definitely *Not* in the Driver's Seat," *Forbes,* January 22, 1979. Material on U.S.–Mexican natural gas negotiations is based in part on this article, as is some information on Mexican development goals.

172 Quotes from two presidents are from "Excerpts from Toasts by Carter and López Portillo," *New York Times,* February 16, 1979.

Chapter 5

175 Numbers of returning immigrants from *Historical Statistics,* 1965, Series C 156–157, p. 64; and Charles Keely and Ellen Percy Kraly, "Recent Net Alien Immigration to the United States: Its impact on

population and native fertility," *Demography,* vol. 14, no. 3, August 1978.

178 General Chapman, as Commissioner of INS, went public with his concern over illegals in 1974. The only figures on the "stock"—that is, the number of illegals in the country at that time—came from testimony before Congress in 1972 by Chapman's predecessor, Raymond F. Farrell, who came up with a figure of about a million. In reviewing how Farrell came up with this number, Keely has written, "It is hardly necessary to go into a detailed evaluation to clarify the unreliability of this estimate." Not only was the figure unreliable, it was too low to serve General Chapman's needs. An estimate that less than one half of one percent of the people in the country were illegals was not likely to persuade Congress to come up with more money for the INS.

178 The text of the news release and an outline of the Darman Report, dated respectively December 8 and 4, 1975, were supplied by the INS.

179 Quotation on General Chapman's budgetary aims from Charles B. Keely, "Counting the Uncountable: Estimates of Undocumented Aliens in the United States," *Population and Development Review,* vol. 3, no. 4, December 1977, pp. 473–481.

179 Figures on apprehensions from *INS Annual Report, 1974,* Tables 23 and 27b.

180 Figure for school-age children of illegals in Texas, *Newsweek,* February 20, 1978.

180 Figure for predicted flow of illegals in 1978, *Newsweek,* February 6, 1978.

180 Figure for illegals in the United States prior to 1970, *Newsweek,* September 26, 1977.

180 1979 flow figure, *Newsweek,* January 1, 1979.

180 Wirken and Hardin figures in Melanie Wirken, "Why We Should End Illegal Immigration," *ZPG National Reporter,* vol. 9, no. 8, October 1977; and Garrett Hardin, "Population and Immigration: Compassion or Responsibility," *Ecologist,* vol. 7, no. 7 and "The Limits of Sharing," *World Issues,* vol. 3, no. 1, February–March, 1978.

181 Figures on technical violations from INS *Annual Report,* 1975, Table 23; concern over children of illegals in Texas schools from *Newsweek,* February 20, 1978; challenge to Tyler, Texas, tuition plan, *Newsweek,* January 1, 1979.

181 Information on illegals in New York from *New York Times,* May 1, 1977.

182 The following discussion leans heavily on Charles B. Keely's excellent critique of estimates of illegal aliens in the United States, "Counting the Uncountable; Estimates of Undocumented Aliens in the United States," *Population and Development Review,* vol. 3, no. 4, December 1977, pp. 473–81. Information is from this source unless otherwise indicated.

183 The story of the illegal who was apprehended five times in one day

was related by INS Commissioner Leonel Castillo on "William
Buckley's Firing Line," viewed on KQED-TV, San Francisco, January 27, 1979.

183   Information on apprehension and deterrent modes from personal
conversation with George Watson, agent-in-charge, Chula Vista
Border Patrol Station, February 2, 1979.

184   The Warren work is unpublished and was privately supplied.
Cornelius's material is from Wayne Cornelius, *Mexican Migration to
the United States: Causes, Consequences, and U.S. Responses,* Migration
and Development Study Group, Center for International Studies,
Massachusetts Institute of Technology, Cambridge, Massachusetts, July 1978, pp. 24ff.

185   Commissioner Chapman's inability to get justification for his figures from those within the INS who were responsible for such
things and his turning to consultants was related, independently,
to us by persons then in the INS.

185   The origin of Lesko's involvements with INS come from Robert
Warren, Planning and Evaluation section, INS, in personal communication. The details of the Lesko estimates are fascinating.
Lesko used what is called a "Delphi panel." In theory, a Delphi
panel is composed of a number of persons familiar with all the
various aspects of some problem, each of whom is asked to estimate
the size of the problem, in this case the number of illegals in the
country, and to state the basis for his or her estimate. After presenting their individual guesses and the reasons for them, a digest of
the opinions is distributed to the panel for comment, and then
another round of estimates is undertaken, and so on until the panel
reaches whatever agreement is possible. Needless to say, a lot of
social scientists have doubts about the usefulness of the Delphi
panel. The Lesko panelists started out with estimates ranging from
2.5 to 25 million illegals and ended up after three rounds with their
final range of 4.2 to 11 million and an average of 8.2 million.

The panelists were not required to reveal the basis of their
guesses, nor did INS reveal their identities. But we were told that
no illegals, no employers of illegals, and no people from the INS
were on the panel—representatives of which groups might have
had some familiarity with the problem.

Lesko Associates also attempted to evaluate the stock and the
flow of illegal Mexican aliens. They based their estimates on man-
ipulations of Mexican census statistics and numbers of apprehensions by the INS. The conclusion was that there were 5.2 million
Mexican illegals in the United States in 1975. Unfortunately, the
technique used in the Lesko study leans heavily on two very shaky
statistics and a baseless assumption. One statistic, the estimate of
the stock of Mexican illegals present in the U.S. in 1970, Lesko put
at slightly less than 1.6 million. This number was obtained by
making unverified assumptions about the accuracy of the Mexican
census. The other questionable number was the ratio of illegals
who escape apprehension to those who get caught at the border.

This was based on untenable assumptions about the uniformity of INS efforts to round up aliens at points in the interior of the United States.

The baseless assumption is that the rate at which illegal Mexicans return to Mexico is roughly that at which *legal* European migrants leave. This assumption goes against all the available evidence, which to the contrary indicates a very high rate of departure. The two shaky statistics and the baseless assumption were combined with an assumed survival rate and the known number of apprehensions to produce the estimate of the 1975 stock of illegal aliens. The Lesko estimate of the illegal population is based on the pyramiding of what are little more than guesses. A detailed analysis of it done by a group at the Bureau of Business Research at the University of Texas at Houston concluded that the 5.2 million almost certainly is an overestimate. (Kenneth Roberts, Michael E. Conroy, Allen G. King, and Jorge Rizo-Parrán, *The Mexican Migration Numbers Game*, Bureau of Business Research, University of Texas, Austin, April 1978, *mimeo.*)

185-86   The budgetary history was supplied by the INS.

186   The reference to Castillo as "Latino activist" is in "A Breakdown in the Immigration System" reprinted from the *Los Angeles Times* in the *San Francisco Chronicle*, World Section, September 10, 1978.

186   Aims of Commissioner Castillo from interviews with him and his staff, August 1978.

187   The Hardin quote is from "The Limits of Sharing," *World Issues*, vol. 3, no. 1, February–March 1978.

187   Quote of the anonymous functionary is from "A Breakdown in the Immigration System," *Los Angeles Times.*

187-88   Information on Residential Survey from "$1 Million U.S. Study Yields Dubious Results," *Washington Post*, December 10, 1978, as well as correspondence and interviews with INS officials. Quotations concerning the "cover-up" and frustrations over the information dilemma are from "Alien Survey: What Caused the Breakdown?" *Los Angeles Times*, February 13, 1979.

188   One agency outside of the INS that is trying to count the uncountable is the United States Bureau of the Census. J. Gregory Robinson and others at the Census Bureau are trying to establish the number of illegals in the country by studying regional variations in death rates. This technique assumes that death records are pretty complete in this country and that, if there is a considerable hidden population in the country, they are not so well hidden that their deaths will not be recorded. Hence, Robinson and others are comparing the U.S. death figures through time on the assumption that unexplained increases indicate a high number of illegals, and from this an estimate of those still living can be made. The most important aspect of this study, as explained to us by one of those who originally designed it, is that it is not intended "to reveal how many fish are in the pond, but whether or not there are whales. People have been saying there are whales out there and we are

seeing if we can find any trace of them." In 1979, when some congressmen were speaking with certainty of great numbers of illegals in the country, technicians at the Bureau of the Census were just beginning to puzzle over techniques for getting at the problem in the first place.

188　Basis for today's most accepted figures is Clarice Lancaster and Frederick Scheuern, "Counting the Uncountable: Some Initial Statistical Speculations Employing Capture-Recapture Technique," paper before the American Statistical Association Annual Meeting, 1977.

189　The Leet criticism was privately supplied.

189　The content of the CIA Report is from *New Times*, August 7, 1978, p. 14.

190　Colby, Wolff, and Marshall quotes are from "Special Report: Illegal Immigration," issued by the Environment Fund, November 1978.

191　". . . contribute much, and require little" quote is from the information packet on Presidential Program on Illegal Aliens, February 1978, p. 3.

191　David North and Marion Houston, *The Characteristics and Role of Illegal Aliens in the U.S. Labor Market; An Exploratory Study*, Linton and Co., Washington, D.C., 1976; Jorge Bustamante, "Emigración indocumentada a los Estados Unidos," *Foro Internacional*, El Colegio de Mexico, vol. 18, no. 1.

192　Cornelius information is from his study, pp. 85ff. This also contains a synthesis of the other work on the subject.

192-93　Chapman's testimony is from "Special Report: Illegal Immigration" issued by the Environment Fund, November 1978.

193　INS Employment figures of illegals from "Special Report: Illegal Immigration," issued by the Environment Fund, November 1978.

193　Information on work available to immigrants is from Cornelius, p. 56; Michael J. Piore, "Illegal Immigration in the United States: Some Observations and Policy Suggestions," *Illegal Aliens: An Assessment of the Issues, National Council on Employment Policy*, October 1976, and "Undocumented Workers and U.S. Immigration Policy," a paper presented at the U.S. Commission on Civil Rights, Symposium on Immigration, New York, September 28, 1977.

193　*Nation's Cities*, vol. 15, no. 7, July 1977. The article by David Nye ("Illegal Aliens: An Urban People Problem") was supplied to us by the publisher, Dorothy Webb.

194　Information on wages from Cornelius, pp. 45ff. This is an excellent overview of the work of others as well as the author's own field work.

195　For information on repatriation, see, "The Repatriation of 1954 and 'Operation Wetback.' "

195-96　Information on wages from Cornelius, pp. 46ff.

196　Funds sent to Mexico estimate is from Martin Tolchin, "Washington Seeking to Repair Schism . . . ," *New York Times*, February 11, 1979. The article quotes political scientist Richard Fagen.

199   The numbers of native-born Canadians and Mexicans from *Historical Statistics, 1975*, Series C 228–295, p. 117. Immigrants from Canada and Mexico, *INS Annual Reports*, Table 13. Population growth rates for Canada and Mexico calculated from base data in "Canada," and "Mexico" articles in *Encyclopedia Brittanica*, eleventh edition; and immigration data, *INS Annual Reports*, Table 13. U.S. population figures from *Historical Statistics, 1975*, Series A 9–22, p. 9, and Population Reference Bureau, *Population Data Sheet, 1976*. Naturalization figures from *INS Annual Reports*, Table 39.

201   Departing immigrants for 1908–1957 from *Historical Statistics, 1965*, Series C 156–7, p. 64; Warren work is in Keely and Kraly.

205   Data on apprehensions of deportable aliens and deportations are from *INS Annual Report*, 1976, Table 23.

205   Information on the length of stay of those apprehended is from "Status at Entry" Section of *INS Annual Reports* for appropriate years.

207   The statement by Galarza is from his *Merchants of Labor, the Mexican Bracero Story*, McNally and Loftin, Charlotte, 1964. This is a key source on the *bracero* program and highly recommended.

207   Quotes on Mexican immigrants of the 1920s from Carey McWilliams, *North from Mexico*, Greenwood Press, Westport, Conn., 1948.

208   McWilliams quote and material on expelling Mexicans from his "Getting Rid of the Mexican," *American Mercury*, March 1933. Reprinted in Wayne Moquin and Charles Van Doren, eds., *A Documentary History of the Mexican Americans*, Praeger, New York, 1971.

209   The quote from the deputy sheriff is from McWilliams, p. 191.

209   More information on unionization of Mexican labor can be found in McWilliams; and in Matt S. Meier and Feliciano Rivera, *The Chicanos*, Hill and Wang, New York, 1972.

211   Cleland quote from *California in Our Times*, Knopf, New York, 1947, p. 262.

212   Some of the material on industry opposition to the FSA comes from Galarza's *Merchants of Labor*.

213   The subsidy estimate is from McWilliams, p. 266; Galarza (p. 84) estimates $55 million for 1942 to 1945; Meier and Rivera, p. 207, gave $113 million for World War II. Whatever the exact cost, it was a substantial subsidy.

213   Wetback statistics from Galarza, Chapter 7.

216   Material on the 1954 expulsion from Operation Wetback from Galarza, *Merchants of Labor;* and John C. Elac, *The Employment of Mexican Workers in U.S. Agriculture, 1900–1960; A Binational Economic Analysis*, University of California, Los Angeles, May 1961 (reprinted in 1972 by R and E Research Associates, 4843 Mission Street, San Francisco) and INS *Annual Reports, 1954*, pp. 31ff, and 1955, pp. 9ff. See also Ralph Guzman, "La repatriaciós forzosa como solución politica concluyente al problema de la immigración ilegal. Una perspectiva historica," *Foro Internacional*, XVIII:3 Enero–Marzo 1978.

216   Data on proportions of farm workers who were *braceros* is from
       Elac, *The Employment of Mexican Workers* . . .

217   For a detailed discussion of biological and social races, see P.R.
       Ehrlich and S. Shirley Feldman, *The Race Bomb, Skin Color, Prejudice
       and Intelligence,* Ballantine, New York, 1978.

217   The Japanese quote is from H. Wagatsuma, "The Social Percep-
       tion of Skin Color in Japan," *Daedalus* 95:420, 1967.

217   For origins of the *Leyenda* see R.D. Carbia, *Historia de la Leyenda
       Negra,* Publicaciones del Consejo de la Hispanidad, Madrid, 1944.
       The text is in Spanish, but the illustrations speak for themselves.
       Lewis Hanke's *The Spanish Struggle for Justice in the Conquest of
       America,* University of Pennsylvania Press, 1949, is the best treat-
       ment of the *Leyenda* in English.

220   Discussion of banditry in part from Manuel A. Machado, Jr., *Listen
       Chicano,* Nelson Hall, Chicago, 1978.

220   Material on Terman from Ehrlich and Feldman, *The Race Bomb,* p.
       51.

221   Discussion of Chicanos in World War II based mainly on Meier and
       Rivera, *The Chicanos,* Chapter 11.

222   The view that Mexicans became a convenient scapegoat after the
       Japanese expulsion is detailed by McWilliams. The reader should
       note that McWilliams himself was an active defender of the Mexi-
       can community at that time and therefore not a dispassionate
       bystander. Material on Sleepy Lagoon and the zoot-suit riots from
       McWilliams from Meier and Rivera, and the Los Angeles papers of
       the period.

223   Material on the Ayres report based on McWilliams, Chapter 12.

227   Mrs. Roosevelt's statements from the *Los Angeles Times,* June 17,
       1943; Hotchkis' reply was the next day, as was the editorial.

227   Mexican-American casualties in Vietnam were detailed by Profes-
       sor Ralph Guzman, *Congressional Record,* 91st Congress, 1st Ses-
       sion, October 8, 1969, reprinted in Moquin.

234   Demographic figures are from John S. Nagel, "Mexico's Popula-
       tion Policy Turnaround," *Population Bulletin,* vol. 33, no. 5 (De-
       cember 1978), Population Reference Bureau. There is of course
       some disagreement among demographers as to exact vital rates for
       Mexico. Some discrepancies are due to different estimates of the
       rate of emigration to the U.S.

234-35 Some historical statistics on Mexico are from Population Reference
       Bureau, *World Population Growth and Response, 1976,* Washington,
       D.C.

235   For an enlightening description of male-female roles and status in
       Mexico, see Thomas G. Sanders, "Mexico," in *Common Ground,* vol.
       II, no. 1, January 1976 (American Universities Fieldstaff), a special
       issue on women's status.

235   Report on UN Fertility Survey is from Nagel, "Mexico's Population
       Policy Turnaround."

235   Mexican population projections from Ansley Coale, "Population
       Growth and Economic Development: The Case of Mexico,"

Foreign Affairs Quarterly, vol. 56, pp. 415–429. Robert W. Fox, "Seminar on Latin American Population Trends and Urbanization" (Inter-American Development Bank, Washington, D.C., 1978); Robert W. Fox, *Urban Population Growth Trends in Latin America* (Inter-American Development Bank, Washington, D.C., 1975).

Chapter 6

241 The facts on which the fictionalized episode is based are from our interviews with both illegals and INS personnel, our visit to the border near San Diego, and the general literature, including, especially, Grace Halsell's *The Illegals* (Stein and Day, New York, 1978). The latter work, although somewhat breathless in style and rather uncritical, is well worth reading for a compassionate illegal-eye view of border crossing. The statistics on Culiacán are from Gene Lyon's "Inside the Volcano," *Harpers*, June 1977.

The information from Judge Rose was a personal communication.

246-47 The figures on farm-worker pay in Mexico and California are from a study by Prof. Refugio Rochin at the University of California at Davis, reported in *Empire Magazine, Denver Post,* July 23, 1978.

The Hunter quote was a personal communication.

254 The story of the rape is from Halsell and "Legal and Illegal Immigration to the United States," a report prepared by the Select Committee on Population, U.S. House of Representatives, Ninety-fifth Congress, 1978.

257 Wayne Cornelius's study is *Mexican Migration to the United States: Courses, Consequences, and U.S. Responses,* Migration and Development Study Group, Center for International Studies, Massachusetts Institute of Technology, Cambridge, Mass., July 1978. For additional information on the attitudes of *mojados,* see the series of articles on illegal immigration from Mexico in *Empire Magazine, The Denver Post,* July 1978.

259 Most of the material on Mexican demography and social conditions was supplied by Robert Fox of the Inter-American Development Bank. Sources include: Robert W. Fox, *Urban Population Growth Trends in Latin America,* 1975; and Robert Fox and Jerold W. Hugeut, *Population and Urban Trends in Central America and Panama,* 1977; both published by the Inter-American Development Bank, Washington, D.C.

260 An excellent study of the relation between land-tenure patterns in Latin America and rural-urban migration is R. Paul Shaw, *Land Tenure and the Rural Exodus,* University of Florida Press, Gainesville, 1976.

262 For a complete explanation of how population momentum works, see P.R. Ehrlich, A.H. Ehrlich, J.P. Holdren; *Ecoscience: Population,*

Resources, Environment, W.F. Freeman and Co., San Francisco, 1977, pp. 208–222.

262   The section on the Mexican turnaround is based on the excellent discussion by John Nagle, "Mexico's Population Policy Turnaround," *Population Bulletin* (Population Reference Bureau), vol. 33, no. 5, December 1978.

262   *Gobernar es poblar* was coined by the Argentine politician and statesman Juan Bautista Alberdi and popularized by Argentine President Domingo F. Sarmiento, in the 1860s. Sarmiento fostered European immigration to Argentina during his presidency (1868–74) in the hope that European culture would civilize the gauchos of his country.

266   A description of the change in education in Mexico can be found in Thomas G. Sanders, "Mexico's Elementary Textbooks Shape Future Citizens," *Common Ground,* vol. III, no. 3, July 1977 (American Universities Field Staff).

273   Bustamante's report is "Emigración Indocumentada a los Estados Unidos," *Foro Internacional,* El Colegio de Mexico, vol. 18, no. 1, 1978.

Chapter 7

276   Names of the Tijuana hotel and those who run it are fictional. This account is a synthesis based on our observations.

277-78   Information for the *Coyotes* section is as follows: The description of Tijuana is from personal observations. The remark of the Mayor of Tijuana about the number of would-be *mojados* and the account of the operation involving a Border Patrol agent on Mexican territory were related to us by Border Patrol personnel. The explanation of the professionalization of smuggling was given by several INS enforcement people, including Charles Sava, Deputy Commissioner for Enforcement, in August 1978. Basic routes, tactics, and problems of *coyotes* are from interviews with enforcement personnel and *mojados.* The proposal to authorize seizure of vehicles used in smuggling is found on page 3 of the Report of the House Select Committee on Population. The discussion of the intent of the INS enforcement effort to complicate the smuggling process is from various INS enforcement personnel, including Deputy Commissioner Sava. A *coyote's* fee (approximately $300) is from interviews with *mojados* and INS enforcement personnel.

281   The Baer story is from *New Times,* January 23, 1978. The names are fictional.

283   The administrative history of the INS is from a statement inside the front cover of the *INS Annual Report, 1975.* The number of entries is from *INS Annual Report, 1976,* p. 4. INS personnel figures are from private correspondence. The figures for deportable aliens apprehended and number of deportations are from *INS Annual Report, 1976,* Table 23.

286   The mission of the Border Patrol, the early history of enforcement

on the Mexican border, and the early and present powers of enforcement agents are from the INS pamphlet "U.S. Border Patrol," revised 1972.

293 The interview with Deputy Commissioner Sava took place in August 1978.

293 The quote on "serving the illegals" was from "A Breakdown in the Immigration System," *World* Section, *San Francisco Chronicle*, September 10, 1978, reprinted from the *Los Angeles Times*.

293 Commissioner Castillo's goals and sense of accomplishment are from our interview with him in August 1978.

294 Commissioner Castillo's interest in the "forgery-proof" identification card for aliens is from the August 1978 interview and from *William Buckley's Firing Line*, KQED-TV, San Francisco, January 27, 1979.

296 Quotations on hopelessness and frustration of the INS enforcement effort are from Larry Romero, "Lenience Blamed . . ." *Fresno Bee*, December 3, 1978.

296 Information in this and the following section is from observations at Chula Vista and from interviews and conversations with personnel there. Additional information on sensors is from a paper by Thomas C. Henneberge, "The Electronic Support Program of the INS," privately obtained.

297 The report by David North is *Illegal Aliens*.

300 Information on replacement fences is from George Watson and Richard Jones, Chula Vista Border Patrol Station and Sector, respectively; Richard Thut, Border Patrol Headquarters, Washington, D.C., and Vern Jervis, Public Information Officer, INS, Washington, D.C. The rumor that portions of the fence were to be electrified and the INS denial were from José Manuel Nava, "Un Millón de 'Mojados' a EU Cada Año," *Excelsior* (Mexico City), October 30, 1978.

Chapter 8

311 For a detailed discussion of the Cornucopian and neo-Malthusian views, see P.R. Ehrlich, A.H. Ehrlich, and J.P. Holdren, *Ecoscience: Population, Resources, Environment*, Freeman and Co., San Francisco, 1977.

312 For details on the transition to a spaceship economy, see Herman Daly's superb *Steady State Economics: the Economics of Biophysical Equilibrium and Moral Growth*. W.H. Freeman & Co., San Francisco, 1977.

312 Population growth projections are from A.O. Tsui and D.J. Bogue, "Declining World Fertility: Trends, Causes, Implications," *Population Bulletin* (Population Reference Bureau, Inc.), vol. 33, no. 4, 1978. This is a very important demographic source; its discussion of implications, however, is laughable because of the authors' apparently complete ignorance of the resource-environment situation.

313   Those interested in the reasons behind our pessimism may wish to consult Ehrlich, Ehrlich, and Holdren, *Ecoscience.*

313   Raspail's book was published in English by Charles Scribner's Sons, New York, 1975.

314   Leon F. Bouvier, with Henry S. Shryock, and Harry W. Henderson, "International Migration: Yesterday, Today, and Tomorrow," *Population Bulletin* (Population Reference Bureau), vol. 32, no. 4, 1977.

315   Canada's new policies are from "Canada Rewriting Immigration Law," *Intercom* (Population Reference Bureau), June 1977. At that time the legislation described was before Parliament but had not yet been passed. Since we have heard nothing to the contrary, we assume it passed without any significant further changes.

315   For Europe's policies, see Leon Bouvier, *et al.,* "International Migration: Yesterday, Today and Tomorrow," and references therein. See also references in Chapter I here.

321   The classic view that Aztec sacrifices were simply to appease their gods has recently been challenged by Michael Harner in "The ecological basis for Aztec sacrifice," *American Ethnologist* 4:117–35, 1977. For an interesting discussion of his still-controversial idea that the need for animal protein tipped the culture into a horrifying pattern of slaughter and cannibalism, see Marvin Harris's eminently readable *Cannibals and Kings,* Random House, New York, 1977, Chapter 9.

322-23   In the technical jargon of demography, replacement reproduction is referred to as a "net reproductive rate of 1."

323   Those interested in the details of the relationships between age composition, net reproductive rate, birthrate, and death rate may wish to consult Ehrlich, Ehrlich, and Holdren, *Ecoscience,* chapter 5.

323-24   The statement on the impact of American population growth is based on the use of per-capita energy consumption as the best available index of impact on both environment and resources. For example, in 1972 the average American used 11,611 kilograms of coal equivalent, while Ecuador used 296, Nigeria 66, Malawi 53, India 186, Burma 58, and Indonesia 133. U.S. impact per capita thus ranges from 39 to 219 times that of those countries, and adding 30 million more Americans is the equivalent of adding 1.17 to 6.57 billion people in those nations. We used the 1–2 billion figure because the larger poor nations tend to be in that range.

325   Estimates of the population impact of immigration are from Zero Population Growth, Inc., "U.S. Population Fact Sheet," August 1978. No details are given of the assumptions made about age composition or fertility of the immigrant group, so these projections, based on Census Bureau statistics and projections, must be viewed as "ballpark estimates."

326   For age structure, see Charles B. Keely and Ellen P. Kraly, "Recent net alien immigration to the United States: its impact on population growth and native fertility," *Demography* 15:267–283 (1978).

326   Data on fertility of women of Mexican origin from Kingsley Davis, "The migrations of human populations," *Scientific American,* September 1974. Fertility of women in Mexico is from John S. Nagel, "Mexico's Population Policy Turnaround," *Population Bulletin* (Population Reference Bureau), vol. 33, no. 5, December 1978.

332   Information on President Carter's proposed immigration legislation comes from his Message to Congress on undocumented aliens, August 4, 1977; 95th Congress, 1st Session, H.R. 9531, A Bill to amend the Immigration and Nationality Act . . . ; Office of the Attorney General, "Illegal Immigration: President's Program," February 1978. Castillo's comment was made on William Buckley's *Firing Line,* Public Broadcasting System, January 1979.

343   The Committee report was *Legal and Illegal Immigration to the United States,* U.S.G.P.O., Washington, D.C., 1978.
Senator Hayakawa's proposal is from Tom Eastham, "How to Stop Illegal Aliens: Hayakawa Has a New Plan," *San Francisco Examiner and Chronicle,* June 10, 1979, p. 8a.

351   Data on physicians from *Report of the Commission on Population Growth and the American Future, 1972.* See especially Judith A. Fortney's article, "Immigration in the United States with special reference to professional and technical workers," in volume I of the research reports.

353   The Commission quote is from the letter of transmittal of the Commission's *Report.*

354   See for an example of planning: "A Model Constitution for the United States," from *The Center Magazine,* publication of The Center for the Study of Democratic Institutions; reprinted in Ehrlich and Harriman, *How to Be a Survivor,* Ballantine, New York, 1971, pp. 166–202. For discussions of the U.S. Government's inability to plan, see Pirages and Ehrlich, *Ark II,* Viking, New York, 1974, pp. 174–178; Ehrlich, Ehrlich, and Holdren, *Ecoscience,* pp. 857–858; Council for Environmental Quality, *Global 2000,* 1979 (in press).

355   Those interested in the general problems of development can find an overview and access to the literature in Ehrlich, Ehrlich, and Holdren, *Ecoscience,* especially Chapter 15.

356   Information on Mexico's pioneer grass-roots development programs is from David Gordon, "Mexico, a Survey," *The Economist,* April 22, 1978; and Alan Riding, "Mexican Rural Program Slows Flow of Emigrants to U.S.," *New York Times,* February 15, 1979.

358   Information on Mexican-American contraceptive use is from B.S. Bradshaw and F.D. Bean, "Some aspects of the fertility of Mexican-Americans," in volume I of the *Research Reports* to the Commission on Population Growth and the American Future, 1972.

RECOMMENDED READING

Azuela, Mariano, *The Underdogs (Los de Abajo)*. New American Library, New York, 1963. Fortunately available as an inexpensive paperback, this book, originally published in 1915, is indisputably the greatest novel of the Mexican Revolution.

Bazant, Jan, *A Concise History of Mexico from Hidalgo to Cárdenas, 1805–1940*. Cambridge University Press, London, 1977. A fine concise treatment of the emergence of modern Mexico by a Professor at El Colegio de Mexico.

Bennett, Marion T., *American Immigration Policies: A History*. Public Affairs Press, Washington, D.C., 1963. The basic reference on policies prior to 1960.

Cline, Howard F., *Mexico—Revolution to Evolution: 1940–1960*. Oxford University Press, New York, 1963. By far the best work on this period by a leading scholar.

Fehrenbach, T.R., *Fire and Blood: A History of Mexico*. Macmillan Co., New York, 1973. A very readable popular history.

Fox, Robert W., *Urban Population Growth Trends in Latin America*, 1975, Inter-America Development Bank, Washington, D.C.

Fox, Robert W. and Huguet, Jerrold W., *Population and Urban Trends in Central America and Panama*. Inter-American Development Bank, Washington, D.C., 1977. Key reference on the demography of America's southern neighbors.

Galarza, Ernesto, *Merchants of Labor: The Mexican Bracero Story*. McNally and Loftin, Santa Barbara, 1964. Basic source on *braceros*, available in paperback.

Halsell, Grace, *The Illegals*. Stein and Day, New York, 1978. Somewhat breathless, but provides a great deal of insight into the lives and motives of the *mojados*.

James, Daniel, *Mexico and the Americans*. Praeger, New York, 1963. Interesting and insightful in spite of its age; unfortunately out of print.

Kiser, George C. and Kiser, Martha W., *Mexican Workers in the United States: Historical and Political Perspectives*. University of New Mexico Press, Albuquerque, 1979. A fine collection that appeared as this book was in proof.

McWilliams, Carey, *North from Mexico: The Spanish-Speaking People in the United States*. Lippincott, New York, 1949. A classic. Greenwood Press paperback edition with a new introduction by the author published in 1968.

Meier, Matt S., and Rivera, Feliciano, *The Chicanos: A History of Mexican Americans*. Hill and Wang, New York, 1972. A good, up-to-date, relatively brief treatment which should be read after McWilliams.

Moquin, Wayne and Van Doren, Charles, *A Documentary History of the Mexican Americans*. Praeger, New York, 1971. A most useful set of readings, ranging from 1536 to 1970. See also Weber, 1973.

Parkes, Henry Bamford, *A History of Mexico*, 3rd edition revised. Houghton Mifflin Co., Boston, 1969. A standard work, interesting reading, covering all of Mexican history. Available in paperback.

Reed, John, *Insurgent Mexico*. International Publishers, New York, 1969. First published in 1914, this book, by the author of *Ten Days that Shook the World*, can give you a feel for the Mexican Revolution.

Ross, Stanley, R., ed., *Views Across the Border: The United States and Mexico*. University of New Mexico Press, Albuquerque, 1978. A wide-ranging collection dealing with various aspects of the borderlands—from migration to health care.

Weber, David J., ed., *Foreigners in Their Native Land: Historical Roots of the Mexican Americans*. University of New Mexico Press, Albuquerque, 1973. Like Moquin and Van Doren, an interesting anthology.

Williams, Edward J. and Wright, Freeman J., *Latin American Politics: A Developmental Approach*. Mayfield Publishing Company, Palo Alto, 1975. Provides fine general background on Latin America.

ACKNOWLEDGMENTS

OUR colleagues at both California State University, Fresno (CSUF), and Stanford University have been extremely generous in supplying us with information, reading portions of the manuscript, or otherwise helping us with the complex job of writing this book. At CSUF these included James Cypher, Don Leet, and Izumi Taniguchi of the Department of Economics; Stephen Benko, James Brouwer, José Canales, and Warren E. Gade of the Department of History; Jesús Luna and Hugo Morales, La Raza Studies Program; Don Broyles, Department of Political Science; Peter J. Klassen, Dean, School of Social Sciences, 1978–79; Richard C. Spangler, Dean, School of Social Sciences, 1977–1978; and Louis Volpp, Academic Vice President. At Stanford they included Cheryl Holdren, Richard W. Holm, and John H. Thomas, and the members of the Population Policy Seminar, Department of Biological Sciences; Donald Lunde, Law School; and Richard R. Fagen, Department of Political Science.

In Washington D.C., we were assisted by Steve Behrens and Phyllis Eisen of Zero Population Growth; Joseph Blatchford, attorney; Jennifer Peck, U.S. Bureau of the Census; James L. Rose, administrative law judge, National Labor Relations Board; Michael Teitelbaum, staff director, House Select Committee on Population; Dorothy Webb, National League of Cities; and Melanie Wirken, Inter-agency Task Force of Immigration. At INS Headquarters, Peter Curral and Robert Warren, Planning, Evaluation and Budget; Edward Jon Guss, former Associate Deputy Commissioner for Planning, Evaluation and Budget; Guillermina Jasso, Special Assistant to the Commissioner; Charles Sava, Deputy Commissioner for Enforcement; Ralph Thomas, Administrative Assistant to the Commissioner; and Richard Thut, Central Office, U.S. Border Patrol were all very helpful.

Other people in the INS stationed outside of Washington went out of their way to give us assistance: at Chula Vista Sector, Richard Jones, assistant chief patrol agent; at Chula Vista Station, A.M. "Skip" Voytush, senior agent, and George Watson, agent-in-charge; and at Fresno, C.V. Hunter, senior agent, Border Patrol, and INS Agent Robert Park.

Several people at El Colegio de Mexico in Mexico City were kind enough to spend time with us and help us to get the perspective of those concerned with migration problems in that nation. We are especially grateful to Victor Urquidi (President), Francisco Alba, and Jorge Bustamante. Our friends Marcos Bogan and Carlos Denton L. (*Instituto de Estudios Sociales en Población* [IDESPO], Universidad Nacional Autonoma, Heredia, Costa Rica) also generously assisted us in understanding the view from south of the border.

We are indebted to Michael E. Conroy, Bureau of Business Research, University of Texas at Austin; Wayne Cornelius, Department of Political Science and Migration and Development Study Group, Massachusetts Institute of Technology; John P. Holdren, Energy and Resources Program, University of California, Berkeley; and Charles Keely, Population Council, for lending us their expertise on certain technical points. Aggie Rose, formerly an organizer for the United Farm Workers, skillfully carried out an interview program for us to provide direct insight into the lives and views of *mojados*. Her contribution was essential.

There were many who helped us but, due to their personal situations, preferred not to be named. One such group were the *mojados* who told us their stories with the candor of honest men and women. Another equally candid group were ranking enforcement personnel of the INS.

In any enterprise like this, certain friends and colleagues not only labor long and hard to improve the quality and accuracy of the manuscript, but also supply moral support that helps bridge the inevitable gaps of despair. In this special category, we would like to express our deep gratitude to Ginger Barber, Virginia Barber Literary Agency; Kathleen Foote Durham, Department of Political Science, Stanford University; William H. Durham, Department of Anthropology, Stanford; Lisa M. Ehrlich, Department of Economics, University of Pennsylvania; Robert W. Fox, Inter-American Development Bank; Gloria Hammond, Ballantine Books; James A. Sandos, Department of History, University of California, Berkeley; Irving Tragen, Deputy United States Permanent Representative to the Organization of American States; and Freeman J. Wright, Department of Political Science, CSUF. We would also like to give special thanks to Leonel Castillo, Commissioner, Immigration and Naturalization Service, who took time from his exceedingly busy schedule to discuss with us the problems faced by his agency.

At Stanford, Jyl Simpson wrestled long and successfully with the horrendous task of turning rough handwritten material into a polished, typewritten manuscript. Jerry Fischer handled a great deal of complicated Xeroxing with skill and cheer. And, living up to its well-deserved reputation, the Falconer Biology Library at Stanford ran down numerous obscure sources, many of them far from the purview of what is normally defined as "biology." In that regard the skill and patience of Claire Shoens is especially appreciated. Carolyn Sherwood; Craig Holdren, Jill Holdren and Evan Lunde helped cheerfully and skillfully with the onerous task of reading proof under pressure of a deadline.

A great many friends and relatives also contributed to our efforts with information, criticism, and understanding. With the certainty that we've forgotten others, we'd like to mention Jane Lawson Bavelas; Betty, Barbara, and Bill Bilderback; Ruth R. Ehrlich; Marilynn Lunde; Anne Murray (Hewlett Foundation); Ruth Simon; Alan Tone; and Polly Webb.

Needless to say, the final responsibility for all views expressed must rest with us. But one of the most cheering aspects of this project was the relative unanimity of the views and reactions of all those who became involved in it. It gives us hope that the problems discussed are indeed amenable to solution.

INDEX